Social History of the
United States

Titles in ABC-CLIO's
Social History of the United States

Social History of the United States
The 1990s

Nancy Cohen

Series Editors
Daniel J. Walkowitz and Daniel E. Bender

A B C · C L I O

Santa Barbara, California   Denver, Colorado   Oxford, England

Library of Congress Cataloging-in-Publication Data

Cohen, Nancy, 1963–
Social history of the United States : the 1990s / Nancy Cohen.
    p.   cm.
Includes bibliographical references and index.
ISBN 978-1-85109-976-4 (alk. paper) — ISBN 978-1-59884-127-5 (set)
EISBN 978-1-85109-977-1 (ebook)
1. United States—Social conditions—1980–   I. Title.
HN59.2.C595   2009
306.0973'09049—dc22   2008032816

12 11 10 09   1 2 3 4 5

Production Editor: Kristine Swift
Production Manager: Don Schmidt
Media Editor: Julie Dunbar
Media Resources Manager: Caroline Price
File Management Coordinator: Paula Gerard

This book is also available on the World Wide Web as an eBook.
Visit www.abc-clio.com for details.

ABC-CLIO, Inc.
130 Cremona Drive, P.O. Box 1911
Santa Barbara, California 93116–1911

This book is printed on acid-free paper ∞
Manufactured in the United States of America

Contents

Contents

Series Introduction

Ordinary people make history. They do so in ways that are different from the ways presidents, generals, business moguls, or celebrities make history; nevertheless, the history of ordinary people is just as profound, just as enduring. Immigration in the early decades of the 20th century was more than numbers and government policy; it was a collective experience of millions of men, women, and children whose political beliefs, vernacular cultural expression, discontent, and dreams transformed the United States. Likewise, during the Great Depression of the 1930s, President Franklin Delano Roosevelt advanced a broad spectrum of new social policies, but as historians have argued, ordinary Americans "made" the New Deal at the workplace, at the ballot box, on the picket lines, and on the city streets. They engaged in new types of consumer behavior, shifted political allegiances, and joined new, more aggressive trade unions. World War II and the Cold War were more than diplomatic maneuvering and military strategy; social upheavals changed the employment patterns, family relations, and daily life of ordinary people. More recently, the rise of the Christian Right in the last few decades is the expression of changing demographics and emerging social movements, not merely the efforts of a few distinct leaders.

These examples, which are drawn directly from the volumes in this series, highlight some of the essential themes of social history. Social history shifts the historical focus away from the famous and the political or economic elite to issues of everyday life. It explores the experiences ordinary Americans—native-born and immigrant, poor and rich, employed and unemployed, men and women, white and black—at home, at work, and at play. In the process, it focuses new attention on the significance of social movements, the behavior and meanings of consumerism, and the changing expression of popular culture.

In many ways, social history is not new. American historians early in the 20th century appreciated the importance of labor, immigration, religion, and urbanization in the study of society. However, early studies shared with political history the emphasis on leaders and major institutions and described a history that was mostly white and male—in other words, a history of those who held power. Several cultural shifts combined to transform how social history was understood and written in the last half of the 20th century: the democratization of higher education after World War II with the GI Bill and the expansion of public and land grant universities; the entry of women, children of immigrants, and racial minorities into the universities and the ranks of historians; and the social movements of the 1960s. Historians created new subjects for social history, casting it as "from the bottom." They realized that much was missing from familiar narratives that stressed the significance of "great men"—presidents, industrialists, and other usually white, usually male notables. Instead, women, working people, and ethnic and racial minorities have become integral parts of the American story along with work, leisure, and social movements.

The result has not simply been additive: ordinary people made history. The story of historical change is located in their lives and their struggles with and against others in power. Historians began to transform the central narrative of American history. They realized that—in the words of a popular 1930s folk cantata, "Ballad for Americans"—the "'etceteras' and the 'and so forths' that do the work" have a role in shaping their own lives, in transforming politics, and in recreating economics. Older themes of study, from industrialization to imperial expansion, from party politics to urbanization, were revisited through the inclusion of new actors, agents, and voices. These took their place alongside such new topics as social movements, popular culture, consumption, and community. But social history remains socially engaged scholarship; contemporary social issues continue to shape social historians' research and thinking. Historians in the 1970s and 1980s who focused on the experiences of working people, for instance, were challenged by the reality of deindustrialization. Likewise, historians in the 1990s who focused on popular culture and consumer behavior were influenced by the explosion of consumerism and new forms of cultural expression. Today's historians explore the antecedents to contemporary globalization as well as the roots of conservatism.

The transformation of the questions and agendas of each new era has made it apparent to historians that the boundaries of historical inquiry are not discrete. Social history, therefore, engages with other kinds of history. Social history reinterprets older narratives of politics and political economy and overlaps both areas. Social historians argue that politics is not restricted to ballot boxes or legislatures; politics is broad popular engagement with ideas about material wealth, social justice, moral values, and civil and human rights. Social historians, naturally, remain interested in changing political affiliations. They have, for example, examined the changing political allegiances of African Americans during the 1930s and the civil rights movement of the 1960s. So too have they examined the relationship of socialist and communist parties to working-class and immigrant communities. At the same time, social historians measure change by looking at such issues as family structure, popular culture, and consumer behavior.

For the social historian, the economy extends far beyond statistical data about production, gross domestic product, or employment. Rather, the economy is a lived experience. Wealthy or poor, Americans have negotiated the changing reality of economic life. Social historians ask questions about how different groups of Americans experienced and resisted major economic transformations and how they have grappled with economic uncertainty. The Great Depression of the 1930s, for example, left both urban workers and rural farmers perilously close to starvation. During the 1970s and 1980s, factories in the Rust Belt of the Midwest and Northeast shuttered or moved, and many Americans began laboring in new parts of the country and working new kinds of jobs, especially in the service sector. Americans have also grappled with the unequal distribution of wealth; some people advanced new ideas and engaged with emerging ideologies that challenged economic injustice, but others jealously guarded their privilege.

As social history has broadened its purview, it has transformed our sense of how historical change occurs. Social history changes our conception of chronology; change does not correspond to presidential election cycles. Social history also changes how we understand sources of power; power is constituted in and challenged by diverse peoples with different resources. Social historians, then, look at the long history of the 20th century in the United States and examine how the terrain has shifted under our feet, sometimes slowly and sometimes dramatically and abruptly. Social historians measure change in complex ways, including but also transcending demographic and geographic expansion and political transformation. How, for example, did the institution of the family change in the face of successive waves of immigration that often left spouses and children separated by national borders and oceans? Or during years of war with rising rates of women's wage and salary employment? Or following moralist reaction that celebrated imagined traditional values, and social movements that focused on issues of sexuality, birth control, homosexuality, and liberation? Historical change can also be measured by engagement with popular culture as Americans shifted their attention from vaudeville and pulp novels to radio, silent films, talkies, television, and finally the Internet and video games. The volumes in this series, divided by decades, trace all these changes.

To make sense of this complex and broadened field of inquiry, social historians often talk about how the categories by which we understand the past have been "invented," "contested," and "constructed." The nation has generally been divided along lines of race, class, gender, sexuality, and ethnicity. However, historians have also realized that analysts—whether in public or professional discourse—define these "categories of analysis" in different ways at different moments. Waves of immigration have reconfigured understandings of race and ethnicity, and more recent social movements have challenged the meanings of gender. Similarly, to be working class at the dawn of the age of industry in the 1900s meant something very different from being working class in the post-industrial landscape of the 1990s. How women or African Americans—to cite only two groups—understand their own identity can mean something different than how white men categorize them. Social historians, therefore, trace how Americans have always been divided about the direction of their lives and their nation, how they have consistently challenged and rethought social and cultural values and sought to renegotiate relationships of power, whether in the family, the workplace, the university, or the military. Actors do this armed with differing forms of power to authorize their view.

To examine these contestations, social historians have explored the way Americans articulated and defended numerous identities—as immigrants, citizens, workers, Christians, or feminists, for example. A post–World War II male chemical worker may have thought of himself as a worker and trade unionist at the factory, a veteran and a Democrat in his civic community, a husband and father at home, and as a white, middle-class homeowner. A female civil rights worker in the South in the 1960s may have seen herself as an African American when in the midst of a protest march or when refused service in a restaurant, as working class during a day job as a domestic worker or nurse, and as a woman when struggling to claim a leadership role in an activist organization.

Social historians have revisited older sources and mined rich new veins of information on the daily lives of ordinary people. Social historians engage with a host of materials—from government documents to census reports, from literature to oral histories, and from autobiographies to immigrant and foreign-language newspapers—to illuminate the lives, ideas, and activities of those who have been hidden from history. Social historians have also brought a broad "toolbox" of new methodologies to shed light on these sources. These methodologies are well represented in this series and illustrate the innovations of history from the bottom up. These volumes offer many tables and charts, which demonstrate the ways historians have made creative use of statistical analysis. Furthermore, the volumes are rich in illustrations as examples of the new ways that social historians "read" such images as cartoons or photographs.

The volumes in this series reflect the new subject matter, debates, and methodologies that have composed the writing of the United States' 20th-century social history. The volumes have unique features that make them particularly valuable for students and teachers; they are hybrids that combine the narrative advantages of the monograph with the specific focus of the encyclopedia. Each volume has been authored or co-authored by established social historians. Where the work has been collaborative, the authors have shared the writing and worked to sustain a narrative voice and conceptual flow in the volume. Authors have written the social history for the decade of their expertise and most have also taught its history. Each volume begins with a volume introduction by the author or authors that lays out the major themes of the decade and the big picture—how the social changes of the era transformed the lives of Americans. The author then synthesizes the best and most path-breaking new works in social history. In the case of the last three volumes, which cover the post-1970 era, scholarship remains in its relative infancy. In particular, these three volumes are major original efforts to both define the field and draw upon the considerable body of original research that has already been completed.

The ten volumes in the series divide the century by its decades. This is an avowedly neutral principle of organization that does not privilege economic, political, or cultural transformations; this allows readers to develop their own sense of a moment and their own sense of change. While it remains to be seen how the most recent decades will be taught and studied, in cases such as the 1920s, the 1930s, and the 1960s, this decadal organization replicates how historians frequently study and teach history. The Progressive Era (ca. 1890–1920) and postwar America (ca. 1945–1960) have less often been divided by decades. This highlights the neutrality of this division. In truth, all divisions are imposed: we speak of long decades or short centuries, and so forth. When historians teach the 1960s, they often reach back into the 1950s and ahead into the 1970s. The authors and editors of these volumes recognize that social processes, movements, ideas, and leaders do not rise and fall with the turn of the calendar; therefore, they have worked to knit the volumes together as a unit.

Readers can examine these texts individually or collectively. The texts can be used to provide information on significant events or individuals. They can provide an overview of a pivotal decade. At the same time, these texts are designed to allow readers to follow changing themes over time and to develop their own sense of chronology. The authors regularly spoke with one another and with the series editors to establish the major themes and subthemes in the social history of the century and to sustain story lines across the volumes. Each volume divides the material into six or seven chapters that discuss major themes such as labor or work; urban, suburban, and rural life; private life; politics; economy; culture; and social movements. Each chapter begins with an overview essay and then explores four to six major topics. The discrete essays at the heart of each volume give readers focus on a social movement, a social idea, a case study, a social institution, and so forth. Unlike traditional encyclopedias, however, the narrative coherence of the single-authored text permits authors to break the decade bubble with discussions on the background or effects of a social event.

There are several other features that distinguish this series.

- Many chapters include capsules on major debates in the social history of the era. Even as social historians strive to build on the best scholarship available, social history remains incomplete and contested; readers can benefit from studying this tension.

- The arguments in these volumes are supported by many tables and graphics. Social history has mobilized demographic evidence and—like its sister field, cultural history—has increasingly turned to visual evidence, both for the social history of media and culture and as evidence of social conditions. These materials are not presented simply as illustrations but as social evidence to be studied.

- Timelines at the head of every chapter highlight for readers all the major events and moments in the social history that follows.

- A series of biographical sketches at the end of every chapter highlights the lives of major figures more often overlooked in histories of the era. Readers can find ample biographical material on more prominent figures in other sources; here the authors have targeted lesser known but no less interesting and important subjects.

- Bibliographies include references to electronic sources and guide readers to material for further study.

- Three indices—one for each volume, one for the entire series, and one for all the people and events in the series—are provided in each volume. Readers can easily follow any of the major themes across the volumes.

Finally, we end with thanks for the supportive assistance of Ron Boehm and Kristin Gibson at ABC-CLIO, and especially to Dr. Alex Mikaberidze and Dr. Kim Kennedy White, who helped edit the manuscripts for the press. But of course, these volumes are the product of the extraordinary group of historians to whom we are particularly indebted:

The 1900s: Brian Greenberg and Linda S. Watts
The 1910s: Gordon Reavley
The 1920s: Linda S. Watts, Alice L. George, and Scott Beekman
The 1930s: Cecelia Bucki
The 1940s: Mark Ciabattari
The 1950s: John C. Stoner and Alice L. George
The 1960s: Troy D. Paino
The 1970s: Laurie Mercier
The 1980s: Peter C. Holloran and Andrew Hunt
The 1990s: Nancy Cohen

Daniel J. Walkowitz, Series Editor
Daniel E. Bender, Series Associate Editor

Introduction: From the New World Order to the New Economy

The 1990s began with an ending—the end of the Cold War. Americans reveled in the giddy promise, the pride and satisfaction of a victory of values, not just might. In the afterglow of triumph, American politicians, the press, and the public gave themselves over to a heady mix of utopianism, opportunism, and national self-congratulation. The social history of the decade unfolded amidst this culturally all-encompassing historical break.

The Cold War had served as one of the principle forces shaping political, economic, and cultural life in the United States in the postwar era. In the years of the Cold War (1947–1989), hundreds of thousands of Americans fought and tens of thousands died in hot wars in Korea and Vietnam. Seventeen trillion dollars of the nation's wealth went to the building of a military superpower. Anticommunist crusades against leftists and progressives in public schools, universities, labor unions, Hollywood, and civil rights and arts organizations shifted American politics to the center and, episodically, to the right. The ever-looming possibility of nuclear war haunted popular culture. The "military-industrial complex"—in President Dwight Eisenhower's memorable phrase—grew to become one of the most powerful sectors of the economy, reshaping whole regions with the infusion of government military investment.

The end of the Cold War represented an opening, an opportunity, which stood ready to be seized. But first, its meaning had to be clarified. Historians generally agree that the Communist regimes of Eastern Europe and the Soviet Union collapsed (between 1988 and 1991) under the strain of their own internal conflicts and contradictions. The end of communism was interpreted in the United

States, however, within the frame of the nation's recent political history under presidents Ronald Reagan and George H. W. Bush. Republicans ascribed the Soviet defeat to Reagan's muscular militarism, but the interpretation did not gain broad acceptance, in part because it was so obviously a partisan one. The explanation that did take hold spoke to a deeper understanding of the character of America. The communist economic and social system had presented an alternative worldview for most of the 20th century. Victory in the Cold War affirmed the political, economic, and moral superiority of America in the global competition for hearts and minds. The mood was captured and memorialized in the much-cited and little-read book *The End of History and the Last Man*, by neoconservative Francis Fukuyama. Fukuyama projected that every nation would emulate the American model of democratic government and capitalist economy. By doing so, war, poverty, oppression, and every other ill that had ever troubled human existence would end.

The triumphalism that greeted the end of the Cold War entertained the potential for two different and contrary responses. In one alternative, the nation's victory could spur Americans to take on even greater national endeavors. Bush's proclamation of a "New World Order" and the liberal quest for bold domestic initiatives funded by the "peace dividend" each anticipated that the collective energy that had fueled American victory in the Cold War would be harnessed to renewed public purpose. As the decade progressed, those who harbored such hopes would be disappointed.

A turn inward, toward private life and private pleasures, was an equally plausible response to victory in the Cold War. During the Cold War, American leaders had extolled capitalism's satisfaction of consumer desires as one of the main virtues of the American system. Who could fault Americans for viewing the end of the superpower conflict as a warrant to enjoy the fruits of their past sacrifice free of cares?

The sense in the 1990s of being poised between two epochal markers—the historical one of Cold War victory, the metaphysical one of the coming millennium—helped spawn a cottage industry in commentary about the meaning and direction of America. By middecade, the triumphant mood had given way to disaffection. Commentators from opposite ends of the political spectrum were lamenting the small-mindedness of the nation's politics and the mood of complacency toward public and political endeavors paralyzing Americans. Roger Rosenblatt, a liberal journalist, ruefully expropriated the decade's colloquial expression of jaded boredom and dubbed 1995 the year of "whatever." He hoped that such apathy toward public affairs would be transitory (Rosenblatt 1996). Andrew Ferguson, a conservative journalist, in 1997 mused regretfully, "An era of tiny commotions lacking great challenges and scandals, villains and causes—affords us a rare respite from the storms of history. Surely over the horizon some large commotions loom, and when they arrive, we'll marvel at our current capacity to make something out of nothing" (Ferguson 1997, 132).

The political scientist Robert Putnam diagnosed in the body politic a more resistant malady. America had become a society of people who "bowled alone"; the voluntary organizations that had sustained civic engagement and enriched communal identity for over two centuries had withered. Democracy was the casualty of the disease (Putnam 2000).

The disaffection had several taproots. One was in the international arena itself. International events quickly lay to rest the quaint notion that history—political and military conflict—had come to an end. In the international arena, the decade saw civil wars, refugee crises, genocide, military coups, nationalist insurrections, and nuclear proliferation. And through it all, relentlessly, 2 to 3 million people died each year from HIV/AIDS. While scientists warned of catastrophic climate change, 9 of the 10 hottest years in recorded history occurred between 1989 and 1999. New viruses that threatened uncontrollable global pandemics emerged. The Cold War was over, but these new international problems were ever-present in the news, distracting the president and Congress from settling down to America's main business at hand—reaping the domestic benefits of Cold War victory. Whether American soldiers actually went to war, as they did in the Persian Gulf and Bosnia and other smaller ventures, or a distant conflict ultimately struck home, as it did with the Middle East conflicts and the 9/11 attacks, international affairs had a powerful influence on the lives of Americans in the 1990s.

It cannot be overstated that few Americans wished to involve themselves deeply in international affairs. Isolationism has a venerable, if checkered, history in American popular culture, and it was evident in the 1990s that many people were tiring of the Sisyphean task of international engagement. But it has been many decades since Americans lived their lives largely untouched by the rest of the world. In the type of work Americans did, the goods they consumed, the people they lived with, the means through which they communicated, the culture they absorbed, and the threats they feared, Americans were enmeshed in a globally interconnected world. The phrase "the global village" was coined in the 1990s. It was a clever one, quickly worn down by overuse to a cliché. Nonetheless, it captured well the social experience of American life in the globalized world culture of the end of the 20th century.

GLOBALIZATION, THE NEW ECONOMY, AND TECHNOLOGY

"We need not shrink from the challenge of the global economy," President William Jefferson Clinton told the nation in his 1997 State of the Union Address. "The new promise of the global economy, the information age, unimagined new work, life-enhancing technology, all these are ours to seize."

Clinton's speech was given a couple years into a phase of economic growth. The economic expansion of the 1990s ultimately turned out to be one of the longest peacetime expansions of the 20th century. The last two years of the decade were awash in celebrations of a "New Economy," as the stock market hit record highs and new technology—"dot-com"—companies multiplied. The official statistics on U.S. economic performance in the 1990s chart a growing, vibrant economy. The media celebrated the boom, adding in a healthy dose of enthusiasm and utopian projection.

Technology was not only the hottest investment ever (until it was not) but also the force enabling, sustaining, shaping, and underpinning the New Economy. The 1990s was a watershed decade in the penetration of technology into all realms of American life. New technologies were invented, and others were made available publicly for the first time. The most significant ones, of course, were the opening of the Internet to commercial use and the invention of the World Wide Web. Yet in the economy, more important was the diffusion of older technologies—computing, robotization, and the like—throughout American factories, offices, and stores. To take one example from the author's life, in my first job out of college in 1985, I typed memos on an electric typewriter, stuffed them in an envelope, and dropped them in interoffice mail. Some hours later, they would be delivered. By the end of the 1990s, email had replaced interoffice mail, and typewriters were collectors' items. To take another example, this time from American public life, the president of the United States expressed shock at the workings of a grocery store barcode scanner while on the campaign trail in 1992. The incident contributed to his electoral defeat, for it was a little late to be so innocent.

In the first decade of the 21st century, Americans have come to take for granted many activities of daily life that were, in 1990, confined to the fantasies of a handful of techies. The spread of new technologies between 1990 and today was unprecedented. Consider that it took 38 years for radio, after its invention, to reach 50 million listeners. Within 4 years of the opening of the Internet to the public in 1992, 50 million people were surfing the web. In 2005, an estimated 1 billion people worldwide were online (*The World Almanac* 2006).

Nevertheless, the changes in the 1990s only went so far. The Blackberry—aka Crackberry—debuted in 1999 with no telephone capabilities. The first iPod went on sale in 2001. Google did not start to turn a profit until 2001, and did not go public until 2004. Technologies and practices taken for granted today, such as the digitization of music, text messaging, and the commercially viable MP3 players, were not broadly available before 2000. Another consideration for assessing the impact of new technology on American social life in the 1990s is that many Americans did not yet have access to the new technologies. Social commentators worried that a "digital divide," mirroring the economic divide between the upper middle class and the rest of America, might become permanently entrenched. Developments since 2000 have not borne out the dire predictions of a technological global divide.

THE ECONOMIC DIVIDE

Before the end-of-decade boom and its utopian technology-driven New Era, the first half of the decade had brought grim times to many Americans. Those memories were still strong in 1997 when Clinton lauded the new globalized world order. His speech was not simply a statement of fact but rather an exhortation to the many Americans who viewed globalization not with anticipation but with alarm and anxiety—and with good cause.

For most of the 20th century, America's international economic and military supremacy had mutually reinforced each other. Even as the collapse of the Soviet superpower seemed to confirm American superiority, the international economy was delivering rude shocks to American workers and businesses.

The American experience of the global economy of the 1990s represented a significant break with the nation's recent past, a past that was in the living memory of many adults. From 1948 to 1973, Americans had enjoyed a broadly shared prosperity that was unparalleled in world history. Postwar prosperity had rested on a high rate of economic growth, high worker productivity, cheap and abundant natural resources (especially oil), and the utter dominance of American industry in the world economy. Even more important were its sociopolitical supports: the power of American unions in core manufacturing industries; the political clout of the national labor federation, the AFL-CIO; the social contract between American industry and those unions; and the broad egalitarian cultural consensus.

The economic woes of the 1970s eroded the social and material basis of what many, in retrospect, viewed as the Golden Age. The social peace between American industry and labor had been founded on sharing the abundance of growth; it disintegrated when growth stalled and a smaller pie was left to divide. Beginning in 1979, first under the leadership of the new Federal Reserve chairman, Paul Volcker, and then more deliberately under the administration of President Ronald Reagan, the United States government and American business reversed many of the policies that had underwritten the shared prosperity of the postwar era. When economic growth was renewed after the deep recession of the early 1980s, it took a new course. Companies merged or moved their operations overseas, and their profits rose; manufacturing jobs disappeared, and blue-collar wages fell.

The 1990s opened with the nation heading into a recession, and the celebratory mood with which Americans greeted the end of the Cold War faded rapidly.

On paper, the recession was a short one. Although economic growth resumed by 1992, Americans in the first half of the 1990s kept losing jobs by the hundreds of thousands, and wages and income remained stagnant. Corporate restructuring and globalization, which had wiped out so many blue-collar jobs in the 1980s, was now taking its toll on the white-collar middle class. This early decade experience sharply undercut the sense of security middle-class Americans had come to take for granted in the postwar era.

The economic expansion of the rest of the decade was truly impressive. However, even though the wealth of the nation increased, it remained distributed in a highly unequal manner, as it had been since the beginning of the Reagan years. As the top 20 percent of the population became richer, the standard amenities of postwar middle-class life—homeownership, good public schools, quality health care, a secure retirement, and college education—slipped out of reach for many middle-income and working Americans.

Most striking about the growth of inequality in the last two decades of the 20th century was its dramatic reversal of postwar economic trends and the de facto repudiation of that era's cultural ideals. In less than 20 years, American society had returned to the extremes of the precrash Roaring Twenties. As the 1990s closed, there were contradictory signs about the direction the future would hold. Middle- and working-class income had started to rise briskly in 1997, and some predicted that, even though the gains of the New Economy had come belatedly to the majority of Americans, income would continue to rise on its foundation. Others countered that increasing levels of indebtedness and skyrocketing costs for health care and child care were eating away at the fairly meager raises gained by the majority. By the middle of the 2000s, it was possible to say that both were right. If trends from the late 1990s had continued, it would have partially arrested the move toward increasing inequality. Instead, economic and political developments—the recession of 2001–2002, the tax cuts of the administration of George W. Bush—wiped out the gains won by most Americans in the 1990s and returned the baseline to the Reagan–Bush years. In the expansion of 2002 and after, as gross domestic product and profits grew at a rapid clip, inequality widened, and median income steadily fell.

America in the 1990s was thus a society materially divided by income and wealth. In similar historical circumstances, Americans had reacted to the accumulation of extreme wealth with populist and progressive movements targeted at the destructive effects of economic inequality. In the 1990s, a few tried to raise the clarion call to a new social activism. Some scholars attempted to educate the public about the facts of the maldistribution of wealth. From the wings of the union movement, local activists won living-wage laws by appealing to their neighbors' sense of fairness that a fair day's work deserved a fair day's wage. Vibrant, if small, student antisweatshop, anticorporate, and radical environmental movements briefly metamorphosed into a larger "antiglobalization" movement that burst on the scene in Seattle in November 1999. Despite these efforts to awaken a broader public, economic inequality remained a minor theme in American political and cultural debate in the 1990s. The corporate scandals that were revealed in 2002 momentarily sparked public outrage, phrased in the classic populist vein of hostility toward the idle rich. But the patriotism evoked by the lead up to the Iraq War quickly put a stop to the reconsideration then underway of the social cost of the 1990s boom.

The economic and political changes reshaping the class composition of American society were registered more personally. The anxiety and insecurity felt by many were revealed in surveys about work and the New Economy; the feelings expressed episodically by the "angry voter." More commonly, when Americans sought to make sense of the changes in American society, it was not through class but rather through the idiom of culture and identity.

DIVERSITY AND DIFFERENCE, COMMUNITY AND IDENTITY

Sometime between the 1980s and the middle of the first decade of the 21st century, "diversity" traveled the path from discovery to unremarkable background banality. The 1990s were, again, as for technology, the watershed decade in this shift. The demographic and cultural reality of Americans in the 1990s was unparalleled diversity. The battles over the significance and effect of diversity seemed essential to the identity and future of the nation. Sorting out the material reality of diversity from the ideological blandishments for and against it is one of the main challenges for a historian of the 1990s.

The remarkable transformation in American family life and the ethnic composition of the nation continued and accelerated in the 1990s. These demographic changes propelled related changes in American beliefs, personal habits, and relationships. All had been under way since the late 1960s. By the year 2000, it appeared that a fundamental transformation in American identity had taken place.

The transformation of the American family in the last two decades of the 20th century was nothing short of revolutionary. Delayed marriage, cohabitation outside of marriage, single motherhood, single householders, a high divorce and remarriage rate, and blended families were all common features of the American mosaic in the 1990s. More significantly, the 1990s was the turning-point decade for the gay family—demographically, legally, politically, and culturally.

The change had begun in the early 1970s, catalyzed by two distinct forces. First, the feminist and gay liberation movements had challenged conventional notions of gender roles and family and thus had created the legal and cultural conditions for individuals to make unconventional choices about sexuality and family formation. And with these new choices went a new approach to child rearing, particularly when it came to raising girls. Second, the long-term changes in the U.S. economy exerted powerful, if unacknowledged sway, over individual choices about family. When wages stagnated in the 1970s, American families kept their incomes from dropping even further by working more. The lion's share of those additional hours were logged by women—wives and mothers who entered the paid labor force, even as they remained largely responsible for caring for children and home. Over the course of the 1980s and 1990s, married women with children increased their time spent in paid labor by the equivalent of two to three extra months a year. While reliable statistics exist for the number of hours worked, it is impossible to quantify the effect of economic strain on individual decisions to forego children, limit family size, marry late, divorce, or never marry. American culture in the 1990s—from daytime TV to academic sociological research—attested that the pressure was generating enormous stress for millions of Americans.

During the quarter-century in which Americans refashioned the family, another fundamental demographic change was underway as well. Immigration, accelerating after the changes in immigration law in the 1960s, created remarkable and unparalleled ethnic, national, and religious diversity in the United States. From 1960 to 1990, 15 million people legally entered the United States to work and live (Daniels and Graham 2001). In the 1990s, the American-born children of these immigrants were reaching adulthood, and an additional 13 to 14 million people emigrated—both legally and without authorization—to America (Passel and Suro 2005). Most immigrants, roughly four out of every five, emigrated from the countries of Latin America and Asia.

The vigorous debate about immigration and ethnicity was at heart a struggle about the nature of American identity. There is no question that the millions of immigrants and their children who joined the American community in the last quarter of the 20th century played an important part in recasting American social and cultural life. To give one dramatic example, in 2000, the children in the Los Angeles public school system spoke over 140 languages. For some Americans, the desire to preserve America as it was led them into a new nativist political movement that sought to close the borders, deny immigrants access to public services, and make English the official language of state. Others welcomed the cultural renewal they perceived would follow in the wake of such a large and diverse infusion of immigrants, and hoped to enlist immigrants in the cause of the New Economy and multiculturalism. Those who directly employed immigrants were wary about entering the political and cultural fray, understanding that their interests were not likely to be advanced by either side. Immigrants themselves followed no single script. Few stepped back to observe that all parties were replaying earlier cultural dramas from the first decades of the 20th century over the practice, effects, and meaning of immigration.

Americans and their leaders were not quite sure whether these changes were destroying America or revitalizing it, increasing tensions or dissolving differences as a postethnic nation took form. In daily life, the young befriended one another, played sports together, listened to one another's music, and, when questioned, revealed that they were less obsessed by differences in race, nation, and language than were their parents. They married with far less regard to their ethnicity of origin and began new American families of their own. The old categories through which Americans made sense of difference had nothing to say about this phenomenon, and the census of 2000 debuted a new classification, allowing people to "self-identify with more than one race." Young people in the West were the most likely to take advantage of the opportunity. Nevertheless, America was far from a postethnic utopia. Membership in white supremacist organizations surged; high schools were terrorized by rival white, African American, Latino, and Asian American gangs. The ongoing and accelerating change in the ethnic makeup of American communities profoundly affected the lives of Americans, from the most intimate questions of friendship and family to the largest matters of government.

Culture and Politics

A soaring crime rate, a persisting crack epidemic, the Crown Heights and Los Angeles riots, an anti-immigrant political movement, pitched and violent confrontations at abortion clinics, and the Oklahoma City Bombing gave the appearance that America in the first half of the 1990s was on a steady course to social chaos and balkanization. By middecade, the signs of endemic social breakdown disappeared. (The correlation with the improving economy, as various chapters will discuss, was quite strong.) Crime rates plummeted, and drug use declined. There were no more riots, and anti-immigrant nativism and right-wing terrorism settled back onto the extremist fringe.

What persisted were the conflicts of the so-called Culture Wars and partisan politics. The public life of the decade in many ways turned on the very question of the object of political action and the purview of the state. Did politics primarily concern classic matters of state, such as economic and social policy and international relations? Or was politics simply Culture War by other means, and the state a battleground over religion, morality, and sex roles?

In a decade when participation in formal politics reached a nadir, everyday life was politicized to a greater degree than ever before in the Culture Wars. The Culture Wars, which began in the 1980s and continue to the present, originated in the opposing worldviews and political programs of the 1960s' New Left and New Right. They found fertile ground in the social, economic, and political transformations in American life of the last quarter of the 20th century. By the end of the 1990s, the Right had become more effective at mobilizing to win political power, yet many of the social and cultural changes first advocated by the New Left—concerning sexuality and gender, family relationships, and popular culture—had been widely adopted by millions of Americans. On the eve of the millennium, it was hard to imagine American society returning to the traditional ways promoted by social conservatives.

Even though the Culture Wars seemed to be all-consuming, the 1990s were still important years for politics in the conventional sense. The election of Bill Clinton as a self-styled "New Democrat" in 1992 raised questions of broad significance. In the 1980s, conservative Republicans had proudly adopted the rhetoric of revolution to describe their ascendancy with Reagan; Democratic liberalism seemed in full retreat. Yet, by the early 1990s, deprived of Reagan's charismatic leadership, the Republican revolution sputtered to a halt, and it appeared that the Republican New Right was about to join New Deal liberals in the graveyard of American politics. In the post–Cold War era, when the historical dividing lines between Democrats and Republicans no longer seemed relevant, what new political identities would emerge in the American citizenry, and how would the political parties adapt? Would the new postliberal, postconservative program—the "Third Way" in Clinton's formulation—become a viable project? Would a resurgent conservatism complete the unfinished Reagan Revolution? While disaffection hardened into a virtual political philosophy within the American citizenry, professional politicians and political activists set themselves to transforming the two political parties. Together these contradictory forces transformed American political life.

Into the New Millennium: An Uncertain Future

During the 1990s, Americans believed the decade to be the dawn of a new era. They saw the end of the Cold War as a historical turning point, creating new possibilities. The palpable sense of the opportunity to be seized, felt by many Americans, was heightened by the millennium fervor that bubbled up by mid-decade. The 1990s, as it was lived, gave every indication of being a watershed decade in American history—the pivot of change from an old America to a new America.

The approach of the millennium fed many projections about America, the world, and the universe that were remote from any grounded sense of how history typically progresses. Once the celebrations of New Years 2000 died down, however, historical time and reality reasserted itself. The 1990s ended not with the second coming or the apocalypse delivered by the Y2K computer virus but with a contested presidential election and the return of an old economy recession.

In 2000 and the first half of 2001, it was a safe bet that the economic dislocations, cultural disputes, and political contests of the 1990s would continue to unfold along a predictable path during the coming years. Electoral politics assumed new urgency when a divided Supreme Court prohibited a vote recount in Florida and in effect handed the presidency to Republican George W. Bush, who had lost the popular vote by over half a million votes to Democrat Al Gore. Anxiety about personal livelihoods reawakened and New Economy fantasies withered, as trillions in wealth and hundreds of thousands of jobs were wiped out by the stock market fall of 2000–2001. Public debate returned to the mundane issues of income inequality, the trade deficit, health care costs, and the loss of jobs to lower-wage production overseas.

People do not live neatly in decades. Rather our lives are punctuated by personal passages and turning points. Social history is particularly attuned to this kind of reckoning of time. Occasionally, however, events in the larger world—history with a capital "H"—jolt us out of the familiar pathways of our lives. September 11 was one of those seismic historical events. For individual Americans, it seemed personally inescapable. It was inevitable that the American government would react, even if there was no predetermined way forward. The terrorist attacks of 9/11 abruptly interrupted the transition that was underway. The 1990s stand as an interval between the Cold War America that Americans left behind in the last month of the 1980s and a future reshaped by the response to 9/11. The greatest conceit of the 1990s was that History Ends. It does not. It will require historians in the future, looking at the years and decades ahead of us today, to determine whether the 1990s was a lost decade or, as it seemed in its midst, the opening of a new age.

REFERENCES AND FURTHER READINGS

Daniels, Roger, and Otis L. Graham. 2001. *Debating American immigration, 1882–Present.* Lanham, MD: Rowman & Littlefield Publishers.

Ferguson, Andrew. 1997. An era of tiny commotions. *Time,* October 27, 132.

Passel, Jeffrey S., and Roberto Suro. 2005. *Rise, Peak and Decline: Trends in U.S. Immigration, 1992–2004.* Washington, DC: Pew Hispanic Center.

Putnam, Robert D. 2000. *Bowling alone: The collapse and revival of American community.* New York: Simon & Schuster.

Rosenblatt, Roger. 1996. To be or not to be . . . whatever. *Time,* December 30, 104(4).

The World Almanac and Book of Facts. 2006. New York: World Almanac.

Issues of the 20th Century

The Economy, Work, and Business

Overview

The longest economic expansion on record in American history occurred from 1992 to 2000, and at the end of the decade, the idea that something fundamental had changed in the economy took hold in the concept of the "New Economy." Was the New Economy new? Each age has its own obsessions, and in the 1990s, the notion of a New Economy held pride of place. The initial outburst of free market triumphalism that had greeted the end of the Cold War helped create the conditions for Americans' fascination with the business of getting and spending; diminished worry about a war between the superpowers also cleared the ground for making other pursuits a national priority. This chapter opens with an examination of the broad economic trends of the 1990s, including the ideas, assumptions, and debates accompanying the cultural invention of the New Economy.

In the 1990s, a key element of the economy, and thinking about the economy, concerned globalization. "The new promise of the global economy, the information age, unimagined new work, life-enhancing technology, all these are ours to seize," intoned President Clinton in his 1997 State of the Union Address. "We need not shrink from the challenge of the global economy." The concept of globalization moved, in the 1990s, beyond the realm of academic investigation to become one of the most hotly debated issues in American life. Americans increasingly understood that their fate was tethered to the world market. The second section in this chapter explores the economic, social, cultural, and political facets of globalization.

1

In the first half of the decade, the combined force of a recession, globalization, and the unprecedented nature of economic recovery sowed broad anxiety among working- and middle-class Americans. This chapter proceeds to examine the transformation of work, first in the manufacturing and then in the service sector. Massive lay-offs in manufacturing over the previous decade and a half had transformed the lives of industrial workers and the communities where American manufacturing had been concentrated. This long-term economic transformation in the 1990s changed the nature of industrial work itself, forced industrial communities to adapt to the changed landscape, and unsettled the lives of American workers. Whereas blue-collar workers had taken the brunt of layoffs in the 1970s and 1980s, in the early 1990s, corporate lay-offs—euphemized in the 1990s as "downsizing"—targeted managers, professionals, and white-collar clerical workers. This section examines the sectoral shift in the American economy and the experience of Americans working in the vast array of service jobs.

The impressive economic expansion of the 1990s was strengthened, and then propelled, by a soaring stock market. Over the course of the boom, the Dow Jones Industrial Average quadrupled, the NASDAQ Composite Index increased tenfold, and $8 trillion in new wealth was generated. The most unusual element of the market boom was the historically unprecedented level of individual investment in stocks: half of all Americans owned stock by the turn of the century. The collapse of the securities markets in 2000–2001 wiped out $5 trillion and threw the economy into recession—and, as the dust settled, generated more sober thinking about the notion of a New Economy. The last section of the chapter examines business from a variety of angles, from the performance of key businesses to the practice and culture of the stock market craze at the end of the decade. The history of the 1990s' economic life would not be complete without a reckoning of the new century's bankruptcies and corporate corruption scandals, which were set in motion during the 1990s boom. The origins of the scandals are addressed in a specific and exemplary case—that of Enron—at the conclusion of the chapter.

TIMELINE

1990	The prototype for the World Wide Web is written by Tim Berners-Lee.
	The recession begins and continues through end of 1991. The recession is exacerbated by large federal budget and trade deficits, built up during the 1980s.
1991	Congress authorizes the National Science Foundation to open the Internet to commercial use.

The NASDAQ Composite Index is at 500 (April).

Unemployment nears 7 percent.

Recovery from the recession begins, as the decline in growth ends.

President George H. W. Bush and Congress reach a compromise to raise taxes and cut spending in order to reduce the budget deficit.

1992   The World Wide Web is available for public use.

Unemployment reaches 7.5 percent as economic growth has resumed, which leads to the invention of the concept of the "jobless recovery."

The presidential election campaign focuses on the economy, and exit polls show that the economy is the most important issue to the majority of voters.

Economic expansion begins late in the year.

The North American Free Trade Agreement (NAFTA), which creates the largest free trade zone in the world between the United States, Mexico, and Canada, is signed by President Bush.

The total federal debt reaches $3.4 trillion, and the federal budget deficit increases to $290 billion.

Wal-Mart becomes the largest retailer in the world.

1993   Commercial services, computer companies, and software developers distribute web browsers to make web surfing possible for people without technical computer knowledge.

Robert Rubin is appointed chair of the National Economic Council.

NAFTA is ratified.

The General Agreement on Tariffs and Trade (GATT) is revised during the Uruguay Round of talks. The revision creates the World Trade Organization (WTO).

The Omnibus Budget Reconciliation Act reduces the deficit, raises taxes on higher incomes, and expands tax credits for low-wage workers.

1994   Average real wages are at a 25-year low.

The Clinton administration spearheads trade negotiations with Japan and China.

GATT is ratified.

The Federal Reserve raises interest rates to slow expansion.

The United States bails out investors in Mexican debt.

1995   The WTO established by GATT comes into existence on January 1.

Real average wages begin to rise.

Shares of Netscape are publicly offered, and on the first day of trading, the stock price rises from $28 to $58. It is the first of the technology IPOs of the dot-com stock market boom.

Stock market rise begins, as NASDAQ hits 1,000.

The Federal Reserve reverses policies over the course of the year, as concerns about inflationary pressures are balanced against the fall of the U.S. dollar in world markets.

1996   Congress passes legislation that deregulates the telecommunications industry.

Robert Rubin is appointed secretary of the treasury in the second term of the Clinton presidency.

1997   The unemployment rate falls below 5 percent for first full year since 1969.

The Taxpayer Relief Act reduces taxes on inheritance and capital gains and provides tax credits for middle-income households.

The United States spearheads an international bailout in response to the East Asian financial crisis.

1998   The first federal budget surplus since 1969 is recorded.

The price–earnings ratio of stocks reaches an all-time U.S. high.

The United Auto Workers (UAW) strike two General Motors (GM) auto parts plants in Flint, Michigan, for seven weeks, idling all of GM's North American factories. GM loses market share in automobiles, which it never regains.

The Federal Reserve and the Clinton administration engineer a bailout of Long Term Capital Management, a private hedge fund, to prevent a collapse of financial markets.

The U.S. Justice Department initiates an antitrust suit against Microsoft.

1999   For first time since 1995, the Federal Reserve raises interest rates in response to the tight labor market.

The Dow Jones Industrial Average hits 10,000 for the first time in history.

Antiglobalization protests take place in Seattle at the meeting of WTO.

The Financial Services Modernization Act repeals New Deal–era banking regulation.

2000   The Dow hits a high of 11,302 (January).

The NASDAQ hits a high of 5,132 (March).

The stock market plunges on Black Friday, April 14, wiping out $2 trillion in investments and beginning a fall that will result in the year's 24 percent decline in the S&P 500 and 60 percent decline in the NASDAQ.

ECONOMIC TRENDS IN THE 1990s: FROM RECESSION TO NEW ECONOMY BOOM

In May 1995, *Fortune* magazine announced, "without the slightest risk of hyperbole, or an outsize sense of self-importance by our magazine, I can tell you that the issue of Fortune you hold in your hands is a historic one. Save it for your grandchildren." The momentous occasion was the magazine's revamping of its 40-year-old Fortune 500 list to mark the discovery of the New Economy. "As our industrial economy yields to a new economy, one much more driven by services and what the software writers call 'pure thought stuff,' let this event mark the watershed" (Huey 1995, 8).

The New Economy was historically significant for its replay of classic American New Era utopianism; it was not a particularly accurate description of the economy. The more prosaic economic statistics of the decade demonstrate that Americans in the 1990s experienced a typical business cycle. A long and vigorous economic expansion was bookended at start and finish by recession.

Recession and the Jobless Recovery, 1990–1991

The early-decade recession was a typical contraction. As businesses experienced falling profits, they ceased buying from their suppliers, froze wages, fired workers, and halted new capital investment. Many businesses went bankrupt. By typical composite measures of recessions, the early 1990s one was in the mid-range of severity for the post-1973 era.

A group stands at Pennsylvania's capitol building protesting unemployment and unfair employment benefits, February 18, 1993. (Wally McNamee/Corbis)

The one new feature of the recession was in the character of its recovery. Even as the official measures showed the nation's economy in an expansion, workers continued to be laid off and unemployment remained abnormally high for a recovery. In short, businesses were growing, the economy as a whole was growing, but workers were still unable to find jobs. Four and a half million jobs were lost between 1990 and 1992, more than were lost during the deep recession of the early 1980s (Johnson 1995). The unemployment rate remained at recession levels, rising from 5.6 percent in 1990 to 7.5 percent in 1992; the long-term unemployment rate doubled, from 10 to 20 percent over the same period. Average wages and median family incomes fell (EPI 2006). Recession levels of unemployment in a phase of economic growth was utterly unprecedented in American economic history. Economists coined the term "jobless recovery" to describe the disjuncture.

Expansion, 1992–2000

Gross Domestic Product (GDP) grew briskly from 1992 to 2000, creating the longest economic expansion in U.S. history. The disjuncture between rising profits for business and hard times for workers persisted well into 1993 and 1994, and uncertainty about the sustainability of growth characterized these years. In

1995, as the expansion kicked into high gear, most economists concluded that the economy was in a healthy growth phase that was likely to continue. By 1996, good times were pronounced more generally throughout the land. Overall, GDP growth averaged 3.7 percent over the entire 1992–2000 expansion. The rate of growth was particularly high, at 4.1 percent, during the latter half of the decade.

By the end of the decade, the U.S. economy was running at full employment, low inflation, and a high rate of growth. The country had not been on such solid economic ground on so many counts since the 1960s. After the initial phase of the expansion, in which job growth stagnated, an all-time record number of 32 million new jobs were created between 1992 and 2000 (Krugman 2003). The unemployment rate fell to 4.2 percent in 1999, its lowest level in 30 years, and continued downward to 4 percent in 2000, the last year of the expansion (EPI 2006).

Recession, 2000–2001

The national economy began to reverse course in late 2000, as the sharp decline in the stock markets ushered in a recession. The U.S. economy was officially in recession from March 2001 to November 2002. This was one of the shortest and mildest recessions on record. Nevertheless, growth in employment again lagged behind GDP growth.

Debates: A New Economy?

The notion that American ingenuity can override the laws of economics is a familiar one in American history, and the New Economy of the 1990s thus was part of a venerable American tradition. Each New Era nevertheless has its own distinctive character. (As it must, or else the idea of its novelty would not be persuasive.) The utopianism of New Economy thinking recalibrated the early decade's notion of the "end of history," and the search for national identity in the moment between the end of the Cold War and the new millennium contributed to the concept's appeal. What gave New Economy rhetoric legs was the way in which information technology, labor productivity, and the booming stock market mutually reinforced each other.

In the New Economy of the second half of the 1990s, technology played the starring role. According to its proponents, new information technology had catalyzed a productivity miracle, which had put the American economy on the road to permanent, uninterrupted prosperity. Technology, likewise, had changed the nature of work itself, and ideas—not material goods—motored prosperity. The New Economy demanded brains, not brawn. At the same time, the flexibility offered by the global economy served the cause of endless growth; with technology and globalization working together, Americans would no longer experience recessions or depressions. Rising incomes and the broad diffusion of stock ownership would bring the interests of all Americans into accord. In the age of the Internet, work was meaningful, workplaces were clean, bosses ruled through consensus, and the distinction between work and play had been erased. The drudgery, conflict, and despoiled environment of the industrial age—and, indeed, of all human history hitherto—had been transcended.

Proponents of the New Economy paradigm translated its core concepts, which derived from economic policy and business cycles, for the larger culture. One of the first to forecast the new age was George Gilder, an evangelical and free marketeer who had previously written books criticizing feminism, welfare, and affirmative action. In his 1989 book, *Microcosm,* Gilder argued that the United States economy had entered a new world in which matter had been overthrown and intellectual capital had become more important than real capital in driving economic growth (Gilder 1989). He celebrated technology's liberation of the individual and its provision of abundant consumer goods. *Forbes* magazine brought Gilder on as a columnist, and from there, he spread the gospel of the technology revolution.

Gilder was a leading force in diffusing New Economy thinking to a popular audience. Alan Greenspan, the chairman of the Federal Reserve, gave it the imprimatur of scientific truth. In December 1996, in a speech accepting an award from the American Enterprise Institute, Greenspan had observed that stock market investors seemed to be under the spell of an "irrational exuberance" (Woodward 2000). The remark caused markets in Japan, the United States, Hong Kong, England, and Germany to tumble, and if Greenspan continued after that to have reservations about the stock market run-up, he kept them to himself. Seven months later, Greenspan was celebrating the nation's economic vitality and popularizing the idea that ongoing economic expansion was made possible by special attributes of the new information technology. The exponential rise in the stock market was henceforth to be understood as a rational market reaction to the "new era" in the nation's economic life.

There were a few critics who questioned the existence of a new age. The economist Robert Shiller warned that the New Economy was nothing more than a house of cards. In *Irrational Exuberance,* Shiller reviewed the history of the relationship between corporate performance and the stock market to demonstrate that stocks were vastly overvalued, and that the country was in the midst of a speculative bubble, not a New Economy (Shiller 2000). Shiller's analysis turned out to be prescient, but at the time, his view was either dismissed or greeted with skepticism.

The implosion of the stock market between March 2000 and April 2001 destroyed the validity of the idea of a New Economy, proving to almost all observers that the boom of the last years of the decade was generated by the force of a speculative bubble. The value of information technology stocks fell with the 60 percent drop in the NASDAQ, and bankruptcy obliterated the overwhelming majority of the dot-coms. So too plummeted the companies' and their leaders' cultural cachet, which had been swelled by New Economy publicity. Also extinguished in the decline were $5 trillion worth of investments. The central contention of New Economy thought—unceasing growth and permanent prosperity—appeared ludicrous in the face of the cascading problems, especially with the revelations from late 2001 through 2002 of massive corporate scandals at New Economy leaders such as Enron, WorldCom, and Global Crossing. After that time, discussion about the American economy returned to more conventional questions and its more established venues. In retrospect, New Economy thinking was no more and no less than a cultural phenomenon of the 1990s—one that reveals significant clues about social life, popular culture, and power, but less about the actual workings of the American economy.

TECHNOLOGY: FROM COUNTERCULTURE TO CORPORATE CULTURE

Work, culture, entertainment, leisure, communication, health, and consumption were all affected by the invention and diffusion of many new technologies in the 1990s. In this chapter, the significance of technology in the economy—on business and labor—is explored. In other chapters, we will turn to the influence of technology in shaping Americans social interaction, leisure, culture, media, and entertainment.

Technology provided new means for communication. Email, cell phones, computerized voice mail systems, and videoconferencing were relatively new, expensive, and rare at the beginning of the 1990s. First adopted widely in business, computers became a common household item as prices for the new goods and services dropped, and by the end of the decade, many Americans could avail themselves of these communication technologies at home as well as at work.

Technology influenced the sense of time itself. The phrase "24/7" came into use in the 1990s. Most important, these new forms of communication broke down the conventional distinctions between the workplace and time at work, and private space and private time. One could work anywhere one could read email and receive cell phone calls. By the same token, entertainment—leisure activities—more readily entered the workplace. One could more discretely email friends than call them; one could surf the web for news, jokes, personal ads, and the like—all while appearing to be diligently at work at the computer. Alternatively, the new technology could be deployed by employers to monitor more closely workers on the job. The new technologies blurred the line between work and leisure. At the end of the decade, Americans were of different minds about whether the new technology had brought unprecedented levels of convenience to their lives or had added to their burdens.

One of the most pervasive influences of the new technology was over Americans' consumption of entertainment. A plethora of new technologies was introduced in the 1980s and 1990s, and as prices rapidly fell, Americans snapped them up. Cable television, diffused widely in American homes in the 1980s, vastly expanded its offerings in the 1990s. At the beginning of the decade, its boosters enthused about the coming 500-channel home. At the end of the decade, Americans complained that there was still nothing worth watching. A majority of Americans owned videocassette recorders at the beginning of the decade, but by the end of the decade, they were replacing them with DVD players, first introduced in 1998. Direct broadcast satellite television customers went from zero to nearly 6 million between 1994 and 1998. Technological breakthroughs in computer gaming in 1989 allowed for the explosion of home gaming systems in the 1990s. The Nintendo system was introduced in 1991. In 1992, Sega released the first system to use CDs instead of cartridges, and Sony introduced its spectacularly popular PlayStation system in 1995. By 1993, 50 million homes had video gaming systems.

Did the diffusion of new technologies in the 1990s revolutionize the lives of Americans, or did Americans merely assimilate the new means into existing routines and patterns? Both sides had advocates. Business analysts widely agreed that technology transformed the workplace and the factory and contributed to the decade's enormous productivity boom. Yet, for Americans in their personal lives, the evidence is more mixed. The new technologies were commonly harnessed to old purposes, which enabled Americans to perform certain tasks more quickly, more efficiently, and more conveniently. The new written language emerging with the ubiquity of text messaging in the mid-2000s was not yet evident in the 1990s. More fundamental transformations of habits, routines, ways of working, relationships, and processing information were a post-millennial phenomenon.

The World Wide Web

The Internet originated as a project of the U.S. military in 1964. Its purpose was to provide command-and-control communications in the event of nuclear war, and it was developed in the Eisenhower era Defense Advanced Research Projects Agency, known as DARPA. Renamed the Internet in 1985, it remained the province of techies, universities, and computer businesses. The National Science Foundation built the high-speed, long-distance data lines through which the Internet could be carried into homes, libraries, offices, and schools, and the costs of the system were shared by the universities, laboratories, and technology corporations that used it. The full potential of the Internet, where vast stores of information were accessible, had yet to be tapped.

The epochal development was the invention of the World Wide Web by Tim Berners-Lee in 1990. Lee wrote the initial Web prototype in 1990 at CERN, the European particle physics laboratory. His key innovation was to structure information as hypertext, which enabled different computer systems and networks to communicate and share information without the use of cumbersome databases that required special terms to be entered. URLs (Uniform Resource Locator), HTTPs (Hypertext Transfer Protocol), and HTMLs (Hypertext Markup Language) were all invented by Berners-Lee.

In legislation spearheaded by Sen. Al Gore Jr. in 1991, Congress authorized the National Science Foundation to open the Internet to commercial use. In 1992, the World Wide Web was up and running. By 1993, an Internet boomlet was on—20 million people worldwide were online. The novelty and the inchoate culture of the new technological world is apparent in the quaint reports from that year. *Time* magazine revealed, "Suddenly the Internet is the place to be. College students are queuing up outside computing centers to get online. Executives are ordering new business cards that show off their Internet addresses" (Elmer-Dewitt 1993). There was still no readily available browser, and the commercial computer services, such as AOL and CompuServe, prevented their customers from directly accessing the Internet.

How would the Internet attain commercial viability when its pioneers conceived of their virtual world as an "open source" democracy where marketing and profiting were anathema and everything on it was available for free? "It's a perfect Marxist state, where almost nobody does any business," one of those pioneers claimed, only partly in jest (Elmer-Dewitt 1993).

The question seems remarkable today, but at the time, it was one that claimed legitimate attention. In the early 1990s, techies imagined themselves to be the 1990s' incarnation of the beatniks or the hippies. Theirs was the "cyberpunk" counterculture, an avant-garde united by their futuristic vision of a "virtual community" underpinned by the new technology. Over the course of the 1990s, this subculture of countercultural techies was transformed. In the early 1990s, *Wired* magazine was a cyberpunk alternative online "zine" for techies; by the end of the decade, it was the industry rag for the dot-com sector.

The transition of the Internet from a futuristic toy of a subculture to a dominant and pervasive communications and information technology occurred between 1993 and 1997. From 1993 to 1994, the commercial services began making the Internet available to customers through easy menus, which saved nontechies from having to learn special programs. Mosaic, the free predecessor to Netscape, became available, and some of the savvier nontechie businesses and individuals starting using it to establish their own Web sites and access the Web (Elmer-Dewitt 1994). Meanwhile, other technological advances made the Web accessible to more people—modem speeds and personal computer power increased, and the browsers Netscape and Internet Explorer became widely available for navigating the Web. Americans with access to the Web from home increased by the millions each year: in 1994, 11 million households had computers equipped with modems; in 1995, 18 million did (Ceruzzi 2003).

In August 1995, shares of Netscape were made available for public purchase, and the dot-com boom was on. The Netscape stock sale was symbolic of the transformation of the Internet and its culture, and its significance in American life. After 1995, Internet pioneers became entrepreneurs. Although the early spirit of antimarket, anarchistic democracy was preserved among a minority—including Berners-Lee—the Internet became for most old and new techies an arena for business opportunity. In 1995, Jeff Bezos quit his home and his job after reading about the annual growth of Internet users, headed for Seattle, and started Amazon.com. Three years later Amazon had 2 million customers and $350 million in sales. Of course, as the dot-com boom and bust proved, many new ideas were duds from a business perspective. Only in the next decade during the so-called Web 2.0 age would the survivors of the stock market meltdown find means to gain real, not just promised, profit.

Impact: The Human Genome Project

Advances in computing made possible one of the most historically and socially important scientific discoveries of all time in the 1990s, one with enormous future economic significance. The Human Genome Project, supported primarily by the governments of Britain and the United States, was established in 1990 with the goal to map the entire genetic blueprint, or genome, of human beings. The process of mapping was done through DNA sequencing. The work was carried out at many laboratories in the United States, England, and other countries; when a gene was mapped, the information was entered into public databases. The work was projected to be completed in 2005 and to cost $3 billion.

In 1998, J. Craig Venter, one of the scientists involved in the project, announced that he was capable of completing the sequencing more rapidly and cheaply through a private consortium. Venter broke with the public project and projected that his company, Celera Genomics, would publish the entire human genetic code within three years at a cost of only $200 million. It was a stunning claim because only 3 percent of the genes of human beings had yet been identified. To achieve its goal, Celera began building the second-largest supercomputer in the world. "We couldn't do it without massive computers," Venter acknowledged (quoted in Johnson 2001).

Given the practical medical applications and the potential profit to be gained from mapping the human genome, the scientific effort metamorphosed into a race between the international Human Genome Project and Celera Genomics, and then between those two entities and two other research lab–pharmaceutical consortiums. In late 1999, the director of the official Human Genome Project announced that they would have a 90 percent complete working draft of the map ready and available to the public by the spring of 2000. Celera was also making rapid advances, and at the same time filing patent applications in the quest to reap profit off of its discoveries. Debate became heated between the two camps with the director of the public project arguing that research would be thwarted by Celera's intellectual property claims on its discoveries, and Venter saying it was a bad idea for genetic information to be controlled by the government (Philipkoski 1999).

Ultimately, the two projects agreed to collaborate, share research, and publish all data free on the Internet. In 2001, the mapping of the human genome was completed, with 30,000 genes identified, far fewer than the 100,000 genes scientists believed to exist. Since that time, major discoveries about the nature and treatment of human disease have been made based on the epochal scientific research accomplished by the Human Genome Project and its offshoots.

GLOBALIZATION

Globalization became a daily reality for ordinary Americans in the decade of the 1990s. Whether they lost a job when the local factory closed, bought clothes at Wal-Mart that were made in China, drove a Japanese car built in America, played Pokemon or Nintendo, collected Hello Kitty accessories, or viewed Anime, rare was the American untouched by the pervasive reach of the global market. The same could not be said of an American living in the 1970s, or even the 1980s. The situation in the 1990s felt paradoxical. The U.S. economy, after the recession ended, was the engine of world economic growth. American businesses were making profits. The U.S. government was the most powerful actor in international economic policy. But American citizens felt buffeted by remote and uncontrollable forces. Although the United States had been the world's leading economic power since World War I, and remained so at the end of the 20th century, no longer did the nation's dominance translate into the fabled American standard of living to which Americans had become accustomed in the post–World War II bounty years.

The Origins of Globalization

Globalization is generally understood to mean the increasing integration of the world economy through the mobility of capital, goods, and people. Most analysts agree that the global integration of markets, finance, and production intensified during the last quarter of the 20th century. Economists, sociologists, and others who analyze statistics on trade and investment continue to debate whether globalization is a qualitatively different organization of the international

Workers put the finishing touches on vacuum cleaners being produced at a new factory in Rosarito, Mexico. (Feature Photo Service/NewsCom)

economy, or just a quantitatively larger expression of the international market that has existed for centuries. Some argue that the extent of globalization has been exaggerated, and that international economic transactions have always been an important feature of U.S. and world capitalism. Their point is a useful corrective to the tendency to deem any example of international economic or cultural relations a case of vaguely defined process of globalization. Nonetheless, the transnational character of world trade and investment in which economic actors are no longer bound to the interests of nation-states represents a new feature of the late-20th-century international economy.

A series of developments in the international political economy over several decades accelerated international economic activity to tip the balance toward what we now routinely refer to as the "global economy." Multinational corporations grew in number and increased their international investment and production; opportunities for direct investment in foreign countries opened; more countries, including the poorest, developed industrial capacity for export; world trade increased; manufacturing declined in the developed countries; and developments in the technology of communications, transport, and production allowed for the global coordination of production and trade.

The quickening of international economic integration and the rise of globalization had multiple causes, but several merit particular notice. First, an essential precondition of globalization was the development, in the countries outside the European, Australasian, and North American industrial core, of the capacity to manufacture industrial products and consumer goods. Industrial development in these nations was made possible by the transformation of their rural areas. Tens of millions of people throughout the world migrated from the countryside to urban areas, bringing a new, cheap labor force into international industrial production. The expansion of the world's industrial capacity vastly increased the competitive pressures on firms in the advanced industrial nations, and the more-recently industrialized countries held several advantages in the race. Second, globalization was stimulated and set on a distinctive path in the 1980s by the governments of the United States and England. Under the administrations of President Ronald Reagan and Prime Minister Margaret Thatcher, financial deregulation, free trade treaties, and tax reduction freed investors in the advanced industrial nations from national regulations and allowed them to seek profit-making opportunities elsewhere in the world.

Americans Experience Globalization

Globalization had a sweeping influence over American economic, political, and cultural life. Deregulation of international finance enabled American corporations to invest overseas more easily. It helped them maintain earnings and profits by lowering production costs, but it was often accomplished at the expense of American workers, who lost their jobs when a factory closed in the United States and opened in a low-wage country. Proponents of globalization argued that Americans were better off overall, as the loss suffered by individual factory workers was more than compensated by the lower cost of consumer goods for the rest of the country. Statistics on international trade give some support to this argument. Americans increased their consumption of foreign-made goods sharply; annual imports over the decade increased from $498 billion to $1.224 trillion worth of goods. Whether it was by choice, as in the preference for foreign-made cars, or for lack of choice, as in the virtual disappearance of the U.S. toy and garment industries, was a subject of heated debate.

Globalization was the most important impetus behind the mass immigration into the United States in the 1990s. Rapid industrial development, combined with international mandates to maintain fiscal austerity, in Asia, Latin America, and the Caribbean propelled millions of men, women, and children to migrate to the United States. (Similar forces sent people from the Middle East and Africa to Europe and from the poorer regions in Asia to the continent's new industrial powerhouses.) New immigrants brought to America their distinctive cultural and religious practices, making the nation more diverse than it had ever been in the past. The postwar era in the United States had been a peaceful interlude in Americans' perpetual struggles over immigration; globalization helped to rekindle a fierce conflict over immigration and American identity, especially as immigrants filled low-wage jobs at the same moment that well-paying blue-collar jobs were being extinguished.

A truly global market in culture, both popular culture and high culture, was created by trade and migration. Some Americans lamented the ways global culture eroded their own traditional ones. Others excoriated the homogenization of world culture, laying the blame at the door of the powerful American culture industry. A few celebrated the diversity, postmodernism, or universalism brought into being by the globalization of culture.

Although globalization exerted powerful economic, demographic, and cultural influence on Americans, critics and proponents alike tended to exaggerate its effect and overlook other forces. Not all immigrants took to the road out of economic necessity; political and religious persecution continued to drive people to seek refuge in the United States, as it had for centuries. Cultural products—music, books, art—have always circulated internationally, and the cultures of people or nations have always been the hybrid fruit of the meeting of cultures. Even in the case that appears to have the most direct connection—the loss of manufacturing jobs—globalization did not do the work alone. More than 3 million manufacturing jobs disappeared in the 1990s, but technological change, not globalization, had rendered some of those jobs obsolete. And if the old industrial powerhouses of the AFL-CIO had been more agile in their response to change, the contours of job loss and wage decline may have looked different. In sum, in every facet of American social life, globalization accelerated and magnified change, but it was not its only source.

Reponses to Globalization

Americans disagreed about the influence globalization had over American politics, social life, and culture. The new and uncertain landscape of the global economy made for strange bedfellows. Opposition to globalization brought together diverse groups with a variety of sometimes contradictory criticisms. The most numerous and powerful constituency against globalization stood in a long tradition of American protectionist sentiment. American business and American workers should be "protected" from the unfair competition of economies with very low wages by tariffs and other measures to stanch the flow of imports. Among more radical antiglobalization activists, who were always in a minority, the main charge against the system was that it exacerbated and entrenched world inequalities and was ravaging the environment of the planet. (And many who agreed with this perspective argued that trade barriers hurt the poor in the rest of the world.) In the antiglobalization camp were labor unionists and workers, environmentalists, progressives, and populists of left and right. Ralph Nader,

Antiglobalization Protests: The "Battle for Seattle"

At the 1999 meeting of the World Trade Organization in Seattle, Washington, tens of thousands of antiglobalization protestors took to the streets for four days of demonstrations. A mass demonstration of such energy and intensity had not been mounted since the antiwar protests of the early 1970s.

Although the movement seemed to burst on the scene as a spontaneous expression of disgust with globalization, it was in fact the fruit of a decade of activism in the student antisweatshop movement, the labor movement, and the environmental movement. The immediate issue was China's application to join the WTO; in the longer view, the issue was globalization itself. Protestors sought a number of specific demands, all of which challenged the dogmatic free market policy then reigning. They called for regulations to preserve the environment, the adoption of labor standards in trade agreements, and the restoration of the right of individual nations to regulate their domestic economies.

The protests drew notice for the diversity of the participants. Large labor unions, environmental groups, and youth were all represented, and the press started referring to the Seattle movement as the "Turtles and Teamsters" coalition. Participants won praise for their ability to transcend divisions that had plagued the Left since the 1960s. But they also drew criticism for the property destruction against corporate symbols, which was carried out by the tiny anarchist contingent within the larger group. To globalization's critics, the Battle for Seattle presaged a new global democracy movement. Large protests five months later in Washington, D.C., and later in Davos, Switzerland, seemed confirmation of the prediction. But within a few years, the roving mass protests had dwindled. Nevertheless, the Battle for Seattle marked a turning point in the debate about globalization. After that, a consensus grew that the global economy should be regulated to preserve international economic stability and to enhance fairness and justice, especially for the world's poorer nations.

icon of the Left, and Patrick Buchanan, icon of the Right, both made the battle against globalization a central cause of the 1990s. The most powerful constituency against globalization was the part of business hurt by foreign competition. They lobbied to arrest globalization with protectionist legislation but kept their distance from the political activists. Although all opponents of globalization tended to be branded as "protectionists," the forces of antiglobalization were more ideologically and politically eclectic than the label suggests.

The proglobalization side was smaller and far less diverse, but what it lacked in numbers it made up for in influence. Free trade was the core principle articulated by the American proponents of globalization; world prosperity and the interests of individual Americans would both be advanced by removing trade barriers and stimulating world commerce. Businesses in the financial sector, economists, and centrist policy analysts and pundits were the most enthusiastic proponents of free trade while the Clinton administration under the guidance of Treasury Secretary Rubin effectively led the battle to loosen restrictions on international trade and investment.

On balance, the proglobalization side scored more victories but did not rout the other side. Most significant, Congress ratified NAFTA and GATT to open markets and deregulated the financial industry, in part to eliminate the remaining constraints on U.S. global capital flows. Nevertheless, the antiglobalization movement made significant gains that would potentially influence the future of the global economy. Through creative protest, they brought public scrutiny to the governing institutions of the international economy—the most insular and opaque governance bodies in the world. They slowed down the race to enact free trade agreements by persuading a majority of Congress to reject fast-track trade talks. The movement won wide acceptance for the position that more regulation of international investment, environmental practices, and labor standards was necessary. They founded a movement for debt relief for poor nations, which by the middle of the next decade, was beginning to gain mainstream adherents. Although it was quite evident by the beginning of the 21st century that globalization would not be turned back, the antiglobalization movement had helped to shift the terms of debate about the influence and future course of globalization.

Globalization and the Trade Deficit

The balance of foreign trade proved to be the weakest element of the U.S. economy in the 1990s. The trade deficit, the excess of imports over exports for all goods and services, stood at $81 trillion in 1990 and grew to hit $378 trillion in 2000. Growth in the deficit slowed middecade with the expansion but resumed its high rate in 1998 as the East Asian Crisis accelerated the trade imbalance and as hard-hit Asian manufacturers reduced prices on already inexpensive consumer goods and industrial products.

The size of the trade deficit and its effect on balance of payments worried politicians and economists. In the broader culture, the trade deficit loomed as another disturbing consequence of globalization. Cheap foreign goods were eliminating good jobs; discount retailers were shuttering small local businesses. In popular culture, Americans bashed Japan at the beginning of the decade and feared a rising China at the end of the decade. China's trade surplus with the United States grew to $28 billion a year by 2001. Although little noted in popular culture, the United States also ran high deficits with Canada and Germany.

MANUFACTURING: WORK AND COMMUNITY

Employment growth in the 1990s continued and accelerated the sectoral shift from manufacturing to services that had been under way in the United States since the 1970s. In 1959, about one worker out of every three had held a job in manufacturing. In 2000, manufacturing provided only about one of every eight jobs while services provided roughly eight of every ten jobs. Nine out of ten jobs created during the 1990s were in the service sector, and the overwhelming majority of these were in the sector's lower reaches. Of the 20 fastest-growing industries, only one was in manufacturing. Overall, employment in manufacturing declined 4.4 percent. Two out of every five miners in the United States lost their jobs in the 1990s. At the start of the 21st century, retail trade alone provided over 4 million more jobs than all manufacturing industries combined (Hatch and Clinton 2000).

The sectoral shift in the American economy brought with it a change in the wages that most Americans could expect from a job. Historically, unions have had less of a presence in the service sector in the United States, and for many people, the move from manufacturing to service work spelled the loss of union wages and benefits. Even in manufacturing, as the unionization rate plummeted 40 percent between 1985 and 2000, wages themselves fell and benefits disappeared (EPI 2006). Although wages and incomes rose in the latter part of the 1990s expansion, millions of people were earning less than they had made at their previous jobs.

Americans, whether in manufacturing or service, worked more hours than they had before, and more than their counterparts in nations with comparable economies. Adding up the additional labor hours of all family members, in 2000, middle-class families worked three months more a year than they had in 1979. Most of the added hours resulted from the labor of married women with children, close to half of whom were in the paid workforce. By the end of the decade, Americans worked on average a month and a half more per year than did their counterparts in the 19 other rich, industrialized countries (Mishel et al. 2005).

Even as the service sector ballooned, the United States remained a manufacturing powerhouse in the world economy, and roughly the same number of people worked in manufacturing in 2000 as in the mid-1960s. In the 1970s and 1980s, the process of "deindustrialization" and the emergence of a "postindustrial society" were subjects of heated social and political debate. The restructuring of manufacturing over the last quarter-century has demonstrated that the terms were misnomers. The transformations in goods manufacturing have nonetheless been profound. For the 18.5 million people employed in manufacturing in 2000, life on the shop floor was very different than it had been for their forebears in 1965. For the many communities that had grown and matured

around the factories of a powerful firm or regional industry, the loss of manufacturing had cascading influences on work, community, family, and public life.

New Relations in Unionized Manufacturing

As American corporations struggled to compete internationally, new relations
between workers, managers, and owners and new techniques of production
replaced old forms. Manufacturers sought to lower wages and increase worker
productivity to maintain profits by holding down costs. Lay-offs, which came to
be known euphemistically as "downsizing," and automation of the labor process
often went hand in hand. Fewer workers were needed to make the finished
product as computer-controlled robotic arms replaced human brawn. The workers who lost jobs to robots were not the only ones affected in the process. For
those remaining to tend the new technology, the old life of the shop—its community, its personal relationships—was irrevocably changed. Such mechaniza-
tion, however, had characterized factory life since the invention of the steam
engine.

Corporate managers' efforts to lower labor costs led them to confrontations
with the once-powerful unions in their industry. In the name of saving the firm
and preserving the remaining jobs, employers demanded concessions from
unions. Contracts reached between unions and corporations during the 1990s

Robots weld cars in a manufacturing plant. (Corel)

contained an array of cost-cutting measures borne by workers: wage freezes, reduced health and pension benefits, reduced compensation and security for newer workers, agreements to outsource jobs to nonunion firms, and the cession of more control over the production process to management. Some companies and unions instead experimented with new forms of cooperation to meet the vicissitudes of global competition. General Motors and the United Autoworkers worked together to create the much-publicized Saturn unit; new plants were built, governed by work rules and benefits that differed from the master union contract in the U.S. auto industry. Other corporations offered employee stock-ownership plans, believing that workers with a vested interest in the firm would be more likely to see the bottom line in the same way that management did. The results of these experiments were mixed and continue to be the subject of disagreement. Assessing the cumulative results of these shifts, it is clear that the balance of power had shifted decisively away from workers toward the managers and owners of American manufacturing firms.

Rebuilding Community after the Factories Close

Many communities had lost virtually all of their existing industrial plants over the 1970s and 1980s. For them, the 1990s was a decade of rebuilding. Regions or cities that had depended on one industry were the most devastated by deindustrialization, and some areas remained depressed in the buoyant economy of the 1990s. In Flint, Michigan, and Youngstown, Ohio, unemployment in the 1990s remained high and intractable. But other parts of the old industrial heartland experienced a revival. Pittsburgh, the city of steel, retooled as a tourist destination and a hub for the New Economy. The abandoned steelworks that had lined the Monongahela River were demolished or turned into theme malls, and downtown office buildings were sandblasted of a decades' soot. Hoping to attract young professionals and suburbanites back to the central city, Pittsburgh boosters touted the clean work of the new infotech enterprises. Employment in the tourism service industry was the more likely destination for former steelworkers and their children. Except for the miles of slag on the outskirts of the city, the industrial presence of the past was cleaned away, and Pittsburgh consistently won awards for being one of the most livable cities in the United States (Savage 2003).

In other places, plant closings and manufacturing flight had occurred in more diverse local economies. Although those who lost well-paying manufacturing jobs suffered, it was still possible to land a service job, even though the wages were usually much lower. More important, a diversified local economy could also provide a foundation for the growth of other forms of manufacturing, particularly of nondurable consumer goods, and in some places, a vibrant manufacturing sector emerged in the wake of so-called deindustrialization. Los Angeles provides an illuminating example of the many forces at work in this kind of transition. In the postwar era, the city had held the rank as the nation's second-largest producer of autos and rubber, and it had been home to a large steel industry as well. By the end of the 1980s, every single one of the auto, rubber, and steel plants had closed. But by the end of the 1990s, the city was the second-largest manufacturing capital of the nation, as food processing, furniture making, garment work, and similar consumer products manufacturing arose. The new manufacturing jobs were nonunion, low paying, and often dangerous, and the workers who filled the new factories were overwhelmingly immigrants from Latin America and Asia. Most were located along the Alameda Corridor, the transportation hub rebuilt with public money to facilitate the movement of international goods from Los Angeles's fast-growing ports to the American heartland. Los Angeles in the 1990s thus provided a model for the adaptation of American manufacturing to globalization. It also, however, stood as an example of the new terms for factory workers in the new global market.

Plant Closings in Shelby, North Carolina

In the spring of 1998, KEMET, a technology firm with a plant in Shelby, North Carolina, announced that it would close its Shelby factory in six months and that 750 of the 950 workers employed there would be laid off. KEMET planned to move manufacturing from Shelby to a plant in Monterrey, Mexico, which the company had opened in 1996. By the end of the transition period, the Shelby building was an empty shell, its machinery packed up and shipped off to Monterrey by the downsized Shelby workers (May and Morrison 2003).

The economic development of Shelby in the postwar era had been fairly typical for a Southern city. Located in the foothills of North Carolina between Asheville and Charlotte, Shelby had once been a rural farming community, where most residents raised cotton. In the 1950s, as it became increasingly difficult to earn a living from the land, textile manufacturers started to relocate to Shelby after closing unionized factories in the North. Textile factory work in Shelby was nonunion and paid lower wages than equivalent work in the North, but it offered a viable alternative for a community that had lost its agricultural livelihood. Other industries followed, and by the mid-1970s, there were close to 100 manufacturing firms with production sites in Shelby. KEMET was one of them, and it was considered to be one of the better, more secure employers in the area.

Work at KEMET represented a hidden side of the technology revolution. While the media marveled about the end of work as we know it with the rise of the knowledge-based dot-com economy, pundits rarely considered the actual physical labor that went into making the material products of computers and electronic equipment. Shelby workers knew better. At KEMET, they made capacitors, an essential element of all kinds of electronic goods. Although they considered it preferable to the dirty work of the textile factories, it was still manual labor conducted on an assembly line.

Like many workers in America who faced unemployment when their employer moved overseas, those at KEMET worried about their families' economic future. KEMET had paid well, and the firm had been one of the few in town to provide permanent, predictable, secure employment. It was also work that required a high level of skill and took place in a clean, safe factory where the managerial supervision was relatively unobtrusive. For all these reasons, to work at KEMET was a mark of prestige in the community and a source of pride to its workers. How would they find equally good jobs? How could their children stay in Shelby when there would be no opportunities for them? What might happen if a family member became sick, now that they had no health insurance from their job? After suffering through the experience of the plant closing, and reflecting on the effect of NAFTA on communities like theirs, many KEMET workers concluded that the prospects for gaining well-paying, skilled manufacturing work were over for them and their children. They planned to use the aid given to NAFTA-displaced workers to pursue education and gain professional skills, hoping in this way to shield themselves from the harsh reality of manufacturing work in the global economy.

The workers of KEMET also felt the loss of something more substantial than their jobs. Their reflections on their fate told a story of a community's values betrayed. In their view, by closing the Shelby plant, the corporate management of KEMET demonstrated that they lived according to a different value system—a "bottom line mentality" (May and Morrison 2003). Echoing an idea of the implicit social contract that had been common in American corporations during the postwar era, KEMET workers believed a company and its employees had reciprocal rights and obligations, and together the success of the enterprise and the vitality of the community would grow. From their perspective, the corporate management of KEMET not only betrayed each of them individually but also the city of Shelby and, more portentously, the nation. Disaffected from their personal experience, those who had been the victims of KEMET's overseas flight predicted that many American companies would take advantage of NAFTA and would act as unpatriotically as KEMET had. The United States would suffer, becoming a "poor country" and one not quite worthy of their devotion. "I can't look at the American flag the same way," explained one woman who had worked at KEMET. "It used to bring tears to my eyes because I was proud of where I lived. It doesn't anymore" (quoted in May and Morrison 2003, 278–279).

Work in the Service Economy

By the end of the 1990s, about 103 million Americans—8 out of 10 workers—held jobs in which they provided services. The debate about the long-term shift from an economy led by manufacturing to one led by the service sector was partially obscured by the exaggerated attention to the short-lived dot-com mavericks. During the dot-com craze, information and technology firms were hailed as the source of the nation's future jobs. But they provided only a small number of new jobs and a tiny proportion of the nation's workforce. About 2 percent of the nation's workers found employment in information and technology companies—compared, for example, to the 17 percent laboring in retail (Henwood 2005; Hatch and Clinton 2000).

Millions of Americans worked as cashiers, nurses' aides, home health care workers, janitors, hotel housekeepers, sales clerks, telephone call operators, data processors, child care workers, waiters, and the like. Almost one out of every five workers—23 million Americans—held a job in retail trade, 8 million of them in places serving food and drink, and most of the rest in stores. Nearly 10 million Americans worked in health services, 3 million of them in the rapidly growing area providing care in the home, in nursing homes, and in other kinds of residential facilities. Five million Americans worked as telemarketers. During the 1990s expansion, more jobs were created in personnel supply services than in any other industry, and by 2000, 3.9 million Americans were working as temporary workers or as an employee of an employment agency (Hatch and Clinton 2000).

Workers in a restaurant kitchen. (iStockPhoto.com)

With so large a proportion of Americans working in a service occupation, the service workforce was as diverse as America itself. When service work is categorized into high-wage, high-skill occupations and low-wage, low-skill occupations, several patterns emerge. The comparatively smaller number of jobs that required a college or advanced degree paid higher than average wages and afforded autonomy, prestige, and opportunity for social mobility were held disproportionately by white Americans, especially by white men. For example, two out of three commodity and securities brokers were white men, one out of four were white women, and only one out of fifty were black women. In the cleaning, caring, and helping occupations, which did not require higher education and paid lower than average wages, Latinos, African Americans, and immigrants held a disproportionately large percentage of the jobs. The income disparity between the two segments of the service labor force was stark. The janitors, maids, and gardeners who maintained the buildings and grounds of financial institutions earned on average $18,000–$28,000 a year while the brokers who worked in the industry earned on average over $100,000 a year (BLS).

Service Work as Knowledge Work

Technology was transforming the American workplace in the 1990s, and the phenomenon spawned utopian ideas about work in the New Economy. Robert Reich, President Clinton's liberal secretary of labor, and Bill Gates, the founder and CEO of Microsoft, shared the view that the knowledge-based jobs of the future would provide satisfying, rewarding, meaningful, and liberating work if only Americans could be adequately prepared to seize the opportunity.

The explosion of dot-coms in the late 1990s tested the theory. Tens of thousands of college-educated women and men in their 20s sought not just jobs but also fabulous fortunes in dot-coms in San Francisco, Silicon Valley, Seattle, New York City, and other enclaves of the infant industry. According to the widely trumpeted popular image, dot-coms were the antithesis of the postwar corporation. Job seekers flocked to dot-coms for the excitement of the hip work culture, where watching TV, playing video games, and Webcasting were considered part of the job. They would gain meaningful work in democratic workplaces run and owned by their peers. They imagined that the stock options they earned in lieu of wages would make them the next celebrated 20-something billionaire, like Netscape's Marc Andreessen and Yahoo's David Filo and Jerry Yang. Persuaded that their work was a mission in the creation of a brave new world, they willingly put in 16-hour days, seven days a week, in cramped, dark, and marginally safe offices, frequently located in former tenement districts. Many college-educated Americans in their mid-20s lived fabulously well for the few years of the dot-com boom, as they earned comparatively high salaries or lived on credit keyed to their assumption of the wealth they would own when their company went public. But, for all but a handful, the dot-com collapse in 2000–2001 wiped out their paper wealth and left them jobless. The mantra of the industry had been that the distinction between work and play had been erased. The promise had been that one could cash out as a millionaire at the age of 30. Overwork and unfulfilled dreams of riches were the reality.

Technology and Service Workers

The daily routine of service work, despite the variety of jobs encompassed, refuted point for point the claims made by New Economy boosters that knowledge work in democratic workplaces was the future of the American economy. Most of the jobs available in service occupations required little skill and only a high school education. Job training typically took place in a few weeks; neither college nor an advanced degree in technology, science, and mathematics were necessary. Work tended to be routinized and repetitive, with little opportunity for the display of individual talent or the realization of personal purpose. Neither advancement nor sizable raises were part of the package in most firms. A woman working in a service job was far more likely to be cleaning offices, hotel rooms, and hospital wards than she was to be writing computer programs in a clean, well-lit office. A man was far more likely to hold a job as a security guard or a janitor than as a securities broker.

While many workers in service industries held jobs that were physically demanding and at times dangerous, others worked in a wide range of jobs that had been changed by the adoption of computer and information technology but not in the liberating ways promised by enthusiasts of the New Economy. For telephone operators, telemarketers, cashiers, data processors, and the like, the new technology intensified their labors, rather than lightening and enhancing them. While one computer program automatically dialed numbers for telemarketers, increasing the number of calls per hour made, another computer program calculated how many calls had been made or how many keystrokes typed by workers to see how diligently and efficiently they labored. It was old-fashioned speed-up in modern guise. In the cleaning, serving, and helping occupations, the old ways still worked well enough for management; maids and janitors were ordered to clean more rooms, nurses' aides and childcare workers assigned to care for more people.

On the job, service workers did not find themselves to be part of a microdemocracy but rather encountered a vast array of old and new mechanisms designed to control their time and monitor their activities. Billed as forces for personal liberation, information and computer technology in fact added new tools to management's arsenal. Where manipulation of the new technology was an essential part of a job—in data entry or telemarketing, for example—the new technology was deployed as a tool for surveillance. At any time, a manager could listen in on the calls made by a telephone operator; supermarket scanners and video monitors tracked the pace of cashiers. New technologies served similar purposes for conventional businesses. Security cameras became ubiquitous in stores, offices, and public places, monitoring the pace and activities of workers. As security guards watched video footage for suspicious behavior, other security recorded their own movements as well. For workers subject to being filmed and listened to, it became difficult to pass along a free coffee to a friend who stopped by the store, take an extra bathroom break to put on a fresh coat of lipstick, or call a sick child at home. Personality and drug tests, developed by the commercialization of biological and psychological science, became widely used by companies to screen out undesirable employees. Even though technology had contributed new tools of worker control, old techniques were not abandoned. Wal-Mart, for example, mixed old and new, installing security cameras in its vast parking lots to track the conversations between union organizers and workers while prohibiting employees from speaking profanely among themselves inside the stores.

Low-Wage Jobs

Among the most exploited in the service sector were poor single mothers, whose already precarious position was exacerbated by the elimination of the New Deal guarantee of income support in the welfare reform legislation of 1996. In 2001, the journalist Barbara Ehrenreich published *Nickel and Dimed,* the story of her foray into the world of low-wage service work. Setting out to examine the conditions confronting the women forced to work by the new welfare rules, Ehrenreich eloquently described the grind of low-wage service work and the lives of her co-workers, who were mostly women struggling to raise children on their own. Traveling to different parts of the country, Ehrenreich took jobs as a waitress, a maid for a housecleaning service, and a sales associate at a Wal-Mart store. Her pay hovered around minimum wage in all these jobs. Neither she nor the women she worked with could make the rent without working two jobs, seven days a week. Instead, many rented rooms in motels and ate fast food because they had no kitchens in which to cook. With no health insurance or paid sick days, they worked while sick, staved off the pain of manual labor with loads of over-the-counter pain medications, and put off doctors' visits for as long as possible. With wages barely sufficient for basic food and shelter, they rode bikes to work or relied on others for rides. They suffered the indignity of arbitrary employers who tested them for drugs, searched their purses, forbid them to talk to each other, and routinely derided, intimidated, and humiliated them. Reflecting on her experience, Ehrenreich posed a poignant question: "If you are treated as an untrustworthy person—a potential slacker, drug addict, or thief—you may begin to feel less trustworthy yourself. If you are constantly reminded of your

Author Barbara Ehrenreich. (AP/Wide World Photos)

lowly position in the social hierarchy, whether by individual managers or by a plethora of impersonal rules, you begin to accept that unfortunate status" (Ehrenreich 2001, 210).

Most workers in the lower-rung jobs in the service sector simply made the best of their individual situation and plugged on. Some, however, turned to unions in their effort to fight exploitation on the job. Just as the American economy was shifting from a manufacturing to a service economy, some national unions refocused their effort on organizing service workers earning low wages. The Service Employees' International Union (SEIU), one of the oldest unions in the nation, achieved the most publicized victory when it won union recognition for thousands of immigrant janitors who cleaned the office buildings of Los Angeles. The Hotel Employees & Restaurant Employees International Union (HERE) planted the seeds for the living wage movement, which then spread to dozens of municipalities through the organizing work of hundreds of community groups and faith-based organizations.

AMERICAN BUSINESS BETWEEN GLOBALIZATION AND THE NEW ECONOMY

After a wave of bankruptcies and downsizing in the early decade recession, American business and the investors who held claims on its profits and earnings did well overall during the expansion of the 1990s. There were notable differences, however, in the performance of the service, manufacturing, and financial sectors.

The key measure of the overall health of American business is the corporate profit rate. After falling during the 1990–1991 recession, it rose steadily until 1997. The driving force was manufacturing, where rising productivity and rising profits sparked the economic expansion in 1993 and sustained it until 1997. The profitability of corporations providing services—excluding financial services—began to rise in 1995 and continued upward until 2000. Between 1997 and 2000,

The Surge of Temporary Employment

On the cusp of the transition from the jobless recovery to the job-generating economic boom, the largest employer in the United States was Manpower Inc., a temporary help agency that had 767,000 individuals on its payrolls (*New York Times* 1996). Temporary work ran the gamut from maid services to data entry to computer programming; thus, generalizations about the nature and quality of life on the job are difficult to make. What is clear, though, is that this kind of work had been insignificant in the postwar American economy—less than half of one percent of jobs in 1973—and that the transformations of the 1980s and 1990s had elevated it to the job of last resort for millions of Americans who had once held steady and secure jobs in corporations.

The surge in temporary help employment in the 1990s was directly related to corporate downsizing. Even though corporations slashed their payrolls, business went on and firms needed the tasks that had once been performed by permanent employees completed. They outsourced those tasks, and temporary agencies supplied the workers to do them. Corporations could save the cost of paying for health insurance, pensions, sick days, and vacation days. They also gained the ability to hedge their bets against the business cycle, avoiding the cost and difficulty of laying off a full-time employee should their business decline. The labor costs were less, and the way in which accounting rules handled contracted work made the bottom-line profits appear stronger. Technology and Internet companies relied particularly heavily on temporary workers. Up to a third of Microsoft's workers at various points in the 1990s were long-term temporary workers; in 2000, these so-called permatemps won $97 million from the corporation to settle a lawsuit charging that the workers were, in reality, permanent ones, and that they had been classified as temps in order to illegally deprive them of benefits.

Flexible employment for corporations often spelled insecurity for temporary workers. Although work differed for the variety of jobs, most temporary workers lacked the benefits and the security that had typically accompanied permanent employment in postwar America. Unlike most other advanced industrialized countries in which the state provided national health insurance, subsidized parental leave, and mandated vacation time, the United States depended on an employment-based system for all of these fundamental needs. Most temporary workers were not compensated on the days they were sick or took a vacation; they had to pay for their own health insurance or risk going without. If the agency could not find them work—for a day, a week, or a few months—they were not entitled to receive unemployment insurance. In this way, business risk was transferred away from corporate stockholders and management and onto workers with no formal institutional claims on the company.

however, manufacturing profitability declined by 20 percent, and the fall in manufacturing profits dwarfed the less dramatic rise in service industry profits. Between 1997 and 2000, if all service and manufacturing corporations are included and those providing financial services are excluded, the overall drop in the corporate profit rate was 10 percent. In sum, if the profits of the financial sector are excluded, corporate profits fell at the height of the 1990s expansion (Brenner 2002).

The fall in manufacturing profit rates took place in 1997, exactly at the moment when productivity, GDP, and demand were soaring; inflation was low; wages were rising; and the stock market was ripping. It should have been the best of times for business. American manufacturers, however, could not sell their goods for a decent profit because they could not raise prices in the face of international competition. The difficulties started in 1995, when wages began their first rise from a 30-year nadir and as the value of the dollar rose (thus making U.S. goods more expensive in the international market). The 1997 East Asian financial crisis, which resulted in those countries dumping their goods into the world market at prices below the cost of production, exacerbated the troubles of American manufacturers.

The boom of the 1990s reached its apex between 1998 and 2000. From 1997 on, with profits in the real economy falling, the stock market and debt-financed corporate and consumer consumption underwrote the expansion. Wall Street, with profit rates leading other sectors in the latter part of the decade, was the star of the 1990s boom. In August 1995, Wall Street took the Web browser company Netscape public. By the end of the day, the stock price had shot up from $28 per share to $58. The stock market boom of the 1990s was on. In the 1980s, finance had begun to rise in importance in the national economy; in 1995, it surpassed manufacturing in its contribution to national income and GDP. Wall Street also attained unprecedented influence over the operation of the real economy, as the fate of corporations producing goods and services increasingly rested on the opinion of investors. The success of finance firms as business ventures themselves, however, rested on shaky foundations. To the extent that their profits were the fruit of a speculative bubble, it was neither sustainable nor a basis for long-term economic growth.

The stock speculation of the late 1990s channeled trillions of dollars into American corporations. The market capitalization of publicly traded corporations increased fourfold over the decade, but much of the new investment, in hindsight, turned out to be over-investment, creating excess capacity in manufacturing and in Internet and telecommunications infrastructure (Stiglitz 2003; Brenner 2002). After five years of rising profits and a high rate of new business starts, the early years of the 21st century were ones of record-breaking bankruptcies, the exposure of massive corporate scandals, and flat and falling real profit rates.

A Portrait of the American Corporation in the 1990s: General Motors, Microsoft, Wal-Mart

Changes in the global economy and the specific strengths of the national economy affected American businesses in varying ways. There were winners and losers in the New Economy and the global economy. General Motors, Microsoft, and Wal-Mart, three leading corporations in key sectors of the American economy—manufacturing, information technology, and retail—are profiled in this section.

General Motors (GM)

In the postwar era, GM had symbolized American economic hegemony and manufacturing prowess. It had been the country's largest employer and largest corporation. At the end of the 1990s, GM still ranked number one in the Fortune 500 listing and remained the world's largest automaker. Nevertheless, the company's decline over the previous two decades had been obvious to all and painful for those who worked for the company or owned its stock.

Although the American auto industry was one of the few manufacturing industries in America to partially withstand the destructive force of globalization, competition had still whittled away its international dominance. Throughout the 1980s and 1990s, GM steadily hemorrhaged market share and workers. In 1991, the company reorganized, laid off 74,000 workers, and replaced its CEO. Over the course of the decade, in an attempt to recover profitability, the company diversified its operations, aggressively pursued ownership stakes in foreign corporations, and built overseas factories in Indonesia, China, and other lower-wage nations.

Nevertheless, neither GM's workers—who went on strike for five weeks in 1998—nor Wall Street were satisfied with the results. Wall Street pressured the company to "restructure" again—that is, to close American plants, lay off workers, and lower wages and benefits. GM staved off the day of reckoning until 2005, when the bankruptcy filing of Delphi, a parts division it had spun off during the late 1990s' restructuring, precipitated a crisis that rippled through the entire U.S. auto industry.

Microsoft

In 1975, a handful of self-described geeks founded the computer company Microsoft. The company soon revolutionized personal computing. By 1993, the Windows system designed by Microsoft was the most widely used computing operating system in the world. By 1995, the company controlled most of the personal computing and office computing market, and its founder, Bill Gates Jr., was lionized as an American hero. In 1998, Gates became the world's first $100 billionaire, and in 1999, Microsoft was the world's most highly valued

Bill Gates, chairman and CEO of Microsoft. (Feature Photo Service/ NewsCom)

company. An early entrant and the clear winner in the computer revolution, Microsoft was also one of the few survivors of the stock market conflagration that took out most of the technology enterprises launched in the 1990s.

One of the strengths of Microsoft, like other technology enterprises, lay in its ownership and control of intellectual property. The creation of such intellectual property—writing software programs and inventing computer operating systems—is the work of a comparatively small number of highly skilled and highly paid workers. The products they created were ones with a high profit margin. Within the Microsoft "campus," Gates's New Economy notion of a "frictionless economy" seemed an accurate description of reality—except for the thousands of full-time, long-term workers classified as temporary workers.

Microsoft's dominance among its competitors, however, was due less to the technological superiority of its products than to the business savvy of its leader. Indeed, Microsoft's business model was that of a classic monopoly. In 1998, the U.S. Department of Justice filed antitrust suits against Microsoft, charging that it had placed a stranglehold on American enterprise with its unfair monopoly practices. In 2001, Microsoft reached a settlement with the justice department over antitrust claims. Other individual settlements with competitors followed.

Although Gates took a large hit with the stock market collapse on Black Friday in April 2000—his personal fortune fell $12 billion in one day—Microsoft weathered the dot-com shakeout and its own legal troubles equally well. For a brief moment in the mid-1990s, the press was full of tales of how expansion of the Internet would lead to the transcendence of the old corporate, commercial ways. Microsoft's trajectory and its continued dominance in its industry instead suggests that the technology revolution did not revolutionize American business practices. Microsoft, as a corporate entity, was a garden-variety corporate monopoly, long identifiable in the American terrain and destined to outlive the dot-com craze.

Wal-Mart

The retail discounter Wal-Mart was the fastest-growing corporation in the fastest-growing sector of the economy. By the beginning of the millennium, it had passed

GM as the largest corporation in the country and in the world. The retail giant creatively combined New Economy innovations and age-old merchant practices. It blazed the way in transforming retail operations through the use of technology but was utterly conventional in its exploitation of its workers, sharp bargaining with suppliers, and cut-throat competition against other retailers.

Wal-Mart revolutionized the logistics of the retail business and created a new paradigm of a consumer-driven supply and demand chain. Traditionally, production drove retail—stores sold whatever was produced. Wal-Mart applied new computer technology to eliminate bottlenecks between suppliers and retailers. It was the first to widely adopt the barcode and track all steps from production to sale in massive databases, which enabled it to compile, analyze, and immediately respond to data generated in each of its stores. Wal-Mart shared its data on consumer preferences throughout its supply chain and, by doing so, was able to drive out middlemen and deal directly with suppliers. With a system for analyzing what sold and what did not, Wal-Mart adapted the "just-in-time" system of global production and transformed the retail industry. By thus eliminating surplus inventory, the bane of retailers, Wal-Mart gained price advantages over its competitors. With these advantages, the company grew rapidly and was soon able to gain the market power to force its suppliers to lower their costs and prices. Each step in the process allowed Wal-Mart to sell its goods for a bit less. In an industry with razor-thin profit margins, slight price advantages made all the difference, and profits grew astronomically from the volume of sales.

Wal-Mart attracted criticism for some of its business practices and the consequences of its success. Small local businesses had difficulty surviving under the new terms of competition created by Wal-Mart, and by the beginning of the new century, video footage of boarded up Main Streets was being disseminated by Wal-Mart's critics as a warning to communities that were contemplating allowing the company to build a store. The company also ran into trouble as it exported certain of the less savory aspects of rural, conservative Southern business culture to the rest of the nation and other countries. In most of the rest of the country, grocery stores were unionized; in Wal-Mart's stores, workers earned wages at or close to the legal minimum wage. And although Wal-Mart was on the cutting edge technologically, its personnel policies clashed with accepted practices of the modern American corporation. Many corporations had voluntarily instituted diversity policies and had found that there were innumerable competitive advantages to be won from the rise of minorities and women in corporate leadership positions. Even though conflicts over affirmative action roiled American politics in the 1990s, and even though there was a long way to go to achieve parity in American business, the tide had turned. Wal-Mart, however, did not join this growing consensus and, according to employees' allegations, discriminated against women, African American, and Latino employees. In 2004, a federal judge certified the largest-ever private civil rights class action case for up to 1.6 million female employees of Wal-Mart in the 1990s who charged that they were paid less for comparable jobs and denied promotions on the basis of their sex. (Wal-Mart appealed the certification of the class action, and the case is still, as of this writing, making its way through the appeals process.)

The Stock Market Boom, 1995–2000

The bull market of the 1990s set many historic records. The Dow Jones Industrial Average doubled between 1992 and 1997 and continued to multiply. When it topped 10,000 in the spring of 1999, it was 10 times its level of 1972. Its 11,302 mark in January 2000 represented a fourfold increase for the decade and a then all-time record high. In 1990, approximately 157 million shares had been traded daily on the New York Stock Exchange; in 2000, approximately 1.04 billion shares were traded on an average day. The NASDAQ, where most of the dot-com and technology companies were listed, increased more than tenfold—from 414 to 5,250—in the same period. Encouraged by New Economy boosters and a cottage industry of market commentators, investors believed that the market was a sure bet and were willing to take historically small returns. As measured by the price–earnings ration of stocks, investors paid roughly two and a half times more for stock than what their counterparts had been willing to pay over the previous century. More Americans than ever before invested in stocks. About half of the population, or 100 million people, owned stock in 2000, compared to only 10 percent who did in 1960. The fall in the markets from August 2000 through 2001 destroyed $5 trillion of wealth—an amount equivalent to 75 percent of the nation's GDP. The drop in the NASDAQ from 2000 to 2001 was the largest-ever one-year decline in a stock average in the United States (Fraser 2005). In the aftermath of the crash, almost all analysts agreed that the boom had been a speculative bubble.

Most of the increase in the stock markets—both in value and in numbers of investors—went into the new technology sector, particularly companies associated in some way with the Internet or telecommunications. Bull market utopianism and hype—of best-selling how-to-buy-stocks books, countless cable financial news shows, and short-lived mass market financial advice magazines— were also concentrated here. Technological utopianism and speculative bubbles have tended to come together in American economic history, and the 1990s were no exception.

The stock market rise, nonetheless, began before the height of the Internet mania. The economic expansion of the mid-1990s was first propelled by the rise in corporate profitability in the manufacturing sector. Investment flowed into the stock market in part because the real economy indicated that profits were growing and there was money to be made through dividends and capital gains. Investors could reasonably expect that the profits of American corporations

Traders on the floor of the New York Stock Exchange (NYSE). (Corel)

would continue to rise. Their optimism, at least initially, was not solely a case of irrational exuberance (Henwood 2005; Brenner 2002).

What role did the Internet play in the fantastic rise in the stock market and the resulting bubble? Undeveloped areas of economic activity tend to attract speculators, and the Internet seemed as good a one as a classic gold rush. The media trumpeted the news that Internet traffic was doubling every three months, or 1,000 percent annually. The accumulating evidence of a "productivity miracle," which theorized that the adoption of new technologies in the production process had caused productivity to rise, appeared to give the fantastic increases in tech companies' value a footing in the real economy. It was, therefore, no surprise that tech stocks rose more than others in the boom of the 1990s. It was also not unusual, from a historical perspective, that precisely these companies were the principle casualties of the market's collapse. Only a small percentage of the dot-com companies that were launched in the bubble survived into the early years of the 21st century. Those that did survive, however—Amazon, eBay, Yahoo—were the bulwarks and leaders of Web 2.0.

Wall Street and the American Corporation
The transformation in the theory and practice of American corporate management rivaled the Internet as a progenitor of the stock market boom and bubble, and provided one of the indispensable ingredients for the market's meteoric rise.

Mergers

The 1990s, like the 1980s, was a decade of merger mania. A large part of the merger activity in the 1990s centered on the industries that were newly deregulated: communications, technology, and the media. The capital for mergers came largely from the increased value of a corporation's own stock in the bull market. CEOs had strong incentives to engage in mergers. Their compensation was linked to share price, they held billions of dollars in options, and the market usually rewarded mergers by ratcheting up share prices. In the most notorious merger of the decade, Steve Case of AOL used his assets to engineer AOL's acquisition of Time Warner, itself a recent creation of the merger of *Time* magazine and Warner Brothers. AOL used stock that was already recognized by some analysts to be inflated to add a tangible asset to its enterprise. The shareholders of Time Warner were the losers. The new AOL Time Warner used a standard accounting procedure of the time, writing off more than $50 billion in losses resulting from the merger. Other companies, including those at the head of the corporate scandals of the early 2000s such as WorldCom and Tyco International, were dubbed "serial acquirers" for their prolific merger activity (Stiglitz 2003).

The new management theory recommended that the interests of corporate executives should be aligned with the corporation's stockholders rather than oriented toward the firm's production and employee relations. The change began in the 1980s, when debt-financed hostile takeovers—leveraged buyouts (LBOs)—shook up corporate America. The investment banks and colorful investors structuring these deals ousted the old corporate management and frequently closed factories to maximize the profits of the new debtholders and owners. The method proved to have its own downside, however, as the level of debt acquired by the new owners proved to be a drag on the bottom line. The approach thus shifted in the 1990s. Investment banks, instead of dismissing the existing corporate leadership, gave the existing leadership the opportunity to perform more ably. Conventionally, success was measured by real growth, sales, or revenues. The new standard by which they would be judged was the company's stock price. As an incentive to corporate executives to focus on the stock market's assessment of their company, stock options became routinely included in executive compensation packages. The value of options soon dwarfed salaries in executive compensation (Henwood 2005; Krugman 2003).

As corporate performance came to be judged more by the standards of Wall Street, corporations became more active market players themselves. A tremendous amount of stock market activity in the 1990s involved corporations purchasing back their own company's shares. The goal of the buy-backs was to ignite a rise in the company's stock price. A self-perpetuating cycle became

The Business of Finance

The internal dynamics of Wall Street cannot be underestimated as a force in the making of the bubble. Just as benefits accrued to the executives of a corporation from engineering a rise in their company's stock price, there was plenty of money to be made by brokerage firms and individual brokers for managing the multiplying number of transactions. New financial instruments, technology initial public offerings (IPOs), and the like increased the daily volume of shares traded on the New York Stock Exchange from 157 million to 1.04 trillion over the decade. Almost every one of these trades brought a commission to an investment broker or firm. Deregulation, which ended the separation between commercial and investment banks, and lax regulation by the Securities and Exchange Commission created an environment rife with conflicts of interest, spotty ethics, and criminality (Stiglitz 2003).

commonplace in the environment of the 1990s stock market boom. Corporate executives announced plans to repurchase the company's stock, and with the announcement, stock prices rose. Executives gained personal profits by exercising their options. Corporate compensation boards, which set the level of executive pay, then rewarded CEOs for the rise in stock price with a raise. The bonus itself tended to be composed disproportionately of new stock options. And on it went. The steep rise in executive compensation in the 1990s was driven in large part by this intimate relationship between corporations and the stock market.

As corporate stock prices assumed greater importance than more traditional measures of business success with investors, a wide disparity opened between real corporate profits and the profits companies reported to investors in their public filings. Whereas real corporate profits stalled between 1997 and 2000—except in the finance sector—during the same years S&P 500 companies reported to investors operating profits of 46 percent, a divergence between real and paper profits greater than had ever been reported (Krugman 2003). With the exposure in December 2001 and after of the scandals in leading corporations such as WorldCom and Enron, it became clear that questionable—and often illegal—accounting practices had enabled failing corporations to present an illusion of spectacular growth in order to stay in the good graces of Wall Street.

Government and the Stock Market Boom:
Deregulation, Laissez-Faire, and Bailouts

The federal government, through a combination of action and inaction, encouraged the stock market boom. As some quipped at the time, there was socialism for investors, the free market for everyone else. The government's indulgence toward the financial markets marked a departure from 20th-century policy, albeit a change that had been in the making since the late 1970s. From the 1930s to the 1970s, New Deal policy formulated as a response to the Crash of 1929 had restrained financial markets and the speculative manias that have historically beset the markets at regular intervals. In the wake of the Great Depression, economic theorists and policymakers throughout the Western world concluded that unregulated financial speculation had an inherently destabilizing effect on the real economy where goods and services were produced and sold. Some of the hallmarks of the early New Deal, banking regulation that separated commercial from investment banking (the Glass-Steagall Act of 1933), investment markets regulation (the Securities and Exchange Commission of 1934), and the reorganization of the Federal Reserve (1935) were designed specifically to curb and regulate finance and speculation. After World War II, the international financial system spearheaded by the United States circumscribed international financial speculation as well. In this tough regulatory environment, the long postwar era was comparatively free of speculative booms and busts.

A new view of finance took shape in the wake of economic woes of the 1970s. Proponents of the free market insisted that taking the brakes off international finance would stimulate the stagnant economy. In accord with this view, the Carter and Reagan administrations initiated banking and financial deregulation. The Bush and Clinton administrations continued to pursue financial deregulation while the Federal Reserve hollowed out the essence of Glass-Steagall. In 1996, the Fed ruled that commercial banks could derive up to 25 percent of their revenue from investment banking. At this threshold, commercial banks could purchase investment banks outright. Greenspan subsequently in 1998 approved the merger of Travelers Group, an insurance company, with Citicorp, a bank, to form Citigroup—even though the merger was technically against the law. The law, not the merger, would be the casualty. With Rubin at the helm, the Clinton administration pushed for the passage of the Financial Services Modernization Act (1999), which repealed what remained of Glass-Steagall. (Shortly thereafter, Rubin returned to Wall Street as the chairman of Citigroup.)

One of the premises of New Deal banking and financial reform had been that regulation could restrain the behaviors that turned booms into bubbles. In the mid-1990s, a number of commentators speculated that U.S. markets might be entering into such destabilizing territory. In September 1996, Greenspan observed in a Federal Reserve meeting "that there is a stock market bubble problem at this point." He also noted that he had the power to slow it down by imposing margin requirements but concluded that the interference in the market might have larger unintended consequences (Greenspan 1996). (Stocks were being bought largely on credit—"margin." Margin requirements would have required investors to put more cash up front, and the requirement would have likely slowed stock market activity.) It left investors curious about whether the

Oracle disapproved of the market rise but most chose to believe that his subsequent New Economy boosterism assured that their investments were considered sound.

The feverish pace of domestic and international investment in the 1990s led to several global financial crises that many observers thought could spiral into serious recession in the real economy if left to take their course. In 1999, *Time* magazine published a cover photo of Greenspan, Rubin, and Lawrence Summers (chair of the Council of Economic Advisors) with the headline "Committee to Save the World." The story applauded their pivotal role in engineering a bailout following the 1998 collapse of the private hedge fund Long Term Capital Management. This was one of several occasions when the Fed, the Clinton administration, and the international lending organizations worked together to prevent a collapse of international financial markets by bailing out investors. (The others were in the 1994 Mexican Peso Crisis and the 1997 East Asian Crisis.) The bailouts, whatever their wisdom as a matter of international financial policy, sent a message to investors that they would be protected from their gambles in the free market.

All told, financial deregulation, lax regulation of the financial industry, praise for the New Economy, and bailouts signaled to investors that the leaders of the United States looked favorably on their activities, would do little to restrain them, and would act to save them from major losses. The federal government thus played a significant role in fostering an environment of carefree speculation and the bubble that ended in a bust.

Alan Greenspan: Chairman of the Federal Reserve, 1987–2006

Americans tend to reward and punish their elected officials for the nation's economic fortunes and misfortunes. Although tax and budgeting policies affect every American in some way, the elected officers of national, state, and local governments have negligible influence over most economic activities and larger economic trends.

Instead, the leadership of the country's central bank, the Federal Reserve, exerts much greater sway over the nation's economic life. The Fed, as it is commonly known, controls the money supply, and in this power lies its ability to influence the business cycle, the level of employment and wages, and business investment. It is also responsible for regulating the nation's banks, a more indirect but nonetheless significant means of influence over day-to-day economic activity.

The Federal Reserve was created in 1913 during an era of social conflict. When populists suggested a plan to control the currency in the interests of debt-ridden farmers, the nation's corporate and financial leaders became anxious about leaving monetary policy under the control of democratically elected officials. The Fed's creators sought to place a nonpartisan, expert, independent authority at the helm of the nation's money supply.

Fed policy is set primarily by its chairman, who is appointed by the president and confirmed by the Senate. During the 1990s expansion, Alan Greenspan served as the chairman of the Fed. He is the only head of the Federal Reserve to have ever been the subject of a popular nonfiction book. The title of the book, *The Maestro,* speaks volumes to the popular acclaim won by Greenspan in the heady days of the New Economy (Woodward 2000).

Greenspan was born in New York City in 1926 to Jewish parents and raised by his mother after his parents divorced. His father was a financier and an amateur stock analyst who, in the 1930s, wrote a book lauding New Deal Keynesian economic policy. Greenspan excelled at math in high school, but his passion was music. On graduating, he went to Julliard to study music. He spent two years there, and then left school to join a jazz orchestra playing regular gigs in New York City. Greenspan realized that he was only an average musician, and in 1945, he left the band and began taking classes at the business school of New York University (NYU), where he earned a B.A. and an M.A. in economics.

Although NYU was a haven for free market conservative economists, Greenspan and his friends were all Democrats and Keynesians at that time. By the early 1950s, Greenspan had been converted to an orthodox free market position himself. After NYU, Greenspan entered the doctoral program in economics at Columbia University, studying with Arthur F. Burns, an economist opposed to Keynesian policies and government budget deficits and who later served as chairman of the Federal Reserve during the Nixon and Ford administrations (1970–1978). However, Greenspan was drawn more to the practical side of economics, and in 1948, he left his studies in order to work for a private firm engaged in economic analysis. In 1952, Greenspan met Ayn Rand, libertarian philosopher and founder of modern American conservatism. It was through conversations and debates with Rand that Greenspan refined his economic and philosophic views and came to share her deep commitment to free market principles. He became an active member of her circle of conservative intellectuals in New York City. Although he was not fully accepted by some of her acolytes, he maintained a friendship and an intellectual bond with her throughout the rest of her life. In 1974, he explained, "What she did—through long discussions and lots of arguments into the night—was to make me think why capitalism is not only efficient and practical, but also moral" (Cassidy 2000).

Greenspan's talent for business forecasting and his mathematical acumen brought him business success. In 1953, a successful bond trader offered him a partnership in his economic consulting firm. Greenspan spent the next two decades at Townsend-Greenspan & Company, where his clients included some of the leading corporations in America. Through his considerable expertise and his winning temperament, Greenspan won access to business and political leaders.

Greenspan first became active in politics in 1968 when he was brought on by the Nixon campaign as an economic advisor. He held a number of positions in the Nixon, Ford, and Reagan administrations. Offered the prestigious post of chairman of the president's Council of Economic Advisors, he informed the Nixon administration that he was a "strict" libertarian. He accepted the position only after winning assurances from the administration that it would not impose wage and price controls during his tenure, as it had done in 1971. Reagan appointed Greenspan to succeed Paul Volcker as chairman of the Federal Reserve, and after approval by Congress, Greenspan assumed the office in August 1987 (Woodward 2000).

Greenspan's first challenge as chairman struck quickly that October. Greenspan responded to the stock market crash of Black Monday by loosening the money supply. Although he was praised for averting a panic at that moment, he was soon criticized for his bungling management of monetary policy and its impact on the recession of 1990–1991. One of his critics was George H. W. Bush, who blamed him for his 1992 defeat (Krugman 1994; Stiglitz 2003).

Greenspan's inauspicious start at the head of the Fed would be largely forgotten as the economy took off, and he was widely celebrated for his helmsmanship of the American economy during the boom. In the past, few Americans had known the name of the Fed chairman. Greenspan, by contrast, achieved celebrity status. Some headlines of the decade illustrate the esteem in which he was held: "The Committee to Save the World" (*Time*), "In Greenspan We Trust" (*Business Week*), "Who Needs Gold When We Have Greenspan?" (*New York Times*). Greenspan himself lent a hand to refining his popular image. He made frequent public appearances, yet he tended to issue pronouncements about the state of the economy in ambiguous and convoluted terms. The press, politicians, and business hung on his words, trying to divine the state of his mind from his impenetrable statements. People started referring to him as the "Oracle."

If there was something fantastical about a celebrity Fed chairman, Greenspan's influence over U.S. economic policy was a substantial and material reality. Most important, his was the most powerful voice demanding deficit reduction. Every sitting president knows that the head of the Fed can quite easily spur good times or provoke bad ones—at least temporarily—with a well-timed change in interest rates. Greenspan and Clinton eventually developed a close and mutually respectful working relationship, but it was critically the threat of Greenspan's displeasure that settled Clinton's early decision to shelve his bigger public investment promises of "jobs, jobs, jobs." In the core responsibility of the Fed, controlling the money supply, Greenspan more or less pursued a conventional approach, although he demonstrated more flexibility than his predecessor did. Inflation remained very low throughout the long boom of the 1990s. However, each time the boom seemed to be raising wages significantly, Greenspan raised interest rates (in 1994, and then in 1999). Interest rate hikes negatively affect wage workers—by increasing unemployment, by increasing the real cost of debt payments, and by depressing wage growth. That workers in the 1990s did not experience greater wage gains during the boom was in significant measure due to convictions in the Fed dating from the 1970s, and shared by Greenspan, that inflation was the greatest threat to the overall national economy (Stiglitz 2003, ch. 3). In bank regulation, a less widely examined role of the Fed, Greenspan oversaw decisions that made the repeal of Glass-Steagall all but inevitable, thus contributing to the momentum for more business deregulation. To this substantial material influence over the underlying forces in the national economy, Greenspan lent his carefully cultivated prestige to the promotion of New Economy boosterism, and he declined to apply any brakes to the stock market boom.

Greenspan's tenure at the Federal Reserve continued into the administration of George W. Bush, and his actions during the Bush years provide perspective on his actions in the 1990s. During the Clinton years, he had insisted on caution, some said deference, toward the markets. He sanctioned his approach by reference to free market principles and the limited role of the Fed and its chairman. But when Bush came into the presidency, Greenspan reversed both of these positions. In 2001, he placed his considerable prestige at the service of the Bush administration's favored initiative, testifying before Congress to endorse Bush's proposed tax cuts. Greenspan ventured beyond monetary matters to argue that the current economic danger was the excessive budget surplus— that is, that the government had too much money—and that tax cuts were sounder economically than spending. While there is a potential connection between budget deficits and the health of the nation's currency—a matter clearly within the purview of the Federal Reserve—how the federal budget is allocated is as clearly a legislative power. When the budget turned from black to red, Greenspan declined to issue his normal warning about the primacy of fiscal discipline and at first remained silent on enacting another round of tax cuts. When he did return to his strictures about fiscal discipline after the nation's budget was deep in the red, he recommended cutting social security—not suspending the tax cuts—to deal with it. Joseph Stiglitz, the Nobel prize–winning economist who served on Clinton's Council of Economic Advisors and as head of the World Bank observed, "Greenspan revealed himself as an advocate of smaller government: both deficit reductions in the nineties and Bush tax cuts in 2001 would lead to a reduced public sector." As Stiglitz noted, this was exactly the "partisan" position of conservative Republicans (Stiglitz 2003, 80).

Greenspan retired from the chairmanship in 2006 with his reputation for brilliant economic stewardship largely intact, but the view would not survive the fall-out from his actions during the Bush presidency. His supporters viewed his reign at the Federal Reserve as one of brilliant leadership in which he steered the economy deftly through several major international financial crises and adeptly managed U.S. monetary policy to sustain the expansion. To them, he earned a reputation as a pragmatic and effective leader who had the courage to break with traditional wisdom about inflation and allow an unprecedented level of economic growth before tightening the money supply. His critics argued that Greenspan unnecessarily dampened wage growth during the expansion out of excessive concern for inflation, fostered a bubble in the stock and housing markets, used his position in an essentially partisan manner to favor conservative policies outside the purview of the Federal Reserve, and—most seriously— made the Fed even more powerful and less democratically accountable. At the end of the 1990s, in a nation whose citizens had historically been suspicious of bankers, financiers, and central banks, the American public largely adopted Greenspan's view of the powerful and unreproachable Fed. But as the housing bubble burst and the world economy faced a credit crisis in 2007, Greenspan's luster faded and a growing body of commentators joined the ranks of his critics.

Popular Involvement in the Stock Market

Never before in American history had so many ordinary Americans invested in the stock market. One in two Americans owned stocks by the end of the decade. As recently as 1985, only about one in eight had. At the height of the bull market, over 100 million men and women owned stocks, 5 million individual Americans engaged in online day trading, and about 30,000 investment clubs met to trade stock tips. Following the market ranked with shopping, gambling, and soccer leagues as a favorite American pastime. On cable TV, financial news programming exploded, briefly displacing soap operas and sports as the most popular form of daytime viewing.

Institutional changes, accomplished over several decades, had acclimated Americans to entrusting their future economic security to the performance of the stock market. Federal legislation governing employee retirement plans, which created tax advantages for investing in 401(k)s, IRAs, and Keoghs, encouraged people to shift their savings from bank accounts to investments. (The savings and loan debacle in the 1980s hastened the transition.) The money set aside for the retirement of union members and public employees had long been invested in the market through pension funds; in the 1990s, those funds grew to approximately $1.4 trillion. Mutual funds and other institutional funds provided the mechanism for pooling savings and minimizing risk, which made it safer and easier for individuals with small savings to invest in the stock market. In 1982, 340 mutual funds operated. By 1998, their numbers had grown to 3,513. The media highlighted stories of intrepid ordinary Americans who ventured into the market with only their native wisdom as a guide—day traders and elderly women in the Beardstown Ladies investment club. In reality, financial institutions managed the investments of the overwhelming majority of investors (Fraser 2005).

Americans rushed into the bull market in the late 1990s believing there was a sure fortune to be made. But the phenomenon could not have happened without a radical transformation in Americans' cultural perception of Wall Street, the stock market, and speculation itself. Wall Street had long been viewed with suspicion in American popular culture. As late as the 1980s, the typical approach to Wall Street in American popular culture was righteous ridicule. Thomas Wolfe's novel *The Bonfire of the Vanities* and the movie character Gordon "Greed is Good" Gecko were two of the most memorable fictional creations of that decade.

All that changed in the 1990s in one of the most dramatic and rapid cultural reversals in American history. Wall Street, which had once been viewed as a principle threat to democracy, now came to be viewed as an arena for the re-alization of the democratic promise. Evoking populist traditions in which the plain people ruled and democracy meant a rough equality of condition, market boosters successfully spread the idea that democracy itself was fulfilled by the wide diffusion of stock ownership. Billionaire investment gurus such as Warren Buffett and Peter Lynch were celebrated as populist heroes who led the armies of the common folk against Wall Street's elitist overlords. Evoking the radical individualist values of the 1960s liberation movements, the tribunes of share-holder democracy portrayed stock purchases as a revolutionary expression of personal liberation. The ubiquitous bromides about "shareholder democracy," "market democracy," and the "democratization of the market" proposed that the American dream had finally been fulfilled through the end of the millennium bull market. Never before had so many ordinary Americans thought this way about finance. It was as if the populist tradition had been turned on its head (Fraser 2005; Frank 2000).

Despite the rhetoric about the market as an arena of democratic equality, the distribution of stock market wealth was highly unequal, even when things were going well. In 1998, just 1 percent of the population owned 48 percent of the value of all stocks while 80 percent of stockholders together owned only 4 per-cent of the total value (Henwood 2005). Not only did middle-class Americans own insignificant amounts of stock compared to the wealthy, they also received meager gains from their investments. The middle fifth of Americans gained only 2.8 percent of the market's rise during the decade, and between 80 and 90 per-cent of day traders lost money. Once the bubble burst, and people relearned the time-tested lesson that the last one in on a Ponzi scheme loses the most, talk of the democratization of the market ceased. Laws governing retirement funds meant that a large proportion of Americans continued to hold investments in the stock market, but the fantasies of instant wealth evaporated as swiftly as the paper wealth itself (Phillips 2002).

Enron and the Roots of Corporate Scandal in the Roaring Nineties
In December 2001, Enron Corporation, a company viewed as the epitome of the New Economy, filed for bankruptcy. On the eve of bankruptcy, Enron was listed in the Fortune 500 as the country's fifth-largest corporation and reported revenues of $101 billion (Stiglitz 2003). By the summer of 2002, three other major New Economy corporations had gone belly-up in some of the largest bankruptcies in U.S. history, and investigations of widespread accounting fraud and company looting had commenced. Criminal cases against some of the most

renowned corporate leaders of the 1990s wended through the courts over the following few years. Ultimately, Kenneth Lay, Jeffrey Skilling, Frank P. Quattrone, Martha Stewart, Bernard J. Ebbers, and others were convicted of a wide range of white-collar crimes, including insider trading, criminal conspiracy, accounting fraud, and looting. Enron was the first to fall and the first in which reports of corporate fraud and criminality were alleged. Enron's founder, Kenneth Lay, had once told the *Economist,* "We were a new-economy company before it became cool" (quoted in Henwood 2005, 34). The other bankruptcies were also in companies that were touted in the late 1990s as the dynamos of the New Economy and the future of American business. Once the exemplar of the New Economy, Enron became and remains the symbol of its corrupt underbelly.

The history of Enron is entwined with its founder, Kenneth Lay. Lay was born in 1942, the son of a poor Baptist preacher from rural Missouri. In the 1960s, he earned a doctorate in economics while working at the Pentagon. After serving as an assistant to a commissioner on the Federal Power Commission in the early 1970s, Lay entered the energy business and pioneered trading methods that limited the risk of pipeline companies. In 1986, Lay became the CEO of the newly named Enron after spearheading the 1985 merger of two natural-gas pipeline companies to form the longest pipeline network in the United States. In the 1990s, Lay transformed Enron from a pipeline company into an energy trading company while, in Horatio Alger fashion, he personally rose to become one of the most celebrated CEOs in the country and one of the nation's leading power brokers.

Enron was praised in the 1990s by business observers for its innovative business strategy. The phenomenal growth of the company, however, resulted as much from political savvy. Enron's rise corresponded to the deregulation of electricity by Congress, which had been accomplished in part by concerted lobbying by Enron itself. One of the first companies to win government approval to sell electricity at market rates, Enron quickly emerged as the most successful energy trading company. The company and its executives contributed hefty sums to election campaigns in the 1990s—between 1989 and 2001, $6 million—and the company also spent millions paying lobbyists to work statehouses and the U.S. Congress. The effect of this political activity on the company's fortunes can be illustrated with one example of Enron's political relationships. In 1992, Sen. Phil Gramm's wife, Wendy Gramm, served as the chair of the Commodity Futures Trading Commission. Enron was a large contributor to Senator Gramm. The commission ruled that Enron was exempt from oversight of its electricity trading futures. Six days later, Gramm resigned from the commission, and five weeks later, she began a tenure on Enron's board of directors. In 2000, Senator Gramm moved legislation deregulating energy trading. Soon after, Enron gained control of California's energy market, even though it owned no power plants, and posted some of its first real profits. In the summer of 2000, with Enron and other companies manipulating the market, Californian energy prices soared, rolling

Kenneth L. Lay, former chairman and CEO of Enron Corporation, declines to testify before the U.S. Senate Committee on Commerce, Science, and Transportation, February 12, 2002. (Martin H. Simon/Corbis)

blackouts hit the state, and the outlay for energy turned the state budget from the black to the red (Henwood 2005; Stiglitz 2003).

After the bankruptcy of Enron, the growth of the company attested to in public filings was revealed to be largely fictitious, and it appeared that Enron's executives were operating what amounted to an elaborate three-card Monty game. In 1999, Enron's board and senior executives waived conflict of interest rules to allow the chief financial officer to create off-the-books limited partnerships, whose main purpose was to make the company's debts and steep losses appear to be profits in public securities filings. The company also began using sophisticated accounting techniques to mask its problems. While Skilling and Lay continued to court new investors, not only by cooking the company's books but also by publicly announcing their own stock purchases, they were surreptitiously dumping over $100 million worth of their own stock holdings. The public and most of Enron's more than 4,000 employees were the unwitting and unfortunate victims. Enron's employees lost their jobs and more than $2 billion worth of pensions. Investors lost over $60 billion, and public pension funds alone lost between $5 and $10 billion. Arthur Andersen, the country's largest accounting firm, collapsed in the wake of revelations of its role in perpetrating the accounting frauds at Enron and other companies.

Roughly six weeks before Enron declared bankruptcy, the Securities and Exchange Commission announced that it had started an investigation into Enron's limited partnerships. And in January 2002, the Justice Department created a special task force to investigate possible criminal activities. By the summer of 2002, former Enron executives had reached plea bargains with federal prosecutors, and arrests and indictments of the company's top executives followed. Ultimately, 24 Enron senior executives and managers pleaded guilty or were convicted of criminal charges. In May 2006, after a 56-day trial, a jury of Houston citizens found their one-time civic leader Kenneth L. Lay guilty of six counts of fraud and criminal conspiracy, to which he could have been sentenced to 165 years in jail. They likewise found Jeffrey K. Skilling, Enron's former CEO and chief operating officer, guilty of 18 counts of fraud and conspiracy and one count of insider trading, to which he could have been sentenced to 175 years in jail. While awaiting sentencing, Lay died suddenly at his home of a heart attack, thus voiding his conviction on a technicality. Skilling was sentenced to 24 years in prison.

While Enron, WorldCom, Tyco, Adelphia, and a few other monumental fraud and bankruptcy cases caught the attention of the nation, the problems in corporate America and on Wall Street were endemic. In the year of Enron's bankruptcy, 270 corporations revised their public filings in earnings restatements—an indicator that loose or deceptive accounting practices might have been involved in the original filing. Every one of the top 10 Wall Street firms in the securities business was implicated in the scandals. To settle the litigation against them brought by New York attorney general Elliot Spitzer, they paid together $1.4 billion in fines and disgorgements (Stiglitz 2003).

BIOGRAPHIES

Marc Andreessen, 1972–

Software Inventor, Founder of Netscape

Marc Andreessen, the inventor and founder of Netscape, was a leader in the development of Web-browsing software during the 1990s. He has been credited with playing a major role in making it possible for personal-computer owners to access the Internet.

Andreessen's fascination with computers began early in his childhood. He wrote his first software program on a school computer while in the sixth grade. While in college, Andreessen worked at the University of Illinois' National Center for Supercomputing Applications. During his work there, he and programmer Eric Bina created Mosaic, the first graphical Web browser that was viable for the public. After graduating in 1993, he went into business with a Silicon Valley mogul, Jim Clark, and they founded Mosaic Communications. After the University of Illinois raised proprietary questions about the pair's use of Mosaic in the name of their new company, they changed their company's name to Netscape Communication in 1994.

To build public dependence on the Netscape browser, the company provided it free to governmental offices and institutions of higher education. For a short while, Netscape reigned supreme. Andreessen became a multimillionaire in 1995 at the age of 24 through the initial public offering of Netscape, becoming the first of the young multimillionaires of the dot-com stock market boom. By that time, Andreessen had won wide honors. He was named one of the top 50 people under the age of 50 by *Time* magazine and was honored as Man of the Year by *MicroTimes* magazine. Netscape was sold in 1999, but Andreessen remained active through several jobs in the computer industry and co-founded OpsWare.

Charles Kernaghan, 1948–

Sweatshop Opponent

Labor activist Charles Kernaghan rose to national prominence in 1996 for his exposure of conditions in foreign sweatshops in which famous American brands were being produced. Kernaghan had been moved to combat sweatshops in the global economy after working in El Salvador as a photographer in 1985. He soon joined the National Labor Committee, where he quickly rose to become the organization's leader. He launched a passionate campaign against American companies' use of inhumane foreign factories to produce goods sold in the United States. His strategy was to reveal substandard working conditions and low pay in sweatshops and to steer brand-name companies away from using these operations to cut their production costs. Among his targets have been retailers like the Gap and Wal-Mart.

Kernaghan won national attention after he testified before Congress that clothes sold at Wal-Mart under the brand name of the popular morning talk-show host Kathie Lee Gifford were produced in Honduran sweatshops. According to Kernaghan's research and the testimony of one of the workers, Honduran children were forced to work 13-hour shifts for less than 50 cents an hour making clothes that bore Gifford's label. Gifford initially denied the charges and threatened to sue the National Labor Committee. She later met with Kernaghan, who brought to the meeting a Honduran teen-aged girl who sewed for Gifford's line. After listening to the girl's story, Gifford promised that she would no longer allow sweatshops to produce her clothing line. However, Kernaghan reported two years later that sweatshops in Latin America and China continued to produce products that bore her name, attributing it to Wal-Mart's refusal to abide by Gifford's promise. In 1998, Kernaghan's organization produced a report, *Behind the*

Label Made in China, which focused on bad conditions in Chinese factories that manufactured products sold under American brand names, including Wal-Mart, Ralph Lauren, and Liz Claiborne. All of these campaigns bore Kernaghan's signature mark. Opposed to boycotts, which he believed punished workers and did little to correct conditions, Kernaghan sought to focus negative publicity on internationally known companies to win reform.

Naomi Klein, 1970–

Author and Antiglobalization Leader

Naomi Klein was a leading intellectual in the 1990s antiglobalization movement. She was a pioneer in formulating the antiglobalization movement's critique of the corporate homogenization of local national cultures. Klein was born of rebel stock: Her parents left the United States and moved to Canada in 1968 to demonstrate their opposition to the Vietnam War. Her mother, Bonnie, became a feminist filmmaker, but Naomi was slow to embrace activism. In high school, she worked for the Esprit clothing chain, and like many teen-aged girls, she frequented shopping malls and thought little about social and political issues. She became an activist after college when she became editor of *This Magazine* in 1993. As a writer and activist, she has raised the alarm about the pervasiveness of corporate branding in world culture. She has encouraged consumers to confront corporations about labor exploitation in the world's sweatshops. Her 2000 book, *No Logo: Taking Aim at the Brand Bullies,* was translated into 28 languages and sold more than 1 million copies. The left wing of the antiglobalization movement embraced Klein's analysis and made it their battle cry. Klein continues to work as a syndicated columnist and author of books on global politics.

Karen Nussbaum, 1950–

Women's Labor Advocate

Karen Nussbaum headed the Women's Bureau in the Department of Labor early in the administration of President Bill Clinton, but her role as an advocate of women workers began much earlier. As a dropout from the University of Chicago, Nussbaum became a clerk-typist at Harvard University. She has traced the seeds of her activism to a day in 1973 when a student entered the office where she was working, looked at her, and said, "Isn't anyone here?" Her feeling of invisibility, as well as dissatisfaction with pay and benefits, led her to join forces with other women in similar circumstances at Harvard, and they formed an advocacy group that soon expanded to include clerical workers in Boston. Subsequently, the Boston group merged with organizations in other cities to form 9 to 5, the National Association of Working Women. That organization joined the

Karen Nussbaum. (William J. Clinton Presidential Library)

Service Employees' International Union, and in 1981, it became District 925 of the SEIU. The group's first goal was to begin a nationwide effort to bring 20 million clerical workers into the union.

In 1993, Nussbaum left her positions as executive director of 9 to 5 and president of District 925 to join the Clinton administration as director of the Women's Bureau, where she served as a strong advocate of women's rights within the Department of Labor. Nussbaum headed a nationwide survey of working women known as "Working Women Count!" the results of which revealed that working women ranked fair pay as their top issue. From her post, she disseminated information about women's rights, pregnancy-related discrimination, and sexual harassment. In 1996 after the election of a reform leadership to the AFL-CIO, Nussbaum returned to the federation to head the Working Women's Department. She later became assistant to the president of the AFL-CIO.

Robert Reich, 1942–

Secretary of Labor

Robert Reich served as President Clinton's first secretary of labor. Reich, who attended Yale Law School with Bill and Hillary Clinton, had gained attention in the 1980s and early 1990s for his books on the economic transformations occurring in the global economy. With his interest in the global marketplace, advocacy of an active government, and call for training Americans for the new, highly skilled knowledge work, Reich was seen as an early theorist of the New Economy and an advocate of a new liberalism.

As secretary of labor, Reich attempted to work within the cabinet to fulfill Clinton's more populist campaign promises. The administration implemented some of his proposals, including tax credits for college tuition, retraining programs for workers, and a minimum wage increase. However, Reich's efforts were often opposed by American business, and he faced criticism from other members of Clinton's cabinet. Reich was unsuccessful in his efforts to fund job training by cutting military spending and his attempt to persuade Clinton to reject welfare reform legislation. Reich left office in 1996 and spelled out his grievances in *Locked in the Cabinet,* published in 1997. In the book, he argued that his experience showed that the federal government was subservient to big business, and the needs of ordinary workers went unaddressed. He returned to university teaching and continued to write about the nation's economy and advocate for workers' rights.

Robert Reich, secretary of labor under President Bill Clinton. (Robert Reich)

Robert E. Rubin, 1938–

Economist and Secretary of the Treasury

Robert E. Rubin was the most influential economic policy advisor in the Clinton administration's economic policy. In January 1993, Rubin left his position as co-chair of the powerful Wall Street brokerage Goldman, Sachs & Company to become Clinton's chairman of the National Economic Council. Bringing the perspective of investors and the financial sector into the inner circles of the administration, Rubin is widely credited with influencing Clinton to alter his economic agenda, abandon populist campaign promises to enact economic stimulus programs, and instead concentrate on deficit reduction. Rubin was a forceful and successful advocate for free trade, business deregulation, fiscal discipline, and other policies associated more with Republican free market conservatives than with historical Democratic liberalism. By the end of the decade, analysts broadly agreed that Rubin was the architect of the proglobalization "Washington Consensus." Critics derisively dubbed it "Rubinomics." Rubin sparred with the more liberal members of Clinton's cabinet, such as Robert Reich, but was the victor. In Clinton's second term in office, Rubin became secretary of the treasury. Rubin left the administration in 1999 to take a top position at Citigroup. He continues to be an important informal advisor to Democrats on economic policy.

John Sweeney, 1934–

Union Leader

Born into a New York City union household, John Sweeney began working for labor unions at an early age and eventually rose to the presidency of the

AFL-CIO. The son of Irish immigrants, Sweeney worked his way through Iona College as a building porter and a gravedigger. After briefly working in a white-collar job at IBM—a nonunion employer—he soon left to work for the labor movement. Within four years, he had risen to a leadership position, becoming in 1960 the contract director for local 32B of the growing Service Employees' International Union. Sweeney rose steadily through the hierarchy of the New York local, serving as an executive board member, vice president, and finally president in 1976. In 1980, he became national president of the SEIU. Under his leadership, the union launched a number of new organizing drives. SEIU engaged in a joint campaign with 9 to 5, the National Association of Working Women, to bring women office workers into the labor movement, and it launched an effort to unionize workers in the nation's biggest chain of nursing homes. In 1986, the SEIU spearheaded a legislative drive called the "Work and Family Campaign," which contributed to eventual passage of federal legislation that established family and medical leaves. At a time when the national labor movement was hemorrhaging members, Sweeney's union doubled its membership, from 625,000 to about 1.5 million members. By the mid-1990s, the SEIU was the third-largest labor union in the United States. In 1995, Sweeney and other labor reformers challenged the sitting leadership of the AFL-CIO. Sweeney won election to the AFL-CIO presidency on a platform to rejuvenate the labor movement. Under his leadership, drives to organize nonunion workers and to engage more directly in politics were undertaken. But by the early 2000s, Sweeney himself faced criticism on many of the same charges issued against his predecessor. In 2004, five major unions, including Sweeney's SEIU, left the AFL-CIO in dissatisfaction over Sweeney's leadership and the recalcitrance of his allies. It was the first major split in the American labor movement since the formation of the CIO in the 1930s. Sweeney remained the president of a smaller federation.

REFERENCES AND FURTHER READINGS

BLS. "Employment, Hours, and Earnings." Bureau of Labor Statistics, U.S. Department of Labor. http://www.bls.gov.

Brenner, Robert. 2002. *The Boom and the Bubble: The U.S. in the World Economy*. London, New York: Verso.

Cassidy, John. 2000. "The Fountainhead." *The New Yorker,* April 24, 162.

Ceruzzi, Paul E. 2003. *A History of Modern Computing,* 2nd ed. Cambridge, MA: MIT Press.

Ehrenreich, Barbara. 2001. *Nickel and Dimed: On (Not) Getting by in America.* New York: Metropolitan Books.

Elmer-Dewitt, Philip. 1993. "First Nation in Cyberspace." *Time,* December 6. http://www.time.com/time/magazine/article/0,9171,979768,00.html.

Elmer-Dewitt, Philip. 1994. "Battle for the Soul of the Internet." *Time,* July 25. http://www.time.com/time/magazine/article/0,9171,981132,00.html.

EPI. 2006. *Datazone.* Economic Policy Institute (cited February 2, 2006). Available from http://www.epinet.org/content.cfm/datazone_dznational.

Frank, Thomas. 2000. *One Market Under God: Extreme Capitalism, Market Populism, and the End of Economic Democracy.* New York: Doubleday.

Fraser, Steve. 2005. *Every Man a Speculator: A History of Wall Street in American Life.* New York: HarperCollins.

Gilder, George F. 1989. *Microcosm: The Quantum Revolution in Economics and Technology.* New York: Simon and Schuster.

Greenspan, Alan. 1996. Transcript. In *Federal Reserve Open Market Committee Meeting.* Washington, DC.

Hatch, Julie, and Angela Clinton. 2000. "Job Growth in the 1990s: A Retrospect." *Monthly Labor Review* 123 (12): 3–18.

Henwood, Doug. 2005. *After the New Economy.* New York: New Press.

Huey, John. 1995. "A New Era Dawns." *Fortune,* May 15, 8.

Johnson, Haynes Bonner. 1995. *Divided We Fall: Gambling with History in the Nineties.* New York: W. W. Norton.

Johnson, Haynes Bonner. 2001. *The Best of Times: America in the Clinton Years.* New York: Harcourt.

Klein, Naomi. 2000. *No Logo: Taking Aim at the Brand Bullies.* Toronto: Knopf Canada.

Krugman, Paul R. 1994. *Peddling Prosperity: Economic Sense and Nonsense in the Age of Diminished Expectations.* New York: W. W. Norton.

Krugman, Paul R. 2003. *The Great Unraveling: Losing Our Way in the New Century.* New York: W. W. Norton.

May, Steve, and Laura Morrison. 2003. "Making Sense of Restructuring: Narratives of Accommodation among Downsized Workers." In *Beyond the Ruins: The Meanings of Deindustrialization,* edited by J. R. Cowie and J. Heathcott, 259–283. Ithaca, NY: ILR Press.

Mishel, Lawrence R., Jared Bernstein, Sylvia Allegretto, and Economic Policy Institute. 2005. *The State of Working America, 2004/2005.* Ithaca, NY: Cornell University Press.

New York Times. 1996. "The Downsizing of America." Series March 3–March 9 and December 29. http://www.nytimes.com/specials/downsize/glance.html.

Philipkoski, Kristen. 1999. "Final Stretch in the Genome Race." *Wired,* October 25.

Phillips, Kevin P. 2002. *Wealth and Democracy: A Political History of the American Rich*. New York: Broadway Books.

Reich, Robert. 1997. *Locked in the Cabinet*. New York: Alfred A. Knopf.

Savage, Kirk. 2003. "Monuments of a Lost Cause: The Postindustrial Campaign to Commemorate Steel." In *Beyond the Ruins: The Meanings of Deindustrialization,* edited by J. R. Cowie and J. Heathcott, 237–258. Ithaca, NY: ILR Press.

Shiller, Robert J. 2000. *Irrational Exuberance*. Princeton, NJ: Princeton University Press.

Stiglitz, Joseph E. 2003. *The Roaring Nineties: A New History of the World's Most Prosperous Decade*. New York: W. W. Norton & Co.

Woodward, Bob. 2000. *Maestro: Greenspan's Fed and the American Boom*. New York: Simon & Schuster.

The New Gilded Age
and the American
Social Divide

OVERVIEW

Even though the buoyant economy of the 1990s lifted incomes and increased wealth, America became a more unequal society in the 1990s. The stock market boom and ballooning pay for corporate executives fueled an explosive growth of income and wealth in the top tier of American society, but only in the last third of the decade did the incomes of working- and middle-class Americans increase. Inequality widened less rapidly than it had in the 1980s, yet the cumulative effect of the boom was to increase the gap between the wealthy and all other Americans.

Who owns and earns what in the United States is fundamentally a question of the distribution of the wealth created by the production of goods and services in the American economy. The widening of the economic chasm between wealthy and ordinary Americans resulted from the unequal distribution of the decade's prosperity, not from economic troubles. In this way, America in the 1990s resembled the buoyant and unequal 1920s. Indeed, the distribution of the nation's wealth had not been so lopsided since that decade.

The late-century economic divide had been opened by Reagan era economic and social policies; it constituted a reversal of the postwar norm and a return to the more typical pattern of industrial capitalism before Western democracies instituted policies of social welfare and economic regulation in the mid-20th century. When economic growth had resumed after the stagflation of the 1970s and the deep recession of the early 1980s, the postwar pattern of distribution had been reversed: the top fifth of the population experienced astronomical income growth while Americans in the middle and lower income brackets saw their wages and salaries stagnate or decline. A comparison of the shares of national income exactly pinpoint the reversal between 1981 and 1982. From 1950 to 1981, the share of national income gained by the middle class (the three middle quintiles of the population) fluctuated little while the share gained by the highest income earners (the top quintile) declined. After the antipoverty programs of the Johnson administration went into effect, the share gained by the poorest Americans (the bottom quintile) also rose. In 1981, the portion of national income gained by the wealthiest 20 percent of the population reached a postwar low. In 1982, the share won by the top quintile began to increase while that of everyone else began to decline. Since that time, with minor exceptions, the share gained by the 80 percent of American households in the first through the fourth quintiles has fallen every year. In 2000, the average income of the top 1 percent of the population was 88.5 times that of the 20 percent of Americans earning the least income—55 times greater than it had been in 1979 (Mishel et al. 2005).

The trajectory of economic inequality, however, was uneven in the 1990s. The trend toward widening economic inequality continued through the recession that doomed George H. W. Bush's presidency. During the remainder of the decade, the economic expansion lifted incomes across the board, and the Clinton administration restored progessivity to the tax system. Nevertheless, economic inequality grew as the boom bestowed more of its bounty on the very wealthy. But it did so at a slower rate, as the wealthy paid more taxes, the working poor gained tax credits, and the income of the middle class grew.

Two developments in particular accounted for the failure of the 1990s' prosperity to be more evenly distributed throughout the American population: globalization and the weakening position of American labor unions. Manufacturing industries, which had paid high wages to union workers, continued to relocate much of their U.S. production overseas and negotiate cost-cutting concessions from their unions on their remaining domestic production. Economic vitality and growth were concentrated in the service and technology sectors, fields with little previous history of unionization and many low-wage occupations. Nevertheless, such shifts in the economy need not have had such a catastrophic effect on American incomes if organized labor had responded more forcefully. Unions certainly lost members to plant closings and capital flight, but they were also cowed by corporate threats to pick up and leave. Ineffective at organizing new members in growing sectors such as retail and technology, unions failed to build a movement for the New Economy.

Nonetheless, the wealth created was so extraordinary during the boom that there remains an important question: why did the incomes of Americans in the middle not rise sooner and higher? Alan Greenspan analyzed the unusual phenomenon as well as anyone. Musing publicly about workers' "heightened sense of job insecurity" and privately with officials of the Fed about the "traumatized worker," he hypothesized that workers were too afraid of losing their jobs to demand raises (Pollin 2003; Woodward 2000). The mass layoffs of the first part of the decade, reinforced by the well-publicized scrutiny Wall Street gave to corporations' labor costs, generated insecurity among working- and middle-class Americans, who showed little inclination to demand wage increases commensurate with their increased productivity. Not until late in the boom, when unemployment fell to a record low, did incomes start rising rapidly, yet the Federal Reserve, concerned about inflation, raised interest rates and nipped the rise in the bud. More than a year before the 2001 recession, the increase in middle incomes had leveled out. The recession of 2001–2002 and George W. Bush's large tax cut on high incomes and investment income sent the country back to inequality levels of the Reagan era, reversing the moderating influences of the Clinton years. By the mid-2000s, the gains of the 1990s had been undone, as inflation eroded the meager increases in wages. Median family income fell in the early 2000s as the income and wealth of the top 1 percent soared.

At the height of the boom in the 1990s, some analysts speculated that the United States might resume the pattern established in the postwar era—buoyant economic growth distributed in a relatively equal manner. With some historical perspective, however, it appears that the latter years of the 1990s were the anomaly, an interlude when the tendency toward widening economic inequality was briefly arrested. The new Gilded Age of the 20th century bore many resemblances to its 19th-century namesake, except for the virtual absence of a democratic challenge to the era's excess, corruption, and inequality.

TIMELINE

1990	Recession begins and continues through end of 1991.
1991	NASDAQ Composite Index is at 500 (April). Unemployment nears 7 percent.
1992	Unemployment reaches 7.5 percent even as economic growth has resumed, which leads to the invention of the concept of the "jobless recovery." The presidential election campaign focuses on the economy, and exit polls show the majority of voters say the economy is the most important issue.
1993	The Omnibus Budget Reconciliation Act reduces the deficit and raises taxes on higher incomes.

The Earned Income Tax Credit (EITC), which benefits low-wage workers, is raised in budget act.

1994   Average real wages drop to a 25-year low.

The Federal Reserve raises interest rates to slow expansion, dampening income growth before expansion has reached middle-income households.

1995   Real wages begin to rise.

Stock market rise begins as the NASDAQ hits 1,000.

The Immigration and Naturalization Service (INS) raids an apartment complex used as a sweatshop in a Los Angeles suburb where more than 70 Thai immigrants are enslaved to make clothes.

The death rate for AIDS reaches a peak at 16.2 deaths per 100,000.

1996   The Republican Congress passes welfare reform, which ends entitlement to support and transforms the American system of public assistance.

The AIDS memorial quilt is displayed for the first time on the National Mall.

1997   The unemployment rate falls below 5 percent for the first full year since 1969.

Taxes on inheritance and capital gains are reduced and middle-class tax credits are passed in the Taxpayer Relief Act.

1998   The price–earnings ratio of stocks reaches an all-time U.S. high.

1999   The Federal Reserve, in response to the tight labor market, raises interest rates for the first time since 1995.

The Dow Jones Industrial Average hits 10,000 for the first time in history.

Antiglobalization protests take place in Seattle at the meeting of the World Trade Organization (WTO).

2000   Unemployment is at 4 percent, the lowest level in 30 years.

The poverty rate, at 11.3 percent, is near the all-time low reached in 1973.

U.S. homeownership reaches an all-time high.

The number of wage workers with less than a high school education is lower in 2000 than in 1990.

The Dow hits a high of 11,302 (January).

The NASDAQ hits a high of 5,132 (March).

The federal budget surplus is in its third year, the longest surplus on record since 1947–1949.

The stock market plunges on Black Friday, April 14, wiping out $2 trillion in investments and beginning the fall that will result in a 24 percent decline in the S&P 500 and a 60 percent decline in the NASDAQ.

WEALTH AT THE END OF THE 20TH CENTURY

By a number of different measures, the income of the wealthiest Americans grew disproportionately. In 2000, the top 20 percent of the population reaped almost half of the nation's total income. The top 5 percent (within the highest quintile) earned fully one-fifth of the nation's income, more than the bottom 40 percent of American households put together. In terms of national income shares, the top 5 percent increased its share while that gained by the 80 percent of American households in the bottom four quintiles fell or stagnated between 1990 and 2000. The change in the distribution of income came primarily at the expense of the middle class, as measured both by their share of national income and by the gap between their wages and the wages of the top 10 percent of income earners. In concrete terms, securities and commodities brokers earned salaries two and a half times the average national wage. Janitors and retail clerks earned less than the federal poverty level for a household of four. Social mobility, thought by some to be a mitigating factor in income inequality, slowed in the 1990s; fewer Americans rose or fell into a different class.

If the United States appears from the data on income distribution to be a divided country, the chasm widens when viewed from the data on wealth. In 1998, the 20 percent of Americans doing the best owned 83 percent of the nation's wealth. The top 1 percent among the top fifth owned 38 percent of all wealth, or twice as much as the rest of American households combined. By comparison, the 20 percent in the middle—the heart of the American middle class—owned 5 percent of the nation's wealth. The top 20 percent increased their net worth 70 percent between 1983 and 2001 while the net worth of the bottom 40 percent plummeted by 44 percent (BLS; Henwood 2005; Phillips 2002; Mishel et al. 2005; EPI 2006).

Table 2.1. Family Income and Wealth (2001 dollars)

The table shows the average real after-tax income of each quintile and the top 1 and 5 percent within the top fifth of the population. Average income and median income are provided for reference. Average wealth figures are for net worth, accounting for total assets and debt.

Quintile	Average Income (2000)	Average Wealth (2001)
Lowest Fifth	$14,100	—
Second Fifth	$29,800	$2,900*
Middle Fifth	$43,000	$75,000
Fourth Fifth	$60,900	$215,300
Top Fifth	$145,400	$490,300
Top 5 percent	$162,925	$1,611,000
Top 1 percent	$886,800	$12,692,100
Average	$58,600	$380,100
Median	$54,191	

*For the bottom 40 percent of households. Among the bottom two quintiles, 17.6 percent had zero or negative net worth.

Sources: EPI 2006; Mishel et al. 2005.

A portrait of inequality can be gleaned from several different measures of the American economy and the income and wealth of Americans. To analyze the distribution of wealth and income, the population is generally divided by households into five parts, or quintiles. Because there is a vast difference in income within the wealthiest 20 percent of the population, many studies also break down the top fifth into the top 10 percent or top 1 percent.

Superstar CEOs and the Explosion of Corporate Compensation

The contours of inequality, and part of its source, can be seen in absolute and relative terms by comparing the compensation of corporate chief executive officers (CEOs) with the average worker in their firms at several hundred of the largest companies. In 1980, CEOs earned, on average, 42 times the average wage of their employees. In 1990, the ratio was 85:1, and in 1995, it reached 141:1. In 2000, after the downturn of the stock market boom, CEOs were earning on average 531 times the amount of the typical employee. The growth in executive pay from 1990 to 2000 was 571 percent; the growth in workers' wages was 37 percent. In comparison, CEOs at the nation's main international competitors were not remotely as well paid as American executives. The ratio of CEO to worker pay in Japan was 11:1, in Germany, 34:1 (Anderson et al. 2001).

The magnitude of the disparity is dramatized by some specific cases. In 2000, the highest paid CEO, John Reed of Citigroup, earned $293 million, a year after financial deregulation, which allowed Citicorp and Travelers Insurance to merge. L. Dennis Koslowski, CEO of Tyco International, who in 2005 was sentenced to 8½ to 25 years in prison for his role in the company's corporate scandal, was paid $125 million in salary and stock options that same year (Anderson et al. 2001).

The success of American corporate executives relative to each other reveals some of the underlying dynamics of the 1990s' economy. CEOs who were able to wrest the largest tax rebates from the federal government also did significantly better, receiving raises close to twice that of their peers. At six companies, in-

Roberto Goizueta, CEO of Coca-Cola Corporation. (George Lange/The Coca-Cola Company)

cluding Enron and Coca-Cola, the CEOs' compensation was equal to or greater than the entire tax break received by the company. Enron received a tax rebate in 1998 of $12.5 million while Kenneth Lay, Enron's CEO, received an $18 million raise and took home a package worth $21.5 million. Coca-Cola's CEO, R. C. Goizueta, earned $111.8 million in the year the corporation received a tax rebate of $72 million (Anderson et al. 2001, table 3.2). Stock options, which served to boost executive compensation while simultaneously lowering a corporation's taxable revenues, accounted for a large part of the rise, especially in the technology sector. Steve Case, the CEO of America Online, earned $117 million in total compensation in 1999, more than 24 times the total annual revenue of the company (Anderson et al. 2000, appendix A).

At the same time that CEOs were being handsomely rewarded, many of them attained a celebrity status, such as had once been reserved for Hollywood stars and starlets and sports legends (Krugman 2003). In the world of business, fame had conventionally been reserved for the entrepreneurial set, not those who topped the unglamorous bureaucracies that made American capitalism churn. The media's burgeoning appetite for stories about celebrity lifestyles spread the news of the conspicuous consumption spawned by the escalating pay. The American public responded, mostly, with admiration—or, at least, with minimal criticism. Only with the revelations in late 2001 about corporate fraud did the tone shift from emulation to disgust.

Consumption

At the end of the 19th century's Gilded Age, the social critic and economist Thorstein Veblen coined the term "conspicuous consumption" to describe the excesses of the Gilded Age elite. The return of indulgent consumerism was one of the conspicuous features of the new Gilded Age of the 1980s and 1990s, but in its late-20th-century incarnation, more people participated and more products were available for those pursuing the material way.

In everyday conversation, people talked of "upscale" places and things—cafes for diners, boutiques for stores, salons for barbershops, lingerie for underwear. Like pornography, you knew it when you saw it. As cigarette smoking became socially taboo, men with disposable income could visit boutiques specializing in cigars, where the magazine *Cigar Aficionado* taught which car, watch, and leather jacket went best with a $30 cigar, and where regular customers were invited into back rooms to sample contraband Cubans. For women with a lot of cash to spare, designer handbags and shoes served the same needs and conveyed the same message of sophistication and discernment. In *Sex and the City,* one of the most popular cable shows of the late 1990s, the defining trait of the lead character was her insatiable desire for $400 Manolo Blahnik shoes. The top half of the population avidly consumed an array of personal services at nail salons, spas, fitness clubs, and luxury hotels. According to Census Bureau data, businesses offering personal services increased their revenues between 40 and 74 percent from 1997 to 2002 (Silverstein and Fiske 2003). At the highest pinnacles of the American wealth pyramid, the very wealthy unabashedly pursued luxury in their travel, personal care, cars, food, and multiple homes. Bill Gates purchased the rights to world-class art archives, digitized them, and displayed them on a 22-foot-wide video display mounted in the reception hall of his 66,000-square-foot waterfront Seattle home. The $15,000 umbrella stand and $6,000 shower curtain only later became symbols of the decade's corrupting excess, after their owner, L. Dennis Kozlowski, went on trial for looting $150 million from his company (Sorkin 2005).

While the wealthiest Americans indulged in a spending spree of historic proportions, families in the upper middle class and upper realms of the middle class injected mass demand into the upscale market. (They were in many ways the successors to the 1980s "yuppies"—no label equivalent to yuppie was coined in the 1990s while the term itself seemed anachronistic and fell into disuse.) The view from business of this kind of consumption, where profit margins were much higher, was positive. Two consultants with the prestigious Boston Consulting Group aptly described the motivation of the consumer in this trend as "trading up." Products that cost more than mass-market goods but less than luxury items, such as Starbucks coffee, Victoria's Secret lingerie, Callaway golf clubs, and Kendall-Jackson wines, were shrewdly marketed. Positioned between luxury and mass goods, they cost more than the average brand yet were affordable

Luxury home in Virginia. (iStockPhoto.com)

to people earning more than $50,000 a year. The superior quality of such upscale goods and the status they bestowed on their owner was part of the appeal, but market research consistently reported that people also felt an emotional connection with the brands (Silverstein and Fiske 2003).

A significant part of the boom in consumer spending was oriented toward the home. At the turn of the 21st century, Americans spent more than double on goods and services for the home than they had in 1970 (Silverstein and Fiske 2003). Some of the spending was to replace labor conventionally done by family members. Overworked middle-class families as well as the wealthy hired immigrant men and women to clean their house, care for their children, and tend their yards. More of the attention lavished on the home, however, was designed to create a haven where any social, cultural, or emotional need could be fulfilled. As Americans spent more time at home and attempted to bring the new luxury and the comforts of personal care within its bounds, they spent a vast amount of time and money on home improvement, most of it on bathroom and kitchen renovation. VCRs, DVDs, home entertainment centers, and computer gaming systems allowed Americans to satisfy much of their desire for entertainment in the home. Consumption of home electronics and technology soared, and builders of large new homes—"McMansions" to critics, or "estate homes" to the builders—included entertainment and media rooms as standard elements in their basic design (Twitchell 2002; Frank 2000).

Americans were fascinated, not dismayed, by all this. Nevertheless, the rising consumption of upscale goods by an increasing number of Americans—and the rising level of indebtedness—engendered criticism from some academics and social critics. David Brooks, a conservative social critic and frequent contributor to *The Weekly Standard,* argued that the lifestyle choices of "Bohemian Bourgeois" or "Bobos" reflected a new elitism, which combined old-fashioned bourgeois materialism with the loose Bohemian social ethic of the 1960s (Brooks 2001). Juliet Schor, a sociologist whose work focused on consumer culture and the middle class, lamented how the old keeping-up-with-the-Joneses phenomenon had intensified as average Americans compared themselves to celebrities instead of their neighbors. She argued that the struggle to measure up was sowing anxiety throughout middle America (Schor 1998). Brooks and Schor, and others in a similar vein, evoked classic American fears of excess materialism that had their roots in the Puritan and democratic traditions (Twitchell 2002; Frank 2000).

THE MIDDLE-CLASS SQUEEZE

As wealth became more concentrated in the last two decades of the 20th century, the American middle class felt the squeeze the hardest. The material struggle of the middle class had profound social, psychological, and cultural effects as well. Work in the postwar American economy had provided the broad middle class unprecedented prosperity, a sense of security, an expectation of continual improvement, and the conviction that one's children would be offered even greater opportunity. The economic woes of the 1970s had undermined the prospects of the millions of blue-collar workers. With the steady and implacable determination of American manufacturers to cut jobs in order to rescue their companies, it was distressingly obvious that the blue-collar path to the middle class was closing. With it vanished a sense of security and optimism, even for those who held on to their manufacturing jobs and the income to support a middle-class living. The blue-collar middle class entered the 1990s chastened—and angry.

As the 1990s opened, the white-collar middle class had just begun to experience similar economic dislocations. Blue-chip American corporations winnowed the ranks of their managers and secretaries, health maintenance organizations imposed market discipline on doctors and nurses, the federal government won deficit reduction by eliminating 1 out of 10 federal workers, and universities replaced retiring tenured professors with temporary workers. Manufacturing firms also continued to shed workers, albeit at about half the pace they had done so in the 1980s. In the second half of the 1990s, middle-class incomes rose, but the middle class slipped in relation to the wealthy. Median income—the amount at which half the population earns less and half more—rose briskly in the second half of the 1990s, from $48,248 in 1990 to $54,191 in 2000 (EPI 2006). Middle-class Americans thus had more money and, in some cases, owned more. However, at the same time, social mobility declined, the numbers of households in the middle class shrunk, and the incomes of the middle class grew at a much smaller rate than those of the wealthy. And even though the boom of the late 1990s briefly turned things around for the middle class, the business cycle of the 2000s repeated the pattern of the recession and jobless recovery of the early 1990s, without out commensurate growth in incomes during the height of the expansion.

Well-being is an emotional state as much as it is an objective one. From this perspective, the 1990s transformed the American middle class. The steady sense of security and optimism that had once permeated the ranks of the American middle class and defined its very being evaporated. Middle-class life, by the end of the century, had become pervaded by risk. Sometimes the risk paid off in hitherto unimaginable wealth—as in the heyday of the dot-com boom. Other times, it spelled uncertain employment, indebtedness, and a sense of being at the mercy of uncontrollable forces.

The Middle Class: Perceptions and Measurements

Most Americans think of America as a middle-class nation, and when asked, an overwhelming majority report their status as middle class. It is an interesting practice culturally, and one that historians and sociologists have investigated at great length. But if we want to examine how Americans fare in relation to each other, it is hardly sensible to define the middle as all but 10 percent of the population. The middle class is broad in the United States; it includes blue- and white-collar workers earning adequate to high wages as well as mid-level salaried managers and many professionals. There are two common measures for distinguishing the middle class from wealthy and low-income households. When the entire population is divided into fifths (quintiles), the middle class comprises households with incomes in the middle three—the second, third, and fourth—quintiles. (The poor are those in the bottom, or first quintile, and the wealthy are those in the top, or fifth quintile.) An additional method, used often in comparative analyses concerned with the level of economic inequality, measures a household's economic position by the ratio of its income to the nation's median income. In these cases, households earning from half the median income to double the median income are considered middle class. Both measures will be employed here.

The State of Labor: Employment, Wages, and Productivity

To the 80 percent of Americans who are not managers, supervisors, or business owners, and who depend for their sustenance on wages from work, the most important measures of economic well-being are the ones that measure pay, the level of unemployment and the numbers of people employed, and conditions at the place of work. Wage rates and their increase over time, the rise and fall in the unemployment rate, the numbers of jobs created and lost, productivity, and the rise and fall in hours worked speak more to their actual experience in the economy than do aggregate statistics such as GDP or per capita income.

By all measures, working people fared poorly in the recession and jobless recovery of the early 1990s. The measures began to turn in a more positive direction in 1994 but barely so, and not in earnest until 1995. Average real wages, after dropping to a 25-year low in 1994, began to rise in 1995, with wage increases for better-paid workers pulling up the average. Once the unemployment rate fell below 5 percent in 1997, wages for all workers rose more briskly, bringing up the median wage and income. The tight labor market of the second half of the decade had especially positive results for African American and Hispanic workers, who experienced their highest rate of income growth in a generation (Mishel et al. 2005). With more jobs available, the percentage of people living in poverty also declined, from 15.1 percent in 1993 to 11.3 percent in 2000. By 2000, employment had grown by 19 percent and 135 million Americans were working, the largest proportion of the total population ever in the paid workforce. With unemployment at 4 percent, its lowest level in 30 years, economists, the media, and politicians celebrated the full employment and rising incomes delivered by the New Economy. Working Americans were inordinately productive, as well. The rate of productivity growth—a measure of how much more is produced in an hour of labor—reached 2.5 percent. Comparing the 1990s productivity rate of growth to the low rate of 1.5 percent during the years of stagnation between 1973 and 1994, economists and business analysts waxed euphoric about a "productivity miracle" (Pollin 2003; EPI 2006).

Clearly, the fortunes of working, middling, and poor families improved in the second half of the 1990s. But many had reason to wonder whether they were in the end better off, as the rising expense of health care and child care and record levels of household debt ate away at raises. Economic growth, furthermore, was purchased more through the exertion of working people than through the miracles of new technology. Productivity, in general, rises through either a more efficient or a more intensive use of labor or machinery. The productivity increase in the 1990s was mostly the result of men and women spending more hours at work. In addition, in historical comparison, the gains resulting from increased productivity were less equitably distributed than in the past as a smaller share went to workers in the form of increased wages, and a larger share went to owners in the form of corporate profit (Pollin 2003).

Nevertheless, the trends compared to the 1980s were positive, and the decade ended with some analysts conjecturing that the three-decades-long stagnation of working- and middle-class incomes had ended. The recession and jobless recovery (2001–2004), however, wiped out the gains of the 1990s. The unemployment rate and long-term unemployment rate rose, the median family income fell, and the numbers and percentage of people living in poverty grew. George W. Bush was the first president since Herbert Hoover to end a presidential term with a net decline in the number of people employed. The trend toward the widening of the economic gulf between the rich and the rest resumed in the first decade of the 21st century.

The Age of Anxiety, 1990–1995

Not since the Great Depression had the white-collar middle class been so buffeted by the ups and downs of the U.S. economy, and not since that time had so many felt so insecure. The insecurity flowed from the mass firings of white-collar workers and professionals by American corporations.

A *New York Times* survey in 1995 captured the distraught mood of Americans. One out of three Americans felt economically insecure. The fear of unemployment hung over the country; two out of every five Americans worried that they would be hit by a lay-off within the next year. Almost four in five worried about saving enough money for retirement. The optimism for a better future that had characterized postwar America evaporated. Half the country thought that the next generation would be worse off, and three-quarters anticipated that the loss of jobs was going to be a permanent problem. Half to three-quarters of working women and men, set against each other in the competition for the remaining slice of the job pie, reported that co-workers were more competitive and that an angrier mood prevailed at work. People who had lost their jobs, and their family members, felt more pessimistic about their own future. They believed in larger proportions that the country was on the wrong track and that they were not as well off as they had thought they would be by this stage of their life (*New York Times* 1996).

Individuals who had been in the path of a "downsizing" narrowed their sights. Chastened, they doubted they would ever find a job that would pay as well as their previous one, and they no longer expected a company to be loyal to them. They cut back on their household expenses and trimmed their dreams. Fearful and cautious about the future, they were willing to give employers more—more of their time through longer hours and shorter vacations, more compliance with the boss—and to cooperate less with their co-workers. They were more likely to be divorced or separated. The children in families that had gone through a lay-off showed realism beyond their years, downscaling their ambitions to fit the family budget.

The atmosphere at work, for those who remained, was pervaded by the experience of job cuts. Many of the workers spared the ax felt guilty and depressed. Younger workers quickly adopted a cynicism and individualism toward corporate America that was new. A 29-year-old college graduate explained, "People aren't going to give 100 percent anymore. . . . I'm not going to be like my dad and work till ten o'clock at night and never see the kids. What for? So I'll be thanked with a pink slip?" (quoted in *New York Times* 1996). An undercurrent of insubordination, at least in spirit if not in action, displaced the old-time corporate loyalty. An anonymously written satiric memo circulated among the employees remaining after the mass cuts prompted by the merger of Chase and Chemical banks asked, "Why am I facing layoffs, why is my career in ruins, why can't I sleep at night?" The answer: "Your largely insignificant life is being sacrificed to bring into existence the best banking and financial services company in the world" (*New York Times* 1996).

The Making of Inequality: Los Angeles, 1990–2000

Mass lay-offs of white-collar workers were unprecedented. Nevertheless, the magnitude of change in blue-collar employment had more impact on the shrinking of the middle class and the widening of the social divide. The changes in Los Angeles in the 1990s are one example of the process by which America became a more unequal society in the late 20th century.

Like all industrial centers, Los Angeles had suffered from industry flight and the loss of jobs in the 1980s, but a strong manufacturing presence remained. The defense industry had continued to thrive as the Reagan administration increased Cold War military spending. Workers in the industry were skilled, unionized, and earned among the highest wages ever paid to manufacturing workers in the United States. But with the end of the Cold War in 1989, federal contracts for the military industry declined. The loss of its main customer hit the aerospace industry in Los Angeles hard; between 1990 and 2000, more than 77,000 aerospace workers lost their jobs. Although companies such as Boeing, Northrop, and TRW continued to run factories in the area, the regional aerospace workforce continued to decrease. The recession of the 1990s, nationally, was deepest in places where military industries were powerful. Unemployment in Los Angeles far exceeded the national level, largely because of job cuts in aerospace. In response to the collapse of the industry and its ramifying effects through the regional economy, more than 1 million workers left Los Angeles. Times were so bad that residents wondered if the region was headed into a full-blown depression.

Nevertheless, as unionized heavy manufacturing virtually disappeared in Los Angeles and many highly skilled workers left the state, fast-growing service and nondurable goods manufacturing industries arose in its wake. The area had several existing economic advantages upon which to rebuild. But the key to continued economic growth was the mass influx of immigrants to the Los Angeles region. Three and a half million immigrants made Los Angeles County their home in the 1990s—a full 11 percent of the nation's entire immigration and 39 percent of California's entire immigration. Of these, roughly 2 million had entered the United States without legal documents (Haydamack et al. 2005).

Economic growth in Los Angeles from the mid-1990s on was founded on low wages and immigrant workers. Whereas the leading industries of the postwar economy—steel, auto, rubber, and aerospace—had raised Los Angeles's workers into the middle class, the new manufacturing leaders consigned their workers to the alarming new category of the "working poor." By the end of the decade, Los Angeles County was the largest manufacturing center in the United States, but the average manufacturing wage was below the national average. A historically diverse service sector also helped to cushion the blow of the devastation wrought by the loss of high-paying manufacturing work in Los Angeles. Tourism and entertainment had always been important industries; the 1990s boom and the new local labor force gave them a boost. The astronomical growth in high incomes also had a profound effect on the service sector in Los Angeles as demand for luxury goods and personal services exploded.

Immigrants filled many of the new and old jobs in both the manufacturing and the service sector, frequently enough displacing native-born white and African American workers. In the construction industry, 15 percent of workers were undocumented immigrants. In the hotel industry, immigrant women and

Immigrant workers lay roof tile. (iStockPhoto.com)

men filled bellhop, housekeeping, kitchen, and laundry jobs once held by union-ized African Americans.

Globalization—expanding transnational economic links, the presence of many immigrants, and the city's emergence as a strategic site in the global economy—enabled some industries to thrive. The ports of Los Angeles and Long Beach became the busiest in the nation, due to the enormous increase in Pacific Rim trade. The new jobs created for truckers, however, did not go to highly paid members of the Teamsters union but rather to mostly immigrant workers earn-ing far less than the hitherto prevailing union wage. The garment industry was the leading example of such a conjunction of local and global forces. The gar-ment industry had formerly provided relatively well-paying union jobs to African American women. In the 1980s and 1990s, the industry returned to its early-20th-century sweatshop patterns—not only in its overseas plants. Nearly 100,000 men and women worked in garment factories in Los Angeles through the 1990s. The overwhelming majority of garment workers were immigrants, close to a third of whom were undocumented. They made less than $10,000 a year, and the industry was rife with violations of wage and health and safety laws.

While the working people of Los Angeles were falling behind, the well off were doing better and better. With a concentration of entertainment industry executives, celebrities, international financial firms, legal services, and real es-tate moguls, the wealthy in Los Angeles were among the most highly remuner-ated in the nation. Beginning in 1999, the United Way of Los Angeles began periodically issuing a report on the state of greater Los Angeles. "A Tale of Two Cities" showed that the county of Los Angeles, the nation's most populous met-ropolitan area, was the nation's capital of inequality and the third most expen-sive place to live. There were a larger number and a higher percentage of very high-income households in Los Angeles than in any other county in the United States. On the other side of the divide, of the county's 9.6 million residents, nearly 1.5 million Angelinos were officially classified as poor, 2.4 million earned under $20,000 a year, 2.7 million had no health insurance, 1.8 million were on welfare, and 236,000 had been homeless over the course of the year. The county's official poverty rate exceeded the nation's by almost 5 percent. One out of every five children in the county lived in poverty, and one out of four was uninsured. The poor, for the most part, worked: almost half of poor families had at least one full-time working family member. While the numbers of the poor and the rich grew and the difference between them widened, the middle class slipped as well. Wages increased only for workers with a college or advanced degree and stagnated or fell for everyone else. Median income in the county fell 10 per-cent during the 1990s, and in 2000 was $12,000 lower than the national median. Among the top 10 industries creating the greatest number of new jobs, 7 of them paid less than $25,000 a year—that is, less than half of the national median in-come. There were extreme income disparities by race and ethnicity as well—

compared to white Angelinos, the median income of African American Angelinos was $22,000 lower, that of Latinos was $20,000 lower, and that of Native Americans was $18,000 lower. At a time when the highest percentage of Americans ever owned their own homes, the price of a median home in the county was one of the highest in the nation, and only a third of Angelinos were able to afford the cost (United Way 2003).

THE POOR

The poverty rate in the 1990s rose and fell with the business cycle. The poverty rate peaked in 1983 at 15.2 percent, and then peaked again in 1993 at 15.1 percent, above the 1966 rate, 4 percent higher than the all-time low of 1973, and even with the previous peak of 1983. Starting in 1994, the numbers of the poor and the poverty rate began to decline again. Between 1993 and 2000, 7.7 million Americans were no longer poor, according to the official poverty threshold, and the poverty rate had fallen to 11.3 percent, close to the all-time low of 11.1 percent in 1973 (EPI 2006).

The economic expansion of the 1990s was partly responsible for the improvement as jobs became plentiful, the unemployed were able to find work, and businesses had to raise wages to attract workers. More important, however, were two federal policies that lifted the incomes of workers earning low wages: the increase in the federal minimum wage and the Earned Income Tax Credit (EITC). Between 1979 and 1989, the minimum wage had lost almost a third of its value through inflation. The legislated increases in the minimum wage between 1989 and 1997 restored some of the lost value and raised the incomes of the millions of adults who worked minimum-wage jobs. The increase in the EITC in 1993 raised the after-tax income of low-wage workers. As a consequence of changes to the minimum wage and the EITC, the share of American workers earning poverty-level wages declined from 30 percent in 1990 to 25.1 percent in 2000 (EPI 2006).

Although there was strong evidence of improvement in the conditions of the poor in America in the 1990s, other statistics suggest that the poor were living in far from ideal conditions and that many other Americans were surviving on the edge of actual sufficiency. First, the official federal poverty threshold is very low and does not reflect significant regional differences in the cost of living. Second, despite improvement for demographic groups that historically had been disproportionately poor, such as African Americans, Native Americans, and children in single-mother households, vast disparities in American society remained. One-fifth of all African Americans were poor in 2000 while less than one-tenth of white Americans were. Third, by comparative standards, the poor in America were doing worse, not better, as the income gap between the poor and the

Low-income housing in Mississippi. (U.S. Department of Agriculture)

wealthy had widened. By international standards, inequality and poverty were most serious in the United States. Among the 20 rich industrialized nations in the Organization for Economic Cooperation and Development (OECD), the United States had the highest proportion of its population in poverty, even as per capita income in the United States was the highest. Despite improvements in the 1990s, 31.5 million Americans were poor at the opening of the third millennium in the richest country in world history.

Is there a conclusion that can be reached from these conflicting viewpoints? Viewed from a long historical perspective, the standard of living of the poorest Americans had improved. "In American's cities, millions of women and men who at the start of the twentieth century would have suffered desperate poverty now, at the turn of the next century, live with a sense of security and in modest comfort," wrote the historian Michael Katz (2001, 17). Nevertheless, the poor and near poor had experienced sharp disruptions in the last 35 years of the 20th century. At the end of the 1990s, with welfare reform accomplished and a booming economy about to bust, fewer Americans were poor, but with social support far more tenuous, they lived with greater uncertainty and insecurity. The poor, those who worked with them to improve their conditions, and scholars who studied poverty and welfare policy looked ahead to the future with trepidation.

Officially, the poor were those with incomes at or below the federal poverty threshold as determined each year by the U.S. Census Bureau. The threshold was adopted in the early 1960s and was based on the amount and proportion

Table 2.2. Poverty in the 1990s

	1990	1993	2000
Percent of population living in poverty	13.50%	15.10%	11.30%
Number of Americans in poverty	33,585,000	39,265,000	31,581,000
Poverty threshold for family of four	$13,359	$14,763	$17,604
Poor as percent of total urban population	19.00%	21.50%	16.30%
Poor as a percent of total rural population	16.30%	17.20%	13.40%
Poor as percent of total white American population	10.70%	12.20%	9.50%
Poor as percent of total African American population	31.90%	33.10%	22.50%
Poor as a percent of total Latino population	28.10%	30.60%	21.50%
Poor as a percent of noncitizen foreign born	n.a.	28.70%	19.20%
Share of single mothers with children among poor	33.40%	35.60%	25.40%
Share of children among poor	20.60%	22.70%	16.20%
Share of elderly among poor	12.20%	12.20%	9.90%
Share of American workers earning poverty-level wages	30.00%	31.50%	25.10%
Percent of population with income at 200% of the poverty level	32.30%	35.20%	29.30%

Source: US Census, EPI, Datazone.

of income a typical family spent on food. At the time it was devised, families spent about one-third of their household budget on food. In recent decades, a consensus has emerged that the threshold no longer adequately measures the cost of living and should be revised. At the end of the century, food accounted for one-fifth, not one-third, of household budgets, and the costs of housing, transportation, health care, and child care had risen. In 1995, experts convened by the National Academy of Sciences recommended that the Census Bureau revise its standard of measurement. The bureau experimented with different measures but by 2006 had not yet adopted a new standard.

Debates: Poverty

In the 1990s, the decade in which the federal entitlement to public assistance was ended, the nature and extent of poverty in America remained a subject of profound disagreement. The debate was particularly racially charged, in part because a disproportionate number of African Americans were poor, and in part because the politics of poverty had run in racial channels since the 1960s. Views about poverty divided along politico-philosophical lines.

On the liberal end of the political spectrum, analysts and advocates contended that poverty was a more serious problem than generally understood, and that the official measures of poverty failed to capture all the poor and the real condition of the poor. A much-cited representative of this position was the Economic Policy Institute (EPI), a nonpartisan think tank. EPI's annual reports, *The State of Working America*, were a leading source for income trends for journalists and policymakers. By underestimating how much it cost to live, EPI economists explained, the official poverty threshold established a poverty line well below the real cost of living, thus undercounting the number of poor Americans and understating the difficulty experienced by the poor and near poor in meeting their needs. EPI further cautioned that even those officially classified as poor were in a comparatively worse situation at the end of the century than they had been in the 1960s. At that time, the poverty threshold income equaled 42 percent of the median family income; in the late 1990s, it amounted to 35 percent of the median family income. Building on a body of international research on "relative deprivation," analysts also explained that, counterintuitively, quality of life is more greatly affected by the social experience of inequality than by absolute measures of wealth and poverty (EPI 2001). Amartya Sen, the 1998 Nobel Prize winner in economics, analyzing vital statistics comparing African Americans and the inhabitants of Kerala, an impoverished state in India, demonstrated that African American women had higher mortality rates than the impoverished Indian women in Kerala. "Being relatively poor in a rich country can be a great capability handicap," he wrote, "even when one's absolute income is high in terms of world standards" (quoted in Cassidy 2006).

Against this view, free market conservatives contended that the poor in America were so well off materially that it was a distortion of language to call the lowest income Americans poor. Instead, they argued that the official poverty threshold overstated the number of the poor and exaggerated the cost of living. This position was most forcefully publicized by fellows of the American Enterprise Institute (AEI), a conservative think tank that is looked to as the leading source for the free market conservative position. AEI scholars argued that the physical and material condition of the poor at the end of the 20th century was better than at any time in U.S. history and superior to that of any other people in the world. Whereas many liberal analysts of poverty focused on the rising cost of services necessary to achieve self-sufficiency—housing, medical care, transportation, and child care—conservatives were more impressed by the low cost of goods consumed by the poor. Conservatives countered that most of those officially classified as poor owned TVs and VCRs; they could shop at retail discounters such as Wal-Mart, which had slashed the price of basic goods like food and clothing; and they received government transfer payments, which subsidized the cost of their food and health care and provided extra cash. Turning on its head the liberal claim that poverty was a relative concept, conservatives proposed that the official classification of the poor in America was meaningless because the so-called poor could own a wide array of middle-class consumer goods.

Parallel to the debate about how to measure poverty and who was poor was another more contentious one about the causes of poverty and its solution. According to liberals, inadequate income—either as a result of unemployment or low-wage employment—made people poor. Therefore, the declining real value of the minimum wage was a prime culprit in the making of poverty: it was worth a fifth less in the late 1990s than in the late 1970s. To take one example, whereas a single working mother earning the minimum wage in 1979 had been able to work herself out of poverty, the wages earned by a similarly situated mother in the late 1990s left her with an income 18 percent below the poverty line. Single women were poorer in part because women were paid less for the same jobs and female-dominated job categories paid less than comparable jobs dominated by men. As married women had entered the workforce en masse to supplement family incomes, it was unremarkable that households with one, not two, breadwinners were more likely to fall into poverty. Likewise, minorities had a disproportionate number of poor families among them because of the long-term effects of historical discrimination, especially de jure and de facto segregation, as well as because of persisting discrimination in the job market. In sum, the causes of poverty were social and political; therefore, society, through the national government, should take responsibility for a solution. The government should alleviate poverty by combating the structural causes of poverty, regulating business to prevent a race to the bottom, strengthening labor laws to protect the rights of workers to form unions, and providing social support and job training for those who remained poor.

The counterargument, most forcefully articulated by conservatives, held that the poverty of individuals was caused by a "culture of poverty." Poverty was not the result of low income, but of dysfunctional culture, itself created by a faulty welfare system. The poor in America were in truth an "underclass" who lived in communities that were culturally impoverished and that failed to provide the cultural models and resources for success to its members. Charles Murray, AEI scholar and co-author of the controversial books *The Bell Curve* and *Losing Ground* and a prominent advocate of the underclass thesis in the 1990s, explained:

> By *underclass* I mean a population cut off from mainstream American life—not cut off from its trappings (television and consumer goods penetrate everywhere), but living a life in which the elemental building blocks of a life—productive work, family, community—exist in fragmented and corrupted forms. Most members of the underclass have low incomes, but its distinguishing characteristics are not poverty and unmet physical needs, but social disorganization, a poverty of social networks and valued roles, and a Hobbesian kind of individualism in which trust and cooperation are hard to come by and isolation is common. (Murray 1990)

In contrast to those who carefully parsed income statistics to determine who was poor, Murray is more concerned about moral indicators such as "criminality, dropout from the labor force among low income young males, and illegitimacy among low income young women" (Murray 1990). Cultural decay, according to Murray and others, was most pronounced among the urban black and brown poor (Herrnstein and Murray 1994; Murray 1984). Government was the problem, breeding dependency and deepening the cultural separation of the underclass from mainstream society. The first step to a solution was to end welfare programs that bred dependency and social dysfunction.

The American public borrowed from both positions to form its opinion about poverty and the poor. Polls invariably showed very strong support—in the 70–90 percent range—for raising the minimum wage, a measure that would raise the incomes of millions of poor, working adults. These views undergirded the launch and growth of the living-wage movement, drawing impetus from a widely held traditional American value that those who worked should be able to earn a living sufficient for family survival. Between 1994 and 1998, 13 cities, including Los Angeles, New York, Milwaukee, and Baltimore, passed living-wage laws that effectively raised the minimum wage for some jobs. By 2002, there were living-wage ordinances on the books in approximately 90 municipalities (Pollin and Luce 1998; Pollin 2003). Although some free market conservatives tirelessly denounced the minimum wage and the living wage, they convinced hardly anyone of their position.

Public acclaim for welfare reform, however, revealed that most Americans no longer approved of paying welfare to single mothers who did not work. Many interests, principles, and emotions converged to propel a debate about welfare into the center of national politics. Nevertheless, the force for change was buoyed by a fairly wide acceptance of elements of the "culture of poverty" thesis on the cause of entrenched poverty.

Welfare Reform

In 1996, President Clinton and a Republican-dominated Congress transformed the 61-year-old system of public assistance for poor families, abolishing the program that had served as the main form of public assistance for poor women and their children and creating a new program of temporary support. Ever since President Ronald Reagan had injected images of "welfare queens" into partisan politics, momentum for welfare reform had been building. The particular inflection of 1990s partisan politics raised it to a central political mission for both Democrats and Republicans. The new program, Temporary Assistance for Needy Families (TANF), rejected the core premises on which Aid for Families with Dependent Children (AFDC) had been erected. By the turn of the century, the 20th-century social safety net for the poor had been radically transformed.

A family on welfare, Oregon, 1996. (David Butow/Corbis Saba)

Although the political struggle over welfare reform was bitterly fought, few denied that AFDC was founded on anachronistic premises. The program, adopted in 1935, had been designed to enable widows to care for their own children, rather than be forced to place them in orphanages. At that time, the gendered division of labor, with wives performing domestic labor in the household and husbands performing wage labor in the market, was then still the norm and the ideal. By the mid-1990s, 98 percent of mothers receiving welfare were unmarried, and almost half of married women worked outside the home for wages (Mishel et al. 2005). Meanwhile, AFDC regulations created for a different time penalized a woman for marrying the father of her children, for working, or for saving enough money to own something as basic as a car. Welfare, moreover, became enmeshed in racial politics and the culture wars, and welfare reform bore the marks of those quite vicious battles. Although the majority of mothers on welfare were white, a disproportionate percentage of recipients were African American or Latino women. In attacking "welfare queens" and cheats, however, Reagan and his followers deliberately fostered perceptions that the problem was one of undeserving African American and Latino women. Nevertheless, the inherent contradiction of the American welfare system, which paid poor mothers not to work and prohibited fathers from living with and supporting their children while working- and middle-class families faced ever-increasing hours at work for stagnating wages, made reform inevitable.

TANF, the new program created by welfare reform, incorporated four essential changes to AFDC. First, TANF rejected the longstanding guarantee of lifetime income to poor mothers with children, known in welfare policy as the "entitlement" to public assistance. No element in the new law was more important than its delimitation of welfare to *temporary* income support. The law allowed a woman to receive public assistance for no more than five years over a lifetime, after which she was expected to be self-supporting.

Second, TANF repudiated the social ideal, dating to the early 20th century, that mothers should stay home and care for their children. Rather, poor mothers should work, and public assistance was to support the mother and children in the transition from welfare to work. TANF required aid recipients to work or participate in work training after receiving two years of benefits. While the program recognized that there were many impediments to a single mother working, by providing for child care, transportation, health care, and training, it abandoned AFDC's support for formal education, encouraging instead job training for a rapid entry into the workforce.

Third, TANF reversed AFDC's de facto marriage penalty, instead proscribing single motherhood and enforcing paternal responsibility. States were given the latitude to experiment with programs that would discourage women from giving birth to children while on welfare. States focused particularly on teenage unwed mothers; some refused benefits to teenage mothers, and some made aid contingent on them living with a responsible adult and attending school. It did not, however, allow states to provide assistance to married couples, but focused instead on making out-of-wedlock births unacceptable. The federal government assumed greater authority over the enforcement of child support laws, traditionally a function of state government, in an effort to identify and locate fathers and hold them responsible for the financial support of their children.

Fourth, responsibility for the design and implementation of TANF programs was transferred to the states as both the federal guarantee of a minimum income and uniform federal regulations were scrapped. The law included, for the states, a mix of incentives and penalties related to the twin goals of America's revamped welfare system: moving welfare recipients into jobs and discouraging out-of-wedlock births. The law enacting welfare reform also cut food stamps and denied a variety of benefits (unrelated to AFDC) to legal immigrants, even though these had little to do with welfare and the perceived problems of the old system.

The Personal Responsibility and Work Opportunity Reconciliation Act of 1996 was a turning point in many respects—in the history of American social welfare, in the history of poverty and the sociocultural understanding of it, and in American party politics. Its influence will reach far into the 21st century. Caught in the maelstrom of partisan politics and the cultural politics of a restructured economy, poor mothers and their children saw fundamental elements of their lives transformed within the space of a brief few years. Americans, approving of the new law by 86 percent, signaled their ideological embrace of the wisdom of the free market, by creating a welfare system geared to the rhythms and ideals of the market.

Organizing to Defend Welfare

With welfare under assault by conservatives, Democrats increasingly eager to overhaul the system, and Republicans ascendant in Congress, a broad range of groups began to work together in 1994 to try to preserve public assistance for poor women and children. Their challenge was to forge enough national strength, in a time of widespread public apathy toward politics, to thwart the drive to reform welfare in a way they viewed as contrary to the interests and needs of poor women.

Because AFDC addressed the needs of poor women and children, feminists and feminist organizations were in the forefront of the campaign to save welfare. The National Organization of Women (NOW), the nation's largest feminist membership organization, redirected its focus in the early 1990s toward issues such as welfare that affected poor and working-class women, and sought to unite with welfare activists on the local and national level. Martha Davis, of the NOW Legal Defense and Education Committee, explained the new direction of the organization: "The punitive welfare measures of recent years have spurred us to take action, since the connections between poor women's experiences and the women's rights issues we have worked on for decades have become so clear" (Davis 1994). In 1994, feminist academics and writers created the Women's Committee of 100, declaring that "a war against poor women is a war against all women" (Kornbluh 1996). On the local level, groups like Vermont's Women United and Wisconsin's Welfare Warriors were organized by poor women, many of them welfare recipients, and they united women in a cross-class alliance to defend poor women.

As the political momentum toward reform grew in 1995 and 1996, religious organizations, unions, child welfare advocates, and African American organizations joined with these feminist groups in a campaign to thwart the passage of a punitive welfare reform law. Primarily, the diverse coalition sought to use the influence they believed they had within the administration and the Democratic Party to win a presidential veto of Republican legislation. They lobbied, they petitioned, they wrote letters, and they held private meetings with administration representatives. But it was not until very late in the game that they tried to mobilize broadly or bring the pressure of direct action to bear on the Democratic Party. The staff of NOW went on a hunger strike and set up a vigil outside the White House—after Clinton announced he would sign the bill. One of the largest unions in the nation activated its phone banks to urge a veto—on the day Clinton announced he would sign the Republican bill. Few imagined that

Clinton would sign a bill he had publicly proclaimed was too harsh, and thus the defeat was attributable in part to a mistaken analysis of the political land-scape (Pollitt 1994). But the issue of welfare reform was not clear cut; opposition to the conservative approach enshrined in the Republican legislation was all that united them. Feminists bitterly divided over the question of whether single mothers should be forced to work; feminists and liberals divided over whether to make common-cause with conservative Catholics who opposed welfare reform, but from a view that presupposed women's traditional role; African Americans disagreed over which would be most harmful to their community, preserving the present welfare system or welfare reform. In the last analysis, the story of the effort to stop welfare reform is one of defeat. But, in retrospect, it is difficult to imagine how a victory might have been wrested in the political and ideological environment of the 1990s.

The Politics of Welfare

By the 1990s, welfare reform was a juggernaut politicians dared not evade. Welfare became a hotly contested partisan political issue because the conservative movement of the 1980s had made the abolition of welfare one of its leading crusades. In the decade, conservatives had accomplished the ideological task of discrediting welfare and the organizing work of creating a constituency willing to make the issue one on which they based their vote. The passage of welfare reform in 1996 was a testament to conservatives' success in moving from a minority social movement to a political powerhouse. Conversely, it represented one of the signal failures of the liberal Left.

In the world of partisan politics, conservative Republicans espied political advantage to be gained from welfare reform, but they equally disapproved of welfare on principle. Welfare was a glaring example for them of all that was wrong with the Democrats' liberalism—its foolish social engineering, its paternalism, its inefficiency, and its violation of the creed of free market individualism.

Public opinion was powerfully influenced by the opponents and critics of welfare, those who conjured up images of lazy, not-too-honest generations of families who had become "dependent" on welfare. "The color of welfare intensified the gulf between its clients and the white working poor and reinforced the conservative attack on AFDC," observed Michael Katz, a leading historian of American welfare (Katz 2001, 322). But the most fertile ground for the critics was in the experience of working- and middle-class Americans struggling to maintain their own standard of living.

Although Democrats remained committed to the principle that the role of government was to provide a safety net for the vulnerable members of society, there was little deep support for AFDC as it was currently operating. For New Democrats, welfare reform was a significant element of their departure from the past, not just a political tactic to win middle-of-the-road voters. Although it was a controversial position to take, some white and African American liberals believed that welfare "dependency" was at least partly to blame for the crisis of the African American urban poor. At the same time, the New Democrats' faith in the market predisposed them against the highly bureaucratized welfare system. Clinton promised in his campaign of 1992 to "end welfare as we know it," by providing training and education to those who needed it and then helping them make the transition to work. He and his advisers made a political decision to devote the first year of his presidency to health care reform. Their defeat on health care, an issue for which there was a popular mandate for change, was an ominous sign for their ability to shape welfare reform according to a vision consonant with traditional liberal or even New Democrat principles. The protections Clinton favored in welfare reform, such as job guarantees, generous subsidies for child care, and job training, would suffer the same fate as health care reform.

It is uncertain whether Clinton could have forged a majority among Democrats for any change to welfare, but when the Republicans took control of Congress in 1994, the matter fell under their control. The Contract with America promised to abolish AFDC, and Gingrich went so far as to call for orphanages to be built and free school lunches to be abolished—earning himself the nickname "The Grinch." During congressional debates on welfare reform, Florida Republican John L. Mica held up a sign, "Don't Feed the Alligators," explaining, "We post these warnings because unnatural feeding and artificial care create dependency" (quoted in Katz 2001, 323). In the fall of 1995, Congress passed a conference bill that bore the imprint of the House Republican hardliners. It would have ended the entitlement to food stamps and Medicaid, turned nutritional programs for children into block grants with reduced funding, and abolished AFDC. The Office of Budget and Management concluded that it would have thrust an additional 1.5 million children into poverty and hurt many who were already poor (Katz 2001). Clinton vetoed the bill in January 1996.

As the 1996 elections approached, Clinton had already vetoed two Republican-designed welfare reform bills, and Gingrich's Class of '94 "revolutionaries" had accomplished nothing from their political manifesto. Both parties were thus looking for a victory on welfare. Congressional Democrats, however, were largely cut out of the process after Clinton made a political decision to work on a bill with Republicans, not his own party. Clinton pushed to eliminate the draconian measures included in the House's version. He proposed amendments to preserve food stamps, benefits for legal immigrants, and support for children after their mothers' benefits expired. Despite the conference committee's rejection of half of his proposed amendments, Clinton announced he would support their final bill, and would try to change it later. On August 22, 1996, shortly before the high season of the presidential campaign, Clinton signed into law the Personal Responsibility and Work Opportunity Reconciliation Act.

After the law was passed in 1996 and Clinton won reelection, Clinton and the congressional Democrats revisited some of the law's provisions that they considered to be most odious. All legal immigrants had been denied all benefits in the 1996 bill. In 1997 and 1998, Congress restored the right of some legal immigrants to receive Supplemental Security Income, food stamps, and Medicaid, but not to the extent that had seemed implicit in Clinton's original promise to right the wrongs of the original bill. Mostly, however, Clinton and Democrats were blessed with a booming economy that brought added tax revenues into the treasury and allowed more money to be put into programs on easing the transition from welfare to work.

As a matter of politics, welfare reform was momentous. One of the defining partisan divides was taken out of politics by Clinton's most successful move of triangulation. But in taking welfare out of politics, American politicians of the 1990s deeded the poorest Americans to the vicissitudes of the market and its unsympathetic judgment and rendered their fate once there politically invisible.

Surviving Poverty

As the government safety net was trimmed, with welfare reform, cuts in food stamps and housing assistance, and the like, the poor in America improvised ways to survive in the absence of these previous forms of public support. They looked to friends and family members and to private charity, as poor people had done before the advent of the welfare state. And they used tools of the new economy, especially credit cards, in an effort to provide basic necessities for their families.

Most poor people lived in those areas bypassed by the New Economy—rural America and deindustrialized zones of inner cities. The urban poor were doubly disadvantaged in the 1990s. Welfare reform and other benefit cuts went into effect just as cities were economically booming—for those hooked into the New Economy. Many working-class and poor neighborhoods were gentrified, and in those that were not, rents skyrocketed anyway. Poor people, forced to make a choice between food, shelter, and medical care, moved in with family members and friends, sleeping on couches and crowding the whole family into an extra bedroom or a garage. Outside of cities, where the cost of housing did not become so much of a problem, getting enough food to survive often posed a challenge for poor people. The rural poor looked for help from soup kitchens run by private charities and churches. The "dominant faces of hunger in America," according to a report by the private hunger-relief organization Second Harvest, "are young, white and female, and they are turning up more in rural areas" (quoted in Katz 2001, 306). Throughout the nation, private and public agencies reported that the number of those seeking emergency shelter or food in the late 1990s had increased by about a fifth. Borrowing money from friends, buying

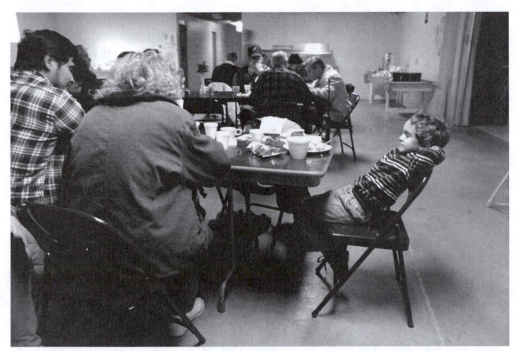

Lunch at the soup kitchen run by Trinity United Methodist Church in Mount Pleasant, Michigan, 1995. (Shepard Sherbell/Corbis Saba)

clothes and household goods second-hand at swap meets and yard sales, street vending, working off the books, and other time-tested strategies for getting by helped poor Americans make up the difference between the cost of necessities and their wages or shrinking public benefits.

The Effect of Welfare Reform on the American Poor

In 1996, AFDC supported 4.8 million families. In 2000, 2.2 million families received TANF (Jencks 2005a). The rapid and steep decline in the welfare rolls surprised everyone. The statistic itself, however, does not reveal why the decline occurred or how poor families who had once received public assistance fared.

There were two possible causes of the decreased numbers of welfare recipients, at least in the first years of the change in the 1990s, before lifetime time limits could have been reached. Women either made the transition to work or they were being denied benefits under the new state rules. Studies undertaken during the first few years of the transition revealed that both were taking place.

Shifting single mothers from welfare to work was an expensive proposition. A number of influences converged in the late 1990s to create the best possible chances for success. The buoyant national economy flooded local, state, and federal treasuries with tax dollars to fund the services women needed, such as transportation, child care, and job training. Unemployment was at a generational low, and with such a tight labor market, there was demand for the least-experienced and least-skilled workers. State welfare offices transformed their own culture and experimented with new and creative ways to help women find and keep jobs. Flush themselves, states added money to child care, transportation, and job-training budgets. Illinois, for example, funded from its own state monies the equivalent of a $22,000 a year child care subsidy. Congress, goaded in part by Clinton's admonitions to make reform work, added more funding to job training in 1997. As the welfare rolls dropped quickly, more money went to each family remaining for the crucial support services to help them make the transition. In the first few years after welfare reform, therefore, those who remained on welfare were often receiving more aid and more social support to make the transition to self-sufficiency (Jencks 2005b; Katz 2001).

At the same time, with the end of the federal entitlement, states were also reducing the rolls through tactics that discouraged eligible families from applying for aid and punished them for often minor violations of the new rules. A 1998 analysis by the *Washington Post* concluded that state sanctions had caused 38 percent of the decline in the welfare rolls (Jencks 2005b). The two sides of the debate faced off again, with those who had assumed welfare was riddled with fraud pointing to the large numbers of people sanctioned as proof of past dishonesty and a sign that the new system was better, and advocates of the poor confirmed in their opinion that reform was primarily about punishing the poor.

Welfare, under both AFDC and TANF, served poor families, and a key measure of the effect of welfare reform is not only how many no longer received welfare but whether the condition of poor families in America improved. The indicators were mixed and remain so to this date. More single mothers worked in the formal economy after welfare reform. The question for them was whether work paid enough to survive, and whether they could hold onto their jobs. Welfare reform coincided with raises in the minimum wage and the EITC, and a large proportion of women leaving welfare found jobs at the minimum wage and were eligible to receive tax rebates under the EITC. Women leaving welfare significantly increased their labor force participation rate, their hours at work, and their income during the 1990s expansion. But studies of several states showed that most earned wages that kept them and their children below the federal poverty line, many lived in worse economic condition than they had while receiving welfare, and they lost ground during the economic downturn after 2000. With wages hovering around the poverty line, women leaving welfare were hard pressed to pay for housing, health care, child care, and transportation. Women who, for various reasons, could not work were plunged into much worse circumstances than they had experienced under AFDC. Individual states provided some exemptions from work requirements, but no state covered all the women who found themselves in such a situation. The most recent studies, which are coming out as the five-year lifetime limit on aid has begun to be imposed, give signs of a newly developing crisis. Neither the minimum wage nor the aid remaining provide poor single mothers a comfortable subsistence, and the juggling act all are engaged in is arduous. But the evidence shows that many of those women who have been unable to leave the welfare rolls, who have been cycling in and out of welfare, are beset by serious and intractable personal problems—such as physical disability, the need to care for a disabled or aged relative, mental illness, or drug addiction—that not only render them unable to keep jobs but also place their children in grave danger.

Another way to examine the effect of welfare reform is to look at indicators of poverty, as half of all poor families were headed by a single woman. After welfare reform, the poverty rate for single mothers dropped significantly, from 42 percent in 1996 to 33 percent in 2000. (The rise in unemployment during the recession of 2001–2002 pushed the poverty rate up.) Other indicators on poverty, such as the adequacy of food and housing, also showed some improvement for single mothers as a whole. Nevertheless, a third of families headed by a single mother remained poor; a total of 3.3 million families were poor, and 1 million families did not have enough to eat. Looking at the situation on balance, Christopher Jencks, a liberal advocate of changes to the old welfare system who opposed the punitive form reform took in the 1996 law, concluded, "The lesson, I think, is that the old welfare system was so awful that even the relatively punitive reforms enacted in 1996 made the average single mother a little better off. Of course, a less punitive system would probably have improved her lot even more" (Jencks 2005b).

Most studies concluded that, among the millions of women and children who no longer received welfare, most were at best marginally better off and most were still struggling economically. As to the effects on children set by the example of a working mother promised by the proponents of the "culture of poverty" thesis, there is little conclusive evidence of either a positive or negative effect. Jason DeParle, a *New York Times* writer who had covered welfare reform, captured the uncertainty and its source eloquently in a book on three former welfare families (DeParle 2004). His friends, he wrote, often asked him how his subjects felt about the change in their life from welfare reform.

> While I had posed versions of the question before, they never seemed to grab [Angie], and I was starting to understand why. On welfare, [she] was a low-income single mother, raising her children in a dangerous neighborhood in a household ruled by chaos. She drank lots of beer. And her kids needed a father. Off welfare, she was a low-income single mother, raising her children in a dangerous neighborhood in a household ruled by chaos. She couldn't pay the bills. She drank lots of beer. And her kids needed a father. "We're surviving!" is all Angie said. "Cause that's what we have to do." (quoted in Jencks 2005b)

It raised the question of what the purpose of welfare reform had been. If it was to reduce poverty, it had done little for those it was intended to help—single mothers and their children. If it was to end welfare dependency and the "culture of poverty," the verdict was out. If it was to impose discipline—"personal responsibility"—on the poor, then perhaps, in a social Darwinian view of things, it was a success.

HEALTH, HOME, AND EDUCATION ACROSS THE AMERICAN SOCIAL DIVIDE

In the 1980s and 1990s, the rise of economic inequality delivered a heavy blow to many middle- and working-class families as their capacity to live the American dream as they understood it eluded their reach. While the income and wealth of the top 20 percent of American households increased, providing them with hitherto unimaginable luxuries, the other 80 percent of American households had an increasingly difficult time securing access to the basic elements of a decent, comfortable, and secure livelihood: health care, housing, retirement, and quality education.

Health Insurance and Access to Health Care

The American health care system was beset by numerous problems in the 1990s, and the "crisis" of medical care emerged as one of the most serious social issues of the decade. Unlike almost all of the rest of the advanced industrial democracies, the United States consigned its citizens' health to the marketplace. The provision of health insurance by employers served as the main prop of the system. In the 1980s and 1990s, as health care costs rose much faster than inflation, employers became increasingly reluctant to shoulder the burden of their employees' health care costs. At the same time, the large national health care corporations, which provided insurance or services to most of those covered by a plan, in effect rationed health care to control costs. Finally, the soaring cost of health insurance left millions of Americans uninsured.

Spending on health care expenditures nearly doubled between 1990 and 2000, and within this total amount, spending on prescription drugs alone tripled, from $40 billion to $121 billion. By the end of the decade, health care spending amounted to $3,955 per capita. As recently as 1980, per capita spending on health care in the United States had been only $931 (National Center for Health 2005, tables 122–127).

To cover the increasing cost of providing health care, insurance premiums rose. The employers who had set the gold standard for employee benefits, the

First Lady Hillary Rodham Clinton speaks at a health care rally at the University of Colorado. (William J. Clinton Presidential Library)

former giants of American industry, were already reeling from other economic woes. The clearest sign of the deterioration of the privately based social welfare system can be found in the statistics on the provision of health insurance by employers. In 1981, 71 percent of workers in the private sector received health care insurance from their employers. By the end of the 1992 recession, the rate had dropped to 58 percent. During the expansion of the 1990s, the rate remained steady at around 58 percent (EPI 2006). More people were covered, as millions of jobs were created, but the fact that the proportion of employees covered did not rise suggested that the system of health coverage through employment was breaking, and only the inordinately tight job market was holding it together. By the middle of the next decade, barely more than half of Americans had health insurance through their jobs.

For millions of Americans, the effect of the changing economics of the provision of health care was felt through the emerging system of health maintenance organizations, commonly known as HMOs. HMOs originated with the Health Maintenance Organization Assistance Act in 1973. Beginning as a relatively insignificant component of health care provision, HMO coverage grew to encompass three-quarters of all covered employees by the late 1990s. In 2000, 82.9 million Americans—one out of three—received their health care through HMOs (National Center for Health 2005, table 136). The systemic shift into HMOs

Buying out of the System: "Concierge Care Medicine"

Some doctors and patients chose to opt out of a health care system fraught with problems of cost, bureaucratic management, and service. In 1996, a Seattle medical group established a new type of practice in which patients paid a retainer fee of $13,000 to a primary care physician, and the physicians in the practice took on no more than 100 patients and ended all relationship with insurers. Commonly known as concierge care medicine, patients received various advantages for the payment of a retainer—immediate access to medical procedures and physician visits, luxurious offices, and around-the-clock email and phone access to their preferred doctor. Critics charged that the practice was creating a two-class system of medicine. Only a couple dozen concierge practices were in existence at the end of the decade, but the practice spread rapidly in the early 2000s. In 2003, concierge providers founded the Society for Innovative Medical Practice Design to promote the expansion of concierge medicine, and the American Medical Association issued ethics guidelines for practitioners operating under retainer contracts.

profoundly changed the relationship between Americans and their doctors and the manner in which they received medical care.

Those who were not provided health insurance through their work either paid for it themselves, received insurance through government programs, or went without. From 1984 on, the percentage of Americans with private health insurance declined, the percentage on Medicaid and other public programs rose, and the percentage of the uninsured rose.

As insurance premiums became more expensive, the numbers of the uninsured increased, from 30 million in 1984 to 41 million in 1997 (National Center for Health 2005). (The numbers dropped briefly during the economic boom between 1998 and 2000, and then rose again.) Many of the uninsured worked in low-wage jobs; one out of four workers earning less than $10 an hour was uninsured. These low-wage workers were not provided with health insurance by their employers or were offered policies that were unaffordable. They often earned too much to be eligible for Medicaid. As the cost of health care rose, political struggles arose over funding for Medicare and Medicaid and the level of services provided to those dependent on government programs. Although the decline in rates of insurance occurred across the board—by income, by race and ethnicity, by sex—the poor suffered the greatest loss. Between 1981 and 1994, their rates of insurance dropped from 38 percent to 25 percent (Collins, Hall, and Neuhaus 1999, charts 5.1–5.10). The federal creation of the State Children's Health Insurance Program (SCHIP) in 1997 and the economic expansion improved rates of insurance slightly—up to 27 percent—but the recession of 2001–2002 caused a decline, and insurance rates continued to fall during the expansion that followed.

The Fraying Social Contract: Employment-Based Social Benefits in a Downsized Age

The slow demise of America's primary system of social welfare gathered force in the 1990s. A social contract between citizens and their government in which essential needs from birth to death were secured provided one of the fundamental pillars of prosperity, security, and stability in the postwar advanced industrial democracies. In providing insurance against sickness and unemployment, security for old age, and various forms of support throughout the life cycle, all countries employed a mix of the public and private sectors. Relative to other OECD nations, however, the United States relied much more heavily on the private sector to fulfill its citizens' social welfare needs. Most Americans received social benefits through their jobs, and the welfare state was largely reserved for those who were not making it in the marketplace. (Only for the elderly did the U.S. take a universal approach.) The social contract in America was more accurately a contract between workers and corporations—often negotiated through unions and overseen by the federal government, which also acted as the insurer of last resort. The agreement seemed straightforward enough: a worker devoted a lifetime of work to a company, and the company in turn took care of his or her health needs and retirement.

The force of economic change combined with the ascendant ideology of the free market undermined the ability and willingness of American corporations to fund their employees' social benefits. Fewer workers received health insurance as part of their compensation, and employers required those who were insured to carry more of the cost. In the same period, millions of those in employer-provided health plans were shifted into HMOs. American business also cut back on pensions for its workers, sharply cutting them in the 1980s, adding some for the highest paid workers during the 1990s' expansion, but in the form of riskier defined-contribution plans rather than the traditional defined-benefit plans that workers preferred. By 2000, fewer than half of American working people had pensions through their jobs (EPI 2006). The strong economy of the late 1990s briefly arrested the tendency toward declining health and retirement provision as employers felt compelled to offer benefits to lure scarce workers. By the end of the decade, nevertheless, the extent of basic health and retirement coverage had narrowed, and the form had changed in a way that shifted risk and cost away from business and onto individuals. Developments in the first decade of the 21st century, particularly the continuing decline of employer-provided health and retirement coverage during an economic expansion, led most observers to the conclusion that the system was broken beyond repair.

America's privately based system had been pioneered in large industrial manufacturing, and although it had spread to other sectors, it had always been most generous in the heavy manufacturing industries in which American supremacy was unrivalled. The gravity of the crisis, likewise, was most strongly felt in these industries.

The developments in the steel industry were exemplary of the underlying economic, social, and political forces eroding the old social contract. As American steel companies suffered losses from global competition, they slashed their workforces—in half between 1980 and 1985, and almost halved again by 2005. The massive downsizing was frequently accomplished by forcing workers into early retirement, which cut current labor costs for companies yet provided pensions and health insurance to the retired workers. By the end of the 1990s, there were three retirees to every active worker in the steel industry. Steel corporations paid for the retirees' health and pension benefits out of current production and out of their earnings from assets, fortuitously ballooning with the stock market boom (Porter 2005).

While the economy overall was growing fast, the East Asian economic crisis devastated the American steel industry. Between 1997 and 2004, 40 companies went bankrupt. On top of this, the bursting of the dot-com bubble wiped out a large proportion of the assets that had been devoted to paying pensions, leaving the industry with billions of dollars in unfunded pension liabilities.

As the venerable Bethlehem Steel showed, one route to recovery was to shed the company's obligations to its former workers. The company filed for bankruptcy in 2001, and the court released Bethlehem Steel from its contractual obligations to provide pension and health insurance for its retirees. The company's retirees were transferred into the Pension Benefit Guaranty Corporation (PBGC), a federal corporation that assumes pension responsibilities when companies terminate plans or are unable to meet their pension obligations. The steel industry handed over 208,000 retirees to the PBGC, and according to the United Steel Workers Union, Bethlehem Steel was responsible for almost half of those. Many former steelworkers found their pensions significantly reduced by the transfer. The retirees were left with virtually no health insurance, even though a quarter of them were too young to receive Medicare. Bethlehem Steel emerged out of bankruptcy through the creation of a conglomerate that joined it with four other bankrupt steel mills. By the mid-2000s, the entire American steel industry had undergone consolidation and restructuring, and the three new conglomerates, Mittal, Nucor, and U.S. Steel, were turning a profit. To achieve this, the new conglomerates cut loose the retirees of the companies they had absorbed, passed their pension obligations along to the federal government's PBGC, and scrapped the old generous system of benefits for their remaining workers. When the American auto industry faced analogous problems in the mid-2000s, it followed the model established by the steel industry.

Health in American Society: Improvements and Disparities

Americans became healthier and lived longer in the second half of the 20th century. Life expectancy rose to 77 years for the population as a whole, and the infant mortality rate, which by 2000 had declined to a quarter of what it had been in 1950, was 6.9 per 1,000 live births. Heart disease, cancer, and stroke remained the three leading causes of death, but as medical care improved, fewer persons died from these conditions (National Center for Health 2005).

Nevertheless, longstanding disparities in the health of Americans by race, ethnicity, income, and education persisted. Despite improvements in medical science, medical technology, and pharmaceuticals, the poor, African Americans, Latinos, Native Americans, and those with less than a high school education died younger, died from treatable diseases at higher rates, and lived in poorer physical and mental health.

The most important cause of the disparities in the health of Americans was limited access to regular and high-quality medical care. Among white Americans,

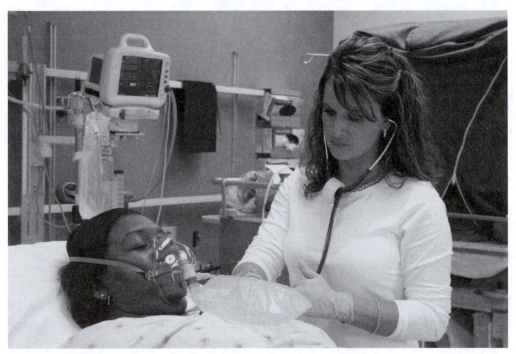

A nurse provides treatment to an ill patient. (iStockPhoto.com)

1 out of 7 adults and 1 out of 10 children did not have health insurance. In contrast, 1 out of 3 Hispanic adults, and 1 out of 4 Asian American and African American adults were uninsured. Among children, 1 out of 3 Latinos and 1 out of 5 African Americans were uninsured; one-third of the insured Latino and African American children were on Medicaid. While Medicaid provided care for some of the Americans living in poverty, the near poor found it difficult to secure medical care. More than 40 percent of low-wage workers had difficulty paying their medical bills or skipped medical care because they did not have the money to pay for it. Roughly every 2 out of 5 African Americans and Latinos did not have a regular doctor. Half of all African Americans relied on emergency rooms, outpatient departments, or clinics for their regular medical care, while only a third of white adults did so. In cities, minorities were much more likely to have to resort to public hospitals obligated to provide care regardless of an individual's ability to pay, and far less likely to receive care at other urban hospitals. African American, Latino, and Native American women were less likely to receive prenatal care in the first trimester of their pregnancies. Fewer than half of African Americans, Latinos, and Asian Americans felt very satisfied with their medical care, and 1 out of 5 African Americans believed that discrimination on the basis of race or income was to blame for the inferior care they received (Collins, Hall, and Neuhaus 1999).

Unequal and insufficient access to medical care resulted in unequal outcomes. On the most important measure of health, life expectancy, African Americans fared the worst. Although life expectancy rose steadily for all groups in every decade of the 20th century, African American men and women, on average, still died younger than white men and women. Infant mortality rates declined and the racial disparity narrowed, but still, African American and Native American infants died at birth at a significantly higher rate than other infants did. African Americans died from stroke, heart disease, cancer, and HIV/AIDS at a much higher rate than white Americans did. Homicide continued to be a leading cause of death for African American and Latino males 15 to 24 years old; the homicide rate for young African American men was more than eight times that for young white men (National Center for Health 2005).

The poor, similarly, were in worse health than the rest of Americans. (Most of the essential health statistics are not collected for different income levels, so statistics for the poor on the most important indicators of health are not available. Labor statistics indicate, however, that education correlates strongly with income, and that those with a high school education or less earn wages near the poverty line.) A mother's education profoundly influenced the survival of her baby. For all demographic groups, the infant mortality rate was lower when the mother had some education beyond high school. The difference for white infants was dramatic. Infants born to white mothers who had not finished high school died at a rate almost twice that of those born to white mothers who had some college education. Men and women with a high school education or less

HIV/AIDS

Medical developments in the treatment of HIV/AIDS, the shifting demography of new HIV/AIDS infections, and the cultural evolution in the view of the disease significantly changed the nature of the AIDS crisis in the 1990s. In the early 1990s, a decade into the epidemic, diverse events and forces acted to reshape Americans' understanding of the disease. Well-publicized cases of HIV infection among nonhomosexuals began to disentangle the troubled connection between government inaction on HIV/AIDS and prejudice against homosexuals. Ryan White, a white teenager infected through a blood transfusion who became a national symbol of the human face of AIDS, died in 1990, and the Ryan White Comprehensive AIDS Resource Emergency (CARE) Act was signed into law that year. CARE funded health care and services for people living with AIDS. The passage of the Americans with Disabilities Act (ADA) protected people with HIV/AIDS against employment and housing discrimination. The basketball star Earvin "Magic" Johnson announced in 1991 that he was retiring from the NBA because he was HIV positive, and President Bush appointed him to the National Commission on AIDS. Johnson then devoted himself to educating the American public about the disease. The burgeoning gay rights movement, particularly the militancy of the group ACT Up between 1988 and 1992, helped cause a sea change in government policy and social attitudes alike.

HIV/AIDS in the 1990s was no longer a "gay disease," not only in popular perception but also in reality. The incidence of HIV/AIDS plummeted among gay men. New infections were prevented by the extensive educational efforts about prevention and community support services within the gay community. But the key development was the middecade discovery of protease-inhibitor drugs and the subsequent adoption of Highly Active Antiretroviral therapy, which provided the first manageable treatment for the disease. A decade earlier, a positive AIDS test was tantamount to a death sentence. By the late 1990s, there were hundreds of thousands of HIV-infected people in the United States and in the world leading normal, healthy, and productive lives. The death rate for AIDS reached a peak in 1995 at 16.2 per 100,000 and then dropped significantly, down to 5.2 per 100,000 in 2000 (National Center for Health 2005, table 42).

HIV/AIDS continued to grow in the United States, but by the early 1990s, the increase was concentrated in minority and poor communities. In reality, AIDS from the start of the epidemic had killed African American and Latino men at a much higher rate than any other demographic group, but this was masked by the higher proportional incidence among gay men. In minority communities, infection was most likely to occur through heterosexual sexual activity or intravenous drug use. Death rates were also significantly higher; some HIV-positive men and women were weakened and sickened further by their drug use while their sexual partners were less likely to have access to health care or to be able to afford the expensive

Continued on next page

HIV/AIDS, Continued

new AIDS drugs. In 1998, pressure from African American leaders and "People With AIDS" activists persuaded President Clinton to declare AIDS a public health emergency in African American communities, thus laying the groundwork for increasing federal funding targeted to AIDS prevention and treatment in minority communities.

The AIDS memorial quilt, begun by Cleve Jones in San Francisco in 1987, was displayed on the National Mall in 1996. Its 40,000 panels attracted more than 1 million visitors. It was the last time it was displayed in its entirety in public. The exhibition, in retrospect, marked a watershed in the reality and the perception of HIV/AIDS. The memorial quilt was an artifact of the first decade of the disease—of its locus in the gay community, of its relentless killing power. By the beginning of 1997, with new and more effective drug therapies becoming the standard of treatment for HIV/AIDS, the shift of new infection and illness in the United States to minority and poor communities, and a changed public attitude toward the disease and people living with the disease, the AIDS epidemic entered a new phase. The hysteria, fear, and prejudice touched off in the early years of the disease had settled into a public mood of acceptance, first of resignation, then briefly of hope—with soon to be retracted claims of an imminent cure or vaccine—and finally to complacency. The "plague" of HIV/AIDS had become a normal part of human life, like cancer or poverty.

died in their prime adult years at a rate twice that of those with more than a high school education (National Center for Health 2005).

Home

Differences in the quality and security of housing were aggravated by the economic cycles of the 1990s, which left some better off and some more insecure. The late-decade economic boom caused housing prices to soar, inflating the wealth of homeowners but making it more and more difficult for working- and middle-class families to purchase or rent decent housing.

In 2000, the homeownership rate in America reached an all-time high—67.4 percent, after rising almost 4 percent in the decade. The overall figure disguised marked disparities. Whereas almost three out of four white households owned their home, fewer than half of African American and Latino households did (Mishel et al. 2005). Discrimination, which had played such a determinative role in postwar residential patterns, was partly responsible for the disparity. A 1989 study demonstrated that half of African American and Latino households faced housing discrimination; another study in 2000 documented that minority homeowners paid higher mortgage rates (Cohen 2003). A more important element in the disparate rates of homeownership, however, was the racial and ethnic income gap. Starting out with less income and wealth, minorities had less ability to purchase homes.

Homes became more expensive in the 1990s. Median home values rose 18 percent over the decade to reach $119,600 in 2000. Compared to 1960, the median home had doubled in value. All homes were not, however, created equal. The value of homes owned by Asian Americans was the highest, at nearly $200,000; African American and Native American homes were worth about $81,000—about one-third below the national median. The value of homes owned by Latinos was also well below the national median. People who lived in major metropolitan areas, where the median home was valued over $150,000,

New suburban homes replace farmland on the west side of Des Moines, Iowa. (U.S. Department of Agriculture)

paid more to buy a home. In the rural south and the Great Plains, home values were far below the national median, less than $75,000. New homes were much more expensive, with the median at $146,300. Not surprisingly, those with the highest incomes lived in the newest single-family homes (Woodward and Damon 2001; Bennefield 2003).

The rising value of homes had mixed consequences for individuals but overall served to widen the social divide. On one side, middle- and upper-class wealth grew as homes increased in value, and many families used their equity in their home to finance their growing consumer purchases. Thus, not only did the real estate market make them wealthier (on paper) but it also allowed them to consume more goods. On the other side, the rising value of homes made it more difficult for people, especially young adults, to make the transition from renting to owning. To achieve their first home, many families moved to exurban housing developments far away from their work or limited their other spending so they could buy a house.

The people most disadvantaged by the rising housing market were the third of Americans who rented their homes. Rents rose during the 1990s, and although there was a slight fall in the proportion of income paid for rent, renters spent a quarter of their income on rent—and often significantly more in some areas. Rental housing ran the gamut from slum to luxury. Those with the lowest income were most likely to live in large apartment buildings or in mobile homes, and the ones most likely to live in crowded conditions (Bonnette 2003). Doubly cursed in the economic boom, renters paid more for housing and fell further behind their fellow citizens whose wealth was increasing as the market value of their homes rose.

While statistics on home values attest to significant economic differences in the nation, other characteristics of Americans' housing choices reveal a deeper social divide. More and more, the very wealthy were isolating themselves in communities of their own kind, reinforcing and deepening residential segregation by class. Not just the rich wanted to keep others out. About one in six Americans at the turn of the 21st century lived in privately managed communities, such as gated communities, which often included their own private security service and other amenities (Cohen 2003). The growth of gated communities reflected fears of social contact with others as well as frustrations with the inadequacy of local government's provision for community life—parks, recreation centers, safe and well-paved streets, and the like. As homes became more unequal, they also became the locus for the increasingly privatized culture of the nation. As the haves found more of their lives satisfied within their private domain, the have nots lived in neighborhoods where they faced drugs, crime, and toxic pollution and where public services were in shambles.

Homelessness

Among the poor in America, the homeless lived with the greatest level of deprivation and the most intense degree of insecurity. Homelessness was a kind of revolving door through which millions of Americans passed every year. On any given night in the United States, 800,000 people were homeless, 200,000 of whom were children. Various estimates determined that between 2.3 million and 3.5 million Americans—or about 1 percent of the U.S. population—were without a home at some point during any given year. A snapshot of any given night would reveal that about half were experiencing their first or second crisis of homelessness, spending as little as a couple weeks or as much as a year without permanent shelter, one-quarter were moving in and out of homelessness frequently, and the last quarter had been continuously homeless for the previous five years. Among the homeless, 40 percent were African American, 40 percent were white, and 11 percent were Latino. At the end of the 1990s, poor Americans were as likely to fall into homelessness as they had been since the beginning of the surge of mass homelessness in the 1980s. Studies showed that from 5 to 10 percent of the poor population experienced some period without shelter over the course of any given year. Services for the homeless had, however, increased significantly (Burt 2001).

Families were particularly vulnerable to temporary homelessness—between 900,000 and 1.4 million children were homeless in a typical year. For the majority of American families who were without a home, they lacked shelter because of poverty and, consequently, an inability to afford housing. Yet they were less likely to be homeless for a long period because they were able to receive public assistance that helped them find permanent housing. Thus, although between one-third and half of the homeless over a typical year were families with children, on any given day, families were only 15 percent of the homeless population.

The homeless population of adults without children was overwhelmingly male and, as with homeless families, disproportionately African American and Latino. On any given day, 61 percent of the homeless were single men, 15 percent were single women, and 9 percent were adults who were together but had no children with them. Ineligible for welfare, half lived in severe poverty, receiving income below 40 percent of the federal poverty line. While poverty

Urban homeless people use shopping carts to transport their belongings and collect discarded goods. (PhotoDisc, Inc.)

was a significant cause of homelessness, mental illness and substance abuse afflicted roughly three-quarters of homeless adults, often in combination, according to self-reporting by homeless adults to providers of services. Only a quarter reported that they had suffered neither substance abuse nor mental health problems.

Federal, state, and local governments, nonprofits, and private charities significantly increased services to aid the homeless in the 1990s. The Clinton administration spent three times as much on homeless services as did the Reagan and Bush administrations. By the late 1990s, there were close to 900,000 beds for the homeless or formerly homeless in emergency shelters, temporary housing, and permanent housing, triple the amount that had been available in the 1980s. But while governments built shelters and assistive housing, they also attempted to drive the homeless out of sight, with sweeps of homeless encampments and police actions against panhandlers. By the late 1990s, 50 cities had enacted antivagrancy laws.

In the 1980s, homelessness had been viewed as a national travesty and a looming crisis. In the 1990s, Americans began treating homelessness as a problem that was likely to persist. Among experts, the consensus by the end of the decade was that only a wide expansion of the stock of affordable housing could solve the problem of homelessness. Yet the prospect of building enough affordable housing expired between the vise of cash-strapped municipalities and a booming housing market. For most Americans, by the turn of the century, the sense of urgency and the sense of outrage about homelessness had faded.

Caring for the Poorest Americans

St. Ann's of Morrisania was located in one of the poorest neighborhoods in the United States. The Bronx Episcopalian church ran a food pantry and a Sunday soup kitchen as well as other educational and social services for the poor families of the area. Many of New York City's homeless had ended up in this section of the Bronx after being effectively driven from Manhattan by anti-panhandling and other ordinances that criminalized their activities.

Twelve blocks away stood New York City's emergency shelter for the homeless. Even though the unit was considered a shelter of last resort, it had a policy of turning away those who arrived without documents, telling them to leave and use the pay phone on the corner to be certified as homeless before returning to the shelter. Near the phone were frequently mothers begging for change—for the phone or to buy food for their children. Sister Katrice, the woman who ran the food pantry at St. Ann's, was a sympathetic witness to the plight of the homeless seeking public shelter.

Sister Katrice, like many other women in poor neighborhoods, lived her life seeking to counter the humiliation inflicted on poor people by so many of society's institutions. She often in the mornings saw mothers and children on the streets, having spent the night there after being denied admittance to the shelter, the children wheezing from untreated asthma and the cold, babies soiled and hungry. Sister Katrice described how mothers were sometimes embarrassed to ask for food, protesting that they had no way to thank her. They would say to Katrice, "'You didn't need to open the door.' I tell them, 'Yes. I did. I *had* to open up. This is a church. God doesn't close the door.'" The ethic of care guiding the actions of her fellow volunteers derived from their understanding of their role in the community. We all "are grandmothers," she explained, "so we're in another generation now and some of us don't have the strength we used to have. But grandmothers have to be there, whether you feel good or not. If a child's mother is using drugs, or sick, or in the hospital, or in some other trouble, and she can't sustain, you have to take her place. You have to be the mother *and* grandmother. Not just for your own. For all" (Kozol 2000, 148).

The Promise of Education, The Crisis of Schools

Of all the social and cultural institutions of America, the public school has always had the greatest expectations placed on it. Schools are to instill in the young the fundamental skills to prosper in the economy, the civic culture that will transmute American diversity into a common "Americanness," and the values of citizenship that will allow American democracy to thrive. Individual economic success, social mobility, national culture, and democratic government all stand or fall on the quality of education.

It is a tall order, and schools have always disappointed. In the 1990s, the demands and hopes became ever more expansive, even as American educational institutions found it painfully difficult to deliver at the most basic level. Schooling—from preschool to graduate level—was beset by numerous problems, and although Americans differed on the nature and cause of the problem, observers across the political and cultural spectrum concurred that the system was mired in a profound crisis. It was also plain that schools were failing some Americans more than others. Schooling, the great social leveler, was instead making more inequality more entrenched.

Publicity given to a variety of indicators shaped the debate about the nature and extent of the crisis. One out of 10 American youth did not finish high school. More men than women dropped out, as did more African Americans than white Americans. The highest dropout rate was among Latinos: nearly 1 out of 3 Latinos left school before graduation. A third, and in some regions more, of American fourth and eighth graders were below proficiency in mathematics. In reading, for every demographic group, fourth graders were not able to comprehend complex writing; African American and Latino fourth graders performed even more poorly, scoring 35 points below white students. American students were falling behind students in the nation's primary competitors, particularly in mathematics and science (NCES 1996, 2003).

As the likelihood of real success in school declined, the importance of education to economic well-being intensified. The changes in the global economy, most analysts agreed, had placed a new burden on education. When American men could gain highly paid employment in manufacturing with a high school degree, a college education mattered less. But as the loss of jobs in manufacturing accumulated, the personal economic cost of educational attainment was amplified. Wages fell for workers who had less than a high school education between 1990 and 2000, even though average wages had increased in the decade, and their income in real dollars in 2000 was lower than it had been in 1975. The premium for higher education likewise rose, as wages for workers with a college or advanced degree increased about 15 percent over the decade (EPI 2006). The solution, which was most fervently advocated by Labor Secretary Robert Reich, was to educate Americans for the higher-level knowledge work in the New Economy. America's competitive advantage would derive from the superior education of its population, and America could retain the best jobs in the new global economy by providing the right kind of education. Although the new technology industries did not create a large number of jobs, the definition of the problem as that of America's very economic survival set the terms of the debate over what should be done to fix America's schools.

Inequality, Race, and Taxes in America's Public Schools

The education crisis was most severe in the nation's cities. Factory closings had eliminated the jobs available to high school graduates and had eviscerated the property tax base through which inner-city schools were funded. In urban school districts, roughly two out of every five children entered school suffering under the burden and stress of poverty. Crime, drugs, gangs, and the inextricable link among them rendered many inner-city neighborhoods and the schools in them dangerous. In the areas where the crisis was the most severe, where one-fifth or more of adults were unemployed, and those who had jobs made the minimum wage, the drug-trade appeared as a more viable route to employment. Those who stayed in school faced innumerable obstacles, not least among them crowded and decaying school buildings, untrained teachers, and shortages of textbooks and computers. If a student made it through to high school graduation, the odds were that he or she had not developed the skills to succeed in college and would be consigned to a minimum-wage job.

Urban school districts were not only poorer but they were also disproportionately minority. After the collapse of de jure segregation, the color line had been redrawn in American schools by suburbanization and white flight. The disparity in the quality of education between the largely white systems in the suburbs and the largely poor and minority systems in the urban core, however, was created as much by tax politics as by economic forces.

Four decades after school segregation was ruled unconstitutional, America's schools remained, in practice, largely segregated. (Lloyd Wolf/U.S. Census Bureau)

School equity legal cases emerged as one of the new civil rights strategies of the 1990s. The intensity of emotions over schools was exemplified by the equity case in New Jersey and its political fallout. In 1990, the New Jersey Supreme Court ruled on a series of cases challenging New Jersey's system of school financing, which provided less funding to poor school districts than to rich ones. The New Jersey Supreme Court agreed with the plaintiffs and required the state to achieve parity in spending between richer and poorer districts. As unequal spending derived from divergent local property tax bases between poor and rich districts, parity entailed increasing the state's contribution to education—by raising taxes or redistributing existing revenues. Politics in New Jersey proceeded to pivot on taxation and education. The legislature raised income taxes to increase school funding, but voters were outraged. The new revenue that was raised to fund poor districts was instead redirected to reducing property and school taxes. The Democratic governor, Jim Florio, who defended progressive tax reform and the plan to equalize school funding, was ousted in 1993 by a Republican, Christine Whitman, who promised to cut the state income tax by 30 percent. The proponents of school equity continued to press their case, and in 1998, the New Jersey Supreme Court struck down Whitman's school spending plan. The funding formula adopted in response reversed the difference, and by 2004, poorer districts in New Jersey were receiving more funding than richer districts. Similar battles were waged in other states. Nationally, by 2001, 20 states, including the populous ones of California, Texas, and New York, were found to have unconstitutional school financing systems. Another 8 states reformed their school finance system without court action. In 1997, poor districts nationally received on average $1,139 a student less than nonpoor districts, or close to half a million dollars for a typical elementary school. Although some progress in narrowing the gap was made at the height of the boom, the funding gap widened again in the subsequent business cycle (Cohen 2003; Brennan 2002).

The school equity cases point to a fundamental fact of American education at the end of the 20th century: the difference in quality between good schools and bad schools was becoming magnified. The search for good schools became the driving concern for parents of school-aged children, regardless of class, race, or ethnicity. Those who could afford to do so moved out of poorly performing school districts into better ones or placed their children in private schools. By the end of the decade, one out of nine American children attended a private school, most commonly one run by a religious group. Those who could not afford to flee bad public schools supported various kinds of change—forming charter and magnet schools, instituting standardized testing, returning to a traditional curriculum, requiring students to wear uniforms, allowing parents to choose their child's school, revamping the governing structure of school systems, and providing vouchers for private school tuition. By the end of the decade, many of these experiments had been tried, but the crisis of schools and education had not been solved.

BIOGRAPHIES

Eli Broad, 1933–

Real Estate and Housing Developer, Philanthropist

Eli Broad made billions of dollars as a businessman and then attracted public attention for spending his wealth as an art collector and a philanthropist. Three years after earning his undergraduate degree in 1954, Eli Broad founded a Detroit construction company that would provide his first million dollars by 1960. Kaufman & Broad became one of the largest homebuilders in the nation. In 1971, Broad moved into the insurance industry, purchasing Sun Life Insurance in 1971 and Coastal States Corporation in 1981. In 1989, Broad divided Kaufman & Broad's business by taking insurance, annuity, and financial services operations and forming a new company, SunAmerica Inc., which he headed. He stepped down from Kaufman & Broad's chairmanship in 1993 although he remained the company's biggest shareholder. He engineered the acquisition of SunAmerica by American International Group (AIG) in 1999 and took a seat on AIG SunAmerica's board while continuing to run SunAmerica until he retired as chief executive officer in 2000. In the 1990s, he was among the richest men in America and was known for his philanthropic projects done on a scale similar to the Gilded Age titans of industry of the previous century. In Los Angeles, he became a formidable figure in reshaping the city's cultural and educational institutions because of the leverage of his philanthropy.

Bernard Ebbers, 1941–

Telecommunications Corporate Executive

Bernard Ebbers was the founder of the telecommunications giant WorldCom, which in 2002 became the largest bankruptcy in U.S. history. Ebbers, who was born in Canada and moved as a youth to the United States, went into the long-distance telephone business in 1983. Before that, he had worked as a milkman, basketball coach, and motel owner. Ebbers's company, based in Mississipi, went on a massive acquisitions spree between 1995 and 2000. In 1997, soon after the passage of the Telecommunications Act, WorldCom took over MCI Communications, the number two telephone company in the United States. The acquisition, which cost $37 billion, was the largest ever in U.S. history. Ebbers, dubbed the Telecom Cowboy, was celebrated as an emblem of the fabulous economic opportunities in the new communications landscape of the dot-com age and the unlikely entrepreneurs leading the New Era. Forbes calculated his personal fortune at $1.4 billion in 1999.

In 2000, after the U.S. government blocked WorldCom's attempt to acquire Sprint Communications on antitrust grounds, the company began to report losses. In the summer of 2002, reports of accounting irregularities began to pour out, and in July, the company filed for bankruptcy. Investigations revealed an $11 billion accounting fraud, and in 2004, Ebbers was charged with conspiracy and fraud related to the accounting scandal. In 2005, Ebbers was convicted and sentenced to 25 years in federal prison. He entered federal prison in 2006.

Marian Wright Edelman, 1939–

Child Welfare Advocate

Marian Wright Edelman was one of the nation's leading advocates for the rights and interests of disadvantaged children. Her activism began in the civil rights movement of the 1960s. In law school, she served on the executive committee of the Student Nonviolent Organizing Committee from 1961 to 1963. After earning her law degree, she went to work with the NAACP Legal Defense and Education Fund in Mississippi, and she became the first African American woman admitted to the Mississippi bar. In 1968, she moved to Washington, D.C., to serve as legal counsel for Martin Luther King Jr.'s Poor People's Campaign. After his assassination, she decided she could be more effective as a political advocate than as a practicing lawyer, and in 1968, she founded the Children's Defense Fund (originally called the Washington Research Project). Edelman promoted federal and state legislation aimed at improving the lives of America's poor children and protecting their interests. Sen. Edward Kennedy once dubbed her the "101st Senator," acknowledging her powerful practical and moral influence on social policy. Edelman, a liberal with roots in the South and intimate knowledge of the region's racial inequities, was close to Hillary and Bill Clinton and served as an informal advisor on social policy to the Clintons. Her husband, Peter Edelman—also a specialist on poverty and social policy—served in the Clinton administration. He resigned in protest over Clinton's signing of welfare reform. In 2000, President Clinton awarded Marian Wright Edelman the Presidential Medal of Freedom, the highest honor the national government gives to civilians.

Marian Wright Edelman. (Centers for Disease Control and Prevention)

Jackie Goldberg, 1945–

Activist and Politician, Author of
Landmark Los Angeles Living-Wage Law

Jackie Goldberg had been politically active since her college days, when she was a leader in the Berkeley Free Speech Movement in 1964. She started her professional life as a high school teacher in Los Angeles. After 18 years of teaching and community activism, she won election to the city's school board and served two terms on the board in the 1980s. In 1993, she won election to the Los Angeles City Council, serving as the first openly lesbian councilmember. She spearheaded many initiatives designed to address the struggles facing the city's working-class and low-income residents. She sponsored and won gun-control legislation to ban "Saturday Night Special" handguns. She authored the city's Living Wage Ordinance, the second living-wage law passed in the nation. In 2000, she won election to the California State Assembly.

Earvin "Magic" Johnson, 1959–

Professional Basketball Player, HIV/AIDS Educator
and Philanthropist, Entrepreneur

The Los Angeles Lakers' Earvin Johnson Jr. earned the nickname "Magic" for his command of professional basketball's courts, but he got a different kind of national attention in 1991 when he revealed that he had been infected with the HIV virus. At that time, Johnson, who had been the first overall pick in the National Basketball Association's 1979 draft, retired while holding the record for all-time assists—10,141, a record that has subsequently been broken twice. Johnson, who says most people expected him to die within a year of his diagnosis, had a sports comeback, when he played on the 1992 U.S. Olympic team and with the Lakers for two brief stints during the 1990s. Since 1991, Johnson's reputation has transcended the one he made for himself in sports. In his hometown of Los Angeles, he emerged as a senior statesmen, widely respected for his entrepreneurial acumen, economic investment, and philanthropic activities in the African American community, and his political involvement in the Democratic party. He gained national and international recognition in the 1990s for his advocacy to raise awareness of the realities of HIV. Speaking at churches, schools, and health care facilities, he has spread the word that a diagnosis of HIV infection need not be a death sentence, and he has sought to raise awareness about behavioral changes that can lower the danger of contracting HIV. Johnson's public advocacy on AIDS played a very important part in the transformation of American public opinion about the disease. Johnson is the author of two books in 1992, an autobiography *My Life,* and *What You Can Do to Avoid AIDS*.

Kevin P. Phillips, 1940–

Author, Former Republican Strategist, Critic of Inequality

Kevin P. Phillips, a prolific writer and keen social analyst, was one of America's leading voices in the 1990s denouncing the nation's growing inequality and its toll on the middle class. In 1990, Phillips published *The Politics of Rich and Poor: Wealth and the American Electorate in the Reagan Aftermath*. He combined statistical analysis—presented as "plutographics"—and moral criticism to document how the rich had gotten richer and the poor poorer during the Reagan years. He issued a rallying cry for a new a populist revolt. The work was surprising and ironic, as Phillips was widely credited with crafting the Republicans' "Southern Strategy" in 1968, which had enabled Republicans to win the presidency in all but one election since that time, and was considered a leading theorist of the New Right. His work of the 1990s, however, showed that Phillips was a classic American populist, and the break with Republicans suggested in the 1990 book did not presage an embrace of Democrats (Kazin 1998). *Boiling Point: Republicans, Democrats, and the Decline of Middle Class Prosperity* (1993) and *Arrogant Capital: Washington, Wall Street, and the Frustration of American Politics* (1994) excoriated both parties. The latter argued that the political gridlock of the 1990s reflected a quiet seizure of power by lawyers, lobbyists, and special-interest groups. He contended that these groups had taken over control of the federal government, making it almost impossible for ordinary Americans to have an impact on the nation's leadership. His influential *Wealth and Democracy* (2002) turned to history in its effort to explain social inequality in the New Economy. "It is hard to imagine that the excesses" of the 1990s, Phillips wrote, "could have developed so destructively if so much knowledge of the past had not slipped away in stock market and 'new era' triumphalism" (Phillips 2002, vii).

William Julius Wilson, 1935–

Sociologist

Sociologist William Julius Wilson was a leading and controversial analyst of race and poverty. By combining elements of the liberal and conservative theories of poverty, he found himself under attack from every direction. His signature thesis on the relationship between class and race was articulated in a 1973 book, *The Declining Significance of Race: Blacks and Changing American Institutions*. He argued that middle-class African Americans faced increasing opportunities but that poverty for others had become a stronger barrier to success than racism. Liberals and some civil rights leaders were concerned that Wilson's theory would reinforce conservative efforts to blame poverty on the poor and further undermine the social safety net. In his 1987 book, *The Truly Disadvantaged: The Inner City, the Underclass, and Public Policy,* Wilson attempted to clarify his position as a liberal, contending that the flight of successful African Americans from urban ghettoes had robbed slum areas of the bedrock principles that made their escape possible. To resolve that problem, he proposed a government investment in the social and economic rebirth of poverty-stricken areas in American cities. To guide the way, Wilson launched the Urban Poverty and Family Life Study, an ethnographic study of 2,500 impoverished Chicagoans and 190 local employers. The study resulted in 21 scholarly papers delivered at the University of Chicago, where Wilson then taught, in 1991. During the 1992 presidential campaign, Wilson acted as an advisor to Bill Clinton and continued to serve as a Clinton advisor after he was elected. However, Wilson expressed disappointment when Clinton signed the controversial welfare reform bill in 1996. He believed the legislation could have devastating effects on many mothers within the welfare system. Wilson wrote yet another controversial book in 1996. *When Work Disappears: The World of the New Urban Poor* asserted that widespread unemployment triggered deviant behavior among residents in urban ghettoes. Wilson, who has taught at the University of Massachusetts as well as the University of Chicago, is currently on the faculty of the John F. Kennedy School of Government at Harvard University.

REFERENCES AND FURTHER READINGS

Anderson, Sarah, John Cavanagh, Chuck Collins, Chris Hartman, and Felice Yeskel. 2000. "Executive Excess 2000." In *CEO Compensation Survey*. Washington, DC: Institute for Policy Studies and United for a Fair Economy.

Anderson, Sarah, John Cavanagh, Chris Hartman, and Betsy Leondar-Wright. 2001. "Executive Excess 2001." In *CEO Compensation Survey*. Washington, DC: Institute for Policy Studies and United for a Fair Economy.

Bennefield, Robert L. 2003. "Home Values: 2000." In *Census 2000 Brief*. Washington, DC: U.S. Census Bureau.

BLS. "Employment, Hours, and Earnings." Bureau of Labor Statistics, U.S. Department of Labor.

Bonnette, Robert. 2003. "Housing Costs of Renters: 2000." In *Census 2000 Brief*. Washington, DC: U.S. Census Bureau.

Brennan, J., ed. 2002. *The Funding Gap*. Washington, DC: The Education Trust.

Brooks, David. 2001. *Bobos in Paradise: The New Upper Class and How They Got There*. New York: Simon & Schuster.

Burt, Martha. 2001. "What Will It Take to End Homelessness?" In *Issue Brief*. Washington, DC: Urban Institute.

Cassidy, John. 2006. "Relatively Deprived." *The New Yorker,* April 3, 42–47.

Cohen, Lizabeth. 2003. *A Consumers' Republic: The Politics of Mass Consumption in Postwar America.* New York: Knopf.

Collins, Karen S., Allyson Hall, and Charlotte Neuhaus. 1999. *U.S. Minority Health: A Chartbook.* New York: The Commonwealth Fund.

Davis, Martha. 1994. "Women on the Move: Civilian Responses to the War on Poor Women." *Social Justice* 21 (1): 102–109.

DeParle, Jason. 2004. *American Dream: Three Women, Ten Kids, and a Nation's Drive to End Welfare.* New York: Viking.

EPI. 2001. "Poverty and Family Budgets." In *Issue Guide.* Washington, DC: Economic Policy Institute.

EPI. 2006. *Datazone.* Economic Policy Institute. http://www.epinet.org/content .cfm/datazone_dznational.

Frank, Robert H. 2000. *Luxury Fever: Money and Happiness in an Era of Excess.* Princeton, NJ: Princeton University Press.

Haydamack, Brent, Daniel Flaming, Economic Roundtable, and Pascale Joassart. 2005. *Hopeful Workers, Marginal Jobs: LA's Off-the-Books Labor Force.* Los Angeles: Economic Roundtable.

Henwood, Doug. 2005. *After the New Economy.* New York: New Press.

Herrnstein, Richard J., and Charles A. Murray. 1994. *The Bell Curve: Intelligence and Class Structure in American Life.* New York: Free Press.

Jencks, Christopher. 2005a. "1990: Welfare Then and Now." *The American Prospect,* June 6.

Jencks, Christopher. 2005b. "What Happened to Welfare?" *New York Review of Books* (December 15). 52 (20): 76–86.

Katz, Michael B. 2001. *The Price of Citizenship: Redefining America's Welfare State.* New York: Metropolitan Books.

Kazin, Michael. 1998. *The Populist Persuasion: An American History.* Ithaca, NY: Cornell University Press.

Kornbluh, Felicia. 1996. "Feminists and the Welfare Debate: Too Little? Too Late?" *Dollars & Sense* no. 208: 24–28.

Kozol, Jonathan. 2000. *Ordinary Resurrections: Children in the Years of Hope.* New York: Crown Publishers.

Krugman, Paul R. 2003. *The Great Unraveling: Losing Our Way in the New Century.* New York: W. W. Norton.

Mishel, Lawrence R., Jared Bernstein, Sylvia Allegretto, and Economic Policy Institute. 2005. *The State of Working America, 2004/2005.* Ithaca, NY: Cornell University Press.

Murray, Charles A. 1984. *Losing Ground: American Social Policy, 1950–1980.* New York: Basic Books.

Murray, Charles A. 1990. "The Underclass Revisited." In *Papers and Studies.* Washington, D.C.: American Enterprise Institute. http://www.aei.org/publications/pubID.14891/pub_detail.asp.

National Center for Health. 2005. "Health, United States, Statistics, 2005: With Chartbook on Trends in the Health of Americans." Hyattsville, Maryland.

NCES. 1996. *NAEP 1994, Trends in Academic Progress: Achievement of U.S. Students in Science, 1969 to 1994, Mathematics, 1973 to 1994, Reading, 1971 to 1994, Writing, 1984 to 1994.* Jay R. Campbell et al., ed. Washington, D.C.: National Center for Education Statistics, Government Printing Office.

NCES. 2003. *Digest of Education Statistics, 2003.* Washington, DC: National Center for Education Statistics, U.S. Department of Education.

New York Times. 1996. "The Downsizing of America." Series March 3–March 9 and December 29. New York: Times Books.

Phillips, Kevin P. 2002. *Wealth and Democracy: A Political History of the American Rich.* New York: Broadway Books.

Pollin, Robert. 2003. *Contours of Descent: U.S. Economic Fractures and the Landscape of Global Austerity.* London: Verso.

Pollin, Robert, and Stephanie Luce. 1998. *The Living Wage: Building a Fair Economy.* New York: New Press.

Pollitt, Katha. 1994. "Subject to Debate." *The Nation* 259 (2): 45.

Porter, Eduarado. 2005. "Reinventing the Mill." *New York Times,* October 22.

Schor, Juliet. 1998. *The Overspent American: Upscaling, Downshifting, and the New Consumer.* New York: Basic Books.

Silverstein, Michael J., and Neil Fiske. 2003. *Trading Up: The New American Luxury.* New York: Portfolio (Penguin Group).

Sorkin, Andrew R. 2005. "Ex-Tyco Officers Get 8 to 25 Years." *New York Times,* September 20, A1(C8).

Twitchell, James B. 2002. *Living it Up: Our Love Affair with Luxury.* New York: Columbia University Press.

United Way. 2003. "A Tale of Two Cities." In *State of the County.* Los Angeles: United Way. http://www.unitedwayla.com/pfdfiles/2003_tale_two_cites.pdf.

Woodward, Bob. 2000. *Maestro: Greenspan's Fed and the American Boom.* New York: Simon & Schuster.

Woodward, Jeanne, and Bonnie Damon. 2001. "Housing Characteristics: 2000." In *Census 2000 Brief.* Washington, DC: U.S. Census Bureau.

Social Movements

OVERVIEW

The social movements of the 1990s traced their lineage to the new social movements of the 1960s. Of course, by 1990, the New Left and New Right were not so new anymore. Rather, they had come of age and now faced questions about identity and purpose. Was it possible to preserve the élan of youth? What might be lost in the move from grassroots voluntarism to formal institutions? What kinds of compromises were legitimate in the move from margin to mainstream? How could they appeal to youth, whose identities had been forged in the post-1960s world? In short, what did it mean to be a mature "new" social movement?

In 2005, at the beginning of George W. Bush's second term in office, and before any histories had been written of the 1990s, many Americans assumed that the Right had been on a steady, inexorable ascent to power since the 1980s. By this logic, in the 1990s, the Right had triumphed over the Left. Such a conclusion was historically inaccurate, and caution needs to be applied to the study of social movements in America's transitional decade.

Of the two most successful movements of the 1990s, one was of the Left and one was of the Right. These movements, the gay and lesbian movement and conservatism, shared many characteristics with each other. They were movements of minorities; they claimed the greatest number of fervent activists; they articulated enormously ambitious goals to recast American society; and they devised a strategic plan to accomplish their goals. Both movements were founded on a broad vision of society, not a "single issue."

The gay and lesbian movement accomplished more in the 1990s for the acceptance of homosexuals in American society than ever before; it also made the greatest advance, on every level, of all social movements of the 1990s. It was, without exaggeration, the "Gay Nineties." Gay and lesbian activists urged Americans to reconsider their prejudice against homosexuality, and millions of heterosexual Americans listened. America experienced a sea change in its view of homosexuals over the course of the 1990s. The change in opinion paid high dividends for the legal rights, political power, and social position of gays and lesbians. This chapter begins with an examination of the gay and lesbian movement.

The Right—the conservative movement—fell and rose and fell again during the 1990s. But it succeeded in forging a powerful minority position in American society and in the Republican Party. In 1992, after George H. W. Bush's electoral defeat, and again in 1998, after the defeat of congressional Republicans, observers from all points on the political spectrum were writing the Right's obituary. The fall from national political power, however, masked the enormous headway the Right made organizing during the decade. The 1990s was a decade of movement building by conservatives toward a very concrete goal: control of the Republican Party and the national government. New Right leaders worked hard to expand the voting base of rank-and-file conservatives, primarily by organizing traditionalist evangelical Christians. Conservative businessmen devoted their capital to building movement institutions and media outlets. Conservative intellectuals energetically worked to rewrite the nation's political narrative and gain a hearing for their views. On the eve of the millennium, conservatives had built a movement and organized a constituency with the power to dictate terms to the Republican Party. They were thus poised to enact their specific goals through the government, should Republicans win political power. The second section of this chapter explores the social movement history of conservatives and the Right in the 1990s.

As both the gay movement and the conservative movement attested, one of the most profound changes of the 1960s was in sexuality and gender roles. The feminist movement had been largely responsible for raising these matters as public concerns. The following section in this chapter examines the state of the feminist movement in the 1990s. Like other liberal and Left movements, feminism became institutionally stronger in the 1990s, but grassroots activism atrophied. Nevertheless, because feminists were one of the prime targets of the culture wars, large feminist organizations preserved more of the social movement spirit than others in the liberal camp, and young women initiated a new phase of feminist activism.

While established liberal and Left organizations blocked many conservative initiatives from being enacted, they tended to lack the dynamism they once had. The section "Liberal Movements in Transition" examines three of the most important historic liberal-Left movements of the 1990s: the labor movement, environmentalism, and new tendencies in black America in the post–civil rights generation. Although public opinion polls showed broad support for workers' rights, environmentalism, and racial equality, the movements for these causes made only halting gains during the 1990s.

The last topic in this chapter explores the fleeting phenomenon of the "men's movement." At its inception, the movement seemed to portend a new social movement with broad and profound appeal, but it turned out to be a passing fad. It was nevertheless a revealing sign of the times.

The history of social movements in the 1990s is at once straightforward as well as an unsolved mystery. Although the 1990s witnessed substantial social movement activity, not a single significant new social movement was birthed in the decade. The 1990s was unique in this regard in 20th-century American history; in every other decade, a new movement emerged or a young movement achieved fantastic success. In the 1990s, two fledging movements—the men's movement and the antiglobalization movement—momentarily held out the possibility of something new, but each foundered in its own way and for its own reasons. Why were the 1990s distinctive? Were Americans too busy clinging to past victories and wrapping up old business—of New Right versus New Left, of sexual revolution and reaction, of labor versus capital—to forge something new? Or did the dearth of new movements suggest a deeper exhaustion with the public and civic sphere? I would speculate that the answer lies in the combined effects of Americans' infatuation with new technology, their New Economy utopianism, and their political disaffection. More time and distance from the events is needed, however, before any more definitive answer can be ventured.

TIMELINE

1990   The Los Angeles immigrant janitors' strike ends in victory for the Service Employees' International Union's (SEIU) Justice for Janitors national campaign.

1991   The "Stonewall West" demonstrations in California protest the governor's veto of gay civil rights legislation.

1992   Presidential candidate Bill Clinton gives a landmark political speech endorsing gay rights.

Christian Coalition candidates win 40 percent of the 500 local school board elections they entered.

The largest-ever abortion rights demonstration is held on the mall in Washington, D.C.

A record number of women are elected to national political office.

Colorado passes an amendment that forbids state and local governments from adopting measures to protect homosexuals from any kind of discrimination.

1993   Lesbian, Gay, Bisexual, Transgender (LGBT) March on Washington is held on the National Mall in Washington, D.C., the largest-ever gay rights demonstration.

Clinton issues controversial policy on gays in the military, abandoning his campaign pledge.

Operation Rescue conducts a seven-city antiabortion campaign.

1994   Freedom of Access to Clinic Entrances Act (FACE) and Violence Against Women Act (VAWA) are passed.

Republicans win control of Congress and set out to enact policies favored by the conservative movement.

The first living-wage law is passed in Baltimore.

1995   The Million Man March is held on the National Mall in Washington, D.C.

Union reformer John Sweeney is elected president of the AFL-CIO.

Fox News and *Weekly Standard* are launched.

1996   Labor, feminists, civil right leaders, and other progressives rally to support Clinton's reelection, despite opposition to his policies.

The Union Summer initiative is launched to train college students to become union organizers.

An increase in the minimum wage is legislated after substantial lobbying by the revived labor movement.

1997   The Teamsters Union launches a successful nationwide strike against United Parcel Service (UPS).

Fast-track trade legislation is defeated by labor lobbying.

Promise Keepers' "Stand in the Gap" rally takes place in Washington, D.C.

The Million Women March takes place to protest welfare reform.

1998   Fast-track legislation is defeated for a second year in a row.

1999   Labor, antiglobalization youth activists, and environmentalists come together in the "Battle for Seattle" protests at the meeting of the World Trade Organization (November).

THE GAY NINETIES

For the gay and lesbian movement, the decade was "The Gay Nineties." Gays and lesbians made huge strides in achieving their goals. Beginning the decade in the midst of the AIDS crisis and mass movement activism, gays and lesbians successfully established the idea that the movement was the next frontier of America's historic civil rights tradition, and that legal discrimination had to go. By the middle of the 1990s, the movement had redefined the goals of gays and lesbians, pushing beyond an antidiscrimination agenda to insist on full inclusion in American society. It was a more difficult case to make to a still-reluctant American public, and the effort intensified the backlash from the religious right. Nevertheless, on balance, in the 1990s the movement advanced more than it was held back by hostile reaction.

The historian John D'Emilio has sought to make sense of the movement's fitful advances over the last three decades by distinguishing between phases of "leaping" and "creeping." The movement's "third leap forward" occurred between the 1987 and 1993 Marches on Washington. In the midst of the AIDS crisis, gays and lesbians strengthened their community institutions, reoriented public opinion, and won resources to stem the AIDS crisis. One of the most important developments in this phase was to bring lesbians and gay men together. Previously lesbians had been concentrated in the feminist movement while the gay liberation movement was a predominantly male affair. The AIDS crisis brought to the movement new gay men, from well-off professionals to working-class African American and Hispanic men, many of whom had been closeted before the disease hit and had felt no need to participate in the movement. Lesbian feminists brought the skills and analysis of political organizers. The new contingent of professional gay men brought funding, connections, and knowledge about how to work inside the halls of power; African American and Hispanic gay men forced a new awareness to issues of race and class. It was an era of militancy and of mass social movement.

The central principle and strategy of the gay and lesbian movement through the early 1990s was to increase visibility. To shift Americans from their deep-seated prejudice against homosexuals, the movement argued, gays and lesbians needed to come out of the closet. When heterosexual Americans learned that their friends, co-workers, relatives, or co-congregants were gay, personal bonds would start to erode unthinking prejudice. October 11 was celebrated as national "Coming Out Day"—the day marked the first viewing of the AIDS quilt

Parents, Families and Friends of Lesbians and Gays (PFLAG) is a national organization that supports the health and well-being of gay people. (PhotoDisc, Inc.)

in Washington and the day of the 1988 march. When celebrities such as tennis star Martina Navratilova and singer Melissa Etheridge came out, the media took notice. But, more important, individual acts of coming out by ordinary gays and lesbians sparked personal transformations in many heterosexual Americans.

A turning point for the movement occurred around 1992 and 1993. A key moment in that shift occurred during the 1992 presidential campaign, as candidate Bill Clinton publicly and unequivocally endorsed gay rights as a new civil rights struggle. As Clinton used his bully pulpit, and gays and lesbians rallied to his campaign, the media completed the shift already under way in its treatment of homosexuality. Once portrayed as freaks and misfits, gays and lesbians were now covered as the family next door. Key to movement success in this phase was the strategic plan launched at the 1989 War Conference. Bringing together 200 national leaders in the gay and lesbian movement, the meeting charted a 10-year plan. It was, in a way, a codification of the insider–outsider strategy being forged in the day-to-day struggle. The plan included mass mobilization and political lobbying, cultural activity, and a sophisticated media strategy.

If the period from 1987 to 1993 was one of "leaping," after Clinton's election and the 1993 March on Washington, the gay and lesbian movement went into a "creeping" phase. One important cause of the decline in social movement militancy was the changing nature of AIDS. The invention of drugs to suppress HIV

Clinton's May 17, 1992, Speech

When presidential candidate Bill Clinton spoke about gays at a Los Angeles fundraiser on May 17, 1992, gays and lesbians were stunned and ecstatic. No straight American politician had ever gone so far in expressing support for gay rights and in extending social acceptance to their gay and lesbian fellow citizens. Clinton no less than defined the cause as one in the eminent civil rights tradition and the struggle to do so as a moral cause. Even the AIDS crisis had done little to erode the deep hostility (or fear) among politicians toward demonstrating support for gays or gay causes. By all accounts, Clinton expressed his true sentiments that night when he said if he had it in his power to end the plague of AIDS, he would gladly renounce his political ambitions. He thereby won a devoted constituency for his 1992 presidential bid. Gays donated $3 million to his campaign, the movement put its considerable expertise at organizing at his disposal, and three-quarters of gays and lesbians voted for him (Kirp 1996).

Clinton brought gay and lesbian leaders into his administration, yet he disappointed the movement and many activists when he retreated on his campaign pledge that gays would be able to serve openly in the armed services. Other acts during his presidency angered them as well, yet overall the movement advanced. Some activists became bitterly disappointed in Clinton. Others thought that they might have overreached, and viewed Clinton's political compromises as unfortunate but necessary. In historical perspective, the example Clinton set for politicians on the night of May 17 had a deeper and more long-lasting impact on American politics and cultural life than did the misstep over gays in the military (Graff 2002).

changed AIDS from a death sentence to a manageable, though still terrible, disease. The rest of the 1990s was one of incremental yet significant change for gays and lesbians, accomplished more by working inside government and business and negotiation than by protest. The new issues were civil unions, gay marriage, and family rights for homosexual couples and their children (D'Emilio 2000; Osborn 2006).

"Stonewall West," California, 1991

California gays and lesbians had long sought as their highest priority a statewide prohibition against discrimination on the basis of sexual orientation. In 1991, the California state legislature finally passed a bill, AB101, to prohibit discrimination in housing and employment. Gov. Pete Wilson had assured Californian gays that he supported antidiscrimination legislation when he had run for office in 1990; however, he vetoed the bill in September 1991.

Outing

The significance attached in the gay and lesbian movement to "coming out" manifested itself briefly in the phenomenon of "outing." Michelangelo Signorile of ACT UP and the magazine *Outweek* was a leading pioneer in the short-lived movement. In March 1990, he wrote a cover story for *Outweek* outing the business tycoon Malcolm Forbes. Within several months, the mainstream and tabloid press were covering the phenomenon of outing itself. According to its proponents, the object of outing, at least initially, was to highlight the hypocrisy of influential closeted gays who often advanced an antigay agenda. The classic case of this kind of political outing was Signorile's exposure that Pete Williams, the Pentagon spokesman during the Persian Gulf War, was gay, was known to many throughout Washington to be gay, and was in the official position of defending the military's ban on homosexuals at a time when the military was expelling dozens of gays and lesbians. When the story about the Pentagon spokesman broke in August 1991 in *The Advocate,* outing became a subject of national debate.

Within the gay and lesbian community, the debate raged as well, for there were many who disagreed with the tactics of the outers. Some argued that the action was justified when it was directed at those who used their positions of power to perpetuate discrimination and hostility toward gays and lesbians. Immersed in the culture wars and the AIDS crisis, gay activists began revealing the identity of closeted Republican political insiders who effectively condoned the hostile policies of the Reagan and Bush administrations. The practice was then extended to Hollywood celebrities and moguls, with the rationale that they should be using their resources and public credibility to aid their dying brethren. After the coinage of the slogan "silence = death" by ACT UP, some argued from that premise that those with special access to the media had a unique responsibility to be forthcoming about their sexuality. Soon, the practice was being deployed indiscriminately, to settle internal scores within the movement or in political contests, even when the protagonists were liberals.

As the gay and lesbian community went through some vicious internal conflict over outing, condemnation from outside the community became more pronounced. The practice quickly fizzled and disappeared from the headlines of the mainstream press. Its defenders insisted, in retrospect, that outing had been a necessary step for breaking open the closet for all gay Americans. Writing in the preface of *Queer in America,* his account of the outing phenomenon within the larger context of radical gay activism and the AIDS crisis, Signorile explained, "I consider truthful discussion of the lives of homosexual public figures as legitimate and significant in the larger aim to give courage to millions of gay people who stay in the closet out of fear and shame: they are not as alone as a homophobic America would have them believe" (Signorile 1993, 35).

The day of Wilson's veto, spontaneous demonstrations erupted in Los Angeles, San Francisco, and Sacramento. Demonstrations, protests, and civil disobedience lasted several weeks and would become known to some West Coast activists as "Stonewall West."

The demonstrations in Los Angeles began in the neighborhood of West Hollywood, home to a large gay male community. A Queer Nation activist had mounted a hunger strike to pressure Wilson to sign the bill. He had set up a tent at a busy intersection, and his place of vigil had become a gathering place for activists. On September 30, the day Wilson vetoed the bill, the gathering turned into a protest. Around the time of the evening rush hour, people started pouring into the streets chanting "We're here, we're queer, get used to it," and calling "out of the gyms and into the streets." One participant described in his diary the scene that night:

> There are perhaps four hundred of us, a motley crowd that ranges from young activists in ACT UP and Queer Nation T-shirts to white-haired Morris Kight, who marched down Hollywood Boulevard twenty years ago in the first gay pride parade in Los Angeles. . . . Two emotions, excitement and fury, carry the crowd forward into the warm autumn night. At the intersection of Santa Monica and San Vicente Boulevard we stop. For a moment it seems no one knows what to do, and then people begin sitting down in the street. Soon we are all sitting, while the sheriffs move at the edge of the crowd, trying to get us back on our feet. Someone begins to chant "our streets, our streets," and it passes through the crowd, until we are all shouting at the grim-faced sheriffs at the top of our lungs, "our streets, our streets, our streets." (Nava and Dawidoff 1994, 245)

While the first night could be deemed a spontaneous protest, after that, the nightly demonstrations were organized by the Los Angeles Gay and Lesbian Center, which left messages on its phone service each day with the location of the night's event. Some nights, 5,000 people were on the streets, covering 10 miles by foot in the city of the automobile. Starting as a protest over Wilson's veto, the demonstrations grew into a broader affirmation of the civil rights of gays and lesbians. They have been remembered since then as a formative moment in the gay and lesbian movement in Los Angeles (Nava and Dawidoff 1994).

1993 March on Washington for Lesbian, Gay, and Bisexual Rights and Liberation

Approximately 1 million people participated in the March on Washington for Lesbian, Gay, and Bisexual Rights and Liberation on April 25, 1993. It was the largest lesbian and gay demonstration ever mounted in the nation, and it attracted far more positive coverage from the mainstream media than any previous public

Gay marine stands with other participants at the 1993 March on Washington for Lesbian, Gay, and Bisexual Rights and Liberation. (Shepard Sherbell/Corbis)

demonstration by gay Americans. The March on Washington was in many ways the capstone of the period of intensive movement building that had commenced with the AIDS crisis and proceeded through the historic political mobilization around Clinton's campaign and election. The purpose of the march, consciously evoking the history of the 1963 March on Washington, was to build momentum for a national gay civil rights bill. Also high on the agenda were the end to the ban on gays in the military and funding for AIDS. A week before the march, President Clinton hosted a White House meeting with a delegation of gay and lesbian leaders, the first meeting ever between a sitting president and gay advocates. Festivities and actions took place in Washington throughout the weekend of the march. Gay veterans held a memorial service at the Lincoln Memorial, AIDS activists surrounded the Capitol in protest, and hundreds of couples participated in a wedding ceremony in front of the Internal Revenue Service. While march participants lobbied legislators who had been supportive of legislation, a handful of legislators came out during the meetings. Signifying the advance in the movement and the rapid change in public opinion, the participants represented the diversity of gay America, and the media treated the march as one in a long line of civil rights demonstrations.

CONSERVATIVES AND THE RIGHT

The conservative movement consolidated its institutions and constituency in the 1990s. As a political movement, conservatism was a coalition of overlapping but often conflicting interest groups and ideological tendencies. The conservative political movement of the 1990s included a wide range of philosophical tendencies—traditional conservatives, libertarians, neoconservatives, paleoconservatives, and the religious right. It encompassed individuals who were active on a specific single cause—such as gun rights, immigration restriction, abortion, property rights, or taxes—and the organizations that were advocates of these causes. As a social movement, however, the center of gravity within conservatism rested in two distinct blocs: the Christian Right and conservative intellectuals.

What made conservatism a social movement, not just a political force, was its mass constituency, composed of nearly 25 percent of Americans who were conservative evangelical Christians. (Another 15 percent of Americans were evangelicals, but of various political leanings other than conservative.) The new Christian Right bore similarities to other identity-based movements, most of which had grown out of the New Left of the 1960s. The Christian Right viewed themselves as a victimized and oppressed minority within America in a way similar to Left identity and civil rights movements. And like those other movements, there was a strong current of separatism. Christian conservatives believed that the moral decline of America brought on by liberalism and the New Left (not distinct in their view) required them to separate themselves from mainstream society if they were to preserve the sanctity and traditionalism of their own Christian families.

A wide array of conservative Christian social and cultural institutions flourished in the 1990s, offering to believers education, leisure activities, entertainment, and news. A new market niche of Christian pop music provided Christian teenagers the opportunity to be like other American teenagers while being shielded from the negative influences of youth culture. Their fathers worked out at gyms and joined bowling leagues held inside the new multiuse complexes built by megachurches. The Christian Broadcasting Network, with its flagship *700 Club* show reaching millions of viewers, provided wholesome entertainment, and a goad to political action, for evangelical families. From these multiple social spaces, Christian Right activists launched their fervent social and political campaigns.

While traditionalist, evangelical Christians provided the ground troops of conservatism, the power within the movement resided in the relationship forged between conservative political strategists, policy intellectuals, and those in American business who hoped to roll back the regulatory and social welfare programs of the government. Antigovernment, free market conservatives wanted to end government economic regulation and social welfare programs. Grover Norquist, head of Americans for Tax Reform, succinctly and memorably described the strategy of the free market wing of conservatism as a strategy to "starve the beast" of government (Liasson 2001). Conservatives witnessed that even Republicans had a difficult time eliminating government programs, and realized that they could accomplish the same goal by depriving the federal government of the money necessary to implement the programs. In one fell swoop, the federal regulatory bureaucracy and entitlement programs would shrink.

Most Americans who were not conservative were exposed to conservatism and learned of its vision and goals through the work of conservative media figures, journalists, pundits, and policy intellectuals. These individuals were self-consciously engaged in ideological work, both to bring the disparate voices of conservatism into harmony and to counter what they perceived to be the "liberal bias" in American society, culture, and politics. Supported by family foundations, corporations, and wealthy individuals, they possessed the resources to broadcast their views widely (Noble 2004). It would be a mistake, however, to attribute their visibility to money alone. They had long been convinced that public opinion was one of the most important battlegrounds of their struggle against liberalism. At the end of the century, the only leftist movement that attached any comparable significance to media work was the gay and lesbian movement. And, in the 20th century as a whole, only the progressive movement of the 1900s and 1910s matched the 1990s' conservatives attention to the cultivation of public opinion.

Conservatism nevertheless faced its own internal divisions. Anticommunism had once provided coherence to the many factions of old and new conservatives. The end of the Cold War removed that glue, and it is not surprising that conservatives were beset by internal conflicts in the first years after the end of the Cold War. The New Right, unlike the New Left, always nursed political ambitions and understood that victory required coordinated action and alliance. When Republicans retook Congress in 1994, Norquist started to convene a weekly meeting in Washington in which conservatives could talk to each other and work out their differences in private. Participants at the weekly meeting included representatives of the think tanks, lobbying organizations, and single-issue groups. Nevertheless, the differences among conservative factions were real. In the brief interlude between the end of the Cold War and September 11, 2001, conservatives looked for a unifying idea. After the steam went out of Gingrich's "Republican Revolution," they lamented among themselves the dangers of fragmentation, straying too far from their base, and the like (Scully 1997). They came closest to finding unity in their battle against the Clintons, who conservatives made into the symbol of all that had gone wrong with America since the 1960s.

The New Christian Right and Christian Education

Since the 1960s, Christian evangelicals of the New Right had targeted the secularism and religious pluralism of mainstream American culture as a threat to

Many Christian Right evangelicals chose to homeschool their children in the 1980s and 1990s. (iStockPhoto.com)

their Christian identity and their prerogatives as Christian parents. By the 1990s, schooling had become one of the central foci of the Christian Right social movement, as activists sought to inculcate Christian youth with "traditional values" and cordon them off from the corrupting influence of the public school system. Homeschooling and private Christian schooling proliferated among Christian Right evangelicals in the 1980s and 1990s. In the 1990s, activists won government approval for their separatist institutions (Bivins 2003).

Education became a key battleground for conservative Christians because that is where they believed that the identity and traditional belief system of evangelical and fundamentalist Christians was being subverted by liberal society. Christian parents objected to a "multicultural" curriculum covering the history and practices of other cultures and religions on the grounds that it fostered moral relativism. When schools allowed homosexuals to be teachers or made available books that treated homosexuality as a normal condition, they protested en masse at school board meetings. They lobbied for science educators to teach evolution as an unproven theory and include in the curriculum the alternative "intelligent design," the 1990s' version of creationism. They opposed sex education, incensed that the public schools were arrogating one of the essential roles of the traditional family. As Tim LaHaye, one of the most influential Christian Right leaders, argued in *The Battle for the Public Schools* (1983), American schools were teaching children "to be anti-God, antimoral, antifamily, anti–free enterprise and anti-American" (quoted in Bivins 2003, 226).

After various earlier forays over the past decade that attempted to convert the public schools to the Christian Right view, by the early 1990s, separation had become the preferred strategy. Christian schools and homeschooling provided parents with a means to limit their children's exposure to ideas that challenged a fundamentalist Christian worldview. These alternative schools would be put at the service of cultivating good Christians and traditional family values; curricula and textbooks promoting Christian views were written and disseminated by Christian Right publishers; organizations such as the National Center for Home Education were founded to monitor legislation and protect the rights of homeschooling Christians. The homeschooling mission and homeschooling curriculum was articulated in the "Twelve Spiritual Goals of Christian Parenting," which included "My child will be sure of his or her salvation." Christian children would experience a seamless unity between religious education and formal schooling, rather than the fundamental conflict they struggled against in secular public schools. One leader of the Christian homeschooling movement claimed that more than 700,000 children were being educated at home (Bivins 2003).

The potential political force represented by Christian Right families became evident by 1992. Success in creating a grassroots base and a national network of schools and homeschoolers allowed the Christian Right to reenter the political contest for control of public education from a position of greater strength. (They had lost a number of political and legal battles in the previous two decades.) In 1992, with assistance from the Christian Coalition, religious right candidates entered 500 local and state races—many of them for school boards—and won about 40 percent of them (Smolowe 1993). Historians debate whether the school board campaign was largely a political strategy of the right wing of the Republican Party, which had fallen from grace in the early 1990s, or whether it represented a genuine grassroots uprising from the base. Regardless, the Christian schooling movement became a formidable power. In 1994, state and regional homeschooling associations, assisted by Christian radio announcements, mobilized more than 500,000 individuals to call their representative in the House to demand a vote against an item within an education bill that they considered inimical to homeschoolers. As a result, the only vote cast in favor of the amendment was that of its original sponsor (Bivins 2003). The quest for school vouchers, which would provide taxpayer funds for private religious education, gained political momentum in the 1990s, as did a new movement to oppose the teaching of evolution in public schools.

Building Conservative Institutions

The New Right devoted effort to a multipronged strategy of long-term planning and institution building, and that focus and its fruits set the movement apart from most social movements of the 1990s. Conservative political action committees, lobbying groups, legal defense organizations, political opinion journalism, mass media outlets, foundations, and think tanks proliferated during the 1990s. Like the movement itself, there was great diversity. The libertarian Cato Institute and the fundamentalist Focus on the Family were very different kinds of institutions with essentially conflicting missions, yet within the conservative movement, they cooperated for the larger purpose of building conservative power. The ability of the New Right to rebound during the presidency of George W. Bush in the 2000s, after its political false starts and wanderings in the 1990s, was absolutely dependent on this strategic focus.

One of the most important types of institutions for the movement, considering the ultimate goal of converting conservative ideas and programs into practice, were think tanks. In the 1990s, the numbers of conservative think tanks increased, their budgets multiplied, and their geographic range expanded beyond the nation's capital into the states and local municipalities. According to a 1999 study, the top 20 conservative think tanks were projected to spend close to $1 billion over the course of the decade. Most of their funds came from tax-deductible donations from corporations, family foundations, and wealthy individuals.

The Heritage Foundation, established in 1973 with assistance from the Adolph Coors family foundation, set the organizational and strategic model for the conservative think tank. Under the same roof, they conducted policy research, ran public relations campaigns, mobilized constituents, and fed a steady stream of news and commentary to the media. Prohibited by federal tax law governing nonprofit organizations from engaging in formal lobbying, the think tanks nevertheless emerged as an influential force at the intersection of the conservative movement and Republican Party policy making. Heritage, the Cato Institute, the American Enterprise Institute, the Manhattan Institute, and the like attained significant influence over federal policy. Unlike the Christian Right's focus on social issues, most of the conservative think tanks devoted their attention to economic and fiscal issues. The primary common goal sought to lower taxes, reduce the role of government in the economy, and reduce funding for social welfare programs. Conservative think tanks were influential in the defeat of Clinton's health care reform, in winning welfare reform and telecommunications deregulation, and in defeating the Kyoto protocol to limit global warming. They also tried to reduce environmental regulation and privatize social security and Medicare, but to little avail (Noble 2004; Schaller and Rising 2002; Callahan 1999). If the conservative think tanks were not as successful in implementing their projects as they would have wished, given a divided government with a Democratic president at the helm, they nonetheless had a large hand in shaping the public debate on the issues. The antigovernment, free market logic uniting disparate policies—such as deficit reduction, tax cuts, cuts in social welfare spending, privatizing Medicaid and Social Security, and industry deregulation—was intellectually refined within the world of conservative think tanks, publicly disseminated

Richard Mellon Scaife:
Conservative Philanthropist

Over the course of 40 years, Richard Mellon Scaife, an heir of the Mellon family oil and banking fortune and owner of the *Pittsburgh Tribune* and other newspapers, donated over $600 million of his personal fortune to conservative causes. Heritage Foundation, the Cato Institute, the *American Spectator* magazine, and Accuracy in Media were a few of the organizations benefiting from his contributions. He served on the board of trustees of Heritage, the Hoover Institution, and Pepperdine University and was the director of the Pittsburgh World Affairs Council. According to *Washington Post* reporters Robert G. Kaiser and Ira Chinoy, "Scaife's philanthropy has had a disproportionate impact on the rise of the right. . . . His money has established or sustained activist think tanks that have created and marketed conservative ideas from welfare reform to enhanced missile defense; . . . organizations and publications that have nurtured American conservatism on American campuses; academic institutions that have employed and promoted the work of conservative intellectuals; watchdog groups that have critiqued and harassed media organizations and many more" (quoted in Johnson 2001, 261–62). Scaife gained public notoriety in the 1990s after several journalistic accounts of his role in planning and funding anti-Clinton initiatives, such as "The Arkansas Project" (of "troopergate"), the Independent Women's Forum, and the legal group assisting Paula Jones in her sexual harassment case against the president.

through their sophisticated public relations arms, and put at the disposal of Republican politicians through their government relations departments. The power of conservative think tanks derived not from a mass constituency but from their strategic approach to ideological work, which combined a commitment to intellectual production through the cultivation of institutions to support it and a savvy approach to the modern media.

Conservatives were active at every level of public opinion, from elite to culture to the mass news and entertainment media. Conservatives could be heard and seen 24 hours a day on popular local and national talk radio and cable news programs targeted to self-identified conservatives. Mainstream newspapers, magazines, and broadcast networks provided a forum for the conservative position to syndicated columnists such as George Will and Robert Novak and pundits such as Ann Coulter. Within the movement, resources were devoted to sustaining elite political opinion journals with tiny readerships, such as the *American Spectator,* the *National Review,* and the new *Weekly Standard.* The conservative opinion journals, in common with their liberalcounterparts, counted their readership in the thousands. The conservative ones, however, were connected to a broader infrastructure and, by comparison, were far more adept at gaining

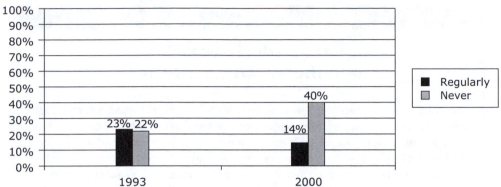

Figure 3.1 *Talk Radio: Percentage of American Public Who Listen Regularly or Never to Talk Radio. At the end of the 1980s and beginning of the 1990s, conservative talk radio seemed the new big thing in the mass media. Rush Limbaugh, the progenitor and symbol of right-wing talk radio, boasted an audience of 20 million in 1993. The phenomenon was short-lived. By the end of the 1990s, political talk radio had shrunk into a marginal force, and only a fraction of Americans continued to listen regularly to it. Cable TV, which took over the style and character of conservative talk radio, had replaced it as the primary medium of mass communication. The potential for the Internet to serve this function was as yet largely untapped. A few entrepreneurial individuals, most notoriously Matt Drudge of* The Drudge Report, *took advantage of the medium. Blogging, however, was definitively a post-millennium phenomenon.* Source: *Bennett 2002.*

a presence for their writers and ideas in the mainstream media to diffuse their ideas more broadly through American culture.

All of this intellectual and publicity activity was made possible by financing made available to movement institutions and individuals for the express purpose of building a lasting and sustainable conservative dominance in American culture, society, and government. Corporations with business before the national and state governments supported think tanks advancing the free market position. A few wealthy individuals and family foundations, such as Richard Mellon Scaife, the Bradley Foundation, the John M. Olin Foundation, the Koch Family Foundation, and the Adolph Coors Foundation, funded a wide variety of conservative causes and institutions.

FEMINISM

After the backlash against feminism in the 1980s, the 1990s was a decade that saw a feminist resurgence (Faludi 2005). Within the feminist movement, it was a time of both consolidation and creative ferment. Organizations founded in the 1960s and 1970s increased their membership, solidified their institutions, and

Rupert Murdoch, Fox News, and the *Weekly Standard*

The conservative strategy to win the hearts and minds of the American public was exemplified in Rupert Murdoch's launch of the cable Fox News Channel and the political opinion journal the *Weekly Standard.* Murdoch was head and majority owner of the News Corporation, one of the world's largest multimedia multinationals. In 1995, he launched the two media ventures, seeking to offer a conservative counterpoint to what he argued was the liberal bias of most media outlets.

Murdoch tapped William Kristol, son of neoconservative Irving Kristol and chief of staff to former vice president Dan Quayle, to be the editor of the *Weekly Standard,* promising him editorial independence. They gathered together conservative journalists Fred Barnes, John Podhoretz, David Brooks, Andrew Ferguson, and others, many of whom were then working as columnists in large national news outlets such as *Time* magazine. The *Weekly Standard* was created to be a conventional political opinion magazine, reporting and analyzing issues from a conservative position. (It also covered social commentary and the arts and culture.) The first issue appeared in September 1995. The *Weekly Standard* had about half the circulation of its liberal competitor, *The Nation,* but gained more circulation for its ideas by its writers frequent appearances on TV and radio commentary programs (Noble 2004; Kristol 2005).

Murdoch's ambitions for a cable news station were larger. In the 1980s, Ted Turner had launched CNN as a television equivalent to all-news radio and won sensational success. CNN nevertheless modeled itself on broadcast news standards in which reporting and opinion were kept distinct. Murdoch wanted to create a similar cable all-news presence but one explicitly conservative. In 1995, Murdoch hired Roger Ailes to head the network. Ailes and Murdoch shared the opinion that the mainstream media was dominated by liberals, and Ailes had experience in the worlds of partisan politics and television production. He had been a media consultant to Presidents Nixon, Reagan, and Bush, had produced Rush Limbaugh's television show, and had run the cable business channel CNBC. Fox News Channel first went on the air on October 7, 1996, with its signature slogan, "Fair and Balanced." The slogan and the format, modeled on conservative talk radio, were Ailes's ideas. Ailes attracted many of his former colleagues at CNBC to the new venture, who also chafed at the perceived liberal bias of other news organizations. In its first years on the air, Fox News trailed in the ratings behind its rivals CNN and MSNBC. That changed when Fox News jumped on the Monica Lewinsky–Bill Clinton scandal in early 1998 before the other networks covered it, and its ratings continued to soar with the station's coverage of impeachment. In those two stories, Fox connected with a conservative audience. By 2000, the network had finally broken even financially and cable systems carried it into 55 million homes. In 2001, it was running even or ahead of CNN in the morning and evening ratings (Auletta 2003).

Rupert Murdoch, Fox News, and the Weekly Standard, *Continued*

With the *Weekly Standard,* Murdoch helped nurture opinion-makers and intellectuals capable of elaborating the intellectual vision and political rationale underlying the conservative program. The project was clearly an important one to him; considered one of the savviest businessmen in the world, Murdoch was nevertheless willing to subsidize the roughly $1 million annual losses incurred by the magazine (Cassidy 2006). With Fox News, which inspired, inflamed, and marshaled the rank and file of the conservative movement through the new technologies of the mass media, Murdoch contributed to the political mobilization of the conservative social movement.

---

gained political influence in Washington. Young feminists, meanwhile, challenged their feminist forebears and proposed revised definitions of feminism. In American politics, feminist issues such as reproductive rights and sexual harassment loomed large, and feminists achieved a prominence in national debates as they were asked to elucidate the meaning and significance of the issues. Feminists, nonetheless, also found themselves on the defensive in the 1990s. Conservatives, among them a newly organized counterfeminist organization, launched a sophisticated assault on feminism and the woman's movement.

Political conflict surrounding two key feminist issues at the end of the 1980s and opening of the 1990s provoked a burst of activism, bringing new recruits to feminist organizations and fortifying the commitment of women who identified as feminists but who had not been activists. For every generation of American feminists, reproductive rights has been a critical issue. It briefly became the single most important issue in the woman's movement, as the Supreme Court appeared to be on the verge of overturning *Roe v. Wade.* Organizations that had been leaders in the struggle to establish and preserve a woman's right to abortion, such as the National Abortion and Reproductive Rights Action League (NARAL) and the National Organization of Women (NOW), grew as young women came to see their reproductive rights threatened. In April 1992, 500,000 people marched in Washington, D.C., to demonstrate their support for preserving a woman's right to abortion. The demonstration was the largest to have ever taken place in the capital. The issues of sexual violence and harassment have also been central to feminism, and in 1991 and 1992, the issues emerged as pressing ones for feminists with the Clarence Thomas–Anita Hill hearings and the revelation of a sexual molestation scandal within the Navy. Many women were outraged at the treatment of Hill by the Senate Judiciary Committee, which dismissed her testimony about being harassed by Thomas and attacked her character in the

Pro-choice rally, Washington, D.C., April 1992. (Corbis)

process. In 1992, the Navy acknowledged that female recruits had been sexually molested by male recruits at the Tailhook Convention the previous year.

The inherently political context of these episodes galvanized feminist leaders to dedicate more effort to political and legislative action. Following the Hill–Thomas case, feminist organizational leaders in Washington were able, as Patricia Ireland, the president of NOW, explained, to "turn public dialogue about sexual harassment and workplace issues into an important victory" (quoted in Frater and Fenoglio 2001). The Civil Rights Act of 1991 provided those alleging job discrimination the right to seek a jury trial and damage awards. Emily's List, a political action committee that funded women candidates for political office, increased from 3,000 to 24,000 members in the year between the hearings and the 1992 election. The national feminist organizations redoubled their voter education and mobilization efforts in the elections of 1992, with significant results. Two statistics stand out in particular: 28 percent of Republican women voted Democratic, and a record number of women were elected to the U.S. House and Senate. It was not excessively hyperbolic of a surprised press corps to dub it the "Year of the Woman." The political momentum continued, and in 1993 and 1994 with a friendly administration in power, effective lobbying by women's organizations helped gain passage of the Family and Medical Leave Act, the Freedom of Access to Clinic Entrances Act, and the Violence Against Women

Act. Ireland believed the latter represented "a conceptual breakthrough," for what it signaled about "our thinking as a culture about family violence" (quoted in Frater and Fenoglio 2001).

Feminism had, by the 1990s, become organizationally and politically institutionalized. The mainstream feminist movement could claim significant gains over the past two decades, such as a record number of women politicians in office, a sweeping revision of American family law, and broad popular acceptance of ideas that very recently had been deemed unthinkably radical. Social issues that feminists had brought into public consciousness roiled the cultural landscape and placed feminists in the middle of heated debates about the nature of American society. These were powerful signs that feminism had come of age; they attested to the success of the Second Wave feminists of the 1960s and 1970s.

Within the woman's movement, leaders of the Second Wave entered a phase of institution building and consolidation. Feminist scholars were at the cutting edge of social analysis as they transformed women's studies into a deeper exploration of gender in human society. Leaders of feminist organizations built the political clout of their organizations while also seeking to broaden their constituency and their focus. Meanwhile, a new generation of young feminists came of age, proclaiming themselves Third Wave feminists and creatively challenging inherited feminist ideas and roles. What did it mean to be a feminist?

From a more ambiguous and critical position, another challenge to feminism emerged from a group of women affiliated with the conservative movement and the 500-member-strong Independent Women's Forum (IWF) (Faludi 1996). These women and their male supporters repudiated the women's movement's claim to speak for American women, arguing instead that the so-called women's movement was out of touch with American women and represented a baneful influence on American society. "In this world, the biggest enemy to truth and common sense and logic is probably feminism," claimed the president of IWF, Anita Blair, in an interview (Goode 1997). Much of the energy of the feminist movement during the decade was consumed in staving off challenges from conservative groups. Feminism itself was contested terrain. And it was ground zero in the culture wars.

American Feminists and the United Nations Fourth World Conference on Women

American feminists in the 1990s broadened their horizon to encompass global issues and to work more collaboratively with women in other countries. The 1995 U.N. Conference on Women in Beijing, China, was a symbolic high point of this evolving relationship. The conference attracted 26,000 women from around the world, a third of whom were Americans. Most of these women were members or activists in women's struggles in their home countries, and they attended the Beijing conference to participate in the Women's Forum, the meeting of representatives of nongovernmental organizations (NGOs). The thousands of women taking part in the Women's Forum hoped to influence the official governmental document to be issued from the conference by the U.N. General Assembly.

In 10 days of meetings, women at the NGO forum shared their experiences from their local settings. American women active in the struggle to achieve environmental justice in the U.S. South met with activists from around the world to discuss strategies for addressing environmental problems that disproportionately harmed poor and minority communities. American women from the Southwest met with women from Pacific islands about the danger to their communities from nuclear testing and nuclear waste. Activists came together over issues such as domestic violence, genital mutilation, and the de facto enslavement of women servants in many parts of the world. They sought to change the world's conventional understanding of these as simply women's issues, and instead to advance the perspective that these were issues of human rights, not women's rights. The official Platform of Action endorsed many of the views that were formulated in the Women's Forum meetings. Most important for the women activists, it upheld the universality of international human rights over nationally particular laws and customs that often denied women's rights (Kaplan 1997).

Third Wave Feminism

A new feminism emerged among young women in the early and mid-1990s. Calling themselves "Third Wave feminists," they perceived themselves to be breaking through the limitations and constraints of the feminism deeded to them by their predecessors. The names of their organizations attested to the spirit of their effort to forge a new feminist identity—FURY (Feminists United to Represent Youth), YELL (Youth Education Life Line), and WHAM (Women's Health Action Mobilization). Many Third Wave feminists understood themselves to be carrying on the legacy of radical feminists who had earlier sought to expand the boundaries of what it meant to be a woman and what it meant to be a feminist. Others, more influenced by dominant media portrayals of stereotypical feminists, were unaware that they were engaging in the debates of their foremothers. The veteran feminist Gloria Steinem cautioned, "Some tactical and theoretical wheels don't have to be reinvented. You may want to make them a different size or color, put them on a different wagon . . . or otherwise make them your own— but many already exist" (Walker 1995, 174).

Although frequently critical of the generation who came before them, by their very self-identification, Third Wavers attested to their place in the continuum of feminist history. They felt, however, that the ascribed role of feminists was limiting them, and limiting to its wider appeal among their peers. Rebecca Walker, daughter of the celebrated writer Alice Walker, explored the struggle many young women and men went through in reconciling their beliefs in women's equality with inherited notions of feminism. "Constantly measuring up to some cohesive fully down-for-the-feminist-cause identity without contradictions and messiness and lusts for power and luxury items is not a fun or easy task." In her travels speaking at colleges, women described their feelings of feminist inadequacy. "I have always believed in equal rights and been involved in speaking up, but I didn't think I could call myself a feminist because I am also a Christian," one shy woman in Virginia told her. Walker's audiences applauded her when she spoke "about all the different things you can do and still be a feminist, like shave your legs every day, get married, be a man, be in the army, whatever" (Walker 1995, 174). Naomi Wolf, a Third Wave feminist who gained broad media attention after her 1991 book, *The Beauty Myth,* agreed that the sentiment was widespread among women of her generation. It was not only the misrepresentation of feminism in the media and the conservative backlash that had led young women to reject the identity of "feminist," even when they strongly supported women's rights. Feminists also had to acknowledge that their own actions had produced this state of affairs (Wolf 1993). The generational divide seemed most pronounced on the related matters of sexuality and female image. Third Wavers reveled in a celebration of sexuality, defending their choice to be heterosexual or bisexual, and insisted that a wide range of female behavior and presentation should be available to feminists. Notwithstanding the protestations of Second Wave feminists that they had been caricatured by the mass media and the conservative backlash, the Third Wave was in part a reaction against the rigidity, ideological conformity, and asceticism of the Second Wave.

Third Wave feminism was essentially a movement of identity politics, 1990s-style, when it was de rigueur to acknowledge the "multiplicities" and "shifting boundaries" of identity. Feminism was part of one's search for an identity that fit; still, feminism had to be personally tailored to fit one's sense of self-hood and all the contradictions of self. Sophisticated enough to understand that the slogan "sisterhood is powerful" was rhetorically useful to their foremothers but in many ways a caricature of Second Wave feminists, Third Wavers nevertheless concerned themselves more with their differences and with how to negotiate them than with an ideal notion of sisterly unity. Identities were multiple—sexual, racial, ethnic, and religious—and in contradiction or uneasy relation with one another. Feminism and its social or political activism, for them, was coalitional; there was not one community of women, but many identity-based groups that formed fluid and shifting alliances. This focus was in part the result of the greater ethnic and racial diversity among them. The combined forces of new immigration, the gains of the civil rights and women's movement for equal access, the increased social tolerance for homosexuality, bisexuality, transgendered identity, and the victories for multiculturalism won by nationalist African American and Chicano student movements had created a generation of young women who were remarkably diverse, self-conscious, and proud.

Like many of the movements of the 1990s that traced their roots to the 1960s New Left, Third Wave feminists believed that cultural activity was a significant form of radical political activity. It was for many Third Wave feminists the essence of their politics and their feminism. One of the first of these new cultural feminisms, the Riot Grrls, emerged out of the punk rock scene in 1991 in Olympia Washington. "Angry grrl" bands like Brett Mobile and Bikini Kill inspired others women musicians and budding young feminists to publish "fanzines" and set up local chapters where young alternative artists with a feminist consciousness could meet and form a community. It was a feminist movement, drawing on "the personal is political" anthem of earlier generations, yet seeking to gain equality within the punk music scene and establish a community of artist activists. Other young feminists were spurred to literary activity. Tali Edut, one of the founders of the *HUES* magazine collective, explained how the mission to create a feminist magazine for young women and "see multiculturalism finally done right in a women's movement" grew out of her personal history reading mainstream women's magazines as a teenager. Her ambitions in 1995, as the magazine had moved from a college to a national venture, were expansive. "In creating a publication that is not just a magazine but a movement, our goal remains to create a new standard of self-acceptance for women" (Edut 1997, 175). Although many Third Wave Feminists no doubt participated in many of the youth social movements of the 1990s—the antiglobalization movement, political contests over affirmative action and immigrant rights, the new labor movement, or the environmental justice movement—there is little record of their participation in more traditional forms of social movement political action for feminist advance.

LIBERAL MOVEMENTS IN TRANSITION

The difficult and ambivalent transition from movement to institution was faced in different ways by many of the 20th century's historic liberal movements. Membership rolls lengthened and budgets ballooned, but throughout the 1990s, liberal, Left, and progressive organizations had difficulty mobilizing their large base and capitalizing on their institutional and political clout.

The troubles that were beginning to be faced by maturing "new" social movements, such as feminism, had long bedeviled the American labor movement. The highly bureaucratized AFL-CIO was viewed by its friends as a dinosaur and by its enemies as a greedy special interest. Longstanding internal dissatisfaction broke forth in 1995, when union reformers ousted the leadership of the national federation.

Environmentalism, ideologically on the liberal end of the American spectrum, was in a position somewhere between the maturing new social movements and the historic and institutionalized labor movement. Although its roots reached back to the conservation movement of the 1910s, environmentalism had been infused with new life, new dynamism, and new mission by 1960s activists. In the 1990s, no single cause enjoyed broader support than environmentalism. National organizations grew in staff and budget, moved further inside the halls of power in Washington, won major legal battles and significant new measures for environmental protection, but inspired hardly a soul. A new movement dynamism, however, emerged on the local level in poor and minority communities. The environmental justice movement—known to activists as "EJ"—galvanized a new constituency for environmentalism and infused new life into the cause.

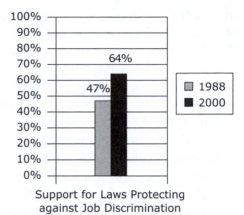

Figure 3.2 *Percentage of Americans Who Support Laws to Protect against Job Discrimination.* Source: *Graff 2002.*

Traditional civil rights organizations, such as the National Association for the Advancement of Colored People (NAACP) and the Urban League, continued to be very active, winning legal cases, performing local economic development, exerting political influence, and counting millions of members. But they were institutions, not social movement leaders, and significant social movement activism and ideological ferment emerged outside their purview.

Shaking Up the House of Labor

By the early 1990s, organized labor had seemingly fallen into an irreversible decline. Unionized blue-collar jobs had been lost to globalization, recession, and downsizing, and corporate managers and Republican politicians had gone head to head with unions and won. The percentage of American working men and women who belonged to unions had dropped steadily and steeply. At the apex of the American labor movement in the mid-1950s, a third of all workers belonged to a union. By 1995, the percentage of unionized Americans had dropped to 14.9 percent (EPI 2006). Unions were failing to recruit new members, and the national leadership of the AFL-CIO appeared paralyzed in the face of the many-pronged challenges to the very existence of unions in America.

On Labor Day 1995, John J. Sweeney, Richard Trumka, and Linda Chavez-Thompson announced that they were going to run for the executive positions of the AFL-CIO against the current leadership. They ran on the slogan "Changing to Organize," promising that under their leadership, the AFL-CIO would make the philosophical, strategic, and financial commitment to organizing millions of new union members. Sweeney was the president of the Service Employees'

International Union (SEIU), which was the only international that had grown substantially in recent years due to its efforts to organize immigrant workers. Trumka, a leader of the Pittston strikes, was the president of the United Mine Workers and known as a militant and a brilliant strategist. The inclusion on the ticket of Chavez-Thompson, international vice president of the American Federation of State, County and Municipal Employees (AFSCME) in San Antonio, Texas, symbolized the reformers' commitment to diversity in the labor movement; no woman or person of color had ever held any of the top offices of the federation. Sweeney's run for the presidency was daring. Lane Kirkland had held the office since 1979, after George Meaney had chosen him as his successor, and although the national labor federation held elections for officers every four years, no one had ever tried to unseat Kirkland. But many unions had been discontented with Kirkland's inaction. The 1994 electoral victory of antiunion Republicans was an additional spur to action. The reform slate won election to the executive council in October 1995. It was the only time in the 20th century that the incumbent president of a national labor federation had been defeated.

The victory infused the labor movement and its progressive allies with hope and energy. Sweeney and the new leadership barnstormed union halls throughout the country in their first months in office, attempting to rally the locals' existing union leadership to the new cause of organizing, political activism, militant bargaining, progressive coalition building and—most difficult of all—internal union reform. At campus teach-ins attracting over a thousand participants each, Sweeney, New Left veterans, professors, and feminist icons, stood together to rally a new generation of youth to the cause of a revived, democratic labor movement. Those over the age of 30 in the room were conscious of being part of a historic moment, in which the combatants in hard hats versus hippies contests of the Cold War and Vietnam era were laying down their weapons to forge a new progressive force. Labor leaders spoke about their commitment to building an inclusive union movement that welcomed women, African Americans, and immigrants. Matured New Leftists explained the historic centrality of the labor movement in American struggles to extend democracy, acknowledging it was a lesson they had ignored in their youthful militancy. The new leadership instituted Union Summer, self-consciously modeled on the Freedom Summer of the civil rights movement, to train a new generation of union organizers. More than 1,000 students signed up for the first year of the program. For a brief moment, supporters speculated about the rebirth of the CIO spirit of the 1930s, which had created the modern labor movement and won the widely distributed prosperity of the postwar golden age (Faux 2002; Moberg 2001; Fraser and Freeman 1997).

Within the labor movement itself, the new leadership redirected the resources of the national federation toward organizing and politics. The tradition of local autonomy is highly prized in the American labor movement; therefore, the power of the AFL-CIO to change the American labor movement is comparatively constrained. Under Sweeney's leadership, the federation voted a special assessment on member unions to raise funds for political mobilization. The political focus paid off. Through get-out-the-vote campaigns and issue advertising, turnout increased among union households and labor-backed candidates won election. The union household share of the electorate rose from 19 percent in 1992 to 26 percent in 2000 (*Nation* 2001). Labor's renewed political focus helped Democrats hold the presidency in 1996 and recapture congressional seats in 1998, though there continues to be debate about the relative significance of the labor vote in those elections. Lobbying by labor won a raise in the minimum wage from a hostile Republican Congress in 1996 and the defeat of fast-track trade authority in 1997 and 1998.

Winning new union members, which could be accomplished only by organizing nonunion workers, proved more difficult. The AFL-CIO encouraged the process by forging stronger and more substantive relationships with other community groups in locales where local unions initiated organizing drives. The burst of living-wage laws passed in the mid- to late 1990s were in almost all cases the fruit of labor, community, and faith alliances. The new leadership of the AFL-CIO also provided financial and political support to reformers within local Central Labor Councils, which in some places such as Milwaukee and Los Angeles became the nerve centers of local progressive initiatives. Whereas locals or internationals were already committed to organizing, as in the case of many SEIU and Hotel and Restaurant workers (HERE) chapters, the AFL-CIO provided invaluable support. The federation began to direct its pension management, research, and communications departments to assist in corporate campaigns intended to bring public pressure to bear on antiunion employers.

The strategy of the new AFL-CIO leadership paid off where there was already a commitment internally to the "new labor movement." In reality, most of the energy for the new initiatives came from the local level, but the encouragement and support from the top helped immensely. Bob King, a regional director of the United Auto Workers, who represented 80,000 workers in the Detroit area, spoke for hundreds of activists who had been dissatisfied with the previous leadership. "We could never have stopped fast track under Kirkland and Donahue. They didn't understand activism, mobilizing the rank and file, building community coalitions; Kirkland could never have created the *presence* that the new leadership built with street actions. Before we were passive, now we're direct and we're loud" (Beasley 1998, 216). When the AFL-CIO wanted to hold local hearings on revising its immigration policy and put a call out for local union members to attend, the Los Angeles County Federation of Labor mobilized 20,000 workers. A similar dynamic occurred with the 1999 Seattle protests. The large labor contingent that received so much media attention in the Battle for Seattle emerged out of grassroots organizing by local labor leaders working in coalition with local environmentalists.

Ultimately, the new leadership of the AFL-CIO was unable to reverse the decline in union membership. Their goal of organizing millions foundered, in part, on the resistance within the local and international unions opposed to the new direction. More important, the legal, political, and business environment was inhospitable to the growth of the union movement. Although surveys revealed that almost half of nonunionized workers wanted to belong to a union, by the end of the decade, union density stood at 14 percent, lower than when the new leadership had taken control. Labor law and its enforcement had evolved in such a way in the United States to allow employers to engage in antiunion campaigns when faced with an organizing drive, to fire workers who were trying to organize a union with little fear of the consequences, and to easily bring in replacement workers when faced with a strike. Each year, almost 10,000 workers involved in union organizing were fired. One survey showed that employers used the threat of overseas relocation in 50 to 65 percent of new organizing campaigns. Even when unions, against the odds, were able to win a union recognition, half of these victories ended with no union contract negotiated (Faux 2002; Pollin 2003).

The labor movement grew in the 1990s for the first time in two decades. More than 265,000 workers joined unions between 1995 and 1999. But population growth, employment growth, and retirements made that insufficient to increase union density, and after 2000, with recession and another jobless recovery, the percentage of unionized workers fell again. By 2001, Sweeney's team at the AFL-CIO faced new dissent as organizing unions became dissatisfied with the slow pace of change in the other locals and internationals, and the latter seethed at the spiraling budget and ballooning bureaucracy of the AFL-CIO office.

"Justice for Janitors" and the Emergence of the New Labor Movement

SEIU "Justice for Janitors" campaigns in Denver, Los Angeles, Washington, D.C., and other cities represented both a strategic shift and a commitment to a new militancy in unionizing. As a matter of national strategy, SEIU decided that "hot shop" organizing was leading nowhere—not to more union members nor to improved bargaining position for current union members. Instead, the international committed to an industry-wide approach to new organizing. In 1986, SEIU launched the Justice for Janitors campaign in Denver, in which the union would seek to organize the largely immigrant nonunionized workforce cleaning America's offices through a new type of campaign focused on the industry and its corporate leaders. As it developed, Justice for Janitors took on the characteristics of a social movement and won enormous public sympathy and solidarity for the low-wage immigrant workers.

A pivotal moment for the campaign occurred in 1990 during a strike in Los Angeles. The local union, SEIU 1877, had lost almost half of its members during the 1980s when the industry underwent a structural transformation. By the late 1980s, most janitors in Los Angeles were immigrant women from Mexico and Central America and most worked for nonunion contractors. On June 15, about 300 striking janitors and their supporters peacefully marched in Century City, one of the central office complexes in Los Angeles. The march was met with police in riot gear, who clubbed the marchers with nightsticks and released tear gas into their midst (Shapiro-Perl 1991). The public outrage that resulted helped the janitors win the strike and union recognition for 6,000 workers. It was the largest immigrant organizing success since the United Farm Workers campaigns in the 1970s. Such grassroots militancy unleashed by the SEIU campaign had become rare in American labor, and many observers noted the parallel with the union drives of the 1930s. But militancy alone did not carry the day in the new globalized economy. SEIU had also mounted a sophisticated international corporate campaign that included solidarity actions by international unions working for the same multinationals in other countries, media relations and gimmicks to win public sympathy, and financial pressure on corporate boards.

The union established the annual Justice for Janitors day on June 15 to commemorate the day of the police beating. The Justice for Janitors campaign won organizing drives in other cities during the 1990s and began to negotiate contracts to improve the wages and benefits of the nation's janitors. In April 2000, another Los Angeles janitors' strike illustrated the gains made by the union and the workers over the decade. Dozens of elected leaders, including every city council member, officially endorsed the strike; some city council members performed civil disobedience in support of the janitors and were arrested. Republican mayor Richard Riordan, who had been at odds with Los Angeles unions for much of his mayoralty, publicly supported the union and the strike and exerted pressure on the city's building owners to meet the demands of the union. Cardinal Mahoney held a special mass for the striking janitors. Vice President Al Gore and Sen. Ted Kennedy came to Los Angeles to speak on their behalf. When the janitors returned to the route of their 1990 march, they were greeted by office workers cheering them from their windows and throngs lining the street in solidarity. Two weeks later, the union had won a wage increase of more than 25 percent for union and nonunion workers alike (Meyerson 2000).

By the end of the decade and the beginning of the 2000s, Justice for Janitors had been diffused broadly in the popular culture, at least in cities where campaigns had been undertaken, and was on its way to attaining the kind of mythic status of key battles of the civil rights movement. A popular bilingual children's book told the story of the 1990 strike from the perspective of the daughter of a Latina janitor who had found her voice as a union activist in the strike (Cohn, Delgado, and Rodriguez 2002). In 2000, filmmaker Ken Loach released *Bread and Roses,* a fictionalized account of the Justice for Janitors struggles in Los Angeles. The film won awards at international film festivals and played throughout the United States in 2001.

The International Brotherhood of Teamsters UPS Strike of 1997

In the summer of 1997, the International Brotherhood of Teamsters led a strike of 185,000 United Parcel Service (UPS) workers. The issue provoking the strike was UPS's two-tier wage and benefit system in which the 60 percent of UPS workers who were classified as part-time workers, yet who worked nearly full-time, were paid less, and received lower pay and benefits. The Teamsters cast the battle as a larger struggle against corporate America's race to the bottom and its jettisoning of the security of American workers. After a two-week-long strike, UPS conceded on virtually every union demand, and the Teamsters had achieved one of the first big strike victories in decades.

The UPS strike was won in large part because of the Teamsters Union's adoption of the techniques of the new labor movement after 1991, when a reform leadership headed by Ron Carey won the top union offices during a federally supervised election. The Teamsters had a reputation as a top-down bureaucratic union out of touch with its members, and allegations of corruption and mafia ties plagued many locals and the international. The reformists within the Teamsters sought to bring more internal democracy to the union, involve members in union decision making, and encourage worker activism. A year before the UPS contract was due to expire, the union initiated member-to-member communications networks, encouraged family members of Teamsters to be active in the upcoming contract battle, and polled members seeking to know what issues mattered most to them. The union simultaneously established a media and international strategy to bring outside pressure on UPS. Rallies were held in seven cities the day before negotiations began, featuring UPS workers speaking about the economic insecurity of part-time work and their worries about health and safety. In short, the Teamsters sought to cast the strike not as a special interest contest between a particular union and a particular company but rather as, in the words of one placard, "Teamsters on Strike To Save the American Dream."

Rallies, petitions, and close communication between the negotiation team and members continued during the negotiations between March and July. In mid-July, with UPS resisting most of the union's proposals, 95 percent of Teamster Union members voted to authorize a strike. On August 3, with the bargaining impasse continuing, the Teamsters went on strike. UPS, in response, ran a $1 million advertising campaign seeking to sway public opinion. But the months of actions and media work by UPS workers had already shaped opinion, and by a two-to-one margin, the public was on the side of the workers. Building involvement and community before the contract campaign also paid off internally for the union. Strikes, particularly in recent decades, have frequently pitted co-workers against each other. But 99 percent of UPS workers participated in the strike and stood on the picket lines or refused to cross them. UPS pilots, who belonged to a separate union, engaged in a sympathy strike and refused to fly. The AFL-CIO coordinated its affiliates to ensure that the UPS workers could continue the strike as long as necessary, winning loan pledges from affiliates for a strike fund of millions of dollars. On August 15, the Teamsters declared that a national "Day for Good Jobs" would be marked on August 22, and prepared for mass community actions around the nation. The management of UPS realized it had lost the battle for public opinion. It agreed to the union's demands on raising wages and pensions, eliminating subcontracting, preserving union control of pension funds, and creating 10,000 full-time jobs—not the 1,000 the company had proposed in its "final offer." Perhaps as important as the bread-and-butter victory was the new life it infused in union members. "I never used to get involved in much of anything but my own private life," Keith Barros told a university audience several months after the strike. "I could just work, come home, watch football, and everything would be just fine. I hope I represent a number of less-outspoken people who are part of the awakening movement to get involved in where we are going as a society" (Whit and Wilson 1998, 254).

Environmental Justice

In areas where poor African Americans and Latinos lived near industrial plants, toxic waste sites, or garbage dumps, a new environmental movement arose. Calling their movement "environmental justice" (EJ), activists sought to demonstrate that environmental hazards and pollution were having a disproportionate impact on minority communities, and to create a new paradigm of environmental activism. By the end of the 1990s, the local, small groups of concerned neighbors and friends had evolved into a national movement of community-based organizations that were redefining the debate in the environmental movement and winning tangible victories. Often the groups targeted polluting facilities in their neighborhoods, engaging in community mobilization and legal action during public environmental reviews. In the first Environmental Protection Agency (EPA) denial of a state-issued Clean Air Act permit citing environmental justice

Homes sit near the Columbus Southern Power Company in Conesville, Ohio. (morgueFile)

concerns, Convent St. James Citizens for Jobs and the Environment, an EJ group in a predominantly African American area of Louisiana, blocked the building of a polyvinyl chloride (PVC) plant in their neighborhood. West Harlem Environmental Action (WE ACT) was a party to a lawsuit against the City of New York for its operation of a sewage treatment plant located in Harlem. Working with the established national environmental organization the Natural Resources Defense Council and other community institutions, in 1993, the groups settled with the City in exchange for a commitment to fix the plant, and they won funds to address environmental and health concerns in the community. By the end of the 1990s, a new generation of environmental activists—young, working class, and minority—were leading the American environmental movement in a new direction.

Debates: Alternative Visions among Black Intellectuals in the Post–Civil Rights Era

In the mid-1990s, people began to speak of a Third Black Intellectual Renaissance as diverse groups of black intellectuals won recognition in popular culture and the mainstream media and generated controversy on many fronts. For the first time in the post–civil rights era, a significant number of African American intellectuals identified themselves politically with the Republican Party and intellectually with the conservative movement. Most prominent among this group were Shelby Steele, Thomas Sowell, and Stephen Carter. Supreme Court Justice Clarence Thomas was perceived as the national symbol of the new tendency, although his intellectual production was minimal compared to other black conservatives. At the same time, on the left, a group including Cornel West, Henry Gates Louis Jr., Patricia Williams, and Derrick Bell challenged the vision, leadership, and program that linked the struggle of black people to the Democratic Party and the welfare state, and critically debated whether political and legal action could ever be the means to racial equality.

Both new directions represented the maturation of the post–civil rights generation and the disappointed hopes of the quarter century past. As we have seen, African Americans, especially those who lived in cities, suffered disproportionately from declining wages, deindustrialization, unemployment, poverty, and urban decay. For poor, urban African Americans, the schools in their neighborhoods were often inferior, and their neighborhoods were besieged by crime and drugs. Rural black Southerners had seen some improvement since the civil rights movement but still were among the poorest and least educated demographic group in the country. The great changes that were predicted to flow from voting rights had not materialized, as gerrymandering had diluted African American political power and African American elected leaders had failed, for a number of reasons, to perform up to expectations.

African Americans, like many other Americans in the 1990s, were disillusioned with politics and government. But, considering how much the black freedom movement had been essentially a political struggle—in both its liberal and radical tendencies—such disaffection had deep and lasting effects on the vision and program of intellectuals most concerned with the condition of black people in the contemporary United States.

Conservative African American intellectuals assessed the state of black America and argued that misguided liberal, Democratic rule had led black people down a yellow brick road. The Democrats' welfare programs created pathological dependency and destroyed the family; affirmative action was unfair, no longer necessary, undermined the American principle of meritocracy, and stigmatized every successful African American. They abhorred what they considered the paternalism of the welfare state. Black conservatives argued that racism was a far less important cause of the subordinate position of African Americans than most thought, and that it was time to stop blaming white America for the crisis of the African American community. African Americans needed instead to accept responsibility for the many problems of their community and renew their moral and practical commitment to individual responsibility. Black conservatives made their philosophical and political home with the free market, antistatist, individualistic, predominantly white conservative movement.

Conservatives, nevertheless, remained a small minority among African Americans in general and among African American intellectuals in particular. On the liberal to left side of the spectrum, there were more voices and more diversity of opinion but likewise a move away from the struggles of the recent past. Some of these intellectuals continued to focus on law, economics, and politics but were critical of the earlier reliance on rights-based legal strategies and welfare state liberalism. The sociologist William Julius Wilson in *When Work Disappears* (1996) combined a structural analysis of the devastating impact of deindustrialization and globalization on urban African Americans with a criticism of the values of the African American urban poor, which he argued had arisen in the wake of endemic unemployment. Roundly criticized for ignoring racial discrimination as a cause of this condition, and sometimes wrongly accused of being a conservative, Wilson in reality favored a revised form of affirmative action, a vigorous program of race-blind public investment to restore decent jobs to the working class as a whole, and the formation of a multiethnic political coalition to address the problem of social inequality.

The dominant tendency among black intellectuals on the left was a turn toward culture and away from politics and law as traditionally defined, practiced, and analyzed. Legal scholars Patricia Williams and Derrick Bell used the techniques of literature—parable, fiction, autobiography, fantasy, and metaphor—in their analysis of law and race. Cornel West, a professor of philosophy, mined the prophetic tradition of African American religion to analyze race and make a more practical connection with the larger black community. Robin Kelley, a historian, studied black youth culture and interpreted its forms as a popular politics of resistance. As one historian reflected, "They seem to be trying to create a new grammar, a new language, to talk about race more deeply and honestly rather than to discuss immediate issues at hand in the same language that has left black people so despairing. They seem to be trying to find, or create, new forms of unity in a society in which radical pluralism may have run its course" (Ayers 1996, 119). In their explorations beyond conventional ways of thinking about race in American, they won near celebrity status. But they also were subjected to withering criticism, especially from other black leftist intellectuals like Adolph Reed, who found the cultural turn fruitless and who themselves remained committed to traditional forms and practices of political social protest.

MOVEMENTS OF MEN

In 1990 and 1991, small groups of American men inspired by Robert Bly's *Iron John* and Sam Keen's *Fire in the Belly* headed off to seminars to discuss being an American man. In 1995, hundreds of thousands of men attended the Million Man March on the National Mall in Washington, D.C. In 1997, hundreds of thousands of men attended the Promise Keepers' "Stand in The Gap: A Sacred Assembly of Men" rally, also on the National Mall.

Was there a Men's Movement? In the early 1990s, many thought the demonstrations of men, as men, indicated that a movement was in formation. The demonstrations from middecade on, however, were very clearly ones of particular types of men whose other identities, as Christian or African American men, for example, were primary. With such vast differences among the distinct expressions of male solidarity, the idea of a "men's movement" vanished by the end of the decade.

Demographically, politically, and culturally, the men's groups were very different from each other. The early decade "Men's Movement," inspired and led by Bly, was ecumenical but spiritual and attracted mostly single, urban, liberal middle-class, and professional men in their late 20s to early 40s. The Million Man March, the first of the public demonstrations, was conceived by Nation of Islam leader Louis Farrakhan and attracted African American men of diverse religious and political views. The Promise Keepers' movement emerged out of an evangelical Christian church, was associated with the new Christian Right, and attracted mostly married, evangelical, middle-aged white men. There was no "men's movement." Rather, there were many identity-based movements of men, which had been self-consciously organized as male-only groups.

Despite these profound differences, the movements shared assumptions about the nature of the problems faced by American men and how to solve them. Most fundamentally, contemporary American men were alienated from the essence of manhood and brotherhood with other men. Rituals designed to help men get in touch with the inner man were common; through drumming, prayers, or cheers, the emotion of loss could be tapped and released. The origin of alienation was in the modern rupture of the relationship between fathers and sons. For the predominantly white movements—the loose one associated with Robert Bly and the more organized Promise Keepers—the break occurred with the Industrial Revolution when fathers went out to factories to work and were henceforth absent to their sons. For African American men, the father-son rupture resulted from slavery and its legacy in Jim Crow and racial oppression.

Because the generational links between fathers and sons had disrupted the traditional means by which such knowledge was passed from generation to generation, men no longer knew exactly how to be men. In addition, feminism had issued alternative rules and norms for women's roles. At best, men were left confused about where this left them; at worst, men's role had been usurped. Each branch of the men's movement approached this issue in different ways.

Men's problems had social consequences, diverting them individually from the true path in life and leaving a society distorted and troubled by the absence of responsible men. Each of the men's movements called on men to engage in rituals of personal transformation as a step to a new way of being a man—in relationship to other men, in relationship to women and children, and in American culture and society. The pervasiveness of spirituality and therapeutic modes in American popular culture were evident in the men's groups' encouragement of self-examination, confession, atonement, public display of emotion, and public pledges to reform.

Between 1990 and 1997, up to 3 million American men responded to diverse and mutually contradictory calls to give public witness to the need for a new American manhood. Countless others participated in reading and discussion groups concerned with the plight of the American man. The participants did not always share the views of the charismatic individuals leading the efforts or of the other men involved. Nevertheless, they were all united by a sense of uneasiness, of uncertainty, about what it meant to be a man in the postfeminist, postindustrial America in which they found themselves. The phenomenon of men's demonstrations peaked in 1997. Just as suddenly as they had appeared, they were gone.

The Million Man March

On October 16, 1995, the Million Man March called by Nation of Islam minister Louis Farrakhan drew between 500,000 and 1 million African American men to a demonstration in Washington, D.C. Fathers and sons, professionals and blue-collar workers, and college and high school students responded to Farrakhan's admonition to come to the nation's capital to "repent and atone," as the Million

Participants gather in Washington, D.C., for the Million Man March, an event organized by Minister Louis Farrakhan as a day of atonement and empowerment for African American men, 1995. (James Leynse/Corbis)

Man March platform put it. Many men were already politically active, and the vast majority of them were voters. A few women participated, but for the most part, women stayed away, as Farrakhan had requested. On the stage were the leaders of the Nation of Islam, politicians, heroes of the civil rights movement, former gang members, and luminaries in the arts. Jesse Jackson criticized the Republican Congress and the criminal justice system. Maya Angelou read poetry. Former gang leaders asked for forgiveness for the damage to African American communities they had caused. Stevie Wonder spoke of the two holocausts that had devastated African Americans and Jews. The crowd burst into sustained and boisterous applause for Rosa Parks. Farrakhan called on the men assembled to repeat after him the following pledge: "From this day forward, I will strive to improve myself spiritually, morally, mentally, socially, politically, and economically for the benefit of myself, my family, and my people."

Specifically, each man pledged that he would renounce violence, drugs, and the abuse of women, and would return home to volunteer in his community, join organizations working for "uplift" and a church or mosque, and register new voters.

The speeches, however, fell lightly on the audience, who found other purposes in the gathering. Indeed, many had left by the time Farrakhan reached the end of his two-and-a-half-hour speech and issued the pledge. One participant reported, "It wasn't uncommon to see dreadlocked youth, proudly displaying the colors red, black, and green in various forms, talking politics and economics with blue-suited professionals. Kids sporting hip-hop gear rapped with older men, who talked to them about hearing and seeing Malcolm and Martin and being in Selma, Washington, and Watts. Followers of Islam discussed religion with Baptists. Instead of marching, a million men found themselves all day long involved in small discussion groups" (McKissack 1995). Participants and the journalists who covered the day universally reported that it was a day of heartfelt fellowship and celebration, a demonstration animated by the joy of recognition and a sense of brotherly solidarity, not by anger or militancy. "I saw no clenched fists," wrote David Ruffin, a journalist who went to the march as a participant (1996).

"Two marches came to Washington," observed an editorial in *The Nation* magazine (*Nation* 1995). "The event on the podium—speeches by the Million Man March's organizers and would-be leaders—naturally caught the media's attention. But the day's long-term significance should more properly be sought in the other march, below the stage, where a mass came together and recognized itself." Until its opening moment, the Million Man March had been surrounded by controversy because it was the brainchild of the leader of the Nation of Islam (NOI), Minister Louis Farrakhan.

Farrakhan's career was riddled with controversy and contradiction. A protégé of Malcolm X, Farrakhan had denounced his mentor as a traitor "worthy of death" shortly before Malcolm's assassination. In the 1970s, Farrakhan had split from the main branch of the NOI after its new leader, Wallace Muhammad, had sought to move the American group into religious agreement with orthodox Islam and had disavowed the separatism preached by his father and longtime NOI leader, Elijah Muhammad. In the 1980s and early 1990s, Farrakhan won broader support for his splinter branch of the NOI and personal acclaim in some African American communities for condemning the drug trade and helping to foster a gang truce in many cities (Marable 1998; Chang 2005). Yet Farrakhan and NOI ministers close to him were on record over many years propagating anti-Semitic and racist theories, calling Judaism a "gutter religion," praising Hitler, condemning homosexuality as "sick," and referring to Korean, Asian, Jewish and other business owners working in African American neighborhoods as "bloodsuckers" (*Christian Century* 1995).

African American and liberal leaders who would ordinarily have been eager to be part of a mass demonstration were in a quandary. Many elements of Farrakhan's ideology—not just the anti-Semitism and homophobia—were repugnant to many of them. Farrakhan's fundamental social philosophy was well to the right of mainstream opinion among African Americans. The minister had called for a day of personal atonement, not a demonstration of political might, and had told African American women to stay home. Yet Farrakhan appeared to have mined a vein of yearning among African American men. After reading the platform of the organizing committee, legal scholar and feminist Patricia Williams observed,

> This basically fundamentalist platform of isolationism, personal responsibility and women-waiting-at-home sounds somewhere between the scripts of the Promise Keepers and the Contract With America. . . . I also worry about a "personal responsibility" march, as some of the organizers have called it, on the site of the civil rights marches of the past. . . . If the marches of the past were about all blacks achieving the full benefits of citizenship, this march of atoning black men seems to insist that "We exist!" "We are

different!" and "We are good!" And there is something about that vision of a march-of-atonement that I find inestimably sad." (Williams 1995)

Internal disagreements and criticism about Farrakhan and the nature of the event, such as those expressed by African American feminists, religious leaders, trade unionists, liberals, and leftists, were buried as the media and leaders of other communities demanded that African Americans repudiate Farrakhan for his racism and anti-Semitism. Many African American leaders believed that a double standard, undergirded by unexamined racist assumptions, was being applied to them. Why were African Americans expected to denounce any African American person who held retrograde views in order to demonstrate their good faith when white Americans were not held accountable for the views of every white racist? Civil rights and feminist leaders split over the question of participation. The NAACP and the National Urban League declined to participate, as did prominent African American feminists such as Angela Davis and Bell Hooks. On the other side, many civil rights activists, African American scholars, and a few feminists participated in the Million Man March, explaining that the march was about the message, not the messenger. It was not lost on them that Farrakhan seemed able to mount the first mass mobilization in years, a task that the traditional civil rights leadership had failed to do throughout the setbacks of the Reagan and Bush years.

Why did up to a million people travel to Washington, D.C., some from as far away as California, to be part of the Million Man March? The testimony of participants captured in press interviews that day and dozens of accounts written by participants in the weeks and months after the march revealed motives that were widely shared. A lawyer from Baltimore explained, "I wanted to show solidarity with other African-American men. I thought it was important to make the statement that there are positive black men in this country and that we're not as negative as the media portrays us" (*Christian Century* 1995). A Washington, D.C., businessman who brought his two sons to the march, echoed this common sentiment of pride in African American history and the dismay of misrecognition. "The majority of us are positive men with good values whose families are foremost in their lives. We are not the drug dealers they show on TV. Throughout history, we have helped build and sustain this nation" (quoted in Ruffin 1996). While the national press had concentrated on the question "would the march be a grand demonstration of anti-Semitism," the participants found the theory that they would be manipulated in such a way silly. Instead, though most of the participants were Christian and Farrakhan was Muslim, the minister's speech connected with the spiritual yearning of many participants (Ruffin 1996).

Opposition to the Republican Right in the brief heyday of the Contract with America also motivated many of the participants who hoped the march would catalyze broad-based political activism. But, even though the Million Man March called forth comparisons to Martin Luther King Jr.'s 1963 March on Washington, there was minimal political content to the day. The pervading themes of the Million Man March were atonement and personal responsibility, to look to one-self and one's brothers, not to the government, for redemption of the African American community. Adolph Reed, one of the sharpest critics of Farrakhan and the Million Man March, argued that the conception of the march was wholly consonant with white conservatism, especially in its endorsement of the culture of poverty thesis and its antigovernment crusade. Such views, according to Reed, "came through clearly in announcements from the podium that the march wasn't a protest march, that the congregants hadn't come to protest anything (actually, as a friend of mine aptly noted, it was the first protest in history where people gathered ostensibly to protest themselves)" (Reed 1995).

The conservatism Reed criticized was not a new invention. Farrakhan's philosophy was solidly in the tradition of African American separatist nationalism. It harkened back to the emigrationist movement of the 1850s and to Garveyism of the 1920s and 1930s, with significant elements of Booker T. Washington's Tuskegee philosophy of economic self-help and political conservatism mixed in. Farrakhan proselytized a conservative worldview in which African American people would achieve salvation through self-help, capitalist entrepreneurship, and the restoration of male authority in the African American family. Farrakhan's racial separatism rejected the central tenet of the civil rights movement. In that tradition, also reaching back into the 19th century, African American people were entitled to the full and equal rights and privileges of American citizenship and incorporation into the nation's civil and economic institutions. Farrakhan's strain of thought was not only more conservative than that of the equal rights tradition, but also profoundly pessimistic. To Farrakhan, separatism was necessary, because white supremacy was intractable (Marable 1998). The greatest irony of the day was that the pessimism inspiring the march was roundly rejected by those who answered Farrakhan's call. Universally, disinterested observers and participants reported the overriding spirit of the day was hope.

The hope born of the experience of the march inspired many to activism upon their return home. Local NAACP and Urban League chapters reported a surge in membership, as did churches and civic organizations. In Macon, Georgia, a local committee of Christians and Muslims working together claimed they had registered 1,000 new voters; the registrar in Macon reported that the proportion of registered eligible voters was higher among African Americans than among whites for the first time ever (Leland and Smith 1996). Voter registration among African American men nationwide increased as many acted on the call to register and get others to register. The effect was notable in the 1996 election. One and a half million more African American men voted than had done so in 1992, even while fewer African American woman and fewer people overall voted that year (Marable 1998). The Million Man March inspired similar demonstrations throughout the decade, such as the Million Women March (1997), the

Million Youth Movement marches in New York City and Atlanta (1998), and the Million Families March (2000), although none reached the size or significance of the first Million Man March.

Promise Keepers

In 1990, a successful and nationally famous college football coach, Bill Mc-Cartney, founded Promise Keepers with the idea of fomenting a mass movement of evangelical Christian men devoted to "Christ-like masculinity." James Dobson, the head of Focus on the Family, provided funding and staff for the embryonic organization, which started as a group of a few dozen men in 1990. In 1991, Promise Keepers attracted more than 4,000 men to a men-only stadium event in Boulder, Colorado. All-male stadium rallies became the group's signature style of mobilization and public presentation. Between 1991 and 1996, the Promise Keepers attracted more than 1 million men to rallies staged throughout the country (Mathisen 2001). By 1996, the organization had an annual budget of $115 million, more than 400 permanent staff, and thousands of mostly female volunteers. In 1997, the group attracted a blizzard of national media coverage for its Washington "Stand in the Gap" rally on the Mall. The event was designed to "present to the Lord godly men on their knees in humility, then on their feet in unity, reconciled and poised for revival and spiritual awakening." Several hundred thousand men participated (Labash 1997).

The Promise Keepers adeptly joined evangelical traditions of camp meetings with contemporary rituals of mass spectator sports to create a phenomenon with great appeal to a particular group of American men. Prayers and witness were orchestrated as mass cheers; exhortations to live a moral life were phrased in the metaphors of sport. The essential vision of the Promise Keepers was embodied in its Seven Promises, which called on men to be moral fathers, husbands, and Christians, according to traditionalist definitions of those roles. Although the media portrayed the Promise Keepers as a mass movement of American men, and in 1997 speculated on its potential for continued growth, the group appealed overwhelmingly to middle-aged, white, married, evangelical men (Mathisen 2001). The 1997 event proved to be the peak of the movement, as membership and attendance at rallies declined thereafter. Plans to stage mass rallies in 2000 were abandoned due to lack of interest.

BIOGRAPHIES

Karen Bass, 1953–

Community Leader and State Assemblywoman

Karen Bass founded one of the leading community-based social justice organizations in Los Angeles. Born and raised in Los Angeles, she worked as a physician's assistant after graduated from the University of Southern California. Working in the nation's largest trauma center when the crack cocaine epidemic struck in the 1980s inspired her to move into community organizing. In 1990, to address the root causes of the crack epidemic in South Los Angeles and propose comprehensive solutions, she and others founded the Community Coalition. Taking inspiration from the early African American civil rights movement, Community Coalition organized African American and Latino residents of South

Karen Bass, founder of the Community Coalition and majority leader of the California State Assembly. (Office of Speaker-Elect Karen Bass)

Los Angeles to improve the community. After the Los Angeles Riots, the organization advocated to stop the rebuilding of liquor stores, which often served as bases for the crack trade's criminal activity, and to devote rebuilding aid to replace liquor stores with nonprofits and businesses that did not sell alcohol. The group also won campaigns on rebuilding dilapidated inner-city schools and welfare rights. Bass was elected to the California State Assembly in 2005. In 2007, she became the first African American woman to serve as majority leader of the state assembly.

Monique Harden, 1968–

Attorney, Environmental Advocate

Monique Harden was a leader in the burgeoning environmental justice movement. Harden was born in San Francisco and raised in New Orleans where her family was originally from. Her great-grandfather had died while building the levees. After college and law school, she returned to New Orleans to work as an organizer in the predominantly African American river parishes. In 1997, while working with Greenpeace in their Toxics campaign, she became involved in a local EJ organization. The community was already subject to 17 million pounds of toxic air pollution from a dozen existing industrial facilities surrounding it when another company sought to build the largest PVC production facility in the world in the area. "To see that some of these industries retain the names of some of these plantations of the areas they built on was just a tremendous blow to me," Harden explained in an interview (Lerner 2002). She subsequently provided legal aid to the group. She continued to work on environmental justice issues in Louisiana, wedding her experience as a community organizer with her legal expertise, and gained a national reputation as a pioneer in the EJ movement. In 2002, she co-founded a public interest law firm in New Orleans to defend and advance the human right to a healthy environment.

Patricia Ireland, 1945–

Feminist Leader

Patricia Ireland became president of the National Organization for Women (NOW), one of the largest feminist organizations in America, in 1991. Ireland, whose mother was a local director for Planned Parenthood in Oak Park, Illinois, first became an activist while working as a flight attendant for PanAm in the 1970s. She was outraged to learn that female employees' spouses were not covered by the company's health insurance while male employees' spouses did receive coverage. She took the case to court with the help of the Dade County, Florida, NOW chapter, and after a court triumph, she decided to become a lawyer herself. While working for a Miami-based law firm, she volunteered much of her spare time to NOW. Her involvement in the organization grew during the 1980s, and in 1987, she became the running mate of the successful NOW presidential nominee Molly Yard. When Yard died in 1991, Ireland became the organization's leader. Under her leadership, the feminist organization experienced a surge of new growth. In 1992, she was one of the leaders of the Washington, D.C., pro-choice demonstration, and she initiated a campaign to connect NOW activists with female candidates. She was instrumental in NOW's campaign to defend abortion clinics against the Operation Rescue's blockade, initiating a program to train thousands of activists to protect abortion clinic workers and women who sought abortions. She was active on international feminist issues, founding NOW's Global Feminist Conference and participating in many forums in Europe and Latin America. She led NOW's effort to establish stronger connections with other civil rights and social justice groups. Her autobiography, *What Women Want,* was published in 1996. She remained president of NOW until 2001.

Bill McCartney, 1940–

Founder of Promise Keepers

McCartney was born in Michigan and raised in a military family. He became a football coach and, as head coach of the University of Colorado team, led his team to 9 out of 10 postseason bowl games, three conference championships, and one national championship. His team, however, garnered negative publicity. In Boulder, his athletes were notorious for violent, criminal, and rowdy behavior. (Two dozen team members were arrested for various crimes ranging from trespass to rape between 1986 and 1989 [Reilly 1989].) At the peak of his football career and national fame in 1990, he published his autobiography, *From Ashes to Glory,* and founded Promise Keepers. In a confessional work, McCartney told how his own spiritual failure had injured his family, his team, and his God. When McCartney founded Promise Keepers in 1990, he was active in the new Christian Right and belonged to the fundamentalist and charismatic Vineyard denomination. He served on the advisory board of Colorado for Family Values as it launched its anti–gay rights campaign to amend the Colorado constitution, and he was active in the pro-life movement (Conason, Ross, and Cokorinos 1996). In 1994, after publicity of his wife's eating disorder and near-collapse emotionally, McCartney resigned from his coaching job to devote himself to his family and to his ministry for Promise Keepers. McCartney was the keynote speaker at all of the group's stadium rallies, and he took on full-time leadership of the organization in 1995. In his 1997 book, *Sold Out,* McCartney revealed his struggles with alcoholism, rage, overwork, and his difficulty in living up to the Promise Keepers' ethic of family responsibility. Media reports at the time revealed other facts of McCartney's family life, which led some to charge him with hypocrisy (*Christian Century* 1997). He continued in the leadership during its decline over the following years and resigned in 2003.

David Noebel, 1937–

Head of Christian Right Ministry

David Noebel was the president of a small religious right organization, Summit Ministries in Manitou Springs, Colorado. The focus of Summit's educational mission was antihumanism, to train Christian youth to deal with secular humanism and other "alternative worldviews." Noebel edited Summit's magazine and authored a number of other books, including *Understanding the Times,* a textbook used in more than 1,000 Christian schools by the late 1990s. Noebel had begun his ministry in Christian Crusade, led by anticommunist Rev. Billy James Hargis, and his political activism in the John Birch Society. In the 1960s, he gained attention among evangelicals for his writings asserting that rock music was a Satanic tool used by communists to corrupt Christians. Because Noebel maintained

David Noebel, founder of Summit Ministries. (Summit Ministries)

his ties to the John Birch society until the late 1980s, he was considered by many evangelicals to be on the fringe. But Noebel won a strong and important endorsement from James Dobson and Gary Bauer, after James Dobson's son attended a training session at Summit. Noebel was active in the antigay movement. In 1977, Noebel wrote *The Homosexual Revolution: Endtime Abomination,* in which he defined homosexuality as one of America's greatest social problems. Noebel was instrumental in the antigay ballot initiative Amendment Two, passed in Colorado in 1992. The amendment forbids state and local governments from adopting measures to protect homosexuals from any kind of discrimination. Noebel and two other men came up with the idea during a meeting in a church basement. Afterward, they formed Colorado for Family Values, wrote the amendment that would appear on the ballot, and began advocating for the measure among evangelicals. They gained initial legal support from an organization funded by Pat Robertson and important endorsements from Bill McCartney and Dobson's Focus on the Family. The measure passed by a more than 100,000-vote margin, a shock to many Coloradans and national analysts, considering Colorado's liberal reputation. Amendment Two was declared unconstitutional in 1996. Noebel remains the head of Summit Ministries, which has added many forms of new media in its educational program (Martin 1996).

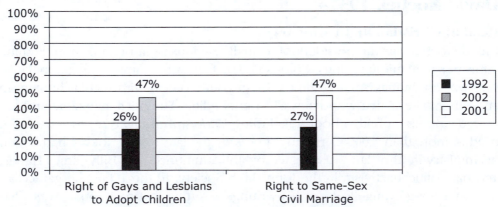

Figure 3.3 *Percentage of Americans Who Support Rights of Gays and Lesbians to Adopt and to Civil Marriage.* Source: *Graff 2002.*

Torie Osborn, 1950–

Leader of Gay and Lesbian Movement

Torie Osborn emerged to national prominence in 1993 when, as executive director of the National Gay and Lesbian Task Force (NGLTF), she helped organize the largest gay rights demonstration ever and brokered the first White House meeting between gays and the president. Osborn became an antiwar activist in college. Like many lesbians at the time, she was a radical and a feminist but remained closeted because she thought revealing it would discredit the causes she fought for. After coming out in the 1970s, she gradually began to focus her energies on lesbian activism. When the AIDS crisis hit in the mid-1980s, she was one of the lesbian feminist leaders who helped bring the gay male and lesbian movements together and broadened the agenda of the movement. After leaving the NGLTF, she wrote *Coming Home to America,* which wove together her own

Torie Osborn, a national leader of the gay and lesbian movement. (Susan Van Horn)

and other activists' stories to reflect on the advances and the remaining challenges of the gay and lesbian movement. Living in Washington, D.C., as welfare reform was passed, she was appalled at the tenor of the debates and decided to turn her organizing toward economic and social justice. She moved to Los Angeles and became executive director of the Liberty Hill Foundation, which funded community-based and grassroots groups working for economic, racial, and environmental justice. She is currently a senior advisor to Los Angeles's progressive mayor, Antonio Villaraigosa. (Osborn 1996, 2006; De Witt 1993).

Andy Stern, 1950–

Labor Union Leader

Reformist labor leader Andy Stern was elected president of the Service Employees' International Union (SEIU) in 1996. Stern had a long history with the union beginning in 1972 as a social worker and later serving as organizing director before ascending to the presidency. In 1995, he directed John Sweeney's campaign to become head of the AFL-CIO. As president of the SEIU and following the path charted by Sweeney, Stern made expansion of membership his top priority and devoted almost half of the union's budget to attracting new members. Janitors and home-care workers were among his primary targets as the SEIU experienced the greatest growth of any union in North America during the late 1990s. The union devoted 11 years of work and more than $1 million to organizing 74,000 home-care workers in Los Angeles—and in 1999, the workers voted to join the union. After Stern's personality and public stands began gathering media attention, he met some criticism that he tried to pressure others to accommodate his positions rather than drawing input from those lower in the union's structure. He acted against corruption within the union, placing some locals in trusteeship. Increasingly disillusioned with the failure of the AFL-CIO under Sweeney to move more aggressively to reform and organize, Stern eventually forced a split in the national labor federation. In 2005, SEIU and six other unions representing 6 million workers left the AFL-CIO and formed the Change to Win coalition.

References and Further Readings

Auletta, Ken. 2003. "Vox Fox: How Roger Ailes and Fox News Are Changing Cable News." *The New Yorker*, May 26, 58.

Ayers, Edward L. 1996. "Black American Intellectuals in the 1990s." In *Social and Secure? Politics and Culture of the Welfare State: A Comparative Inquiry*, edited by H. Bak, F. L. V. Holthoon, H. Krabbendam, E. L. Ayers, and Netherlands American Studies Association, 119. Amsterdam: VU University Press.

Beasley, Noel. 1998. "'On the Front Lines': The Labor Movement around the Country." In *Not Your Father's Union Movement: Inside the AFL-CIO*, edited by Jo-An Mort, 213–222. New York and London: Verso.

Bennett, Stephen Earl. 2002. "American's Exposure to Political Talk Radio and Their Knowledge of Public Affairs." *Journal of Broadcasting and Electronic Media* 46 (1): 74–86.

Bivins, Jason. 2003. *The Fracture of Good Order: Christian Antiliberalism and the Challenge to American Politics*. Chapel Hill: University of North Carolina Press.

Callahan, David. 1999. "$1 Billion for Conservative Ideas." *The Nation*, June 1, 21.

Cassidy, John. 2006. "Murdoch's Game." *The New Yorker*, October 16, 68–85.

Chang, Jeff. 2005. *Can't Stop, Won't Stop: A History of the Hip-Hop Generation*. New York: St. Martin's Press.

Christian Century. 1995. "Marchers Make Pledge." *The Christian Century,* November 1. http://findarticles.com/p/articles/mi_m1058/is_n31_v112/ai _17611068/pg_1.

Christian Century. 1997. "PK Message Strikes Close to Home: Lyndi McCartney, Wife of Promise Keepers Founder Bill McCartney, Experienced Eating Disorders and Contemplated Suicide, According to an Interview in the *New York Times.*" *The Christian Century,* December 10, 1151(2). http://findarticles.com/ p/articles/mi_m1058/is_n35_v114/ai_20114096/pg_1.

Cohn, Diana, Francisco Delgado, and Luis J. Rodriguez. 2002. *Sí, se puede! = Yes, we can! Janitor strike in L.A.* El Paso, Tex.: Cinco Puntos Press.

Conason, Joe, Alfred Ross, and Lee Cokorinos. 1996. "The Promise Keepers Are Coming: The Third Wave of the Religious Right." *The Nation,* October 7.

D'Emilio, John. 2000. "Cycles of Change, Questions of Strategy: The Gay and Lesbian Movement after Fifty Years." In *The Politics of Gay Rights,* edited by Craig A. Rimmerman, Kenneth D. Wald, and Clyde Wilcox, 31–53. Chicago: University of Chicago Press.

De Witt, Karen. 1993. "Gay Official Has the Look of Apple Pie and the Outlook of a Revolutionary." *New York Times,* April 24.

Edut, Talit. 1997. "*HUES* Magazine: The Making of a Movement." In *Third Wave Agenda: Being Feminist, Doing Feminism,* edited by L. Heywood and J. Drake, 83–102. Minneapolis: University of Minnesota Press.

EPI. 2006. *Datazone.* Economic Policy Institute. Available from http://www .epinet.org/content.cfm/datazone_dznational.

Faludi, Susan. 1996. "Where's the Feminist Conspiracy?" *The Nation,* April 29, 5–6.

Faludi, Susan. 2005. *Backlash: The Undeclared War against American Women.* New York: Anchor.

Faux, Jeff. 2002. "Solidarity Ever?" *The American Prospect,* November 30.

Fraser, Steve, and Joshua Benjamin Freeman. 1997. *Audacious Democracy: Labor, Intellectuals, and the Social Reconstruction of America.* Boston: Houghton Mifflin.

Frater, Elisabeth, and G. I. A. Fenoglio. 2001. "Surveying Feminism's Progress: Interview with Patricia Ireland." *National Journal* 33 (26): 2120.

Goode, Stephen. 1997. "Armed with Common Sense, Anita Blair Attacks Feminism." *Insight on the News,* 31(3).

Graff, E. J. 2002. "How the Culture War Was Won." *The American Prospect* 13 (19): 33–36.

Johnson, Haynes Bonner. 2001. *The Best of Times: America in the Clinton Years.* New York: Harcourt.

Kaplan, Temma. 1997. *Crazy for Democracy: Women in Grassroots Movements.* New York: Routledge.

Kirp, David. 1996. "Perfect Enemies: The Religious Right, the Gay Movement, and the Politics of the 1990s." *The Nation,* September 9, 44–48.

Kristol, William, ed. 2005. *The Weekly Standard: A Reader: 1995–2005.* New York: HarperCollins.

Labash, Matt. 1997. "What Is—or Who Are—the Promise Keepers?" *Weekly Standard,* October 6, 24.

Leland, John, and Vern E. Smith. 1996. "Marching into Macon." *Newsweek,* October 7, 63–64.

Lerner, Steve. 2002. Interview with Monique Harden. California: Commonweal.

Liasson, Mara. 2001. Interview with Grover Norquist. In *Morning Edition, National Public Radio.*

Marable, Manning. 1998. "Black Fundamentalism: Farrakhan and Conservative Black Nationalism." *Race and Class* 39 (4): 1–22.

Martin, William C. 1996. *With God on Our Side: The Rise of the Religious Right in America.* New York: Broadway Books.

Mathisen, James A. 2001. "The Strange Decade of the Promise Keepers." *Books and Culture* 7 (5): 36.

McKissack, Fredrick, Jr. 1995. "Thanks a Million." *The Progressive* 59 (12): 23–25.

Meyerson, Harold. 2000. "The Red Sea: How the Janitors Won Their Strike." *Los Angeles Weekly,* April 28.

Moberg, David. 2001. "The Six-Year Itch." *The Nation,* September 3/10, 11–16.

Nation. 1995. "Outmarching the Hatred (Million Man March, October 16, 1995)." *The Nation,* November 6, 521–523. http://findarticles.com/p/articles/mi_hb1367/is_199511/ai_n5580399.

Nation. 2001. "Let's Get Organized." *The Nation,* September 3/10, 3.

Nava, Michael, and Robert Dawidoff. 1994. *Created Equal: Why Gay Rights Matter to America.* New York: St. Martin's Press.

Noble, Charles. 2004. *The Collapse of Liberalism: Why America Needs a New Left.* Lanham, MD: Rowman & Littlefield.

Osborn, Torie. 1996. *Coming Home to America: A Roadmap to Gay & Lesbian Empowerment.* New York: St. Martin's Press.

Osborn, Torie. 2006. Interview. Los Angeles, September 7.

Pew Center. 1999. "Retro-Politics: The Political Typology, Version 3.0." Washington, DC: Pew Center for the People and the Press.

Pollin, Robert. 2003. *Contours of Descent: U.S. Economic Fractures and the Landscape of Global Austerity*. New York: Verso.

Reed, Adolph, Jr. 1995. "Black Politics Gone Haywire." *The Progressive* 59 (12): 20–22.

Reilly, Rick. 1989. "What Price Glory?" *Sports Illustrated*, February 27, 32–34.

Ruffin, David C. 1996. "The March: A Million Men Signal Resurgent Advocacy." *The Black Collegian* 26 (2): 136–139.

Schaller, Michael, and George Rising. 2002. *The Republican Ascendancy, 1968–2001*. Edited by J. H. Franklin and A. S. Eisenstadt, *The American History Series*. Wheeling, IL: Harlan Davidson.

Scully, Matthew. 1997. "The New Malaise?" *National Review* 49 (20): 30–32.

Shapiro-Perl, Nina. 1991. *Justice for Janitors: Si, Se Puede! Yes, We Can!* Service Employees' International Union (distributor), video recording.

Signorile, Michelangelo. 1993. *Queer in America: Sex, the Media, and the Closets of Power*. New York: Random House.

Smolowe, Jill. 1993. "Crusade for the Classroom." *Time*, November 1, 34–35.

Walker, Rebecca, ed. 1995. *To Be Real: Telling the Truth and Changing the Face of Feminism*. New York: Anchor Books.

Whit, Matt, and Rand Wilson. 1998. "The Teamsters' Fight at UPS." In *Not Your Father's Union Movement*, edited by Jo-An Mort, 179–188. New York and London: Verso.

Williams, Patricia J. 1995. "Different Drummer Please, Marchers!" *The Nation* 261 (14): 493–494.

Wolf, Naomi, et al. 1993. "Let's Get Real about Feminism: The Backlash, the Myths, the Movement." *Ms. Magazine*, September/October, 34 (10).

The Politics of Transition: Redefining Political Identities

OVERVIEW

American political life in the 1990s was propelled by two powerful and contradictory forces. In politics and government proper, professional politicians and political activists set themselves to transforming the two major political parties. Among the citizenry as a whole, however, political disaffection and disengagement prevailed.

From a historical perspective, Americans were comparatively less interested in government, elections, and civic organizations than they had been in the past. Political engagement had been declining over several decades and by many measures hit a nadir in the 1990s. Disaffection hardened into a virtual political philosophy of its own; fewer voters than ever showed up for elections.

The Democratic and Republican parties each underwent fundamental transformations in the 1990s. Each party entered the 1990s internally rent, with the fragile relationships among its constituents endangering the prospects of electoral success. For Democrats, the defeat of the party's two most recent presidential candidates called into question the viability of the already frayed New Deal coalition and the New Deal legacy of liberal social reform. Republicans, on the other hand, were for the first time in more than half a century facing the tensions of victory. The alliance of disparate factions that had brought Ronald Reagan to the presidency began to unravel during the presidency of George H. W. Bush.

Although there were moments of high drama when it appeared that one party—or one faction within it—had triumphed, the decade as a whole was one of stalemate. In 1992, the implosion of the Republicans and the election of President William Jefferson Clinton led commentators to pronounce the death of conservatism and herald the birth of a new Democratic Party. Then, in 1994, Georgia representative Newt Gingrich led another self-proclaimed Republican "revolution"; with victory, Republicans speculated about the end of the two-party system and openly doubted the legitimacy of Clinton's claim to be president. Clinton himself was reduced to claiming the president was "still relevant." The Democrats recovered in 1996 and again in 1998, but through distinctly old-fashioned campaigns that called into question the supposed triumph of New Democrats. The campaign for the presidential election of 2000, which began in 1998, seemed a replay of earlier battles, only less interestingly and engagingly so. In the 1990s, Republicans hoped to institutionalize the Reagan legacy, as Democrats had done after Roosevelt's presidency. They failed. The Democrats hoped that Clinton's presidency would restore them to political hegemony. It did not.

Stalemate was the result of the decade's political competition, but the day-to-day activity and spirit within the parties was anything but staid. To the contrary, as we have seen in the previous chapter on social movements, it was a decade of political ferment. Centrists, New Deal liberals, and progressives debated each other about the substantive direction for the party, as they worked together to keep Democrats in office. The centrists, led by Clinton, dominated the party apparatus through the decade, even as the liberals and progressives performed the yeoman work of voter mobilization. The loss of the presidency in the contested election of 2000 rekindled the party's internal contention. As 2001 opened and Republican George W. Bush was inaugurated, the different factions of Democrats had fought each other to a draw. Within the Republican Party, the internal factional battle was less visible to the public but more decisive. The Republican Party was utterly and rapidly transfigured, as the Right, organizing from the bottom up, routed moderate Republicans and won control of the Republican Party.

Nevertheless, the frenzied activity within the parties occurred within a broader social milieu of pervasive disillusionment with the political system. The opinions of the majority of Americans toward politics ranged from disregard and apathy to distrust, anger, and cynicism. Most Americans who were eligible to vote did not; when people turned their attention to politics, they had little good to say about their elected officials or the functioning of the various levels of government they depended on. The political culture of the 1990s was forged out of this seemingly odd conjuncture of public detachment and political innovation. Indeed, the two currents significantly reinforced each other at every turn.

This chapter opens with an examination of Americans' political views, sensibilities, and opinions over the course of the 1990s followed by a chronological review of the political transformations that occurred in the 1990s. The chapter examines the state of the Republican coalition; key events during George H. W. Bush's presidency; and the mood of Americans in the 1992 election year, their experience of government and its failures, and the consequences of the Bush presidency for both political parties. The processes through which the Democratic and Republican parties were transformed and the consequences of this process for national partisan divisions are also discussed. The last section examines the impeachment of President Clinton from the perspective of social and cultural history by situating the politics of scandal in the context of the media culture and partisan divisions of the late 1990s.

TIMELINE

Late 1989   Berlin Wall falls (November 9–10).

The United States invades Panama in largest military operation since Vietnam War (December 20).

1990   The Americans with Disabilities Act is passed.

Saddam Hussein, dictator of Iraq, invades neighboring Kuwait (August 2).

President George H. W. Bush declares a "New World Order" and engages in diplomacy to build an international coalition against Iraq.

Bipartisan agreement to increase taxes to reduce the federal budget deficit is signed by Bush, who thus breaks his "Read my lips—no new taxes" campaign pledge.

1991   The United States launches war against Iraq and wins a quick victory in what is known as the Persian Gulf War.

Anita Hill alleges sexual harassment by Clarence Thomas in hearings before the Senatate Judiciary Committee.

Antiabortion group Operation Rescue mounts a four-city civil disobedience campaign.

David Duke, former Grand Wizard of the Ku Klux Klan, wins the Republican primary for governor of Louisiana.

A failed coup attempt in the Soviet Union results in the dismantling of Communist rule and dissolution of the union into separate republics.

1992   A Los Angeles riot rages for five days after a Ventura County jury finds four Los Angeles police officers not guilty of beating an African American motorist, Rodney King (April 29).

Democrat William Jefferson Clinton is elected president, defeating Republican incumbent Bush and independent H. Ross Perot.

Amendment Two to the Colorado constitution is passed, prohibiting antidiscrimination statutes to protect gay and lesbian rights.

President Bush finalizes agreement on the North American Free Trade Agreement (NAFTA) after failing to win reelection.

Strategic Arms Reduction Treaty, the first ever to dismantle nuclear weapons, is ratified by U.S. Congress.

Bush pardons Reagan officials involved in Iran-Contra scandal.

1993   The World Trade Center in New York City is bombed (February).

Clinton's economic stimulus package is filibustered and defeated.

Clinton's budget, which reduces the deficit and increases taxes, is passed by Congress.

The Brady Handgun Violence Protection Act and the Family and Medical Leave Act, both previously vetoed by Bush, are signed by Clinton.

Hillary Clinton's Health Care Reform Task Force unveils a plan for universal health care (September).

Republicans Richard Riordan and Rudolph Giuliani elected as mayors of Los Angeles and New York, respectively, after running tough-on-crime campaigns.

Clinton champions NAFTA, which is ratified over significant Democratic opposition (December).

News about the Clintons' Whitewater investment is first revealed (December).

1994   Clinton health care reform is defeated.

The Whitewater investigation begins.

The Omnibus Violent Crime Control and Prevention Act, including funding for more police, and the Violence Against Women Act are passed.

Anti-immigrant Proposition 187 is passed in California.

"Three Strikes and You're Out" law is passed in California.

Uruguay Round of trade negotiations under the auspices of the General Agreement on Trade and Tariffs (GATT) are completed and signed by the United States in April. The agreement creates the World Trade Organization (WTO), which begins operation on January 1, 1995.

Republican congressional candidates issue a Contract with America.

Republicans sweep national and state elections, and Georgia representative Newt Gingrich becomes Speaker of the House.

The Christian Coalition emerges as the leading political organization of the Christian Right.

1995   Timothy McVeigh and Terry Nichols bomb the Oklahoma City Alfred P. Murrah Federal Building.

The United States brokers the Dayton Accord for Bosnia, and U.S. troops are sent to Bosnia in peacekeeping mission.

The federal government is shut down, precipitated by budget impasse between House Republicans and Clinton.

1996   The Personal Responsibility and Work Opportunity Act is passed, reforming welfare.

The Supreme Court declares Colorado's Amendment Two unconstitutional in *Romer v. Evans*.

The Antiterrorism and Effective Death Penalty Act is passed.

The Telecommunications Act deregulates the communications industry.

Ralph Nader and H. Ross Perot mount third-party presidential races.

Clinton defeats Republican Robert Dole and is reelected president.

1997   The Taxpayer Relief Act of 1997 reduces taxes on inheritance and capital gains and provides middle-class tax credits.

Congress holds hearings on campaign finance reform.

1998   Clinton is investigated in the Monica Lewinsky sex and perjury scandal.

Former wrestler Jesse Ventura is elected governor of Minnesota.

Campaign finance reform legislation passed by the House is filibustered to defeat in the Senate.

Republicans lose 10 House seats in the midterm election.

Gingrich resigns as Speaker of the House.

Lame-duck House votes articles of impeachment against Clinton.

A surge of Latino voters returns Democrats to statewide power in California.

1999   Gingrich resigns his House seat amid corruption charges involving his political action committee (January).

The Senate impeachment trial of Clinton ends in acquittal (January–February).

The Financial Services Modernization Act is passed, repealing the last remaining regulations of New Deal era Glass-Steagall banking legislation.

The 2000 presidential campaign begins with George W. Bush emerging as the early front-runner.

Mass demonstrations against globalization take place at World Trade Organization meeting in Seattle (November 28– December 3).

ISSUES, VOTING, AND VIEWPOINT IN THE AMERICAN PUBLIC

Shaping political culture and political contestation in the 1990s was Americans' widely shared mood of disillusionment with politics, politicians, and government. In the first half of the decade, as many Americans parried the economic blows of the recession and jobless recovery, political disillusionment expressed itself in the phenomenon of the "angry voter." In 1992, one survey showed three-quarters of American voters believing that "government is pretty much run by a few big interests looking out for themselves," a rise of 20 percent in only eight years. Other polls and surveys confirmed its conclusions. In 1964, 76 percent of Americans had trusted government "to do what is right" "most of the time" or "just about always." By 1992, only 29 percent did. Between those two dates were the debacles of Vietnam and Watergate, the years of stagflation and malaise (Judis 2000). Nonetheless, voter turnout in 1992 indicated that angry Americans still believed their vote mattered; 55 percent of eligible voters came out to the polls, a level that had not been matched in a presidential election

Arkansas governor and Democratic presidential candidate Bill Clinton addresses a campaign rally, 1992. (Corel)

since 1972. In 1994, disaffection showed itself in the unanticipated Republican sweep of congressional and state elections and a drop in turnout to 36.6 percent. Voter turnout continued to plummet, dropping to 49 percent of eligible voters in the 1996 presidential election, its lowest level since 1924. Hardly a third (32.9 percent) of Americans who could vote did so in 1998, a low not registered since the wartime election of 1942 (U.S. Bureau of the Census 2000, Table 479, p. 291).

Although the 1990s was a decade of declining interest in and trust of politics, politicians, and government, a minority of Americans remained engaged in the political sphere. Those who considered politics a vital part of their daily life devoted much of their energy to a struggle to reorient the political parties. Like the broader public, they believed something had gone wrong in American democracy. Their solution, however, was not to opt out but rather to contend for democracy's soul, to return the American government to its proper course, and to rekindle the political spirit of their fellow citizens. In their engagement with the political process, conservative New Right activists and liberal and progressive activists shared a common experience. Millions of their disaffected compatriots agreed with them about the need for change. By the end of the decade, Americans were mostly satisfied economically, no longer so angry about government, and more prone to trust it to do something to help the vulnerable. But they remained dissatisfied with the political system and politicians: 54 percent wanted a third party to arise (Pew Center 1999).

On many of the issues contested by political activists, there was indeed wide agreement among the American public. By substantial majorities, Americans wanted the environment cleaned up and protected, Social Security and Medicare preserved and strengthened, the minimum wage raised, and the influence of money and lobbyists in the political system restricted. Polls, surveys, news reports, anecdotal stories, and community initiatives all confirmed broad consensus on these matters. Yet they were all hotly contested politically because powerful business interests stood to lose from these measures. Proposals to privatize Social Security and Medicare; the defeat of legislation to raise the minimum wage in the late nineties; repeated administrative, legal, and political conflicts over environmental regulation; and the filibuster of campaign finance reform legislation all reflected the jockeying of business groups, not an outpouring of popular disgust at government activism. Although the conservative movement had spent 15 years attempting to hone political disaffection into an antigovernment philosophy, polls showed that Americans' belief in governmental activism grew over the 1990s (Teixeira and Rogers 2000).

On cultural issues on which most Americans agreed or felt apathetic, a similar dynamic unfolded when a politically mobilized and energized minority sought to change the status quo. Conservatives hoped to end affirmative action and to outlaw abortion. Gays and lesbians hoped to expand the civil rights of gay people and gain greater acceptance in American society. Interestingly, though these groups were on opposite sides of the so-called Culture Wars, each gained political ground. Support for equal rights for gays rose spectacularly during the 1990s, especially among young people. Support for the right to abortion as laid out in *Roe v. Wade* eroded. At the end of the decade, a majority still supported a woman's right to abortion in the early stages of pregnancy, but agreement with the feminist view—as advanced by the pro-choice movement—that women should have self-determination over their reproduction plummeted. These issues, such as abortion, the status of gay Americans, and affirmative action, were the flashpoints of the Culture Wars and are examined in more detail in the last chapter. Here, it is important to underscore that significant change in public opinion on these issues occurred because of political mobilization. It is unlikely that such a rapid change in opinion would have taken place without active movements that sought to influence opinion and institute their goals politically.

Whereas activists had inserted particular issues into national debate that only a minority considered to be of vital importance or relevant to their lives, other issues such as crime, guns, trade, and welfare deeply worried and divided Americans. These issues thus became driving ones in politics, determining how people would vote and how they appraised their elected leaders.

Finally, there were issues that dominated the news but actually mattered little to the vast majority of Americans, except as objects of entertainment and fascination. Most of the political "scandals" fall into this category. Forces as dis-

Table 4.1. Public Confidence in Government, Public, and Other Institutions

Institution, ranked from most negative to most positive	Strongly positive	Strongly negative
Political organizations, e.g., Republican or Democratic parties	15	43
Congress	15	39
Organizations that advocate a particular cause	20	30
Federal government	23	31
Major corporations	24	27
Organized labor	25	29
State government	26	26
Media	29	30
Public society benefit, e.g., civil rights, social justice, community improvement organizations	31	21
Public higher education	51	12
Military	54	12
Religious organizations	55	12
Small businesses	56	8
Private higher education	57	8

Note: The survey questioned respondents whether they had a "great deal," "quite a lot," "some," or "very little" confidence, or "no opinion" about 27 institutions. The table above includes results for the top 5 and bottom 5 institutions, and 3 of the 17 institutions that fell in the mid range. The strongly positive column includes those who answered that they had a great deal or quite a lot of confidence; the strongly negative column includes only those who answered very little.

Source: Independent Sector, The Gallup Organization, *Giving and Volunteering In the United States, 1996.*

parate as the adoption of new communications technologies, corporate consolidation of the media, and the activism of wealthy movement partisans pushed political scandal to the forefront of the mainstream media. Although Americans avidly consumed the spectacles, few cared much about the issues they raised. In retrospect, the press's coverage of the many fill-in-the-blank-*gates* only deepened most Americans' cynicism about politicians and the political system. Poll results over the course of the most covered and potentially most serious scandal, the Clinton-Lewinsky case, suggest that most Americans concluded "a pox on both your houses." The incessant media coverage of alleged scandal was an unreliable barometer of American opinion in the 1990s.

In a middecade Gallup survey on Americans' confidence in their social, cultural, economic, and political institutions, Americans reported the least amount of confidence in Congress and the political parties, and the most in private higher education and small business (see Table 4.1). The survey further demonstrated that the dissatisfaction with government and politicians was complemented by a deep suspicion of the civic organizations most frequently charged as "special interests" (organized labor and major corporations) and those associated with political advocacy in the broad sense. This table includes all categories in which 25 percent or more—or one in four Americans—expressed a negative view. For comparison, it includes the ratings of the three institutions that inspired the greatest level of confidence: private higher education, small businesses, and religious organizations. When the positive and negative views are taken together, the survey as a whole suggests more than just dissatisfaction with formal politics. It reveals a profound alienation from the public sphere all together.

Crime

In 1994, nearly two out of five Americans surveyed thought crime was the most important issue for government, and about one out of three believed crime was the most serious problem facing their own community. "No subject generates more concern than violent crime, none touches people more deeply and personally, none triggers more emotion," the journalist Haynes Johnson observed after talking to hundreds of Americans in his travels during 1992. "More than any issue . . . the growing specter of violence leads people to think that something fundamental has been broken in America" (Johnson 1995, 13). Essentially, Americans believed that their government had failed them in one of the most basic tasks of any organized state—protecting life, property, and public safety.

These views reflected the reality that all types of crime had in fact been increasing and spreading geographically since the mid-1980s. There were fewer places to escape from its dangers. "When I was a boy my mother went anywhere she wanted to in this town and she never locked the door. Now I worry about somebody going in there and robbing and killing her," J. L. Chestnut, a black lawyer who lived in Selma, Alabama, told Johnson. "There are drugs everywhere in a little town like this. Basically, they come out of the ghettoes of Chicago and New York and Detroit" (Johnson 1995). Many Americans shared Chestnut's fear as well as his perception about the origin of crime. In addition, random and unusual acts of violence seemed to be occurring more frequently in part because the news media dwelled on the stories. America had the highest murder rate in the world. Cases, such as the slaying of a white three-year-old girl by Latino gang members who opened fire on her family's car after they had gotten lost and turned onto an unknown Los Angeles street, or that of the mother, Susan Smith, who drove her two children into a lake and deliberately drowned them, were sensationalized by the media, but the facts were all too true.

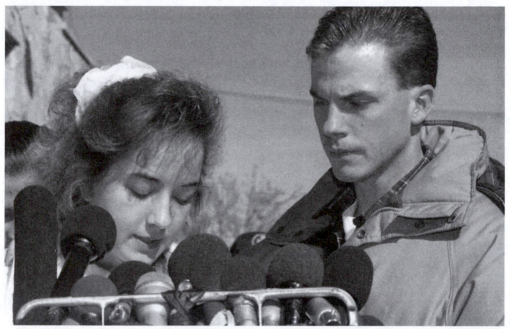

Susan Smith speaks at a press conference. (Spartansburg Herald Journal/Corbis Sygma)

Notwithstanding some highly publicized suburban incidents, crime remained most prevalent in urban America. The crack epidemic of the 1980s had spawned an increase in violent crime, much of it committed by heavily armed, drug-dealing gang members. Drug dealing was a lucrative but illegal occupation, and turf wars between rival syndicates rendered many poor urban neighborhoods unconscionably dangerous places to live. City governments, which suffered steep losses in revenue early in the 1990s, were already struggling to provide basic services like trash collection; they floundered when it came to public safety. As rising urban crime rates seemed to be transmogrifying into larger urban disorder, voters in the nation's two largest cities opted for change. In the mayoral election after the Los Angeles Riots, the city elected a moderate Republican businessman, Richard Riordan, rejecting the liberal successor to five-term Democratic mayor Tom Bradley. After the Crown Heights riots, New Yorkers ousted the incumbent Democratic mayor David Dinkins in favor of a successful criminal prosecutor, Rudolph Giuliani. Both Riordan and Giuliani promised to put more cops on the street to make their cities livable again.

Nationally, forces converged in the 1990s to elevate the issue of crime to the level of an apparent national emergency and to prompt the adoption of a new approach. For nearly a quarter of a century, Republicans had employed racially coded rhetoric on the subject of crime, arguing explicitly that Democrats' social liberalism coddled and encouraged criminals and implicitly that most criminals were African American. Over time, Republicans discredited the liberal view that crime was best dealt with by addressing its root causes, limiting access to guns, and rehabilitating convicted criminals. Republicans insisted instead that crime would fall by putting more police on the street, allowing them freedom to do their job, and deterring criminals through long prison sentences and the re-institution of the death penalty.

The pendulum swung definitively toward the Republicans' tough-on-crime approach after several notorious, yet very different, crimes. The first was the abduction, rape, and murder of 12-year-old Polly Klaus by a paroled rapist in 1993. Within months, 72 percent of Californian voters approved a sweeping initiative requiring lifetime imprisonment for repeat offenders. After passage in California, the "Three Strikes and You're Out" law quickly became a national model adopted by the federal government and almost half the states by the end of the 1990s. Two terrorist acts, the attack on the World Trade Center in 1993 and the Oklahoma City Bombing of 1995, precipitated federal action. The Omnibus Crime Act of 1994 and the Antiterrorism and Effective Death Penalty Act of 1996, both proposed and defended by a Democratic administration, institutionalized the public's clamor for harsh and long punishment.

As with so many complex and controversial social problems, political action on crime lagged behind the actual trend of crime and the public's opinion about it. At the high tide of political reaction in 1994, with the country eager to punish criminals and politicians anxious to comply, crime went down, falling to the level it had been in 1988. The decline was not an aberration; crime plummeted for the rest of the decade. Between 1991 and 2000, the violent crime rate fell 33 percent and the homicide rate fell 44 percent. Overall, the incidence of crime fell 27 percent, and the crime index rate reached its lowest point since 1972 (Crime in the United States 2000). In short, the worst was over. By 2000, the views of the American public on crime and punishment had shifted. Only 11 percent thought that crime was the most important issue for government. A majority had reconsidered their support for some of the tough measures instituted in the 1990s and believed that government should focus on addressing the root causes of crime.

The consequences of America's rush to adopt tough measures against crime were profound. Between 1990 and 2000, 400 new correctional facilities were built, and the nation's prison population nearly doubled. With 6.5 million men, women, and teenagers incarcerated or on parole in 2000, the United States had 3.1 percent of its population under correctional supervision. Many of the new policies, especially the differential handling of drug-related offenses, had a disproportionate impact on minorities. With penalties much higher for possession or sale of crack cocaine (used by the black and brown poor) than for powder (used by the white middle class and wealthy), African Americans and Latinos came to account for 57 percent of the country's prison population (U.S. Bureau of the Census 2000).

The Appeal of Independent and Third-Party Candidates

The 1990s brought a wave of independent political candidacies and forays into third-party politics not experienced at such high levels since the 1930s and, before that, in the Progressive era. The disparate efforts spanned the political spectrum, from far right to moderate left and much in between. Third-party and independent candidates shared little besides the desire to dislodge the established political parties and "insider" politicians, and the ambition that animates all who seek high political office. Yet the remarkably strong response of the American public to many of these candidates revealed the depth of national political disaffection in the decade.

H. Ross Perot set the mold for independent candidacies and at the same time revealed the limits of its practical effects. Running as an independent in the 1992 presidential election, Perot won supporters for his anti-Washington populism and plainspoken Americanness. Yet it was his personal fortune that kept his campaign alive in the media, funding the arsenal of television advertising and the provisional campaign organization "We the People." His personal fortune was also used in 1996 to create a formal political party, the Reform Party, which served as a vehicle for his personal presidential bids and was deployed for other third-party candidates at the local level. Money allowed Perot to spread his message and create an institutional mechanism for other outsider candidates. Without it, Perot could not have had the impact he did. Nevertheless, his message resonated with a sizeable minority of voters. In contrast, other wealthy candidates flopped during the decade.

Perot's constituency tended to be independent centrist white men who were disillusioned with both parties and felt that America was in decline. A minority among a similarly situated group of disillusioned white men were drawn not to centrists like Perot but instead to right-wing populists. Patrick Buchanan, who moved from Republican insurgent in 1992 to Reform Party independent over the course of three presidential elections, was the most successful at harnessing this sentiment for political gain. Buchanan drew attention and condemnation for expressing prejudice toward feminists, gays, Jews, and immigrants. But many voters drawn to his candidacy were indifferent to these cultural appeals. Instead, they appreciated him for his opposition to free trade and his muscular statements in favor of protecting American workers from overseas industry flight. Buchanan proudly proclaimed himself to be on the right, but in historical perspective, his candidacy stood within the enduring populist tradition spanning right to left.

Independent Jesse "The Body" Ventura, elected governor of Minnesota in 1998, also stood on that ambiguous and multivalent populist ground. Ventura, a former professional wrestler and occasional actor, won the governorship of Minnesota in a three-way race by defeating a sitting mayor and the son of former Democratic vice president Hubert Humphrey. Ventura's unexpected and much analyzed political rise seemed at first to confirm the consensus among historians and political commentators that what remained vibrant of the populist tradition was its right wing. On closer examination, Ventura defied that view. Contrary to the national media portrait that the brazen, outspoken, former wrestler was a right-wing demagogue, in his home state, voters perceived Ventura as a tough liberal. He publicly supported the rights to abortion, gay rights, gun control, and the legalization of medical marijuana. He was a Vietnam War veteran, yet he opposed the Persian Gulf War. He was against capital punishment and an array of measures favored by the religious right, such as school vouchers and prayer in school. His strongest support came from young voters and new voters, and he split the vote of women. Although his persona was one of a working-class tough guy, he won a majority of those who thought things were going well in Minnesota and those personally doing well, and lost among voters with less than a high school education (Wills 1999).

Reforming Elections

Polls and surveys in the 1980s and 1990s consistently revealed that Americans strongly disapproved of the apparatus of election financing and legislative favor and vigorously supported campaign finance reform. Public dissatisfaction crested in 1996 as House races became more expensive than ever and allegations of illegal foreign contributions plagued the Clinton campaign. The two major parties, for example, raised $445 million for the 1992 elections and $755.5 million for 1996 (U.S. Bureau of the Census 2000, table 482, p. 294). The contributions and spending reached record levels for a midterm election again in 1998, and it was only after this election that momentum for reform grew within Congress itself.

Americans wanted to limit the money raised and spent in campaigns; they had no love for political action committees, lobbyists, or special interests. There was not a single specific reform that a majority did not support. Reforms proposed to reduce the donations of the largest contributors—major corporations, wealthy candidates, labor unions—were supported by margins ranging from 66 to 80 percent. While Americans unambiguously favored reform, they just as clearly held a jaded view of their elected representatives' willingness to do something about the problem of money in elections. An absolute majority believed that neither Clinton nor the Republicans would deliver campaign finance reform, and two-thirds thought that the congressional hearings of 1997 would yield no more than a "partisan attack" by the Republicans (Shaw and Ragland 2000).

The doubts of the American public were confirmed in the last three years of the decade when a bipartisan campaign finance reform measure was proposed in both houses. In 1998, the House passed the measure that would have regulated so-called soft money and issue advertising. Introduced in the Senate as the

McCain-Feingold bill, the Republican leadership mounted a filibuster. Supporters were in the majority but fell eight votes short of ending the filibuster. The scenario was repeated in 1999, when the same legislation was again filibustered to defeat.

THE WANING OF THE REAGAN REVOLUTION

Republicans celebrated the start of the new decade in high spirits. Ten weeks earlier, the Berlin Wall had fallen, and Republicans claimed a party victory. The first eight months of 1990 augured another decade of triumph. Mikhail Gorbachev instituted multiparty competition in the USSR, ending the monopoly of power held by the Communists since the Revolution. Communist regimes throughout Eastern Europe fell peacefully and were replaced by popular governments. Even South Africa's apartheid gave signs of ending as the ruling party released Nelson Mandela from prison. East and West Germany moved toward reunification. But everything turned around between August and December of 1990. On August 2, Iraq invaded Kuwait, setting off a crisis in the oil-rich Middle East. America began preparing for a post–Cold War hot war. A new kind of international chaos loomed.

Upon Saddam Hussein's invasion of Kuwait, the Bush administration turned its attention toward a grand conception of a "New World Order" and the more prosaic diplomatic task of building a post–Cold War international alliance. The earlier and smaller military ventures in Grenada and Panama by Reagan and Bush had already demonstrated that Americans had put much of their Vietnam disillusionment with the American military behind them and would "rally around the flag," as the oft-repeated phrase had it. Nevertheless, a mood of anxiety pervaded the country in the months leading up to the Persian Gulf War. Iraq, everyone knew, would be no Grenada.

Ordinary Americans feared not only war in the Middle East. More important, domestic problems—decaying cities, a failing health care system, soaring federal and state budget deficits, plant closings and mass lay-offs, and political and business corruption—soured the national mood. It is not by oversight that domestic landmarks make no appearance in the catalogue of early post–Cold War triumphs. Bush's four years in office were not happy ones domestically.

Two weeks before the Persian Gulf War began in January 1991, *Time* magazine named its 1990 "Men of the Year—The Two George Bushes." In retrospect, it was a prescient piece of journalistic analysis. With the lightning-quick victory of the United States in the war, Bush's approval ratings rose to the highest level ever recorded for a sitting president. But the Man of the Year issue of *Time* in 1991 more perceptively tapped into a deeper mood in the country. One of the George Bushes, according to *Time,* "finds a vision on the global stage; the other

American troops on the move in the Persian Gulf War, 1991. (Department of Defense)

still displays none at home" (Church 1991). Depicting a leader who seemed to care little about ordinary Americans, senior writer George J. Church wrote, "His domestic policy to the extent that he has one, has been to leave things alone until he could no longer avoid taking action. That strategy of deliberate drift burdens the nation with a host of problems that have become worse over the past decade: drugs, homelessness, racial hostility, education, environment" (Church 1991). Twenty-two months later the American public would reach the same conclusion.

The Reagan Coalition Fractures

Bush unskillfully presided over the disparate alliance of various kinds of conservatives, business leaders, and social moderates that uneasily made their home together in the Republican Party after Ronald Reagan. With Bush at the head of the party, the tensions and disagreements within were all too public. Piqued already that Reagan had done so little to enact their agenda despite the critical role they played in his rise to the presidency, conservatives barely tolerated Bush. For his part, Bush attempted to meet conservative demands on key issues to hold their support through his presidency and reelection bid. Bush opposed gun control legislation spearheaded by former Reagan press secretary James S.

Brady, who had been paralyzed during John Hinckley's assassination attempt on Reagan. He proposed a constitutional amendment to ban flag burning. He appointed an outspoken opponent of abortion, Clarence Thomas, to the Supreme Court. None of these positions had majority support in the American public but each was a litmus test for a specific conservative interest group. Despite these gestures, the Right began to break ranks with Bush. The first to balk were the small number of conservative isolationists who opposed American involvement in the Gulf. Then, when Bush reluctantly agreed to tax increases as part of the 1990 budget deal, conservatives deserted him in droves.

Business, an equally important constituency of the Republican Party, split over the wisdom of pursuing Reagan's economic policy into the changed environment of the 1990s. Over the course of Bush's presidency, as trade and budget deficits soared, businesses failed, and once-powerful manufacturing industries disappeared from the United States, some business leaders became convinced that the country needed a new approach. The dogmatic antitax and antiregulation stance, associated with Reagan's supply-side economics, seemed to them counterproductive in the contemporary global economy. The once solidly Republican business community started to splinter. In 1992, leaders of the Council on Competitiveness, made up of corporate executives, most of whom had been lifelong Republicans, endorsed Clinton (Judis 2000).

After 11 years of governance once hailed as a "revolution," the alliance over which Reagan had presided had fragmented, leaving the Republican Party weakened. Close associates of Reagan and Bush had been brought down in political and business scandals, sullying the record on which Republicans would have to run. The fiscal and economic policies of the Reagan administration had been abandoned, widely discredited among the American public and repudiated by many lifelong Republican business leaders and academics. Even the apparent success of Republicans on foreign policy was transmuted into a weakness in the electoral arena. The end of the Cold War removed the most important unifying issue—anticommunism—that had once kept Republican factions together. At the same time, the aftermath of the Persian Gulf War rekindled Americans' skepticism about military intervention in foreign lands and politicians who would lead them into such adventures.

Republicans, Taxes, and the Federal Budget Deficit

"Read my lips—no new taxes," Bush had famously promised in the 1988 presidential campaign. His primary victory was widely attributed to the pledge, and so too was his victory over Dukakis seen to be proof of the wisdom of his antitax stance. But by 1990, the federal budget deficit had grown to $221.2 billion. The deficit was almost entirely the creation of the Reagan era—it had nearly tripled between 1981 and 1990 (U.S. Bureau of the Census 2000, table 532).

With the economy faltering in 1990, opinion makers, business leaders, and leaders of both political parties knew that something must be done. But no one stood to gain from it politically. For Republicans, the policies responsible for the ballooning deficit—massive military spending combined with enormous tax cuts disproportionately benefiting the wealthy—had been essential to holding together the coalition that had brought Reagan and Bush to power. Any fix for the problem meant alienating one or another constituency, at the potential cost of reelection. For Democrats, the crisis atmosphere generated around the problem of the deficit set a precedent that fiscal prudence should be a priority over public investment. It was a notion that would sharply limit the money available for domestic spending—the peace dividend—for as long as a deficit existed.

Ultimately, President Bush and the Democratic-led Congress negotiated a budget compromise that raised taxes and reduced government spending. But by doing so, Bush broke his 1988 campaign promise. The tax increase set in motion the political unraveling of the Reagan coalition. Led by House minority whip Newt Gingrich, attacks by conservative Republicans cost Bush a 20-point decline in his approval rating.

Gender and Race in American Politics: The Clarence Thomas–Anita Hill Hearings and the Supreme Court

In 1991, President Bush nominated Clarence Thomas to the Supreme Court to fill the spot vacated by the retiring justice Thurgood Marshall. Thomas was put forward by the Republican Right, and it was widely understood at the time that Bush was making amends for increasing taxes and for his previous appointment of Supreme Court Justice David Souter, who had not voted with the conservatives on the court. The key issue, as all parties understood, was abortion. The goal of the Right was to secure a conservative Supreme Court majority to overturn the 1973 ruling in *Roe v. Wade* that women had a constitutional right to an abortion. Thomas's nomination, however, became a flashpoint in the nation's conflicts over race, sex, and the relations between men and women in American society after feminism.

When Marshall announced his retirement, there was a broad consensus, among Republicans and Democrats and white and black Americans alike, that an African American jurist should be appointed to succeed him. Likewise, across the political spectrum, it was understood that the fate of the liberal and civil rights jurisprudence pioneered by Marshall was uncertain. Thomas's record, however, strongly suggested that he was deeply conservative, close to the religious right, and opposed to affirmative action and abortion. He was on record praising Louis Farrakhan, the controversial leader of the Nation of Islam, and attacking Thurgood Marshall and other civil rights leaders. After his nomination, many civil rights and women's organizations announced their opposition. Since Thomas had been a federal judge for just two years, many in the legal profession also expressed concern that he was too inexperienced to serve on the Supreme Court.

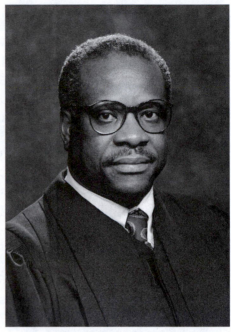

U.S. Supreme Court Justice Clarence Thomas. (U.S. Supreme Court)

Thomas's confirmation was politically critical to the Bush administration because it hoped to remain in the good graces of voters and leaders on the Republican Right. Expecting the confirmation hearings to hinge on abortion, White House advisors to Thomas honed a strategy drawn from lessons learned from the defeat of nominee Robert Bork in 1987. Understanding that the Senate would reject any nominee who explicitly announced opposition to *Roe v. Wade* and other landmark civil rights cases, the advisors instructed Thomas to rebuff as inappropriate questions about how he would vote on the Court, to disavow earlier positions as reflecting only his status as an employee of the Reagan administration, and to invite scrutiny on his character, where his image as a devoted family man and his personal Horatio Alger story would win the day (Wills 1995).

During the weekend before the scheduled Senate vote, the subject quickly changed when *Newsday* and National Public Radio (NPR) reported allegations that Thomas had sexually harassed a former employee. Anita Hill, a University of Oklahoma law professor who had worked for Thomas at two federal agencies during the Reagan administration, had submitted an affidavit, which detailed incidents between 1981 and 1983, to the Senate Judiciary Committee after interviews by the FBI. Hill, like Thomas, was African American and held conservative legal and political views. The Judiciary Committee ignored the report. After the story broke, feminist leaders and seven women House members marched to the Senate and demanded hearings on the matter.

In October 1991, in three days of nationally televised hearings in front of the all-male and all-white Senate Judiciary Committee, Thomas pronounced, "I am not going to allow myself to be further humiliated in order to be confirmed." Into an atmosphere already supercharged with the controversial subject of sexual harassment, Thomas upped the ante with a charge of racism. "I will not provide the rope for my own lynching," he pronounced. The allusion to the history of lynchings of black men following false charges of rape by white women was stunning. In response, African American scholars observed that no black man in American history had ever been lynched based on accusations from a black woman. "A black woman, herself a victim of racism," wrote law professor Kimberlé Crenshaw, "was symbolically transformed into the role of a would-be white woman whose unwarranted finger-pointing whetted the appetites of a racist lynch mob" (quoted in Wills 1995).

Hill took the stand and told the committee that Thomas had badgered her to date him and had repeatedly made lewd comments to her, among them describing sexual acts, his own sexual prowess, and scenes from pornographic films. Thomas and his supporters on the committee questioned Hill's motives and alluded variously to her as a disappointed suitor or one with sexual problems of her own. Feminists observed that such charges were typical of what women faced in rape trials and in sexual harassment cases, and it was no wonder that Hill and most other women were reluctant to come forward and thus court public humiliation. In response to Hill's testimony, Thomas repeated his charge in a subsequently famous attack on the committee for perpetrating "a high-tech lynching for uppity blacks who in any way deign to think for themselves, to do for themselves" (quoted in Wills 1995). The hearings closed with no resolution or agreement about whether the allegations were true or relevant to Thomas's confirmation. The Senate voted, by a margin of 52–48, to confirm Thomas to the Supreme Court.

The Anita Hill–Clarence Thomas hearings attracted tremendous public attention and were the source of enormous divisiveness; they virtually single-handedly made the subject of sexual harassment a national issue. Before the hearings, sexual harassment was a concept almost unknown outside legal and feminist circles. Afterward, every American knew what it was and had a strong opinion about it. For those who doubted the truth of Hill's allegations, the hearings were more evidence of how feminists turned any innocent act of a man toward a woman into a source of conflict. In the antifeminist movement, the Hill-Thomas hearings became a symbol of everything that was wrong and harmful about feminism. The episode also became a flashpoint of the broader Culture Wars, in which Hill and her defenders were seen by opponents as the embodiment of the liberal, politically correct establishment. Articles and books poured forth on the subject for several years after. For many women, the Senate's disregard of the charges and its treatment of Hill sparked outrage and a new attention to issues of gender inequality. Most analysts agree that the hearings influenced voting in 1992, when the gender gap reached close to 20 percent and a record number of women were elected to Congress. Not only did they mark the beginning of heightened awareness about sexual harassment; legal filings charging sexual harassment multiplied rapidly.

TURNING POINT YEAR: 1992

The year 1992 was a turning point in post–Cold War America. Problems, conflicts, and divisions dominated the American consciousness for most of the year. Fears of decline and hopes for renewal unfolded in the midst of a particularly consequential presidential campaign that would determine whether the Republican Party could consolidate its hold on power and secure its place as the dominant political party in the nation. What direction the United States would take in the new post–Cold War world seemed to hinge on the outcome of the election.

To most Americans, the most pressing and most disconcerting issue was the condition of the economy. The 1990–1991 recession defied expectations about how the economy functioned in the normal business cycle, as unemployment continued to rise even as the gross domestic product showed economic growth returning. With ruthless corporate downsizing, soaring health care costs, stagnating income, and rising unemployment, Americans felt insecure and disillusioned. Some found a scapegoat in Japan, accusing that country of causing America's economic decline.

To many Americans, the nation's culture was in as serious decline as was the economy. The Culture Wars over multiculturalism, feminism, the National Endowment of the Arts, and political correctness were a recurring theme in the headlines between 1990 and 1992. But to most Americans, controversies over history textbooks or the National Endowment for the Arts were irrelevant compared to the tone of commercial culture and its effect on youth. Explicit sex and graphic violence were everywhere in American movies, television, video games, and popular music, and television news shows had taken a turn toward sensationalism in their drive to win market share. American youth were spending more time watching television and playing video games, where parents had no control over their exposure to sex, violence, and vulgarity. Like many generations of parents before them in American history, 1990s' adults believed things had gotten much worse since they had been young.

Fissures in American society between the sexes were vividly exposed. The Hill-Thomas hearings and the subsequent confirmation of Thomas had galvanized feminists on the issues of sexual harassment and abortion. There was a pervasive bitterness among people who disagreed about the bounds of appropriate sexual conduct. As evidence of the pervasiveness of sexual violence and harassment, women pointed to the conviction of boxing champion and celebrity Mike Tyson on rape charges and the 1992 government report that detailed the sexual molestation of 26 female Navy recruits at the Navy's Tailhook Association Convention the previous fall. Conservatives, many men, and a handful of prominent antifeminist women accused them of humorlessness and authoritarian predilections.

America's long-simmering racial tensions erupted in April with the Los Angeles Riots. In 1991, a videotape of Los Angeles police officers beating an African American man, Rodney King, had been broadcast throughout the world. On April 29, 1992, the trial of those officers ended in an acquittal by an all-white jury. By that evening, what would become the largest riot in American history was in full flower. Although the Los Angeles Riots of 1992 turned out to be an isolated event, many Americans at the time worried this was only the beginning of nationwide urban unrest. Occurring in the midst of the presidential campaign, the Los Angeles Riots provoked a nationwide debate on the condition of urban America and the state of African American popular culture, bringing out into the open feelings about race—"the American obsession," as Studs Terkel aptly called it in his 1992 book (Terkel 1992).

Although the riots had many taproots beyond historic white-black conflict, they nevertheless exposed the depth of alienation and anger among poor urban African Americans in the wake of the Reagan Revolution. Race war, however, appeared more likely to be instigated by white supremacists. David Duke, a former Grand Dragon of the Ku Klux Klan, had won the Republican primary for the Louisiana governorship. After losing in the general election, he announced he would run for president in the Republican presidential primary. Although the Republican Party disavowed him, he nevertheless won 10 percent of the vote in Mississippi, and the Klan boasted it was having fantastic success recruiting in its campaign to create "1,000 David Dukes."

In these ways, 1992 was a particularly disturbing year for Americans. (Internationally, it was also a terrible year, with the siege of Sarajevo in the former Yugoslavia and clan war in Somalia. Each would lead to the deployment of American troops on peacekeeping missions.) Troubles such as these created an opportunity for the little-known governor of Arkansas, Bill Clinton, to win the presidential election of 1992. The year was a watershed in American political life, the election a definitive turning point in the transformation of the political parties, the redefinition of American political identities, the rise of the boomer generation to political maturity and power, the politicization of the Culture Wars, and the forging of a third way in social and economic policy.

Voter Discontent and the 1992 Presidential Campaign

By just about every account, American voters in the first half of the 1990s were angry. As early as the fall of 1991, it had become evident that American discontent had made Bush vulnerable to defeat. In a special election to fill a vacant Pennsylvania Senate seat, Bush's former attorney general was defeated by a Democrat, who ran against the Reagan-Bush record and boldly advocated expanded liberal programs that spoke to the new insecurity of the middle class. At the same time, the right wing within the Republican Party got into position to take Bush down as Patrick Buchanan and David Duke entered the Republican presidential primary. As fall turned to winter, Bush's prospects looked even worse. In the New Hampshire Republican primary, with all the advantages of incumbency, Bush won only 53 percent of the vote while Buchanan won 37 percent. On the campaign trail, Bush appeared to be profoundly out of touch. In one of the most publicized incidents, he made a televised campaign stop in a grocery store and expressed shock at the checkout line scanners and the cost of milk. It was new to him, but to no one else in the nation, and the episode seemed to confirm the nagging suspicion among voters that the president was ignorant of their daily experience of economic insecurity. No improvement was in sight, and polls revealed that 80 percent of Americans were dissatisfaction with the state of the nation.

In their disaffection, American voters were more prone than usual to look to a political outsider, and the presidential election of 1992 attracted unlikely contenders. Jerry Brown, former governor of California, mounted a populist-styled progressive challenge within the Democratic Party. Democratic front-runner Clinton also convincingly portrayed himself as a Washington outsider, undercutting Brown's most appealing selling point. In the Republican field, Buchanan more than any other candidate appealed to the resentment felt by Republican-leaning angry voters. The consummate outsider of the year, of course, was Texas billionaire Perot. Perot was the only one of the contenders financially capable and temperamentally inclined to run a campaign outside of the two major parties. When he unexpectedly withdrew his candidacy during the Democratic convention, it left the race to Clinton and Bush.

The contrast between the youthful Clinton, the poor-boy-made-good from Hope, Arkansas, and the elder patrician, Bush, could not have been more stark. While Clinton jazzed it up playing saxophone on a popular late night television show, every TV-watching American learned that their current president had not had to buy his own food or enter a grocery store in decades. In the first presidential election held since the advent of commercially driven 24/7 news, the candidates' image and personality assumed an outsized importance.

Each campaign spoke to the voters' discontent. The Clinton team targeted voters' economic worries, especially the pervasive insecurity felt by the middle class. Employing populist rhetoric at many turns, Clinton attacked elites, promised to "put people first," and proposed an economic stimulus program of public investment and job creation. While he was courting working- and middle-class voters with populist themes, he also promised to support NAFTA and deficit reduction, stances that pleased prominent corporate leaders who backed and funded his bid for the presidency. Clinton would become known in his presidency for his strategy of "triangulation," or what he and his compatriots in the Democratic Leadership Council termed the "New" Democratic direction. To win back white Democratic men who had often voted Republican since 1980, he also promised a middle-class tax cut, to put more police in the streets, and to "end welfare as we know it." In controversial moves of symbolic politics, Clinton made a special trip home to Arkansas to witness the execution of a severely mentally retarded African American man and pointedly attacked a female African American rapper during his speech to Jesse Jackson's Rainbow Coalition. On other social issues, however, Clinton was a solid social liberal; he earned the devotion of gay rights organizations for being the first national presidential candidate to proudly welcome their support, and he won the backing of feminists for a strong record on woman's issues. Though many Democrats were dismayed with Clinton's tepid support for many of their traditional economic programs, his accommodation of white moderates on crime and welfare, and his ties to business interests, they chose to mute their criticism and remain unified in order to win back the White House.

Although every indication from the press, and the polls, was that the economy was the overriding issue for voting Americans, Republicans ran their campaign on the cultural divide. With the economy in recession and his party in disarray, Bush banked on mobilizing social conservatives as his best hope for victory. While Clinton's colorful campaign advisor James Carville kept everyone on the message "It's the economy, stupid," Republicans relentlessly attacked Clinton's character and focused on disputed cultural issues in their campaign for "family values." In August, Americans were privy to what seemed to be the crack-up of the Republican Party at the Houston nominating convention. Leaders of the religious right and antifeminism—Pat Buchanan, Pat Robertson, Marilyn Quayle—spoke during the prime-time slots while Log Cabin Republicans (gays), moderates, and the still-large pro-choice contingent were shunted out of sight. The party's platform was also testimony to Bush's capitulation to the right wing of the party. Buchanan, given the opening night prime-time speech in lieu of Ronald Reagan, set the tone of the convention: "There is a religious war going on in this country for the soul of America. It is a cultural war, as critical to the kind of nation we shall be as the Cold War itself, for this war is for the soul of America. And in that struggle for the soul of America, Clinton & Clinton [Bill and Hillary] are on the other side, and George Bush is on our side" (quoted in Wills 1992, 366).

Clinton won the election with 43 percent of the popular vote. Bush garnered only 37 percent, the lowest share for a Republican since the party had split in the three-way contest of 1912. Perot, who had dropped out of the race during the Democratic convention and reentered it in the fall, won 19 percent of the popular vote. His was the second-best showing for a third-party candidate in U.S. history. Exit polls confirmed that the economy was the preeminent issue of the election with roughly half of all voters citing it as their most important concern. Voters who felt that their own situation was worsening favored Clinton by a 5:1 ratio. Millions of so-called Reagan Democrats moved back to the Democratic line, gaining Clinton the broadest support a Democrat had won since the civil rights legislation and social movements of the 1960s. The all-Southern ticket, with Tennessean Al Gore Jr. in the vice presidential slot, also paid off for Democrats, as they picked up six Southern and border states that had been voting Republican for several cycles. Women continued voting as they had during the years of Republican dominance, preferring the Democratic ticket by a 22-point margin.

The 1992 Elections and the Unsettled State of National and Local Politics

The 1992 elections ushered in a new phase of electoral and party politics, not only in the presidential race but also in congressional and state elections. Americans repudiated the Reagan Revolution by their presidential vote in 1992. But it was not clear whether the Democratic Party would regain its status as the dominant party of the 20th century. The year was one of political change more broadly, but with no single direction. Congress saw a turnover of 123 seats, but most of those were open seats and only a handful of incumbents were defeated. Democrats retained control of both Houses, but they lost nine House seats. The new class of Democrats was much more diverse than any previous Congress—there were a record number of women, African American, and Hispanic politi-

cians elected. The victory of the socially liberal baby boomers Clinton and Gore, who promised they would create a cabinet that "looked like America," and the election of a younger, more diverse Congress, suggested that the American public had accepted many of the changes brought about by the Left social movements of the 1960s and after. Yet at the same time, the Republicans newly elected to Congress were more conservative and more ideological than their predecessors were.

Ambiguous results at the state and local level, in retrospect, provided the first glimpse of the volatility and divisiveness in the American electorate that would come to characterize America in the first decade of the 21st century. There was little turnover in governorships and statehouses, with Democrats retaining control of the overwhelming majority, but there were local stirrings that boded

President Bill Clinton and Vice President Al Gore walk on the South Lawn of the White House, August 10, 1993. (William J. Clinton Presidential Library)

ill for Democrats. Fourteen states approved congressional term limits (which were later ruled unconstitutional) at a time when Democrats held majorities in the Senate and the House. Antigay initiatives were on the ballot in four states and municipalities. Oregon voters defeated one while Colorado voters passed a constitutional amendment (Amendment Two) to overturn local ordinances providing equal civil rights to gays. (In 1996, the Supreme Court ruled it unconstitutional.) In a sign of things to come, antiabortion activists gained control of the Kansas Republican Party after a summer of Operation Rescue protests at abortion clinics. Christian Right candidates won approximately 40 percent of the 500 school board races they contested (Smolowe 1993).

REMAKING THE POLITICAL PARTIES: THE DEMOCRATS

The 1990s was a transitional decade for the Democratic Party. The attempt to transform the party issued from the highest levels of the party leadership. In the parlance of the decade, the struggle pitted "new" Democrats—centrists—against "old" Democrats—New Deal liberals and 1960s progressives. Under Clinton's leadership, the centrists made significant headway in defining the party's philosophy and policies. Nevertheless, other constituencies within the Democratic Party remained vibrant, contesting the move to the center. Despite the repeated pronouncements by Clinton and allies about the triumph of New Democrats, the party remained a big tent for many different ideological tendencies and a diverse constituency.

Although Democrats aired their disagreements publicly and, often, with acrimony, the differences between so-called old Democrats and new Democrats were far less than those that were at the same time dividing and reconstituting the Republican Party. Although there were individual exceptions, every Democratic faction supported consumer rights, worker safety, and environmental regulation. All strongly supported the legal and political changes wrought by the civil rights movement. All supported workers' rights, progressive taxation, and programs to increase the incomes of the working and middle class. On many social issues and Culture War hot buttons, the distinctions among Democratic factions were subtle. Centrists, liberals, and most conservatives supported the preservation of *Roe v. Wade,* but some Democrats advocated more restrictions on the practice of abortion and a more limited interpretation of the landmark Supreme Court decision. A handful of Democrats favored ending affirmative action, many thought it should be "mended, not ended"—as Clinton adroitly proposed—and others wholeheartedly supported it. Gun control set urban Democrats at odds with rural Democrats, but there was a wide middle ground between them. Set against the contemporaneous move right in the Republican

Party and the virtual purge of Republican moderates, these were differences in degree, not kind.

The subject of greatest contention was economic policy. Although some Democratic centrists insisted that social liberalism had alienated Middle America and that the party needed to "get Right" on the social issues, the main divide in the party was really over economic issues. When Clinton entered office, many traditional Democrats thought that the economic insecurity they faced was a result of globalization. Many of Clinton's advisors, however, embraced the promise of globalization. The fights over free trade treaties in Clinton's first term would expose these divisions and play a large part in the setback Democrats met in the elections of 1994.

Clinton, New Democrats, and the Democratic Leadership Council

Clinton's election was widely perceived as not only a personal victory but also one for the centrist Democratic Leadership Council (DLC). Founded in 1985, the DLC sought to forge a new base of political power within the party. The group brought together politicians, policy intellectuals, and corporate funders. The group's regional base was the South, where Democrats had historically been more conservative than the rest of the party, and where white voters were exiting the party in droves since President Lyndon Johnson pushed civil rights legislation through Congress. Bill and Hillary Clinton were founding members, and Bill Clinton served as the body's president in 1990 and 1991. In its first year, more than 100 politicians joined the group; many of these were from the South or the Sunbelt (Baer 2000). Clinton maintained his ties to the DLC and the group took much credit for his successes. In retrospect, however, the DLC was only one of many influences on Clinton's presidency. Clinton, who was universally recognized as one of the most talented politicians of his age (by friend and foe alike), could never be simply the creature of a minority interest group within the party. Clinton worked with and listened to the DLC as he believed the situation warranted; he cherry-picked the DLC ideas he liked and ignored the rest. He frequently consulted other constituencies and policy advisors, and his cabinet included liberals as well as centrists.

Nonetheless, the centrist tendency promoted by the DLC exerted enormous influence within the Democratic Party in the 1990s. Convinced Democrats could win in the post-Reagan world only by attracting social moderates and disaffected independents, the DLC hoped to shunt aside several historically powerful liberal constituencies. Tactically, the DLC recommended that Democrats change course on a number of issues, such as capital punishment, welfare, and affirmative action, all of which were close to the hearts of Democratic liberals and progressives (Judis 2000). The debacle of Michael Dukakis's 1988 presidential

Robert Rubin, one of the chief architects of President Bill Clinton's economic policy, served as secretary of the treasury during Clinton's second term. (U.S. Department of the Treasury)

campaign was their touchstone in this regard. In that election, Bush and other Republican groups had tarred the Democratic candidate as a tax-and-spend liberal who was soft on crime. The infamous use of the Willie Horton ads, featuring an escaped African American rapist, was rightly condemned as racist. Nevertheless, the ads worked to the Republican advantage. The DLC argued that in order to make the party appealing to Reagan Democrats—white, working-class men who had seemed to respond to such Republican social and cultural appeals—and the many swing voters who had no strong party affiliation, the party had to move to the center.

In the late 1980s and early 1990s, the DLC's research wing, the Progressive Policy Institute, articulated a practical strategy for electoral victory and a vision of a revised liberalism. Although its program included communitarian initiatives, such as a national youth service program, the essential innovation of the DLC was to abandon the New Deal legacy on economic regulation and social welfare and shift the party toward a pro-business stance. Impetus for such a move also came from other sources, especially sectors of the business community.

Creating an International Free Market: Origins of the 1990s "Washington Consensus"

The globalized economy of today is largely the creation of self-proclaimed conservatives who, beginning in 1979, worked to reverse the domestic and international economic policies that had governed the world economy during the postwar era. The new turn was most closely associated with its leading advocates, Reagan, Federal Reserve chairman Paul Volcker, and British prime minister Margaret Thatcher.

Together in the early 1980s, the American and British governments embraced the "free market," rejecting Keynesian and social welfare policies that had been universally followed from 1945 to 1979. The international economic order created by the United States and the industrialized nations of Western Europe after World War II had been designed to prevent a repetition of the 20th century's catastrophes. Domestic national stability would be ensured through social wel-

fare programs and regulation of business; international stability would be overseen by international financial institutions and secured through strict control of
currencies and capital flows. The new generation of free marketeers who rose
to power in the late 1970s and early 1980s rejected these policies and the very
premises on which they were based. They argued that excessive regulation of
capital and the misguided attempt to maintain full employment through fiscal
and monetary policy caused economic stagnation. Prosperity could be restored
only through the adoption of free market principles; private investment would
drive the economy once capital was freed from restrictions, and the benefits
would "trickle down" to the working majority. In pursuit of this objective, the
governments of Reagan and Thatcher reduced welfare and other forms of social security, lowered taxes on the income and property of the wealthy, deregulated and privatized industry, and employed the power of the government to
break strikes and weaken their nation's labor unions. In the international arena,
they sought to open all countries to unrestricted trade and private, direct foreign investment. The International Monetary Fund (IMF) and the World Bank,
influenced largely by the United States through its control of the largest bloc of
votes, required countries that sought assistance to eliminate budget deficits,
reduce social spending, privatize national industry, open their nation's industry
to direct foreign investment, and deregulate the private sector. By the end of
the 1980s, much of Latin America, Africa, the Caribbean, and some Asian countries had gone through such a structural adjustment program imposed by the
international lending and development agencies. The same policy would be
imposed on the former Communist countries after the Cold War ended.

The free marketeers expected not only that developing nations would live up
to the dictates of fiscal austerity, minimal economic regulation, and open markets but also that the advanced economies would do so as well. The Reagan
administration introduced a novel set of domestic economic policies, "supply-
side economics," which were bitterly debated but prevailed during Reagan's
presidency and into the first years of the Bush administration.

As Americans celebrated the arrival of a new decade in 1990, two years of
anemic economic growth turned into a recession. The return of hard times in
the 1990–1991 recession opened the possibility that new leaders would reject the
economic policies of the Reagan era. The retreat from supply-side economics
began under Bush and was symbolized by the 1990 budget deal to raise taxes.

In 1992, Clinton won election largely on his populist-sounding campaign on
the troubled economy. Clinton also ran, however, as a new kind of Democrat,
one willing to reexamine the verities of Democratic New Deal economics and
entertain new constituencies. Led by investment banker Robert Rubin, who
Clinton named as chair of the National Council of Economic Advisors and later
treasury secretary, the Clinton administration pursued the trade, fiscal, social
welfare, and regulatory policies that were consonant with the global vision of
the conservative Republican free marketeers who preceded them. The Federal

Reserve, under Alan Greenspan, although independent of the administration, managed monetary policy and the regulation of the nation's banks in a manner consistent with such a free market vision. Gradually, in the mid-1990s, as the Clinton administration's economic priorities emerged, the term the "Washington Consensus" came into use to describe the bipartisan acceptance of the economic policies spearheaded by the administration. By some of its domestic critics, it was dubbed "Rubinomics," and in most of the rest of the world, this policy order was known as neoliberalism.

Clinton Democrats regularly spoke about charting a "Third Way" between the old New Deal liberalism and Republican free market conservatism. As Clinton's skillful thwarting of Republican attempts to undermine the universal social welfare programs of Medicare and Social Security and his tax hikes on the wealthy show, the Third Way was not just a slogan. The Third Way was, however, strongly opposed by liberal and progressive Democrats, especially on trade. The Clinton administration made some concessions and lost a few legislative battles over the Democrats' new direction on economic policy. Nevertheless, from a longer historical perspective, the Clinton Democrats in the 1990s built on, rather than repudiated, the system that had been forged by conservatives to undo the postwar liberalism of their Democratic forebears. Ultimately, the Clinton administration placed the power and authority of the U.S. government behind a global economy ruled by the free market, even as it cautiously sought to moderate some of the market's more adverse social consequences.

Health Care Reform

The crisis in America's provision of health care and health insurance had been one of the leading issues in the 1992 election, and Clinton had promised that health care reform was on the top of his agenda calling for putting people first. Universal health care, provided or financed by national government, was the norm in the industrialized world. Past Democratic administrations had proposed it and had been turned back.

Could the Third Way deliver to the anxious middle class? Could a major new social welfare program spearheaded by the government be achieved in the contemporary political environment when belief in liberalism and activist government had been undermined by conservative attacks? Should the market be enlisted to deliver social benefits? Health care reform proved to be the first litmus test of the New Democratic approach to social welfare.

President Clinton placed the first lady, Hillary Rodham Clinton, at the head of a 500-person task force to study the issue and propose health care reform. In the fall of 1993, the task force issued its recommendation for a market-based system of "managed competition," including universal coverage for the uninsured. Insurance companies would continue to be the intermediaries between patients and doctors while the federal government would use its leverage to regulate the quality of service provided, to negotiate fees to lower costs, and to provide coverage for the uninsured. The plan included an employer mandate, thus building on America's primary system of employment-based insurance by adding a compulsory element to it. The plan gave a leg up to health maintenance organizations (HMOs), which were then not yet as dominant as they would become by the late 1990s. Liberals would have preferred a universal single-payer system, like the one in use in Canada, but that was vulnerable to the Republicans' charge of "socialized medicine." The Clinton plan, in contrast, proposed using the power of the government to make the market work better. Polls at the initial release of the proposal showed two-thirds of Americans favored the plan and only one-fifth opposed it (Judis 2000).

Ultimately, health care reform was killed by well-organized opponents. Business opposition played a large role in the defeat. Large insurers initially supported the plan, but the smaller ones in the Health Insurance Association of America (HIAA) opposed it. The HIAA spent $50 million to defeat the plan, $15 million of it on a television ad campaign that featured a worried middle-aged couple named Harry and Louise questioning the plan. Polls showed public support dropping dramatically after the ads aired. Pharmaceutical companies and the National Federation of Independent Business, which represented small businesses, launched massive lobbying campaigns against the measure. Large companies that did not provide insurance to their employees, such as Wal-Mart, Marriot, and Pizza Hut, were more discreet in their efforts, meeting privately with Republican representatives. For these industry groups and companies, simple self-interest dictated opposition to health care reform.

Although moderate Republicans were initially disposed to compromise to reach bipartisan agreement on health care and the administration was willing to negotiate, conservative Republican activists calculated that any legislation would advantage Democrats and had to be resisted. In unveiling health care reform, Hillary Clinton had presented it as "the Social Security Act of this generation, the reform that would establish the identity of the Democratic Party and be the defining legislation for generations to come" (quoted in Judis 2000, 86). New Right publicist William Kristol agreed and, in a private memo that was distributed widely, warned that Clinton's universal health care plan "will revive the reputation of the party that spends and regulates, the Democrats, as the generous protector of middle-class interests. And it will at the same time strike a punishing blow against Republican claims to defend the middle class by restraining government" (quoted in Dionne 1996). Members of Grover Norquist's Wednesday group organized business opposition and lobbied Republicans with the message that no compromise would be acceptable. Norquist's group also kept reports about suspicious doings of the Clintons at the top of the news in the right-wing press, with the intent of discrediting the first couple as untrustworthy. For example, it was in the months when the Clinton health care plan was being publicly debated and polling well with the public that accusations about Vince Foster's murder and "troopergate" first surfaced and charges about Whitewater were revived. As the Democratic political journalist John Judis observed, the claims "recalled the scurrilous Republican attacks against the New Deal in the late 1930s" (Judis 2000, 86). By February 1994, the plan was dead and it was never brought to a vote (Starr 2007).

Globalization and Trade Policy: Party Divides and the Economic Divide

The fundamental division in the Democratic Party, the one that provoked the epic debate about the soul of the party, was over economic matters. Historically speaking, the working class constituted the base constituency of the "old" Democratic Party. New Deal economic regulation and social welfare policies had been crafted with their interests in mind. In the globalized world of the 1990s, industry flight had made trade the most critical issue to blue-collar Americans, and there was strong protectionist sentiment within the rank and file of the party. The New Democrats, however, sought to realign the party with corporate America and Wall Street; they favored a new economic policy to unleash American business in the global economy, which, as Clinton saw it, was the "best engine of prosperity." Practically, that meant free trade internationally, more business deregulation domestically, and, at the least, a distancing from the party's working-class and labor union base.

The Clinton administration championed globalization, and its international economic policy sought to remove trade restrictions to help American corporations succeed in the global marketplace. Over the course of two terms in office, the Clinton administration avidly promoted international free trade through the adoption of multilateral and bilateral trade agreements. The administration counted as its major successes the passage of NAFTA, the creation of the World Trade Organization out of the Uruguay round of trade negotiations, and trade normalization with China.

Many Democrats remained adamantly opposed to free trade. NAFTA proved particularly treacherous for the administration. In response to Democratic opposition, the Clinton administration had been forced to find a congressional majority among Republicans. The Democratic election defeat in 1994 was widely attributed to Democrats' disaffection with Clinton for his failure to deliver on many of his promises to restore middle-class security set against the zeal with which he led the campaign to ratify NAFTA. As a movement rose against globalization and the labor movement experienced a burst of vitality in the late 1990s, the administration met defeat on some of its free trade initiatives, most notably on its effort to gain fast-track authority in negotiations of trade treaties. The WTO meeting in Seattle in 1999 was designed to showcase Clinton's legacy of advanc-

Democrats and Social Liberalism: Gay Rights and Women's Rights

Gays had supported Clinton strongly in the campaign, with funding and with voter mobilization, and Clinton immediately moved to fulfill his campaign promise to open the armed forces to gay Americans. The military leadership, led by Chairman of the Joint Chiefs of Staff Colin Powell, resisted and publicly rebuked Clinton. Instead of risking a showdown with the military, Clinton issued the infamous "don't ask, don't tell" policy. The armed services could continue to enforce their ban on homosexuals, but they could not ask a member of the services whether he or she was gay. The compromise pleased no one.

Liberal and progressive Democrats were angered and disappointed that Clinton could crumble so easily; gay activists were infuriated. Clinton's appointments, however, of an unprecedentedly diverse cabinet and of Supreme Court Justice Ruth Bader Ginsburg signaled that he would be a reliable bulwark against conservative attacks on abortion and affirmative action. Feminists developed a strong working relationship with the administration and, in 1993 and 1994, helped gain passage of the Family and Medical Leave Act, the Freedom of Access to Clinic Entrances Act, and the Violence Against Women Act. With some trepidation, they continued to support him. Many feminist and gay rights leaders who had worked for decades in advocacy organizations went to work in the executive agencies of the Clinton administration. Outsider movements gained insider access for the first time.

ing free trade. Instead, it marked a watershed in the quest to put some brakes on unfettered globalization.

Refining the Third Way: Taxation, Environmental Protection, and Industry Deregulation

The New Democratic vision was one of the middle road—between Republican free market conservatism and Democratic economic liberalism. The Clinton administration rejected the more radical ideas and policies of the Reagan and Bush administrations. Nowhere was the break with the previous administrations clearer than in tax policy and in environmental protection. But on budget politics and the regulation of industry, the administration drew heavily from the Republican model and broke with its own party's traditions.

Taxes

Early in his administration, Clinton sought to bring the progressive principle back into the tax system. The 1993 budget, the first budget under his watch, increased tax rates on corporations and the wealthiest 3 percent of the population and levied a 10 percent surcharge on incomes over $250,000. The tax system was also employed to raise the incomes of the working poor by expanding the Earned Income Tax Credit (EITC) for low-wage workers. Pressure to focus on deficit reduction sunk Clinton's promised middle-class tax cut before it could be proposed. It, too, would have made the tax system more progressive. Not a single Republican voted for the budget, which included tax increases.

Republicans exploited the issue of taxes in the 1994 election and falsely charged Clinton with having raised taxes on the middle class. The new and emboldened Republican majority afterward tried to achieve large tax cuts, primarily for the wealthy, in their 1995 budget package. The Clinton administration outmaneuvered congressional Republicans in the budget showdown of 1995 and killed the proposed tax cuts.

The Clinton administration subsequently moved to appease elements of the Republican coalition on taxation, in part hoping to take the wind out of charges of raising taxes on the middle class. Child and education credits in the Taxpayer Relief Act of 1997 effectively lowered taxes for middle-class families. But in terms of revenue, the act's reduction of inheritance and capital gains taxes, which primarily benefited the upper fifth of the population, accounted for the largest proportion of the tax cuts.

Even with the concessions made to the antitax forces within the Republican Party, the poorest 20 percent of American families benefited the most from Clinton's tax policy. Middle-class families experienced a slight decrease in their taxes. Taxes rose only for the top 20 percent of families, with the wealthiest families among them experiencing higher rate increases. The top 1 percent, whose taxes had been reduced 9 percent under Reagan, experienced a 5 percent rise in taxes under Clinton. The Clinton administration thus took an initial step in reversing the Reagan tax legacy.

Environmental Protection
The Clinton administration rejected the conservative contention that environmental, health, and safety regulations constituted restrictions to market freedom. Clinton changed the course set by his predecessors in many specific cases in these areas. Through executive order, he expanded worker safety regulations to include repeated stress injuries, covering pink-collar office workers and blue-collar food processors at the same time. He rebuffed the perennial attempts by congressional Republicans to open the Arctic National Wildlife Refuge to oil drilling and resisted some of their attempts to attach antienvironmental riders to other bills. Secretary of Energy Hazel O'Leary initiated the Openness Project. Appeals to national security had exempted the Atomic Energy Commission and the Department of Energy from environmental regulations and the public review associated with environmental laws. O'Leary declassified the agency's records, thereby making public hitherto secret programs that had endangered public

health. She also moved to apply environmental regulations and clean up toxic pollution at sites under the department's authority. Clinton protected more land from development than any other president in the 20th century. He was unwilling, however, to expend the political capital necessary on the Kyoto Treaty limiting greenhouse gas emissions. Against Gore's strong objections, Clinton refused to submit the treaty to the Senate for a vote.

Arctic National Wildlife Refuge valley in the summer. (U.S. Fish and Wildlife Service)

Deregulating Industry

The deregulation of industry, which had begun under Carter and accelerated under Reagan and Bush, continued during the Clinton administration. The most significant acts of the Clinton administration completed the already far advanced deregulation of communications, media, and banking. The Telecommunications Act of 1996 deregulated the residential phone and cable TV industries and eliminated ownership limits on broadcast television and radio stations dating from the 1930s. The Financial Services Modernization Act of 1999 was the last step in the dismantling of New Deal era banking regulation. The process was already well advanced by the action of the two previous administrations, and by the Federal Reserve's interpretation of its role enforcing banking regulations.

The Telecommunications Act illustrates the convergence of New Economy ideology and the politics of the Washington Consensus. Passed by a bipartisan majority, Clinton extolled the measure, promising that by freeing market "competition" the act would unleash "innovation" and a communications revolution. Backers claimed it would spur technological development of telecommunications, promote consumer choice, and lessen costs. The industries affected had lobbied for a decade to achieve these measures and were generally happy with the legislation. Critics warned it would speed the consolidation of media companies and lessen the number and diversity of sources to which Americans could turn to for news and independent programming. Consolidation of media companies quickly followed the act's passage, but the optimistic economic forecasts also seemed to be vindicated as investments flowed into the telecommunications industry and the dot-com boom seemed a blessing. By the end of 2001, however, the industry had collapsed. One of the 1990s telecommunications leaders, WorldCom, was the biggest bankruptcy ever in U.S. history; another 22 telecom companies also went bankrupt. Telecom companies lost $2 trillion in market capitalization, and half a million people in the field lost their jobs (Stiglitz 2003).

Divisions and Debates within the Democratic Party

Out of the presidency for the previous 12 years, Democratic voters and politicians alike opted for unity during the 1992 election campaign. But the tactical unity masked real differences within the party. While the DLC led the charge to reinvent the Democratic Party, the activist base and many of the senior party leaders in Congress and the governors' offices remained committed to the social and economic policies of New Deal liberalism and to the reforms won by the civil rights and social movements of the 1960s and 1970s.

Most important to the Democrats' electoral future was Clinton's ability to deliver on his promises to the middle class. There were a few small victories in the first two years in office, such as the passage of more progressive taxation and the Family and Medical Leave Act. Republican opposition exercised through a Senate filibuster, however, removed from Clinton's economic plan many of the items the administration had planned to restore middle-class security. The defeat of health care reform was a major blow in 1994, an election year. Disagreements among Democrats in Congress—over crime, health care, trade, and the budget—played a role in the legislative defeats. That same year, the Fed raised interest rates, slowing economic growth and job creation before the tentative economic expansion had raised incomes. From the perspective of voters, Clinton's meager accomplishments were not enough. In 1994, some Democratic voters simply stayed home and did not vote, while many in the white working class repudiated the Democrats and voted Republican, clearing the way for the Republican sweep of Congress, governorships, and statehouses (Teixeira and Rogers 2000).

From 1994 until the end of the decade, even though Democrats remained loyal to Clinton, the party was consumed by internal squabbles. As E. J. Dionne, one of the leading centrist Democratic political journalists of the decade, wrote, "Among liberals, and among Democrats of all stripes, solidarity has become an antique notion" (Dionne 1995). Democrats had a proclivity for publicly airing their disagreements. The dilemma of the party was on public display in the 1996 presidential election. Liberals and progressives viewed Clinton's welfare reform act and punitive crime legislation as draconian acts that violated the party's principled commitment to security for the poor and to civil liberties. Nonetheless, congressional liberals and the Clinton administration had worked together to defeat all of the Contract with America items as originally proposed and, most important, to preserve Medicare against Republican cuts. The question for all was whether it was more important to defeat conservative Republicans or to wage a struggle for control of the party. In 1996, most liberal, progressive, labor, civil rights, and feminist leaders supported Clinton, although they were dismayed over Clinton's triangulating centrism. Jesse Jackson's speech at the Democratic convention expressed their perspective. He counseled "smiling through the tears. . . . I do not like the signing of this welfare bill, but I will not give up the ship" (quoted in Corn 1996). The sentiment was repeated in many variations throughout the campaign.

With Clinton's reelection in 1996, the DLC claimed victory in internal party struggles but conceded that it was a group of leaders and thinkers awaiting a mass following. Indeed, old-style Democratic politics had rescued the floundering party in 1996. The AFL-CIO, under a new reform leadership, had persuaded member unions to fund political advertising and voter mobilization to defeat Republican incumbents and committed the federation to working in concert with other progressive organizations. After a long-existing split between labor

The rise of a new labor movement and the political mobilization of Latinos after the passage of Proposition 187 helped turn California from a solidly Republican state to a solidly Democratic state between 1990 and 2000. Here, two pivotal leaders in that transition, Antonio Villaraigosa and Miguel Contreras, talk during a rally with UNITE laundry workers. (Slobodan Dimitrov)

"Triangulation": Welfare Reform

Clinton's effort to survive politically after the 1994 election yielded the most significant act of social policy undertaken by his administration: welfare reform. Clinton and his advisers, especially the controversial Dick Morris, took the 1994 election as an object lesson in the virtues of centrism. The effort to chart a new philosophical and political course between liberalism and conservatism, with which Clinton began his presidency, transmogrified into a political strategy of "triangulation." Clinton feinted right of congressional Democrats and left of congressional Republicans. Most important, he sought to co-opt the issues on which Republicans siphoned off Democratic voters—crime, welfare, and a balanced budget. When necessary, he ignored the base of the party or circumvented Democratic politicians, insisting always that his centrism was better situated to win back swing and centrist voters in the upcoming elections. In some cases, like welfare reform, he sacrificed his own stated principles for the sake of a political victory; several liberal members of the administration quit in protest over his signing of the 1996 legislation.

Welfare was one of the most contested social issues within the Democratic Party. It divided self-identified moderates from liberals and progressives—and all too often, white from black Democrats. Welfare reform powerfully affected the lives of millions of Americans, and its consequences continue to unfold in contemporary America.

and the groups that had grown out of the 1960s New Left, the diverse liberal constituencies within the party were tentatively beginning to work in concert.

The dispute over who had really won the election and where the party could find new Democratic voters echoed through the rest of the decade. The DLC posited that, with declining interest in politics and voting, the margin of victory for Democrats would come from the cosmopolitan, upwardly mobile New Economy professionals. "America is becoming more affluent and the number of upper-middle-class voters is expanding," according to Al From (quoted in Borosage 1999). Liberals and progressives countered that there were more potential votes for Democrats among the millions of working- and middle-class voters who had deserted the party or stopped voting altogether, and that a renewed commitment to restoring economic security would bring them back. The DLC claimed credit for the 1998 midterm defeat of congressional conservatives. Progressives pointed out that it was their leaders in Congress who had led the fight against the right-wing impeachment drive, had changed the administration's views on privatizing Social Security and Medicare, and had stalled unpopular free trade initiatives and won a commitment to improve labor and environmental protections in future trade agreements. Increased voter turnout for the Democrats in 1998 among Latinos, African Americans, women, and union members, all of whom voted Democratic by large majorities and were most opposed to Republican initiatives, gave credence to the latter claims.

Democrats of all persuasions agreed that the stalemate within the party left it at the end of the decade without a clear program, strategy, or vision. Public squabbles dominated the lead-up to the 2000 election. The vice presidential candidate, Joseph Lieberman, took every opportunity to prove he was a cultural and religious conservative, hostile to the social liberals of the party. Some progressive leaders declared that the party had betrayed them. The close popular and electoral vote of the 2000 election, which George W. Bush ultimately won after the Supreme Court ruling in *Bush v. Gore* to stop the vote recount in Florida, was at least partly due to the internal divisions within the Democratic Party.

Progressives, the Democratic Party, and Ralph Nader's Presidential Bids

Democratic Party progressives were the ones most threatened by the centrist tendencies within the party in the 1990s. Especially in its DLC articulation, centrism specifically targeted the progressive-left positions on the economy, social welfare, racial justice, criminal justice, and, to a lesser extent, feminism and gay rights. Progressives faced the dilemma throughout Clinton presidency of whether they would be more effective working within the party, registering protests with occasional votes for third-party candidates, or forming a new party altogether. They were also bitterly divided among themselves.

The question rose to the fore in the presidential elections of 1996 and 2000, when Ralph Nader ran on the Green Party ticket with a message tailored toward disaffected progressives. Nader had been a pioneer of the consumer rights and environmental movements and was widely respected for his integrity, his commitment, and his effectiveness, even among those who did not share his goals. Unlike the other alternative or third-party candidates of the decade, he neither had a devoted constituency (like David Duke or Pat Buchanan), nor won people over with his quirky charm (like Ross Perot or Jesse Ventura). He nevertheless was a political force and his lackluster campaigns, arguably, by splitting the Democratic vote in 2000, have had a lasting impact on American history.

REMAKING THE POLITICAL PARTIES: THE REPUBLICANS

In 1992, the nation elected a Democratic president as the national media focused on the ugly public divorce between the hapless George H. W. Bush and the Republican Party's angry conservatives. Meanwhile, under the radar, Christian Right and antiabortion activists won control of Republican state and local committees, election to political office, and passage of antigay ballot initiatives. The organizational élan that the Right demonstrated locally in 1992 went national in 1994, as Republicans took control of Congress for the first time in a half century, and Republican congressman Newt Gingrich noted the mandate they had won and declared the triumph of a Republican-led New American Revolution. The Republican Party was utterly remade in the 1990s by New Right grassroots activists and movement leaders, and the strategic coordination between the two. In the preceding chapter, we examined the New Right as a social movement; this section examines the political objective and effect of conservative organizing. Republican electoral victories in 1994 and 2000 resulted in part from earlier grassroots organizing within conservative issue organizations and traditionalist religious groups. Kansas provides a case study of the entry of activists into local Republican politics. On a national level, the major shift in the fortunes of the two parties resulted largely from the move of white Southern men into the Republican Party and the ascendance of the party in the region on that basis. Lobbying groups run by powerful conservative leaders, such as Pat Robertson and Ralph Reed's Christian Coalition, played an important role in transmitting the local power shift in various states to Washington and forging the disparate state Republicans into a cohesive force. By the late 1990s, most moderate Republicans had been replaced by conservatives, and the national party had a distinctly conservative cast (Hacker and Pierson 2006). Although the Right remained a numerical minority among Republican voters and in American society and New Right politicians during the 1990s were unpopular and unsuccessful in governance, conservatives had become the gatekeeper of the Republican Party by the end of the decade.

Operation Rescue and the Transformation of the Kansas Republican Party

In the summer of 1991, the militant antiabortion group Operation Rescue called for a "Summer of Mercy" in Wichita, Kansas. Seeking to duplicate their efforts in Atlanta in 1988 and Los Angeles in 1990, the group called for citywide acts of civil disobedience against abortion clinics. At the time, politics in Kansas was characterized by a bipartisan consensus, in which both parties were led by moderates. Local, state, and national offices were divided between Democrats and Republicans, each party was itself dominated by centrists, and both parties were pro-choice. Government and business leaders of both parties disapproved of the tactics of Operation Rescue and sought to organize a unified civic response to inform the out-of-staters that they were not welcome. When thousands of protestors showed up in Wichita, newspapers warned of the danger of religious fanaticism and insisted that the local citizenry opposed the demonstrations (Frank 2004).

Although many of the protestors were from out of state, Operation Rescue nonetheless attracted some of the citizens of Wichita. Kansas had long been a hotbed of Protestant evangelicalism, but it was not until the Summer of Mercy that deeply held religious feelings were channeled into politics. The city was brought almost to a standstill by the mass civil disobedience of the antiabortion activists. Pro-lifers were lying under cars, picketing doctors' homes, chaining themselves to fences, and going to jail in droves. At antiabortion gatherings throughout July and August, including one that drew 25,000 people and would be remembered as a catalytic moment, conservative organizers went among the activists to encourage them to sign up—for political action. The mailing list of Kansans for Life grew by 10,000 within weeks of the rally, and the list was then put to electoral use.

A year later, in August 1992, the rank-and-file antiabortion activists had won control of local Republican committees, capturing the majority of precinct positions in an otherwise lightly attended primary election. After winning control of the party machine, insurgents defeated moderate Republicans in the primary and then went on to victory in the general election for the state legislature. The 14-year-incumbent Democratic Speaker of the Kansas House, for example, lost his seat to a carpet layer with no previous political experience.

Intense political infighting within the Republican Party between the new conservatives and the established moderates ensued. In 1994, the conservatives swept state and national offices, making Kansas a virtual one-party state and installed their members in Kansas House leadership positions and issued a "Contract with Kansas." By 1996, Kansas's U.S. congressional delegation was 100 percent Republican and 100 percent antiabortion, and conservatives were conspicuously freezing moderates out of positions of influence. The internal conflict within the Republican Party persisted and became increasingly bitter. When moderates regained control of the party organization in elections in 1999, the conservatives ignored their electoral defeat and set up their own organization.

The 1994 Election

In the elections of 1994, Republicans routed Democrats and took control of both houses of Congress for the first time since Eisenhower's presidency. Although the Republican leadership interpreted the win as a mandate for the bold conservative vision proclaimed in Georgia representative Newt Gingrich's "Contract with America," the deeper cause was the persisting economic insecurity of many Americans and their disappointment that the change promised by Clinton had not materialized. Although the mythology of the contract continued to circulate over a decade later, scholars are unanimous that it was an insignificant factor in

Republican Speaker of the House Newt Gingrich, Republican National Committee chair Haley Barbour, and Republican representatives Dick Armey, Dennis Hastert, and John Boehner at a press conference on the Contract with America. (Erik Freeland/Corbis)

the election. Most voters never heard of the contract—until after the Republican victory and their claims that the election was a mandate to enact the contract (Hacker and Pierson 2006). The 1994 election had the effect of arresting the developments set in motion by the Democrats' 1992 victory. Less clearly a referendum on American opinion than some wanted to claim, the election was nevertheless absolutely critical in shaping the political and media culture of the remainder of the decade.

Republicans claimed a national mandate, but the evidence of the shifts in electoral support in the elections between 1992 and 1998 suggests that more voters were registering their dissatisfaction with Clinton in 1994 than were endorsing the agenda of the Gingrich-led Republicans. Widespread apathy was reflected in low turnout in 1994: voter turnout dropped to 38.7 percent, around the same level as that for midterm elections since the 1970s but well below the turnout for the 1992 presidential election. Some key Democratic constituencies stayed home, while others, especially the white working class, repudiated the Democrats and cast their lot with the Republicans. These traditionally Democratic constituencies increased their support for the Democrats and Clinton in 1996 and 1998, however, after they witnessed the Republicans in power. A minority of voters were clearly aware of the changes promised by the conservative House leadership. Conservative voters were mobilized by the National Rifle

Association, the Christian Coalition, and conservative talk radio and television hosts. For the first time, Republicans were able to mount get-out-the-vote drives that were as successful as Democratic ones had been for decades. Roughly two-thirds of gun owners and those who listened to talk radio voted Republican. The combined effect of lower-than-normal Democratic voting and historically high conservative voting produced small margins of victory for Republicans in many local races.

Regional Focus: The South Turns Republican

At the beginning of the 1990s, the Democratic Party dominated local and state politics and the congressional delegations from Southern states, as it had since the birth of the "solid South" in the era of Jim Crow. By the end of the 1990s, the "Southern Strategy" pioneered by Richard Nixon in 1968 had come to fruition. The South had turned from solidly Democratic to solidly Republican, as white voters deserted the party that had institutionalized the legal and political changes won by the civil rights movement.

Since 1968, when Nixon had made racially coded appeals to white conservatives about busing, crime, and "big government" and George Wallace had mounted an explicitly segregationist independent candidacy, Democratic presidential candidates had fared poorly in the South. Native sons like Jimmy Carter and Bill Clinton made some headway, but non-Southern candidates were trounced. In 1994, Republicans extended their success at the presidential level to the congressional level, for the first time since Reconstruction winning a solid majority of the seats in the Southern states' congressional delegations. In the largest-ever House freshman class, the Georgian Gingrich welcomed such Southern conservative firebrands as Tom DeLay (Texas), Robert L. Barr (Georgia), and Steve Stockman (Texas). Governorships and statehouses also turned over. The reversal in the region was a lasting one (Schaller and Rising 2002; Lamis 1999).

The transformation of Southern party politics had been under way for almost two decades and had been spurred by a combination of forces. The most important cause of the shift was the resistance of white Southerners to black equality. The restoration of civil rights and the re-enfranchisement of African American Southerners with the Civil Rights Act and the Voting Rights Act passed in the Johnson administration spawned a backlash among white Southerners. African American voters turned to the Democratic Party, which supported civil rights, and white voters began to look elsewhere. Two decades of race-based political appeals by Republican candidates persuaded the majority of white Southerners to leave their historical party affiliation behind. These white Southerners also tended to be evangelical or fundamentalist Protestants, and the increasing ties between political evangelicals and the Republican Party deepened their sense of cultural affinity with Republicans.

The Christian Coalition

The Christian Coalition was a voter education and lobbying organization created to harness the beliefs and fervor of Christian conservatives for political purposes. Founded in 1988 by Pat Robertson and Ralph Reed in the wake of Robertson's failed presidential bid, the Christian Coalition set out to build on, but also to adapt, the model of Jerry Falwell's Moral Majority. The goal of the Christian Coalition was to mobilize religious activists to win control of the Republican Party at the local, state, and federal level to forward their "pro-family" cultural and social agenda (Layman 2001). During the 1990s, the Christian Coalition was acknowledged as the leading political organization of the religious right.

The Christian Coalition, consciously seeking to expand the Christian Right voting bloc through a coalitional approach, deliberately departed from the pioneering work of Falwell's Moral Majority. Falwell's Moral Majority had been based in the fundamentalist churches of his Baptist Bible Fellowship denomination. The Coalition, in contrast, attempted to build interdenominational chapters and to overcome the divisions among different denominations of conservative Protestants and between Protestants, Catholics, and Orthodox Jews. It trained its activists to mute any rhetoric of fundamentalism in order to appeal to other religious conservatives. The organization was relatively successful in attracting orthodox Pentecostal, fundamentalist, and evangelical white Protestants, but less so in convincing African American evangelicals, Catholics, and Jews to join. In an additional departure, Reed steered the Christian Coalition to expand its purview beyond core cultural issues to take on other issues, such as tax credits for families, welfare, and crime, in line with other branches of the conservative movement. Reed also sought compromise on some cultural issues, for example, disavowing interest in a constitutional amendment to ban abortion. In retrospect, these latter moves were strategic rather than principled; the opponents of abortion proved far more successful in winning piecemeal restrictions than they had in the quest to ban abortions all together. Compared to other Christian Right organizations (such as the Family Research Council), the Christian Coalition was relatively quiet about homosexuality. It sought, in short, to chart a more pragmatic course in order to enhance its influence within the Republican Party, not always to the approval of its grassroots base (Layman 2001).

The Coalition catapulted into the political headlines in the 1994 election for its purported success in turning out Christian conservatives to vote for Republicans. The Coalition was originally organized as a tax-exempt nonpartisan organization. Its main activities were to produce "score cards" and voter education guides informing voters of candidates' stands on key "pro-family" issues. These guides were then distributed free to conservative churches to disseminate them among voting congregants. The Christian Coalition claimed to have distributed 30 million voter guides in the 1994 elections and 45 million in the 1996 election. Opinion varies on the influence of the group. In one reputable survey, one in five voters reported basing their voting decision on the guides (Manza and Brooks 1999).

The Christian Coalition, Continued

By late 1997, the Christian Coalition had gone into a tailspin. Reed left the organization in 1997 to become a political consultant. The new leadership discovered that the organization, which had once boasted chapters in 48 states, 2.8 million members, and a budget of $26.5 million, was more than $3 million in debt. In 1999, amid more troubles, disgruntled former staff informed a *New York Times* reporter that only 7 state chapters were still viable and that many of their earlier claims about membership and influence had been deliberately inflated. "We never distributed 40 million guides," the Coalition's former national field director told the *New York Times.* "State affiliates took stacks of them to recycling centers after the election. A lot of churches just put a pile of them on the back table. I never considered effective distribution anything short of inserting them into church bulletins, but in very few churches did that actually happen." In 1997, the Internal Revenue Service denied the Christian Coalition's application for tax-exempt status, stating that its work was not nonpartisan but favored the Republican Party. That decision led many churches, concerned about their own tax-exempt status, to thereafter decline the Coalition's request to distribute voter guides (Goodstein 1999).

Although the Christian Coalition faced difficulties as an organization in the late 1990s, it had performed a critical function in organizing religious conservatives, especially evangelicals, as a solid Republican voting constituency. Reed and Robertson remained powerful political figures even after they left the organization, and many other organizations existed by the turn of the millennium to activate the religious vote. Although the majority of evangelicals in America continued as in the past to remove themselves from politics, in the election of 2000, 73 percent of evangelical voters voted for Bush. They provided him with 40 percent of his total vote, although they made up only 25 percent of the electorate. Almost four out of five evangelicals who voted for Bush reported that they had received political advice from a religious source, such as their pastor, the Christian Coalition, or voter guides placed in their church (Kellstedt et al. 1994).

New social relationships, unrelated to the South's historical legacy of slavery and segregation, accelerated the political transformation. Many middle-class white Americans from other parts of the country moved to the booming new suburbs of the South in the 1980s. Southern-style racial politics held little interest for them, relatively unburdened as they were with the unique regional history of the South. But these new migrants tended to be conservative on most issues. The Republican platform, particularly its probusiness, antigovernment, antitax economic conservatism, was thus inherently appealing. Leaning independent or Republican, they saw little to change their mind among Southern Democrats, consumed as they were by factionalism between white moderates and officeholders and the African American voters who inevitably provided them the margin of victory.

The final cause of the political realignment in the South was redistricting after the 1990 census. Few African Americans had won election in the South in the 15 years since the passage of the Voting Rights Act. Under legal order and political pressure, Southern states redrew district lines after the 1990 census to create districts with a majority of African American eligible voters. (Judicial orders enforced this as a remedy in some cases while legislatures took the lead in others.) An African American candidate would be more likely to win election, the theory went, in a district with a majority of African American voters. The theory proved correct. The remaining districts, however, had far fewer African American voters, and with overwhelmingly white populations, Republican candidates handily won election over white moderate Democrats. Redistricting, adopted to enhance the political power of African American voters, ironically proved to be the tipping point for turning the South Republican (Lamis 1999).

PARTISANSHIP AND THE CLINTON SCANDALS

The Republican "New American Revolution" led by Gingrich was short-lived. Just two years later, Clinton coasted easily to reelection over Senate leader Republican Bob Dole. The quick turnabout was not just a preference for Clinton over Dole, but rather it reflected Americans' identifications with the political parties; 1995 was the only year between 1989 and 2000 that more people identified themselves as Republicans. In 1996, Republicans had lost favor and more Americans again identified themselves as Democrats. (The largest percentage of Americans claimed they were independent or "other.") The Democratic advantage continued through the remainder of the decade (Pew Center 1999).

The problem for Republicans was that their congressional leaders had overreached, and had done so on matters dear to a majority of Americans—Medicare and Social Security. Democrats rebounded and conservatives were rebuked. Although Republicans remained the majority in the House, Clinton had demonstrated that he would outmaneuver them on every important conservative initiative. Therefore, after the eclipse of the Gingrich moment, Republicans and conservatives faced the problem of being essentially the minority party in America and trying to keep their fragile coalition together with no prospect of delivering political victories. It was in this electoral context that the so-called Clinton scandals came to dominate American political life.

Republicans frequently used investigations into the Clintons to shore up their most enthusiastic conservative constituents, keep the administration off kilter, and hold their fragile coalition together. The conservative movement, particularly, avidly lodged charges against the Clintons and worked tirelessly to keep accusations alive. As Richard Mellon Scaife, one of the largest funders of conservative causes, told a guest at a private luncheon in 1994, "We're going to get Clinton." Scaife remained true to his word (Johnson 2001, 11). He funded the "Arkansas Project," which disseminated the troopergate accusations, from which the Paula Jones sexual harassment case arose, and the Vince Foster suicide conspiracy theory. (Foster was a former colleague of Hillary's and an old family friend of the Clintons who went to work in the White House with them. Suffering from depression and the pressure of accusations against him and the Clintons, he committed suicide. The Right charged that he had been murdered to cover up his knowledge of the Clintons' nefarious doings, and investigation of the charges was bundled with Whitewater.) Another beneficiary of Scaife's money was Judicial Watch, which charged that Commerce Secretary Ron Brown had been murdered—not accidentally killed in a plane crash—to prevent him from revealing knowledge of the Clintons' crimes. Details of the role played by conservative activists, funders, and leaders in the Clinton scandals can be easily found in many journalistic accounts and popular histories of the Clinton years (Stewart 1996; Toobin 1999).

A pliable media was the unwitting accessory to the conservative movement activists, reporting every rumor that might, if substantiated, raise questions about wrongdoing. As the late journalist Lars-Erik Nelson wrote in one of several acute analyses of the role of the press in the new media world, "In the current ethics of the press, there need be no actual misdeed to set the bloodhounds baying; there need be only an appearance, perhaps a slowness or clumsiness in responding to a false charge, and we are off and running" (Nelson 1999).

The "scandals" were distracting to the nation and certainly eroded Clinton's reputation and support for his presidential agenda. Opinion remains mixed about whether the scandals, especially the Clinton-Lewinsky affair, played a significant role in the 2000 election.

The Whitewater Case

The Clintons faced reports of scandals and charges of corruption from the time of the 1992 presidential campaign until their last acts in the White House. The train of investigations began with reports of an Arkansas real estate investment in the 1980s. In March 1992, *New York Times* reporter Jeff Gerth detailed rumors about a real estate investment of the Clintons in "Whitewater," and questioned the propriety of the deal and the Clintons' relationship with an Arkansas banker. In 1993, with new reports on Whitewater coming out, Republicans alighted on the so-called scandal and other accusations emerging in the right-wing press about Bill's illicit sexual affairs and Hillary's past practices as a lawyer in Arkansas. The

Clintons, in what would come to be considered one of their biggest missteps, resisted discussing the Whitewater investment. By doing so, they prompted many to wonder whether there was indeed something to hide.

After pressure from Republicans, Clinton agreed in January 1994 to a special counsel investigation, and Attorney General Janet Reno appointed Robert Fiske Jr. to the position. Fiske, a Republican, went about his work in a professional, nonpartisan manner. He quickly completed a report confirming that Vince Foster had committed suicide. Six months into the investigation, after Clinton signed the reauthorization of the independent counsel statute that had lapsed, a court dominated by Republican judges removed Fiske and named Kenneth Starr to replace him (Toobin 1999).

Kenneth Starr, who had personal and professional ties to some of the conservative campaigns to discredit Clinton, interpreted his role as independent counsel exceedingly broadly and used his powers in that office to pursue all allegations against the Clintons, no matter how remote their connection to his original charge to investigate Whitewater. It was in this way that Clinton's sexual relationship with Monica Lewinsky became a public matter, and that sex would become the catalyst for the first impeachment of a president since the 1860s.

Impeachment and American Popular Opinion

Between 1995 and 1997, President Clinton engaged in a sexual affair with Monica Lewinsky, a White House intern in her 20s. Distraught after the affair ended, Lewinsky confided in Linda Tripp, a co-worker at the Pentagon. Both of them had once worked in the White House; Tripp had been transferred for blatantly partisan activity and hostility toward the Clinton staffers. Nursing resentments and cultivating ties with right-wing activists, Tripp promised them she would help provide material to undermine the Clintons. She coaxed Lewinsky to tell her stories over the phone while she recorded the conversations on tape; she insisted that Lewinsky keep evidence of her encounters with Clinton and later instructed investigators what to ask for. Working closely with Lucianne Goldberg, a literary agent in New York with close ties to right-wing activists, she persuaded Lewinsky to tell her story to Michael Isikoff, a reporter for *Newsweek* (Johnson 2001, chs. 8–9; Toobin 1999).

When the magazine decided to hold the story until it could undertake further fact-checking, the Internet's pre-bloggers took over. On January 17, 1998, shortly before midnight, Matt Drudge posted his report on *The Drudge Report,* a right-wing Web site, charging that *Newsweek* had killed a story about a sexual affair between the president and a White House intern. Other anti-Clinton Web sites immediately circulated the story. The mainstream broadcast and print media, uncertain what to do in the face of the scoop, decided to report the fact that rumors were circulating. Clinton gave his State of the Union Address 10 days later, and polls afterward showed his public approval rising from an already high 57 percent to 73 percent. A majority also said that anything that might have happened with Lewinsky was a personal matter (Berman 2001).

The Lewinsky case had become public in large part because Starr, whose investigations into the Whitewater and Vince Foster cases were proving to be dead-ends, chose to take information about Lewinsky and seek powers to investigate. Starr learned of the allegations from conservative activists working with Tripp. The activists had contacted Starr's office in early January, providing information about Clinton's affair with Lewinsky and Clinton and Lewinsky's depositions in the Paula Jones civil case, hoping to interest the independent counsel's office in it. (Clinton and Lewinsky had separately testified in depositions in that case that they had not had sexual relations. Much of the debate of the months of the scandal concerned what sorts of sexual activities amounted to sex.) There was in fact no connection between Whitewater and the Paula Jones case, but Starr nonetheless decided to seek authority to include the Jones case in his investigation, thus opening up the possibility of charging Clinton with obstruction of justice. The course of events was complex and often unseemly—it included an 18-hour FBI interview with Lewinsky, in which her requests to contact a lawyer were repeatedly rejected, and the deposition of a sitting president in a civil case unrelated to his public responsibilities about matters that a vast majority of Americans told pollsters they considered to be private and personal matters.

For the next year, the Lewinsky scandal dominated the news. The new media culture, in which the ability to win market share trumped old journalistic values, had matured over the decade. Shows that had been launched during the O. J. Simpson case were joined by new ones of a similar format, such as Fox's *Hannity and Colmes,* but which were more openly partisan.

On September 9, 1998, Starr submitted the independent counsel's report, which had begun as an investigation into the Whitewater deal. His report stated that the investigation had revealed "substantial and credible information" that Clinton "committed acts that may constitute grounds for impeachment," including perjury, obstruction of justice, and engaging "in a pattern of conduct that was inconsistent with his constitutional duty to faithfully execute the laws." All of the counts concerned actions regarding the Jones and Lewinsky cases, not Whitewater, nor any act undertaken by Clinton in his official duties as president. On September 11, 1998, every Republican and all but 63 Democratic representatives voted to make *The Starr Report* public on the Internet, before any of them or the president and his lawyers had read it. The report outlined 11 possible grounds for impeachment, but the real meat of the report was in its graphic descriptions of sex, which Starr had decided to include in the report (Starr et al. 1998).

Despite the revelations, polls consistently showed that Americans continued to support the president throughout the months of 24/7 coverage of the Lewinsky

*Supporters of Bill Clinton rally outside Congress during impeachment proceedings.
(Brooks Kraft/Sygma/Corbis)*

scandal and were disgusted by Starr's handling of the case and Republican attacks on Clinton. They revealed that more than two-thirds of Americans had a
favorable view of Clinton's performance as president although many disapproved
of his personal behavior.

The verdict of the 1998 election came down hard on the Republicans, who
were avidly pushing for Clinton's removal. Democrats picked up five seats in
the House and lost none in the Senate. The night of the elections, Gingrich announced his resignation from his position as Speaker of the House. At the time,
he explained that he faced opposition in the ranks for their debacle, but in January 1999, he resigned his seat as well, following revelations of a six-year-long
sexual affair with a young congressional aide and the start of a federal investigation into a fundraising scandal involving his political action committee.

Although the election and polls clearly showed that Americans wanted Clinton to remain president, Republican House Majority Whip Tom DeLay and
Senate Judiciary Committee Chairman Henry Hyde pushed for impeachment.
On December 11, the lame duck House in a party-line vote voted four articles
of impeachment against Clinton. The tragedy of impeachment quickly turned
to farce. On the same day as the impeachment debate, a New York newspaper
reported that Republican Speaker-designate Bob Livingston had engaged in sexual affairs. In a final act of misplaced self-righteousness, Livingston cast his vote

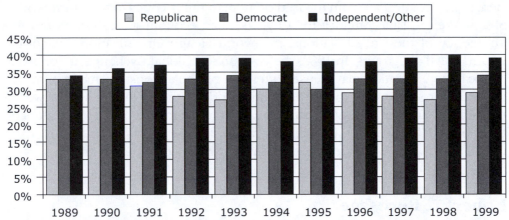

Figure 4.1 *Political Party Identification in the 1990s (percent). More Americans identified themselves as Democrats than Republicans in every year but one in the 1990s. In 1995, as Republicans under Gingrich took control of the House, the GOP became the majority party. Democrats quickly retook the lead by 1996, helping to propel Clinton's reelection. Americans widely blamed Republicans for the shutdown of the federal government in the winter of 1995–1996, and part of the decline in GOP identification is attributable to that event. The pronounced radicalism of the Republican majority after 1994, however, also convinced many Democrats that the danger of the new Republican Party outweighed their disappointment in Clinton. As important in the shifting numbers of Democrats and Republicans was the fact that roughly a third of voting-age Americans identified themselves as independent.* Source: *Pew Center 1999.*

to impeach Clinton, resigned his office, held up his personal courage as an example to the president, and demanded Clinton resign. He was booed by his House colleagues. The Senate trial was held after the seating of the new Congress in January. It lasted 37 days and ended with the Senate's acquittal of Clinton on both remaining articles of impeachment. Ultimately, despite seven years' worth of investigations by independent counsel Kenneth Starr, which cost $56 million in federal funds, and several congressional investigations, all charges against the Clintons were dismissed for lack of evidence.

BIOGRAPHIES

Medea Benjamin, 1952–

Antiglobalization Activist and Green Party Leader

Human rights activist Medea Benjamin was one of the leading organizers of the antiglobalization protests in Seattle in 1999 and a proponent of Ralph Nader's 2000 Green Party presidential race. From the time she finished graduate school,

Benjamin's political activism focused on human rights issues in the Third World. She worked in Latin America for 10 years as an economist and nutritionist for an agency of the United Nations, the World Health Organization, and other international aid groups. In 1988, she co-founded Global Exchange, a nonprofit advocacy organization that focused attention on the actions of American multinational corporations in the developing world. In the 1990s, Benjamin was a prominent leader of the antisweatshop movement and one of the originators of the "fair trade" movement. In 2000, she ran for U.S. Senate as a Green Party candidate and was a leading advocate of Ralph Nader's presidential bid.

Robert L. Borosage

Writer and Founder of Progressive Political Organizations

Robert L. Borosage was a leading progressive writer within Democratic circles in the 1990s. Beginning his career as a lawyer, in 1974, Borosage founded the Center for National Security Studies, an organization devoted to calling attention to the tensions between civil rights and the growing national security powers of the federal government. In the 1980s, as director of the Institute for Policy Studies, his work focused on opposition to President Ronald Reagan's military interventions in Central America and nuclear arms buildup. At the end of the Cold War, Borosage was a leading proponent of the peace dividend. He worked on the political campaigns of progressive Democrats such as Paul Wellstone, Carol Mosely-Brown, and Barbara Boxer. Throughout the Clinton years, as a writer and organizational leader, he was a prominent critic of the Democratic Party's centrist turn. Unlike other progressives, he remained committed to the Democratic Party.

James Dobson, 1936–

Christian Right Leader, Child Psychologist

James Dobson was one of the most influential leaders of the social movement of Christian conservatives, and he was instrumental in the movement's effort to institute "family values" through the political system. The son of a Pentecostal minister, Dobson first achieved prominence through his distinctive version of child psychology. After earning a Ph.D. in psychology and working at Children's Hospital in Los Angeles in the 1960s, he published *Dare to Discipline* in 1970. In the book, Dobson wed the doctrine of traditional evangelical Christianity to psychology, advocating a return to strict child-rearing practices. By doing so, Dobson rejected the dominant paradigm of nurturance in place since the 1950s publication of Dr. Spock's books. Dobson's work appealed to conservative Christian families, who had always been uncomfortable with the liberal approach of Spock and his followers. Dobson continued to write books on the Christian family and he founded Focus on the Family, a Christian ministry based in Colorado Springs, and the Family Research Council, the lobbying arm of the Christian Right. Under Dobson's leadership, Focus on the Family became in the 1990s one of the most influential and powerful organizations of the Christian Right. By the end of the 1990s, the organization had a budget of $113 million and a staff of 1,300 people. Dobson's influence derived from the popularity of his books and his radio and film broadcasts among Christian conservatives. The audience for his radio show was five million, his 15 books sold several million copies, and his film series was viewed by 70 million people. Dobson's positions on social, cultural, and political issues derived from a literalist reading of the Christian Bible and evangelical Christianity. He vigorously opposed abortion, gay rights, stem cell research, the Department of Education, and sex education; he advocated a return to traditional gender roles and traditional marriage, school vouchers to fund private religious schooling, and psychological counseling to cure homosexuality.

Ruth Bader Ginsburg, 1933–

Justice of the Supreme Court

Ruth Bader Ginsburg, appointed to the Supreme Court by President Clinton in 1993, was the second woman to serve on the U.S. Supreme Court. Ginsburg was

born and raised in a Jewish family in a working-class neighborhood of Brooklyn. After receiving her law degree at the top of her class at Columbia, Supreme Court Justice Felix Frankfurter rejected a recommendation that Ginsburg be his clerk, saying he would not hire a woman. Ginsburg first worked as a legal secretary and then won a clerkship with a U.S. District Court judge. Ginsburg became a professor of law at Rutgers University in 1963. At that time, she was one of only 20 women law professors in the nation. In 1972, she joined the faculty at Columbia Law School, where she was the first tenured female professor. In that same year, she became the first director of the American Civil Liberties Union's Women's Rights Project, which she directed until 1980. In the 1970s, she argued six women's rights

Ruth Bader Ginsburg. (Richard Strauss, Smithsonian Institution, Collection of the Supreme Court of the United States)

cases before the Supreme Court and won all but one. Her litigation pioneered new legal rights for women, but she often used male plaintiffs to make the case that gender discrimination in law—even when purportedly to benefit women— was based on stereotypes and generally unconstitutional. President Clinton appointed her the Supreme Court. At the time, she was considered to be a moderate who would help bridge the divisions between the liberals and conservatives on the court. Her decisions have tended to align with the liberal justices, and she remained a strong advocate of women's rights, especially as the Court shifted in a conservative direction in the 2000s.

Grover Norquist, 1956–

Conservative Leader

Grover Norquist was one of the single-most powerful leaders of the New Right in the 1990s although he did not become more widely known until after George W. Bush's election in 2000. As Rush Limbaugh wrote in the jacket blurb on Norquist's self-published 1995 *Rock the House,* Norquist "is perhaps the most influential and important person you've *never* heard of in the GOP today." Norquist was already a libertarian when he entered college, and he began his political activism in the College Republicans. In 1981, he ran the campaign for Jack Abramoff to become president of the organization, and after Abramoff won, he appointed Norquist the group's executive director. Norquist moved to Washington and became deeply involved in Republican politics as Ronald Reagan assumed the presidency. In those years, Norquist adopted what would be his singular focus on the free market: eliminate taxes and reverse decades of business regulation and social welfare programs. In 1985, Ronald Reagan's chief of staff tapped Norquist to head an advocacy group the administration was setting up, Americans for Tax Reform, and Norquist has headed the organization since then. Norquist originated the idea of issuing a no-tax pledge to Republican politicians and was wildly successful in securing a signed pledge from Republican local, state, and national politicians. In the late 1980s, Norquist became close to Newt Gingrich and in 1994 was an early advocate of the Contract with America. After the Republicans took control of the House, Norquist began convening a weekly meeting of conservative leaders of all stripes. In the Wednesday meetings, social conservatives, neoconservatives, libertarians like Norquist, and single-issue advocates met privately to reach a common political strategy on their divergent goals. Leading Republican politicians often sat in on the meetings. Norquist dubbed the group the "Leave-us-alone-coalition." Impartial analysts and partisans across the political spectrum agreed that Norquist's group was critical in bringing cohesion to the conservative movement and translating the movement's goals into political policy. Norquist was very close to the second Bush administration and gained notoriety in the early 2000s for his hyperbolic rhetoric against government regulation and Democrats. In 2005, he was implicated in the Jack Abramoff corruption scandal.

Kurt Schmoke, 1949–

Mayor of Baltimore, Dean of Howard Law School

Kurt Schmoke served as the mayor of Baltimore throughout the 1990s and attracted national attention for his unconventional and often daring approach to governance. Schmoke was elected as the city's first African American mayor in 1987. At the time, Baltimore had exorbitantly high poverty rates, was wracked by violent crime and gangs, and many of its residents were afflicted with drug addiction. The problems were especially severe among the African American inner-city poor, where the crack epidemic of the 1980s had exacerbated the city's historical legacy of poverty and Jim Crow. Schmoke, who hailed from the city's African American middle class and had an impressive academic pedigree, immediately set to work on tackling the multiple crises. He first provoked outrage by telling the National Conference of Mayors that the subject of drug decriminalization should be discussed because doing so might prove more effective at reducing the criminal infrastructure that had grown powerful on the illegal drug trade. In his first term, taking on powerful interests in the teachers' unions, he privatized several failing schools, and he pushed educators in other schools to follow private school curricula. He established controversial needle-exchange programs for drug users in an effort to stem the spread of HIV/AIDS among drug addicts and their unwitting partners. He oversaw the establishment of reading programs to boost the academic performance of poor students. Schmoke was reelected twice in 1991 and 1995, but in 1999, bombarded with criticism for incompetent management and blamed for not doing enough to solve Baltimore's intractable problems, he chose not to seek a fourth term. In 2003, he became the dean of Howard University Law School.

Antonio Villaraigosa, 1953–

Democratic Politician

Antonio Villaraigosa was one of a generation of young Latino politicians who rose to political power in the 1990s in California. Born to Mexican American parents in Los Angeles, Villaraigosa was raised by his mother in East Los Angeles, a poor predominantly Latino section of the city. He became politically active in college, joining a radical Chicano rights organization, and then, like many future Los Angeles progressives, went to the People's College of Law. He worked as a union organizer, and, highly effective as a coalition builder and organizer, he began to broaden his interests and his connections in Los Angeles. He joined the American Civil Liberties Union board in 1988, won election to the organization's presidency in 1993, and then ran for a state assembly seat in 1994. He won the race in a difficult campaign against another Latino candidate. Like Tom Bradley, the city's former African American mayor, Villaraigosa assembled a coalition of ethnic voters (in this case Latino) and liberals (mostly Jewish), and added to it strong support from the city's increasingly dynamic labor movement. In 1996, he was chosen to be the Democratic majority leader in the assembly, and in 1998, he won election to the speakership of the assembly. He spearheaded progressive legislation on urban parks, health care for the poor, education, and the environment. In 2005, Villaraigosa was elected the first Mexican American mayor of Los Angeles since 1872. With his classic American life story of humble origins to fame—a story he told many times on the campaign trail—Villaraigosa became a role model to millions of Latinos and immigrants in California.

REFERENCES AND FURTHER READINGS

Baer, Kenneth S. 2000. *Reinventing Democrats: The Politics of Liberalism from Reagan to Clinton*. Lawrence: University Press of Kansas.

Berman, William C. 2001. *From the Center to the Edge: The Politics and Policies of the Clinton Presidency*. Lanham, MD: Rowman & Littlefield Publishers.

Borosage, Robert L. 1999. "Democrats Face the Future." *The Nation,* February 8, 11.

Church, George J. 1991. "A Tale of Two Bushes." *Time,* January 7, 20.

Corn, David. 1996. "What's Left in the Party?" *The Nation,* September 23, 20–22.

Crime in the United States: Uniform Crime Reports. 2000. Federal Bureau of Investigation, U.S. Department of Justice.

Dionne, E. J., Jr. 1995. "Why We Need a Second Party; When Will the Democrats Organize?" *Commonweal* 122 (18): 8–9.

Dionne, E. J. 1996. *They Only Look Dead: Why Progressives Will Dominate the Next Political Era*. New York: Simon & Schuster.

Frank, Thomas. 2004. *What's the Matter with Kansas? How Conservatives Won the Heart of America*. New York: Metropolitan Books.

Goodstein, Laurie. 1999. "Coalition's Woes May Hinder Christian Right." *New York Times,* August 2, 1.

Hacker, Jacob S., and Paul Pierson. 2006. *Off Center: The Republican Revolution and the Erosion of American Democracy*. New Haven: Yale University Press.

Johnson, Haynes Bonner. 1995. *Divided We Fall: Gambling with History in the Nineties*. New York: W. W. Norton.

Johnson, Haynes Bonner. 2001. *The Best of Times: America in the Clinton Years*. New York: Harcourt.

Judis, John B. 2000. *The Paradox of American Democracy: Elites, Special Interests, and the Betrayal of Public Trust*. New York: Pantheon Books.

Kellstedt, Lyman A., John C. Green, James L. Guth, and Corwin E. Smidt. 1994. "Religious Voting Blocs in the 1992 Election: The Year of the Evangelical? *Sociology of Religion* 55 (3): 307–326.

Lamis, Alexander P. 1999. *Southern Politics in the 1990s*. Baton Rouge: Louisiana State University Press.

Layman, Geoffrey C. 2001. *The Great Divide: Religious and Cultural Conflict in American Party Politics, Power, Conflict, and Democracy*. New York: Columbia University Press.

Manza, Jeff, and Clem Brooks. 1999. *Social Cleavages and Political Change: Voter Alignments and U.S. Party Coalitions*. New York: Oxford University Press.

Nelson, Lars-Erik. 1999. "Undemocratic Vistas." *New York Review of Books*, August 12.

Pew Center. 1999. "Retro-Politics: The Political Typology, Version 3.0." Washington, DC: Pew Center for the People and the Press.

Schaller, Michael, and George Rising. 2002. *The Republican Ascendancy, 1968–2001*. Edited by J. H. Franklin and A. S. Eisenstadt, *The American History Series*. Wheeling, IL: Harlan Davidson.

Shaw, Greg M., and Amy S. Ragland. 2000. "The Polls-Trends: Political Reform." *Public Opinion Quarterly* 64: 206–226.

Smolowe, Jill. 1993. "Crusade for the Classroom." *Time*, November 1, 34–35.

Starr, Kenneth. Office of the Independent Counsel (1994–), United States Congress House. Committee on the Judiciary. 1998. *The Starr Report: The Official Report of the Independent Counsel's Investigation of the President*. Rocklin, Calif.: Forum.

Starr, Paul. 2007. "The Hillarycare Mythology: Did Hillary Doom Health Reform in 1993?" *The American Prospect* 18 (10).

Stiglitz, Joseph E. 2003. *The Roaring Nineties: A New History of the World's Most Prosperous Decade*. New York: W. W. Norton & Co.

Terkel, Studs. 1992. *Race: How Blacks and Whites Think and Feel about the American Obsession*. New York: New Press.

Toobin, Jeffrey. 1999. *A Vast Conspiracy: The Real Story of the Sex Scandal that Nearly Brought Down a President*. New York: Random House.

U.S. Bureau of the Census. 1998. *State and Metropolitan Area Data Book 1997–98,* 5th edition. Washington, DC: U.S. Census Bureau. http://www.census.gov/prod/3/98pubs/smadb-97.pdf.

U.S. Bureau of the Census. 2000. *Statistical Abstract of the United States, 2000.* U.S. Dept. of Commerce, Economics and Statistics Administration. Washington, D.C.: U.S. Census Bureau. http://www.census.gov/prod/www/statistical-abstract-1995_2000.html.

U.S. Department of Justice. 2000. "Crime in the United States: Uniform Crime Reports." 2000. Washington, DC: Federal Bureau of Investigation, U.S. Department of Justice.

Wills, Garry. 1995. "Thomas's Confirmation: The True Story." *New York Review of Books,* February 2.

Wills, Garry. 1999. "The People's Choice." *New York Review of Books,* August 12.

Private Life: Family, Community, Culture, and Entertainment

OVERVIEW

The previous chapters examined economic and public life in the 1990s. This chapter and the next turn to Americans' personal lives—their primary relationships, communal institutions, and pastimes.

It is impossible to discuss Americans' family, community, religious, and personal lives without giving pride of place to diversity. Diversity was one of the key words of the 1990s. It described the reality of American communities, beliefs, and experience; it stood as an ideal for some, a challenge for others, and something to fear for a minority.

Yet at the same time, other typical experiences of the 1990s made Americans more similar to each other. Geographic mobility erased many of the historical distinctions among residents of different regions. Suburbanization, especially in its newest form of "exurban" real estate development, colonized large swaths of American farmland, leaving fewer rural Americans and creating nearly identical exurban communities dotting the landscape. Globalization and the practices of American multinationals offered Americans of all regions, religions, and ethnicities the same brands to buy in the same stores. New technologies that sped the transmission of knowledge and trends globally, corporate mergers in the entertainment industry, and the ongoing commodification of culture offered an unprecedentedly uniform global culture. These developments were a powerful countervailing force against diversity's tendency to accentuate difference.

Thus, as Americans became more diverse, economic and cultural forces dissolved difference. The contrapuntal dance between diversity and homogenization powerfully shaped Americans' experience in the 1990s, particularly in their lives outside of work and politics.

On the most intimate level, Americans were experiencing unprecedented differences in their family lives. The transformation of the American family in the last quarter of the 20th century was nothing short of revolutionary. This chapter begins with an examination of the array of American family and household types and the changing nature of experience throughout the life cycle. Discussions of family, gender, and sexuality are followed by explorations of various subjects along the life cycle, such as parenting, childhood, the teenage years, and aging.

Historically, one of the major differences among Americans has originated in the regional cultures of the country. The distinctiveness among regions declined throughout the postwar era. One could persuasively argue that, by 2000, regional differences had disappeared. The 1980s and the 1990s, especially, marked the point of no return. The next section in this chapter examines American lives as they were situated in specific locales. The common theme that emerges in these discussions of farming and the rural life, sprawl and exurbanization, new urbanism, migration into the Rocky Mountain states and urban America is the obliteration of historical local cultures, the losing battle to preserve them, and the pervasive sadness over the loss.

Immigration has been the other major source of America's historical diversity. The country is currently in the midst of one of its largest waves of immigration, and at this writing, immigration is currently one of the most divisive issues in American politics. The subject is covered in its own chapter, yet it should be read as a companion to this one.

After examining Americans in the places they live, this chapter then turns to one of the essential communal and affective associations for Americans: religion. The topic encompasses an examination of the demography of religion, broad trends in religious belief and experience, and the specific practices of several religious groups. Immigration enormously expanded the diversity of religions and religious practices common in the United States. At the same time, Americans across many different religions were turning to a more experiential and spiritualistic form of religious expression. Nowhere were the creativity and contradictions forged out of the crosscurrents of diversity and homogenization more evident.

In the final topic, this chapter turns to the practices and habits of Americans in the part of their lives they routinely called their "free time." The sections in this topic describe most of the main areas of activity—films, books, television, sports, shopping—and explore some of the common themes, practices, and tendencies. Popular culture and leisure, where the marketplace and the diversity of Americans intersect most potently, was inevitably an arena where diversity and difference flourished. One of the decade's most profitable commercial innovations, niche marketing, attested to the fundamental differences among Americans. Nonetheless, popular culture and commercialized entertainment were the primary common ground on which Americans of different backgrounds met. And it was there, more than in any other arena of life, that difference and diversity were eroded.

TIMELINE

1990   The American population reaches 248.7 million.

Reform Judaism allows gays and lesbians to be ordained as rabbis.

Tim Berners-Lee writes the initial protocol for the World Wide Web.

1991   Basketball star Magic Johnson reveals he is HIV positive.

Legislation spearheaded by Sen. Albert Gore opens the Internet to commercial use.

1992   The World Wide Web is released.

Ice T's song "Cop Killer" stirs controversy over rap music and artistic expression.

Hurricane Andrew hits the American Southeast.

1993   Mosaic Web browser is made available free. The first radio and television programs are aired on the Internet.

The Family and Medical Leave Act is passed, which requires employers to provide unpaid time off for the care of family members.

The United States Holocaust Memorial Museum, located on the National Mall in Washington, D.C., opens.

Toni Morrison wins the Nobel Prize for literature.

1994   Netscape Web browser is offered for sale.

Sexual abuse of children by Catholic priests is first revealed.

Professional baseball players strike.

Sports and television celebrity O. J. Simpson is arrested and charged with the murder of his ex-wife and her friend.

1995   Netscape makes its initial public offering.

Microsoft releases Internet Explorer and bundles it with the Windows operating system shipped in new computers.

Amazon.com goes online.

O. J. Simpson's trial takes places in Los Angeles.

1996   The Federal Agriculture Improvement and Reform Act overhauls the agricultural subsidy policy.

Oprah Winfrey's book club begins, and the first book featured, Jacquelyn Mitchard's *Deep End of the Ocean,* hits number one on the *New York Times* best-seller list.

1997   Smart Growth and Neighborhood Conservation Initiatives, Maryland, is passed to limit sprawl and control development.

1999   The U.S. women's soccer team wins the World Cup.

Forty-two percent of American households own personal computers, an increase of 75 percent since 1994.

Shooters at Columbine High School kill 12 students and 1 teacher and wound nearly two dozen before taking their own lives.

2000   The American population reaches 281.4 million, the largest census-to-census increase in history (13.2 percent, 32.7 million people).

AMERICAN FAMILIES AND THE LIFE CYCLE

The most profound demographic change in the 1990s was the continuing de-cline of the traditional nuclear family. Historians of the American family have shown that the traditional family was typical only for a brief interlude in the postwar period; nevertheless, it has remained an ideal for many Americans and was held up as the norm throughout mainstream culture. Real practice in the 1990s was far from the ideal. In 1960, nuclear families constituted 45 percent of American households. By 1980, they had shrunk to 30 percent of households, and by 2000 to 24 percent (Johnson 2001). Numerically, married couples and their children accounted for slightly over half of the nation's population in 2000. Among those who lived in other familial arrangements, some did so because of the difficulties of life in the nuclear family. Half of all marriages ended in divorce, a proportion that had stayed relatively constant since the 1970s, and at any given

In the 1990s, single-parent households made up 16 percent of the American population. (iStockPhoto.com)

moment, about one-tenth of the population was divorced. Families in which a single parent was raising children made up 16 percent of the population, and in three-quarters of those, the family was headed by a woman. An indeterminate number of Americans lived in what had come to be known as blended families, in which remarriage or cohabitation after divorce brought children from multiple families together with one parent and one stepparent. Multigenerational families accounted for 3.7 percent of all households (U.S. Bureau of the Census 2000, table 55). Looked at another way, two-thirds of the 72.1 million children in the United States lived in families headed by a married couple, one-quarter lived in families headed by a single parent, and 6 percent lived in families with two unmarried parents (Simmons and O'Neill 2001).

By 2000, the second-largest household type in the United States was not a family at all. In one-quarter of American households, a man or woman lived alone. Their numbers had grown 23 percent over the decade, reaching approximately 27 million individuals, or one-tenth of the population, by 2000. By comparison, the 1950 census had found singles to constitute only 9 percent of the nation's households. Their growth reflected demographic trends at each stage of the life cycle. Americans married later, and many lived alone before they did so. Some marriages broke up after children became adults, and many middle-aged singles were divorced men and women. The 35 million elderly Americans who made

Table 5.1. Unmarried Partner Households in the United States

Unmarried Partner Households

Male and female	4,881,377
Both male	301,026
Both female	293,365
Total	5,475,768

Sources: QT-P18. Marital Status by Sex, Unmarried-Partner Households, and Grandparents as Caregivers: 2000, based on a data set from Census 2000 Summary File 3 (SF 3); Tavia Simmons and Martin O'Connell, "Married-Couple and Unmarried-Partner Households: 2000," Census 2000 Special Reports, issued Feb. 2003.

up 12 percent of the American population constituted about a third of single households. Women far out-numbered men, and a large proportion of them were widows.

While the traditional nuclear family was declining, new types of families arose. About 5 percent of adults lived with another adult to whom they were not married. For the first time in American history, significant numbers of single persons and gay couples reared children. Many single mothers were single by choice, not because of an accidental pregnancy or a failed heterosexual relationship. Only a decade earlier, women who wanted children but were not coupled with a man had few opportunities to bear and raise children. In the 1990s, women sought out the new reproductive technologies to bear children or took advantage of the global market and relaxed laws to adopt children on their own. Gay men and women formalized their relationships in commitment ceremonies, won domestic partnership and civil union rights in some states, advocated for equal rights to marry, and formed families with children. Lesbians had the option of using the new reproductive technologies or, like gay male couples, could adopt children. It was evident in gay enclaves that there was a baby boom afoot.

The diversity of the American family was not random. Different ethnic groups had distinct patterns. Non-Hispanic white Americans married and divorced at the highest rate. Asian Americans divorced at less than half the rate of white non-Hispanic Americans. Hispanics married at higher rates, had more children, and divorced at a somewhat lower rate than most other groups; 45 percent of African Americans never married. Immigrants and second-generation Americans were much more likely to live in extended or multigenerational households. There were regional variations as well. Utah had the highest rate of marriage in the country while marriage rates were lower in most counties on the east and west coast and in New England. California had the largest number of unmarried-partner households; Utah and Alabama the lowest number of them. Singles and gay families were much more likely to live in a large city. The South had the highest percentage of children living outside of married-couple families. Almost all children in the central Great Plains and the inland western states lived in families headed by married couples. Family patterns also varied by educational and income levels. Women with more education and higher income married later, delayed child rearing, and had fewer children (Spain and Bianchi 1996). Most teenage births were to poor women.

American Marriage and Divorce in Comparative and Historical Perspective

Historical comparisons and developments are often tracked against the period immediately preceding, and for much of this book, we have focused on developments contrasting the last two decades of the 20th century with the postwar era (1945–1973). For the subject of marriage and sexuality, however, such an examination is revealing but also somewhat misleading. There were sharp differences in marriage rates, age of first sexual intercourse, and age of first marriage between these two periods. Often attributed to the sexual revolution by critics, these changes produced tremendous cultural conflict in the United States (Fukuyama 1999).

A longer historical perspective on the subject, however, demonstrates that it was the postwar period that was unusual rather than the decades of the sexual revolution (Therborn 2004). The American experience of 2000, statistically speaking, was more similar to that of 1900 than it was to that of 1960. At the end of the 20th century, the median female age at first marriage was 25; in the first two decades of the 20th century, it hovered around 24. But in 1960, with early marriage at its peak rate, the median age of marriage was 20. From a somewhat different statistical angle, fewer than half of American women in 1900 were married by the age of 24; in 1960, nearly three-quarters of women were married by that

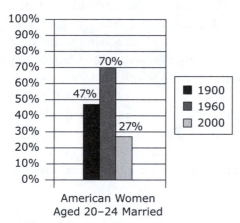

Figure 5.1 *Marriage Delayed, But Strong.* Sources: *U.S. Bureau of the Census 2000, table 55; Therborn 2004.*

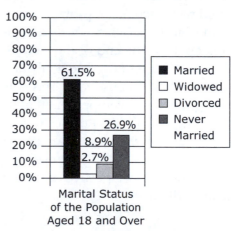

Figure 5.2 *Marital Status of the Population Aged 18 and Over (1999).* Sources: *U.S. Bureau of the Census 2000, table 55; Therborn 2004.*

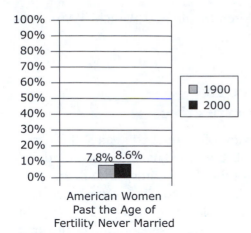

Figure 5.3 *Percentage of American Women Past the Age of Fertility Never Married.* Sources: *U.S. Bureau of the Census 2000, table 55; Therborn 2004.*

age. In 2000, just slightly over a quarter of American women were married before the age of 25. The trends in Western Europe and other areas of Anglo settlement, such as Australia, moved in parallel with these trends in the United States. Everywhere in the developed world in the post–World War II period, more people married and did so at a younger age, compared to their counterparts of the first third of the 20th century. The zenith in most countries was in the 1960s to early 1970s (Therborn 2004).

Although late-20th- and early-20th-century marriage patterns were similar, at the end of the century, Americans divorced more frequently. In the mid-1990s, about half of all marriages were statistically likely to end in divorce (Therborn 2004). Traditional conservatives and communitarians decried the collapse of marriage and the negative effect of divorce on children. Several considerations should be taken into account when evaluating debates about the effect of divorce on children. First, against the supposedly soaring divorce rates of the end of the century, it is useful to keep in mind that high death rates at the beginning of the century more frequently left children permanently bereft of one or both parents. Second, most divorced men and women remarried or hoped to remarry, and many cohabitated with each other, providing two adults in the household for children. Third, rising life expectancy levels and declining mortality had created a new phenomenon by the end of the century, albeit one several decades in the making. Married couples now frequently faced 20 to 30 years of married life without any children in the household. This was one of those changes that had only subtly and gradually developed but that had profound implications for the nature and meaning of daily life. Practically and statistically, divorce did not necessarily split a family with children under 18 in the household. Finally, marriage was still a strong, vibrant institution, even if premillennium American marriage looked alien from the perspective of the 1950s ideal of early marriage and proscription against divorce.

New Frontiers in Parenthood

Although most children in America were born to married parents, a notable and significant trend in the 1990s was the decoupling of child rearing from heterosexuality and the nuclear family. The expansion of new reproductive technologies, from the simple method of artificial insemination to the complex medical intervention of in vitro fertilization, severed the once-necessary link between heterosexual sexuality and the reproduction of the species. The legal, cultural, and political expansion of adoption, especially through adoptions of foreign-born children by American adults, also reinforced the trend. Americans who had previously had to forego parenthood—older women, women without a male sexual partner, gays and lesbians—had now gained the opportunity to forge a family with children through several different avenues.

The vast majority of America women had children at some point in their life. In 1992, only 16 percent of women aged 40–44 were childless (Spain and Bianchi 1996). Yet, as more and more women delayed childbearing into their late 30s and early 40s, new technologies to treat infertility became highly sought commodities. In the mid-1990s, more than 9 million women, or 15 percent of those in their reproductive years, took advantage of fertility treatments. The number of clinics offering in vitro fertilization and other techniques multiplied eight times between the mid-1980s and mid-1990s, to top 300 (Stephen and Chandra 2000).

Women in heterosexual relations sought medical assistance when infertility left them unable to conceive and carry a baby. But the more significant consequence of the rapidly developing technology was that it allowed single women and lesbian women to carry their own biological children. Many used the relatively simple technique of artificial insemination, and sperm banks increased in number and in their sophistication in choosing and marketing "donors."

One of the hot-button social issues of the 1990s was out-of-wedlock birth, or, in other words, childbearing by unmarried women. Babies born to unmarried women had risen from 11 percent of births in the 1970s to 28 percent of all births by the early 1990s. Although there was a lot of hand-wringing about the purported problem, and the issue powerfully shaped the debate about welfare reform, the United States was not unusual compared to industrialized countries. In almost every country of the developed world, between one-quarter and one-half of all births occurred outside of marriage.

The Gay Family

Surveys in the mid-1990s indicated that approximately 3 percent of Americans considered themselves lesbian, gay, or bisexual. It was estimated that there were approximately 2 million gay parents in the nation, some living as couples, and some raising children as single parents. Although some gay activists claimed that the true percentage of gays in America was closer to 10 percent, international comparisons confirm the likely validity of the lower 3 percent figure (Wald 2000; Therborn 2004).

The novelty of the gay family and the persisting social and legal proscription of homosexuals meant that many family practices taken for granted in heterosexual

Gay fathers hold their 2-month-old adopted daughter. (Tomas Van Houtryve/Corbis)

married families were areas of uncertainty and precariousness for gay couples and their children. For heterosexuals, visiting one's wife in the hospital, inheriting one's husband's property automatically and without taxation, adopting a child, receiving health insurance through one's mother's job, were all taken as part of the natural order. In fact, such practices, customs, and privileges, though nurtured in affective relationships, were founded on American family law, as legislated and enforced by the government.

In 2000, 20 states continued to criminalize private sexual contact between adults of the same sex. Although typically not enforced, such laws remained on the books, and state laws thereby sanctioned different treatment of heterosexual and homosexual couples. Gays faced obstacles in adoption; two states still prohibited gay adoption, but most made it far more difficult for a gay couple to adopt a child. And a partner of a gay parent had to go through a co-parent adoption in order to gain a legal relationship with one's child. State laws were silent or discriminatory on other central areas of family practice, such as inheritance, child custody, and medical responsibility (Wald 2000).

Women, Work, and Family

As in the decades previous, most American women married and most had children. But, in the 1990s, mothers and married women participated in the labor force in record numbers. While mothers and wives increased their work outside the home, neither the division of household labor between men and women nor American public policy supporting families changed fundamentally. For working mothers, particularly, the balance between family and work became at once a practical, material, emotional, and—for many—a political issue.

Sixty percent of all women worked in the 1990s, compared to just 45 percent as recently as 1973. Wives worked 919 hours a year in 1979 compared to 1,384 hours in 1999. The entry of wives and mothers into the paid labor force, especially in middle-class families in the last three decades of the century, resulted in those families increasing their yearly work hours by, on average, five additional months. Middle-class wives put in 12 more weeks of full-time work between 1979 and 2000 (Mishel et al. 2005).

Child care became a critical issue for working mothers. In 1990, 3 out of 4 mothers with preschoolers worked, compared to 1 out of 10 who did so in 1950. Some families with flexible work schedules were able to split child care between the mother and father. Some had relatives who could stay in the home and care for the children. Still, almost two-thirds of working mothers sent their children out of the home to be cared for, either to another home or to a group center. Working women lamented that quality child care was not available or too expensive to afford, and studies from the 1970s to 1990s showed that women dropped out of the labor force, chose part-time over higher-paid full-time work, and made other critical decisions about their work based on their concerns about child care. A U.S. Department of Labor study showed that families in which women worked in the labor force identified child care as the most important issue (Spain and Bianchi 1996). The United States was the only industrialized country without child care and parental leave policies. While the Family and Medical Leave Act of 1993 required employers to provide time off, it was unpaid leave.

Despite the entry of women who were mothers and wives into the paid labor force, women remained largely responsible for the domestic labor of child care and housework. Throughout each decade of the 20th century, housework had become physically less demanding, yet the amount of time spent on housework only declined in the 1970s with women's mass move into the labor force. Women reduced their hours of domestic labor by about a third in the last quarter-century, and men increased theirs, but women continued to devote double the amount of time that men did to household chores. Though the division of household labor by gender narrowed slightly, as measured by time spent, it persisted in the division of tasks. Women continued to perform about three-quarters of cleaning, cooking, shopping, and household management while men focused on helping with child care and home and yard maintenance, performing about 40 percent of that labor. Variations among families had more to do with ideas about relations between the sexes than it did with the material contribution women made to household finances through their work. Men shared more equally in

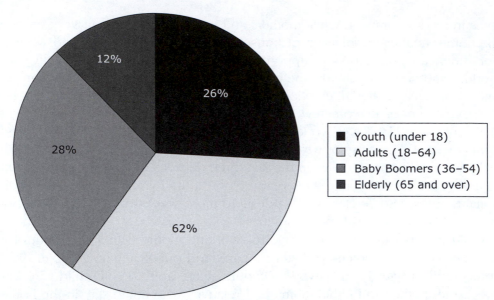

Figure 5.4 *Age Breakdown of the U.S. Population (2000)*. Sources: *U.S. Bureau of the Census 2000; Meyer 2001*.

household labor in families that believed in egalitarianism between the sexes; men performed less of the housework and child rearing in families that believed in traditional divisions and differences between the sexes (Bianchi, Robinson, and Milkie 2006; Spain and Bianchi 1996).

Were families moving toward an equal division of work and household labor, or was the double-shift of women entrenched? No clear trajectory had emerged at the end of the century, and sociologists debated which pattern would prevail. Some argued that families would make an economic calculation and assign household labor to the spouse paid less in the labor market, whether it was the man or woman. Others found evidence that the gender wars of the workplace and the insecurity of the globalized economy created a situation where household labor became an arena for the "symbolic enactment of gender relations" (Spain and Bianchi 1996, 232).

To the surprise of both independent analysts and partisans in the gender wars both, even as families spent less time on housework and they clocked more hours at work, they spent more time with their children—playing, chaperoning, teaching, and caring for them. In 1965, mothers spent an average of 10 hours a week on child care. In 2000, married mothers spent an average of 13 hours a week on child care activities, and single mothers spent an average of 12 hours a week. A large jump in the hours spent on child care took place between 1995 and 2000. The change was surprising, considering that most mothers did not work in 1965 and the era was one in which the stay-at-home mom was a cultural ideal. Working mothers spent more total time than fathers or stay-at-home mothers engaged in paid labor, housework, and child care. The workweek for a working mother averaged 71 hours in 2000 while that for a mother not in the labor force was 52 hours. Working mothers sacrificed personal time in order to devote time to their children while holding down a job and performing most of the housework (Bianchi, Robinson, and Milkie 2006).

The Childhood and Teenage Years

The lives of American children in the 1990s were structured, supervised, monitored, regimented, and commodified to a greater degree than ever in the past. Such an approach to childhood—to preparing the next generation for its adult responsibilities—was, however, a continuation of trends long in evidence in the entire developed world. As the historian of the family Goran Therborn observed, "in the course of the 20th century, children became more costly, more scarce, more valuable, more unruly, more powerful" (Therborn 2004, 285). In the 1990s, the economic insecurity of the first half of the decade and the economic flush times of the New Economy equally reinforced the cultural focus on childhood development.

Parents continued to rely on child-rearing manuals for advice on how to raise children, as they had done throughout the postwar era. In the 1990s, however, the debates about raising infants and young children were inflected by the legacy of feminism and consumed with the question of the role of working mothers. Every few months, one of the nation's leading magazines would run a provocative cover story on fathers, mothers, or children, such as *Time*'s fall 1990 special issue, "Women: The Road Ahead," or its May 24, 1993, article on "Kids, Sex and Values." In doing so, they accurately captured the zeitgeist of American family life.

Children of elementary school age experienced constant supervision by adults. The free, unstructured, unsupervised time of childhood, when children were largely left to their own devices in their own play, almost entirely disappeared in the 1990s. The days of most children were divided between school, supervised after-school activities, structured group activities, homework, and leisure time in the home under parental supervision. In school, time for recess and the arts shrunk as standardized testing and funding cuts converged to focus educational resources and time on the core disciplines. Pressure to excel at school intensified. For 70 percent of American children, when the school day was over, their mothers and fathers were at work. Because of real—and imagined—threats to children left alone, the days of playing with friends on cul-de-sacs, public playgrounds, and urban streets were over. Parents, when they had the means, placed their children under adult care in the two- to four-hour gap between the end of school and the end of work. Most children therefore went from the institutional setting of school to some form of supervised activity.

Children chase a soccer ball. A child's free time was greatly reduced in the 1990s as parents opted for structured group activities and activities with more supervision. (iStockPhoto.com)

The economic position of a child's family profoundly shaped the content of those supervised hours. Children of working-class families went to subsidized public school after-school programs, to Boys and Girls Clubs, to Police Activities Leagues, and the like. Middle-class children participated in American Youth Soccer Organization (AYSO) leagues, which had 3 million registered players in 1998, and group arts and recreation classes in their communities (Oxoby 2003). Their mothers often arranged their work schedules to leave time in the afternoon to be with their children, and one of the decade's most recognizable social types was the so-called soccer mom, the middle-class, white suburban mother who shuttled her children to soccer practice and similar activities. Wealthy children frequently had babysitters and nannies to shuttle them between private lessons and private tutors.

The nature of the American workplace and the absence of public family policy to support families thus significantly affected the nature of childhood. But economic pressures and evolving cultural norms and expectations equally contributed to the regimentation of childhood. Parents were not only worried about the physical safety of their children but also about their future emotional health and material success. Although the United States had the most parsimonious family policy of any developed nation, American culture was highly child-centered. Smaller families, the changing economy, and broadly diffused cultural expectations converged to intensify the pressure on parents to invest time and resources in the cultivation of their children's talents and on children to excel. The cost of college skyrocketed at the same time the baby boom peak population made admission to colleges extremely competitive. With the erosion of the blue-collar road to middle-class security, a college degree became ever more necessary to ensure a decent living in adulthood. Teenagers who demonstrated a wide array of talents and activities moved ahead in the college admissions race. Particularly among the upper middle class, the college competition began in the elementary school years.

Playtime, what remained of it, became more commodified and, in that way, more similar to adult leisure activity. In their spare time, children largely played with commercially produced toys and games and consumed commercially produced music, videos, television shows, and movies. In 1993, Americans spent $15 billion on toys (Oxoby 2003). Historians of popular culture note the popularity of Japanese products in the decade, such as Hello Kitty accessories for girls and Pokemon cards for boys, or teenage boys' response to the improvements

Winners of the Spice Girls look-alike search in New York, 1998. The four Spice Girls look-alikes were chosen from more than 2,000 entrants to appear in a national commercial launching the Toymax Spice Girls product line. (NewsCom)

Generation X and Generation Y

For a brief moment in the 1990s, people in their late teens and early 20s were labeled Generation X, after a novel by Douglas Croupland. The defining characteristic of the generation was purportedly its aimlessness, its self-conscious distance from the concerns of the baby boomers who preceded them. As interest in "Gen X" proliferated across the culture, with magazine cover stories scrutinizing its meaning and advertisers shaping campaigns around the notion of a Generation X market, the label became so broad as to become meaningless, and it slipped from usage. An attempt to label the next youngest cohort Generation Y was virtually dead on arrival. A perusal of newspapers and magazines published in the 1990s will yield many references to Gen X and some to Gen Y. Curious readers who enter this world should be warned that contemporary observers had as little idea of its meaning as they do.

A Columbine High School student, who escaped during the massacre, finds her mother outside the school, April 20, 1999. (Tom Cooper Sentinel/Corbis Sygma)

in video-gaming, or the mass popularity of a Disney's animated blockbuster. From the perspective of social history, however, what is significant is that child's play had become more and more shaped by the marketplace. In association with and reinforcing the evolving market penetration of childhood, advertisers aimed their appeals directly at children and youth in recognition of their record levels of purchasing power. School districts that were strapped for cash began in the 1990s to allow corporations to post ads in hallways, buses, and school buildings. It was the decade that the tie-in ad campaign came into its own. Classic 20th-century games such as Monopoly or Operation were repackaged in movie- or television series–themed editions, books of classic fairy tales pictured Barbie as the female heroine, and kids' meals at fast food restaurants came with made-in-China toys of recent movie characters.

Teen Violence and the Columbine Shooting

The United States had the highest rate of teen violence and gun use of any industrialized nation. The problem increased in the 1990s, and it became a pressing subject of national debate. Cities, and poor neighborhoods in cities, had always suffered from teen violence, often connected to gang activity. The introduction of crack cocaine in the 1980s combined with the intensification of the "War on Drugs" led to a peak in crime and violence from the mid-1980s to 1994. A large proportion of crimes were committed by young men. Gang rivalries became more deadly as the economic stakes rose—with the drug trade—and guns became more powerful and more widely available. Homicide was the leading cause of death for African American teenagers and the third leading cause of death for white teenagers. Crime in urban areas dropped precipitously in the second half of the decade, reaching its lowest level since the early 1970s, and fewer teenage boys committed murder or were killed.

A rash of murders and school shootings committed by white suburban teenage boys in the late 1990s touched off a national obsession with teen violence and the psychological condition of teenage boys. The most serious case occurred on April 20, 1999, in Littleton, Colorado. On that day, two suburban, middle-class teenage boys who were students at Columbine High School entered the school carrying semiautomatic weapons, shotguns, and 50 bombs, and went on a shooting rampage. They killed 12 students and 1 teacher, wounded nearly two dozen others, and then killed themselves. News crews had hurried to the school during the siege to broadcast scenes of it throughout the nation. Americans were horrified at the brutality of the attack, its seeming mindlessness, and the access that teenagers had to weapons. The shooters left no clues behind about their motive. Public opinion eventually settled on the theory that the boys were social outcasts, subjected to ridicule by popular athletes, and had broadcast their antisocial tendencies by wearing black trench coats and acting sullen. In its aftermath, schools installed security measures, such as metal detectors, and began closely scrutinizing their student bodies for signs of antisocial behavior.

Within families, the trends in the lives of children discussed here held true for teenagers as well, but class mattered more each year. As middle-class and wealthy children became older, parents' concerns shifted from safety and emotional development to that of ensuring success. Supervised activities for fun, such as soccer league, were replaced by activities for personal development—serious competitive sports, SAT tutoring, volunteer work to enhance a college application, or the refinement of musical, athletic, or artistic skills. Conversely, for poor families, particularly urban minorities, concerns about safety increased for teenagers. Inadequate public schools, urban unemployment, and the prevalence of the drug trade and gangs created a hazardous terrain for teenagers to navigate. A young African American inner-city man was more likely to end up in jail than in college. For those who made it through high school, the path to a decent living ran through years of 70- to 80-hour weeks combining part-time community college with full-time work. Of course, the very nature of American adolescence was the struggle to escape from these adult-imposed strictures and to strike out on one's own and shape one's identity in relation to peers.

Sexuality among Teens and Young Adults

The sexual revolution of the 1960s continued to shape American sexual behavior in the 1990s, even as cultural conservatives waged campaigns to abolish premarital sex. The increase in premarital sexual activity began in the late 1950s and accelerated in the 1960s with the lifting of the legal ban on contraceptives and the technological innovations in birth control. In the early 1970s, about a third of American women had premarital sexual intercourse; in the 1980s and 1990s, about half did. A national sample in 1992 concluded that 53 percent of American women had sexual intercourse before the age of 18. Sexual activity among teenage males and females was not very different; in 1995, 49 percent of female teens and 55 percent of male teens had ever had sex. Teenagers in the early 1990s were somewhat more sexually active than teenagers in the late 1990s (Abma 2004). Most probably, campaigns against teenage sexuality and fears about AIDS and other sexually transmitted diseases together worked to affect this change.

As Americans had sex at a younger age and married at an older age, young American men and women experienced a longer period of premarital sexual activity than had their parents' generation. With sexual initiation separated by many years from marriage, they were also far more likely to have multiple sexual partners in their lifetime. Marriage remained the ideal and actual ultimate object for Americans, but the new normal for Americans, both statistically and morally, included sex outside of marriage (Therborn 2004).

This development was in accord with every other developed nation, but America was more traditional than most of its counterparts. One-fifth of 18–24 year olds reported that they were virgins at marriage. "Virginity pledge" campaigns by religious groups sought to boost these numbers, but even though many teens took the pledge, the National Longitudinal Study of Adolescent Health found that 88 percent of the 12,000 teenagers surveyed in the federal study had broken their pledges and had sexual intercourse before marriage (Altman 2004).

The United States also had an unusually high rate of teenage births—double that of comparable countries—yet rates dropped dramatically in the 1990s. From 1990 to 2002, teenage pregnancy rates in the United States declined: among

Aging

The numbers of Americans over the age of 65 reached a record level in the 1990s. According to the 1990 census, 31 million Americans were over 65; in the 2000 census, 35 million elderly Americans were counted (He et al. 2005). With the aging of Americans and changes in family households and relationships, questions about how to care for the elderly as they became ill or too frail to care for themselves dominated Americans' perception of age and death. The 1980s had witnessed an explosion in the number of nursing homes and the number of men and women residing in them. In the 1990s, 4.5 percent of the elderly were living in nursing homes, but most of those who needed assistance were being cared for by relatives or paid caregivers in their homes.

The vast majority of American men and women over the age of 65, however, were healthy, active, and living independently. With lifespans having increased significantly over the century, and dramatically in the last couple of decades, a new interest in the quality of life in the later years emerged. How could older people live fulfilling lives, unhindered by outright discrimination and cultural assumptions that older people were in a waning phase of life? How could American society instead harness the wisdom and experience of older Americans?

Betty Friedan, the author of *The Feminine Mystique,* which had done so much to spur Second Wave feminism, turned her considerable skills of provocation and literary talent to aging and "ageism" in *The Fountain of Age.* Friedan's book was based on recent scientific findings about the nature of aging, interviews with men and women over 65, and her own experience of ageism as she passed the age of 60. Age and aging, in Friedan's analysis, had its own "mystique." It "is perceived only as decline or deterioration from youth" and its victims are "rendered helpless, childlike and deprived of human identity or activities," so that they "don't remind us of ourselves." As an alternative, Friedan proposed a different conception of the later years as a stage in the life cycle in which new emotional and intellectual capacities emerge. Having entered her old age with anger at society's treatment of the elderly, she found cause to revel in the experience of being old (Friedan 1993, 302).

African American teenagers by 40 percent, among white teenagers by 34 percent, and among Hispanic teenagers by 19 percent. In the debates about welfare, many critics decried the high rate of births to single teenage mothers in the African American community. But even white American teenagers had a higher rate of teen births than any other Western European country. Studies revealed that two-thirds of these teenage births were unwanted, suggesting that the United States' high rate of teenage births resulted from inadequate sex education or lack of access to contraceptives rather than to fundamentally distinct patterns of sexual behavior (*U.S. Teenage Pregnancy Statistics* 2006; Therborn 2004).

THE AMERICAN LANDSCAPE: PLACE AND LAND

The lives of Americans have always differed profoundly according to place, and in this regard, the 1990s was no exception. But several trends in the 1990s homogenized the physical, social, and cultural landscape of the nation.

First, a look at the demographics of the national landscape: How did Americans disperse among cities, suburbs, and rural areas? In an ever-mobile society, where did Americans move from and to? Of the 281.4 million people living in the United States in 2000, approximately half lived in suburbs, a third lived in cities, and a fifth lived in rural America. Americans continued to be a geographically mobile people; in the second half of the decade alone, 46 percent of the population moved (Katz and Lang 2003). Native-born Americans tended to move to Sunbelt suburbs while immigrants tended to settle in urban areas or in farming districts. African Americans, in a reversal of the mid-century migration to the North and West, returned to Southern states. Well-educated, middle-class African Americans were the ones who tended to migrate to the South, and Southern cities such as Memphis and Atlanta were the prime destinations. In a related development, metropolitan residential areas became more racially integrated. But segregation by income widened, if at a somewhat lesser rate than in the 1980s.

A majority of Americans lived in suburbs, and suburbs grew twice as fast as central cities in the 1990s (Katz and Bradley 1999). But polls revealed that was not what people would have ideally preferred. An equal number would have liked to live on a farm as appreciated suburbia—25 percent each. More, 37 percent, idealized the small town, according to a 1997 Gallup Poll (*Wilson Quarterly* 1997). By the end of the decade, large proportions of Americans living in metropolitan areas that had experienced massive exurban development considered sprawl to be one of the biggest problems of their region (Williams 2000).

Urban America registered both growth and decline in population. Some older midsize cities, such as Philadelphia and Detroit, lost population during the decade, but other cities experienced a population and economic growth as central cities were revitalized and people moved back downtown. Sunbelt cities in the South and West, such as Houston and Phoenix, grew spectacularly although much of their growth was of a suburban rather than urban character. With the economic boom of the decade, the cost of real estate skyrocketed in urban centers such as New York, San Francisco, Boston, and Chicago where so much of the New Economy took place. These cities become largely unaffordable to the middle class, and by the beginning of the new millennium, urban populations were divided between the relatively wealthy and the relatively poor (Berube 2006).

National and global economic forces powerfully shaped America's social landscape in the 1990s. The development of new exurban housing developments in undeveloped rural land beyond the existing suburban ring placed more and more American families in similar communities where few signs survived of the particular regional environment or culture. National home builders such as the Toll Brothers, one of the originators of the "McMansion," or KB Homes, who catered to slightly more modest tastes and more limited incomes, cultivated a national market, building Tudors or Cape Cods wherever they acquired land. Urban gentrification and economic globalization together eroded much of the difference between one American city and another. Corporate chains grew healthily, often at the expense of local small businesses. The distinctive character of many neighborhoods of America's cities was obliterated when Starbucks or Barnes & Noble moved in down the block. Technological developments, particularly in communications, severed the age-old relationship between place of work and place of residence imposed by the constraints of physical distance and transportation. Men and women in booming businesses could now live in rural splendor or small-town familiarity while maximizing their earnings at the same time. Conversely, the new technology enabled the labor-power of the ever-growing numbers of Americans incarcerated to be made available to entrepreneurs. Prisons became host not only to small industries and local manual labor demands, as in age-old practices, but also to direct marketing call centers.

At the end of the 19th century, Americans worried about the "closing of the frontier" and the limits it would impose on the nation. At the end of the 20th

Housing developments stretch out to form suburbs in the desert around Las Vegas, Nevada. (iStockPhoto.com)

The Exurbs: Key Statistics, 2000

"Sprawl" was the choice critical word to describe the phenomenon of the growth of exurbs. Similar to postwar suburban development, exurbs were developed in relation to urban centers but were located significantly farther from the core and tended to include larger homes on larger tracts of land.

 Exurban population: 10.8 million.

 Growth rate 1990–2000: 31 percent.

 Exurban population as percentage of metropolitan area population: 6 percent.

 Regional distribution of exurban population: South, 47 percent; Midwest, 24 percent; West, 15 percent; and Northeast, 14 percent.

 Acres of land per home in exurban census tracts: 14.

 Average acreage of land per home nationally: 0.8.

 Percentage of exurban workers who commute to urbanized core for work: 52.

 Percentage of exurban workers who commute one hour or more to work: 11 percent.

century, Americans faced the question of limits in a new way. Rapid and extensive suburbanization in the 1980s and 1990s had converted millions of acres of open space and rural farmland to exurban housing developments. An American Farmland Trust survey in 1997 estimated that 1 million acres of agricultural land was developed for suburban housing every year (Williams 2000). The new development required water and energy, while residents of the far-flung exurbs used more oil to heat their larger homes and to fuel their larger vehicles for longer commutes to work. The desert metropolises of greater Las Vegas and Phoenix alone grew 83 and 45 percent, respectively, during the 1990s. The 1990s was, nevertheless, the decade when awareness of the relationship between land use, transportation, and housing development and its impact on community and the environment became a mainstream worry and more concerted action and conscious land-use planning was initiated. No measure symbolizes this better than the construction of a subway in Los Angeles, the original antiurban sprawling suburban metropolis.

The Changing Rocky Mountain States

During the early 1990s, the six Rocky Mountain states of Montana, Idaho, Wyoming, Utah, Colorado, and New Mexico experienced a population and economic boom while the rest of the country remained mired in the jobless recovery. The new migrants to these states tended to be relatively well-off professionals who wanted to escape the hassles of urban and suburban life to live in the wondrous natural landscapes of the rugged West. Unlike earlier back-to-nature movements among urban Americans and thanks to the new technologies, these migrants were able to maintain their urban careers in their new rural homes. To them, the majority of whom were Californians, the region offered good schools, open space, outdoor recreation, the end of long commutes, and the restorative tonic of small-town life. In addition to those who chose to settle permanently in the Rocky Mountain states were many wealthy individuals and celebrities locating their second or third home in particularly beautiful towns, such as Jackson Hole, Wyoming, or Boulder, Colorado.

The Rocky Mountain region, however, was historically the home of the most rugged and individualistic of America's Westerners. Its economy had long been centered on resource extraction—mining, fishing, logging, and ranching. Generations of men had earned their livelihood pitting themselves against the forces of nature to wrest the earth's riches for human gain. The gulf between the cosmopolitan, professional newcomers and the long-time residents was wide. William Kittredge, the Western writer, wrote pointedly about the clash between them. "Imagine it. You've spent your life in a town by the river where the cottonwood leaves flash in the evening breeze. . . . You hate to see your paradise overrun by latecomers from seaport," even though one understood that the newcomers were saving the local economy as the old "resource colony" one collapsed (Kittredge 1993, 27). Although laws preserving the natural wonder of the Rockies were "a good thing," the livelihoods of ranchers, miners, and loggers were being eviscerated by many disparate forces, not the least of which was the new economy the urban migrants brought with them. "A lot of locals, former loggers and miners and such, are likely to end up in the servant business, employed as motel clerks and hunting guides, and they know it. It's not hard to figure why many people in the Rockies hate this wave of outlanders with such passion" (Kittredge 1993, 27).

Changes in Rural America

The 20th century's ongoing transformation of rural America reached a turning point in the 1990s. A significant majority of Americans, about 6 of every 10, lived in rural areas in 1900 while less than one-quarter did in 2000. The decline of farming was even more dramatic: less than 2 percent of the country's labor force worked in agriculture in 2000, compared to 41 percent in 1900; the number of farms fell 63 percent over the century; and farming was the main economic activity in 2000 in only 20 percent of rural counties (USDA 2005).

For Americans, the idea of rural life had always evoked an image of life devoted to the land, but by the 1990s, the reality was far from the imagined ideal. In 1940, 31 million Americans lived on farms, and 9 out of 10 of those farm residents worked in agriculture. By 1991, only 5 million Americans lived on farms.

Half of those found employment outside of the agricultural sector while two-thirds of farmers did not live on a farm. As a whole, only 7 percent of rural Americans gained their livelihood through farming and related industries. In rural America, as in the rest of the American social landscape, residence and workplace were separate. Observing that the lives of rural Americans were no longer bound up with farming, the Census Bureau ceased collecting data on people who lived on farms and ceased publishing its 45-year-old annual publication about them. In an understated epitaph for a lost rural America, the government's demographers explained that "farm residence no longer tells us much about farmers" (Dorcth, 1994, 21).

Not only did America's farming population decline precipitously but the very significance of agriculture to the rural economy, to the national economy, and to the nation's social and cultural landscape also changed dramatically. Granted there were many forces at work that caused this change, from technological advances to demographic shifts to secular economic change. One of the most important forces was the residential real estate market. America's farmland had become the new frontier for exurban housing development. Between 1950 and 1997, 20 percent of America's farmland disappeared, transformed into housing developments farther and farther from the metropolitan areas that had once formed the core from which suburban development grew (Williams 2000). The economics of farmland conversion were compelling to both developers and farmers. Farmland was particularly attractive to developers, for it had already been cleared, flattened, and drained. Farmers made greater profits by selling land for development than from the agricultural commodities they could produce; as the population of farmers aged and neared retirement, selling land for development seemed a wiser economic strategy than leaving it to children uninterested in or unable to farm the land. And development had a snowball effect on the agricultural economy of a rural locale. Property taxes increased as land values rose from housing developments; struggles over water supply between farmers and developers became endemic in the arid West; the more intensive production on lands that remained, gained through chemical fertilizers and pesticides, exhausted the land more rapidly. Local businesspeople that served farmers, such as creditors, seed companies, or machine suppliers, had a more difficult time making a livelihood, and many left or failed in the agricultural economy. The remaining farmers, those who persisted, found their communities bereft of the services they needed to run their farms, traveling farther and paying more for seed, machines, and fertilizer. It was as if the American farm was being slowly whittled away—one slice, floods, next slice, an offer one couldn't refuse, next, falling commodity prices, next, the federal government "reform" of the farm subsidy system. And so on. The strong old trunk of the American farm was reduced to a slender and delicate twig, apt to snap at any moment, at least according to the ominous predictions of some of its tribunes.

By the turn of the 21st century, the extensive development of the American countryside for nonrural uses was so far advanced that the Census Bureau decided that its traditional system of classifying American land and lives was obsolete. In June 2003, the category of "micropolitan" was invented to acknowledge that the exurban-type development in hitherto rural tracts had made certain rural counties resemble metropolitan ones more than they did rural ones. Once these borderlands of micropolitan areas were removed from the rural classification, the land area of rural America had shrunk for the first time to less than half of the continental United States. In popular parlance, these regions were known as exurbia—in short, the reference points were the far away metropolitan center around which the lives of exurban residents orbited, just as their suburban predecessors had.

What replaced farming as a way of life for Americans living in the shrinking areas still deemed to be rural? In general, the rural economy became more similar to the metropolitan economy, but those counties that were closer to metropolitan areas or boasted natural amenities weathered the transition better. Lifestyle-conscious, well-off urban consumers provided a stimulus to farms located nearby, which could vastly increase their profits by switching to organic production for farmers' markets and health food stores. Quaint small towns and stunning natural landscapes attracted metropolitan tourists and exiles, and many rural locales gained a new life by adapting to them. Rural counties less blessed by proximity or nature had a rougher go. In more densely populated rural areas, such as the coastal South, the shift from better-paid industrial work to low-wage industrial work and services was analogous to what urban and suburban Americans faced under deindustrialization. Food processing, an industry that bridged agriculture and the burgeoning service sector and which was partially shielded from the vicissitudes of globalization, provided jobs for 1.7 million Americans— or roughly twice as many waged and salaried jobs provided by farms (Economic Research Service 2000; Hatch and Clinton 2000).

In those counties in more difficult straits, still reeling from the rural economic crisis of the 1980s, government officials and residents were willing to look at less appealing options in order to provide employment, shore up an almost nonexistent tax base, and revive dying towns. Every year in the 1990s approximately 25 new prisons opened in rural counties. (The prison-building boom tapered off in the late 1990s as crime rates dropped nationwide.) Prisons provided jobs for local residents. The wages were low, acknowledged economist Thomas Pogue, but "it's a more stable industry for a town than a manufacturing plant . . . [and] these prisons are being located where people don't have much of a choice" (quoted in Kilborn 2001). The property taxes they paid and the concession fees towns levied on prisoners' phone calls and vending machines infused county treasuries with the funds to pay for local schools, police, and road building. For example, in Sayre, Oklahoma, population 2,881, home to a privately run prison housing almost 2,000 inmates, the prison paid nearly $7 million in wages to 270 local residents, and revenues from its operation increased the city's budget 60 percent in less than five years (Kilborn 2001). Another option for rural towns was to provide land for warehouses for retail companies (especially Wal-Mart) that needed to distribute overseas goods throughout America. The massive complexes and the traffic from a steady stream of 18-wheelers moving cargo containers disrupted the rhythm, pace, character, and environment of rural life. But survival often seemed a more important social good, one worth sacrificing the quality of rural life. Over the course of the 1990s, even as rural poverty rates dropped substantially, one-quarter of rural counties lost population, some by more than 5 percent (McGranahan and Beale 2002).

Family Farming

Small, family farms accounted for 9 out of 10 farms in America, and family farmers owned almost 7 out of 10 acres devoted to agricultural production in the United States. Industrial farms, whether owned by families or not, however, were responsible for two-thirds of America's $191.5 billion worth of production of agricultural goods.

Family farms, with their limited production, could not sustain household expenses through farming alone, and most were dependent on additional income from other sources. Government farm subsidies helped small family farms, many of which could not cover their cost of production, remain viable. Family members worked outside of the farm sector and supplemented family income with wages and salary from other employment (USDA 2001).

Aerial view of a farm in Chippewa Falls, Wisconsin. (U.S. Department of Agriculture)

New Urbanism: Recreating the Small Town Community

"New Urbanism" was a movement of planners and architects that emerged in the 1990s to promote the conscious recreation of small town life in new planned mixed developments. Architects Andres Duany and Elizabeth Plater-Zyberk pioneered the New Urbanism.

Combining a communitarian and an environmental ethic, they proposed that America's current land-use policies of "sprawl" degraded the physical environment and thwarted a sense of community and civic engagement among neighbors. Some of the central practical ideas of New Urbanism were to foster a public realm where people could congregate; to build homes walking distance to shops, work, and leisure and civic activities; and to situate homes more densely to encourage neighborly interaction. Benefits would accrue to the environment as polluting and resource-wasting commutes were minimized, and to individual psyches as the richness of community replaced the anomie of suburban isolation. In 1993, New Urbanists founded the Congress for a New Urbanism to promote and disseminate their theory and practice. It could be argued that "New Urbanism" was a misleading name for the movement, for it sought to change the nature of new suburban development, not renew America's cities. Instead of replicating one exurban housing development after another, New Urbanists recommended that planners and developers should seek to create small town–like communities each time they undertook new development. To accomplish such a goal required a level of planning far beyond what the economics of real estate dictated unaided. Zoning laws were the primary means available to shape suburban development.

Table 5.2. America's Ten Largest Cities, 2000

City	Total Population
New York, N.Y.	8,008,278
Los Angeles, Calif.	3,694,820
Chicago, Ill.	2,896,016
Houston, Tex.	1,953,631
Philadelphia, Pa.	1,517,550
Phoenix, Az.	1,321,045
San Diego, Calif.	1,223,400
Dallas, Tex.	1,188,580
San Antonio, Tex.	1,144,646
Detroit, Mich.	951,270

Source: U.S. Census Bureau.

With the economy—and the housing market—booming in the 1990s, Duany and Plater-Zyberk's alternative model of residential development won adherents but not necessarily of the sort they sought. The Disney Corporation was the most avid and influential promoter of the New Urbanist idea. In the 1990s, it began construction and settlement of Celebration in Florida, an entirely new and fully planned community for 20,000, designed to look and feel like a turn-of-the-20th-century small town with Victorian homes and a small town downtown. Ultimately, the Disney Corporation appropriated some of the sentiments of New Urbanism but little of its alternative planning ethic. The town where Celebration pioneers lived and worked turned out to be only the first phase of a larger commercial, retail, and industrial development slated to grow to 7 million square feet (Hayden 2003, 212).

RELIGION

In the 1990s, Americans remained a religious people, as they had been for most of the nation's history, yet the religions Americans practiced and the character of American religiosity had changed significantly. About 93 percent of Americans believed in God or a higher power, a percentage that had stayed relatively constant since the mid-1970s. The vast majority of Americans—77 percent—identified themselves as Christians, with roughly two-thirds of these Protestants and one-third Catholics. Jews accounted for about 2–3 percent of the population; Muslims, a somewhat smaller percentage. Nationally, those holding no religious preference rose from 7 to 14 percent in the decade, with the greatest increase among Protestant-raised believers. A third of Americans changed their religious affiliation over the course of a lifetime. Only 7 percent of American adults did not believe in God or doubted the existence of God (Roof 2000; Hout and Fischer 2002, table 1).

In comparison to many other countries, the United States has been religiously diverse. Diversity in American religion took on in the 1990s a new pluralistic character. As the religious scholar Dana L. Eck explained, "As we begin a new century and a new millennium, we in America are on new religious terrain. America has truly become a multireligious nation" (Lindner 2000, 362). Since the 1960s, there had been a marked increase among Americans in the practice of Eastern religions, and among African Americans in the practice of Islam. But the depth and breadth of religious change resulted more profoundly from the global diffusion of peoples and religions following the Immigration Act of 1965. Immigrants from China, Vietnam, Korea, India, and other Asian nations were Buddhists, Hindus, Sikhs, and Jains. Muslims from South Asian, Iran, Arab countries, and Africa likewise practiced the vast array of Islamic traditions. By the end of the 1990s, there were an estimated 2 to 3 million Buddhists in America, 2 million African American Muslims, 1 million Muslims of immigrant descent, and 1.6 million Hindus. The status quo of traditional American religious pluralism among Protestants, Catholics, and Jews was equally shaken up and transformed. Catholics from the Philippines, Central America, Mexico, and Brazil brought different practices, beliefs, and politics to the American Catholic church once dominated by descendants of Irish and Italian immigrants. Immigrants who were the descendants of those converted by Protestant missionaries from the mainline churches in the 19th and early 20th century discovered their native denominational church in America to be alienating, and founded their own ethnic United Church of Christ and Presbyterian congregations. Moderately religious and Orthodox Jews alike felt betrayed by the died-in-the-wool atheism of the Russian Jews they had rescued from Soviet anti-Semitism. There was a world of difference in belief, practice, and experience between immigrant Muslims and indigenous African American Muslims. The immigrant practitioners of these di-

Muslim women walk with a child near the Golden Gate Bridge in San Francisco. (iStockPhoto.com)

verse traditions likewise faced a challenge to their native ways. The religious pluralism of America was for the most part unknown in their home countries. In the United States, they encountered people of other faiths in their urban neighborhoods and workplaces, and perhaps for the first time encountered different practices and interpretations of their own religion. Some observers believed this multicultural and multireligious environment provided ideal conditions for the blossoming of "religious vitality" (Roof 2000).

Debates: Religious Experience and the Changing Religious Landscape

Historians and sociologists of religion debated in the 1990s how to make sense of the contradictory evidence about the significance of religion in American life. Outside religious circles, it appeared that a rapidly growing and powerful conservative Protestantism had come to define American religion and the role of religion in public life. The 1990s were the heyday of the lobbying groups the Christian Coalition and Focus on the Family, of "megachurches" with membership in the many thousands and multimillion-dollar annual budgets, of the acrimonious public debate about "family values" shaped by those who read the

Bible literally. It was the decade when Pope John Paul II sought to turn back
Vatican II and enforce conservative and traditional church teachings, especially
on sexuality, birth control, women's roles, and abortion. Within all of the historical major religions in the United States—Protestantism, Catholicism, Judaism,
and, to a smaller degree, African American Islam—the orthodox and doctrinaire,
and to be frank, the intolerant, appeared to be flourishing. Pope John Paul declared that contraception was evil during a whirlwind tour through America. A
Google search on some of the early-decade religious public figures who gained
notoriety—Pat Robertson, Meir Kahane, Khalid Abdul Muhammad—will quickly
reveal the family resemblance.

But underneath the surface, and less noted in the popular media, was a complex and shifting religious environment. When scholars looked at the evidence
of religious belief and practice, they noted that the evidence was contradictory.
Was American religion flourishing or stagnating? For several decades, membership in the mainline liberal churches had declined and membership in evangelical and conservative churches had increased, leading many to speculate on
an underlying shift from liberal to conservative in America's dominant religion,
Protestantism. Some argued that there was a religious revival centered in the
evangelical movement, closely associated with the New Right; others responded
that even that growth had not arrested the trend under way since the 1960s of
falling institutional membership and participation. Another study argued that the
association between the political right and religion was not leading to religion
gaining ground but rather to disaffection by a growing number of Americans.
The sociologists Michael Hout and Claude S. Fisher, observing statistical evidence
that the proportion of Americans with no religious preference doubled in the
1990s after remaining constant since the mid-1970s, hypothesized that the identification of Christianity with the political right in the decade was the most important cause of the shift. "Organized religion linked itself to a conservative social
agenda in the 1990s, and that led some political moderates and liberals who had
previously identified with the religion of their youth or their spouse's religion
to declare that they had no religion," they argued. For up to half of those declaring no religious preference, they concluded, "it was a political act, a dissent
from the affinity that had emerged between conservative politics and organized
religion" (Hout and Fischer 2002). They emphasized, however, that these people were estranged from organized religion, and that the majority of them believed in God or considered themselves spiritual. The proportion of these adults
without religion that held an unfaltering belief in God surged, from 13 percent
in 1991 to more than 29 percent in 2000.

The Princeton Religion Research Center and the Gallup index, two of the
most trusted surveys on American religion, and additional academic surveys
seemed to suggest that belief and religious affiliation had been declining since
the 1960s. The scholar David Roozen, analyzing this index, distinguished clear
differences among generations, with the youngest baby boomers reporting the

least interest in religion (cited in Roof 1996). But other surveys revealed Americans to be a highly religious people, especially compared to their counterparts in the developed Western world. Attempting to assess the conflicting evidence, the sociologist Wade Clark Roof wrote, "No one knows if the self-reported figures on religious attendance and membership are more inflated now than in the past, but it appears that sizable numbers of Americans today certainly take some liberties in describing their religious lives" (Roof 1996). My own review of the various surveys of religious belief, practice, identity, and institutional membership have left me skeptical that we can make reliable conclusions about such seemingly simple facts as how many self-identified Protestants, Catholics, Jews, Muslims, Hindus, and Buddhists lived in the United States. Roof aptly observes, "Sorting out actual religious commitments from the subjectivity and nostalgia surrounding religious identities in a country where religious language is typically cast as 'preferences' . . . all makes for a complex situation" (Roof 1996).

In short, there was a significant divergence between what quantitative data—from surveys, institutional censuses, etc.—and experience, observation, and qualitative analysis revealed. Books about religion, spirituality, and angels were flying off bookstore shelves; Americans regularly peppered their speech with spiritual references; no politician could risk a giving a major public address without mentioning God at least once. Scholars of religion hence looked for new ways to understand American religiosity. Harvey Cox, Wade Clark Roof, Catherine Albanese, Robert Wuthnow, Meredith B. McGuire, and Donald Miller, among others, proposed that the old analytical paradigms, focused on religious institutions and the mind of religious believers, were inadequate to make sense of the religious landscape that had been emerging since the late 1960s. Acknowledging that the long history of religious practice recorded shifts among different possible emphases, these scholars argued that there was strong evidence that the United States had entered an "experiential" phase in its religious culture. Spiritual meaning was not gained through the persuasion of the mind, or the cultivation of faith, but rather in Cox's words, through "emotional, communal, narrational, hopeful, and radically embodied" religious practice (Cox 1995). American religious practice registered "a mode of spirituality that places primacy not on reason, not even on belief system, but rather on a mystical-experiential stance which . . . is deeply liberating and empowering, and something of a protest against existing religious language that has turned stagnant or been corrupted" (Roof 1996).

While mainline churches and established congregations lost members and the members they retained were middle-aged or elderly, religious communities and congregations that offered an experiential mode of practice attracted baby boomers and their children in large numbers. Important experiential or spiritual movements of this sort arose within American Protestantism, Catholicism, and Judaism. The Catholic *cursillo* and Jewish Renewal movements were very similar to the larger and more visible new Protestant movements. Scholars observed that the spiritual, experiential impulse animating this growth was not limited to organized religion. A similar spirit clearly promoted the diffusion of New Age beliefs and practices. Sociologists also found the impulse in civic organizations, such as Habitat for Humanity, which enlisted volunteers in the practice of building homes for the poor, and in business, such as in the Lotus Development corporation's creation of a "soul" committee to probe the values underlying its management practices (Roof 1996). Those who had come of age in the 1960s, a generation that had rejected authority, hierarchy, proscribed morality, and the like, turned to practices in which the emotions and the body were engaged when they faced the perennial question of the meaning of life and one's place in the world. They imbued everyday activities with the significance of a spiritual quest; they had become "seekers" for meaning and self-transcendence.

Some scholars ventured that the new experiential mode represented a transformation of American religious life, with one claiming it to be a "second reformation" (Miller 1997). Most, however, viewed the period as one of flux and change, and asserted that it was unclear how this evolving mode of religious practice would develop in the future. As Roof, one of the preeminent religious scholars of the decade, told his colleagues, "The religious terrains in the United States are changing, and so must our maps of those terrains. The maps are yet to fully evolve, but there must be some clues in the details around us" (Roof 1996).

Evangelical Protestantism: New Paradigm Churches

The transformation of Protestant worship in "new paradigm churches" and the soaring popularity of those churches among baby boomers and their teenage children attracted wide attention in the 1990s (Miller 1997). Although derisively characterized as "megachurches," the rise of these new, nondenominational churches were significant indicators of evolving American religious beliefs and practices and the cultural significance of organized religion in American life at the end of the 20th century.

Southern California nursed three of the churches that would grow to become the largest and most important national congregations: Calvary Chapel, Vineyard Christian Fellowship, and Hope Chapel. Each was founded between 1965 and 1974 by charismatic preachers dissatisfied with the nature, character, and structure of the churches in which they had been raised.

Influenced by the values of the 1960s counterculture, and appropriating its cultural practices, the new paradigm churches transmuted that heritage of radicalism and individualism into a communal and often socially conservative template for life. Like many of their generation, pastors and members of new paradigm churches sought authenticity, healing, and personal meaning in their lives; they likewise rejected tradition, authority, hierarchy, and convention (Miller 1997). In their view, the mainstream and mainline Protestant denominations, with their stale ritualism, authoritarian clergy, and bloated bureaucratic hierarchies, had strayed from the true meaning of Christianity. The new paradigm churches sought to foster an unmediated individual relationship with God and Jesus. Their founders and pastors cultivated an atmosphere of informality, humility, and spiritual egalitarianism among congregants. They valued an extroverted spirituality, rooted as much in the body and emotions as in the mind. Where they parted company with the counterculture, however, was in their conviction that the personal quest for authenticity and meaning should not be oriented toward self-realization but rather toward a life devoted to Christ within the congregation's communal life.

While the cultural practices of these churches were very much attuned to modern—or more accurately, postmodern—ways, the Christianity preached and practiced was traditional and fundamentalist. Contemporary music was integral to worship and services; electric guitars replaced organs and pop melodies displaced the traditional hymnal. Worship services would often begin with a guitar player leading congregants in a half hour of group praise singing. This would be followed by a teaching period, led by the pastor, who would interpret a passage of scripture in a humble, conversational, and down-to-earth style. It would often be followed by a call for anyone to come forward to initiate a commitment to Jesus. More joyous music followed, and in some churches, the service ended with a period of ministry, which in some charismatic churches included healing rituals and speaking in tongues. The Sunday service, however, was only one small part of life in these churches. For many members, their deepest connection to the church and the congregation came through weekly Bible study in smaller groups in homes. The churches also hosted a wide array of social, recreational, and cultural activities for members by age- and interest-group (Miller 1997). As the emphasis on the weekly service and on home Bible study groups shows, biblical study of the true Christian life was the foundation of these churches' practice. And the Christianity preached and practiced in these churches was that of a literalist reading of the gospel and the traditional family and social values supported by such an approach. For all the ways these churches approached people from their contemporary situation—encouraging informality, popular culture, therapeutic and confessional social interaction—the essential appeal was that they offered a "powerful sense of life's purpose" and a clear instruction on how to live a moral life (Miller 1997, 301).

The new paradigm churches were churches of the "born again," that is, Christians who had undergone a conversion experience in which they had taken in the Holy Spirit and become transformed from a "sinner" to be "saved." Of the members of Calvary, Hope, and Vineyard, 93 percent were sure they had been born again, and another 5 percent thought that they had been (Miller 1997). Conversion initiated a life transformation. The past was sin and selfishness; the future, after being born again, was to be devoted to serving God. The guide for one's new life of service was the Bible, and the locale was the Christian community of

Crystal Cathedral, Garden Grove, California. (iStockPhoto.com)

the church. "Discipleship" and "accountability" were watchwords within these churches. A man who devoted himself to God showed personal discipline and responsibility toward one's family and community. He sought guidance from his spiritual mentor in the church and, above all, served God (Miller 1997). Home to an almost uniformly born-again membership, actively proselytizing for individuals to step up to an intimate relationship with Christ, and nurturing a community in which spirituality and Christian commitment were seen as a seamless part of a whole life, these churches were far more hospitable to the born again than were mainline churches and even many of the more established evangelical and fundamentalist churches.

The 1990s was a decade of explosive growth and enormous popularity for these churches and others like them. In the early 1990s, "crusades" held in stadiums and amphitheaters brought out hundreds of thousands of people in attendance, where charismatic pastors called individuals to their "appointment with God" to be saved. Surveys showed that about 1 out of every 20 or 30 people stepped forward, and about 10 percent went through a serious process of conversion (Miller 1997). Christian rock concerts, sponsored by these pastors and including preaching and calls to conversion, attracted more than 50,000 seekers at a single event (Miller 1997). In the mid-1990s, there were more than 1,000 churches belonging to these three movements—600 churches in Calvary, 400 in Vineyard, and 50 in Hope Chapel (Miller 1997). Calvary had also launched churches in other countries. The home churches of each movement had huge weekly attendance—for example, between 6,500 and 12,000 people attended weekly services at Calvary's Southern California churches (Miller 1997).

Jewish Americans: Religion and Peoplehood

What did it mean to be Jewish in America in the 1990s? Historically, cultural or ethnic Jewishness had been the central element of Jewish identity to the majority of Jewish Americans who were secular or barely observant. But by the end of the 20th century, the cultural experiences and social environment in which ethnic Jewishness had flourished into the postwar era had vanished. Ironically, assimilation into the American economic and social mainstream and the erosion of distinctive Jewish cultural practices left the practice of Judaism as a religion as one of the few remaining avenues for the expression of Jewish identity. The dilemma is captured by the fact that Jews in the 1990s had a higher rate of synagogue affiliation than at any other time in the 20th century but attended services far less frequently than any other religious group in the United States (Laderman and León 2003). With such uncertainty about what constituted Jewish identity and so little remaining cultural specificity to Judaism, concern about losing the young was rampant among Jewish leaders. A 1990 community survey had shown an intermarriage rate of 52 percent; a survey later in the decade of younger Jews suggested that their Jewish ethnic identity and attachment was far weaker than that of their parents. The leaders of community organizations poured energy and money into programs to reclaim the young—day schools, summer camps, youth groups, and trips to Israel (Seltzer and Cohen 1995; Wills 1998; Grossman 1999).

Jewish Americans nevertheless felt a strong collective identity, even if they disagreed about what constituted it. The force of cohesion, bringing almost all American Jews together in a shared identity and project, was the memory of the Holocaust and the preservation of Israel as the state of the Jewish people. Jewish identity through Holocaust remembrance reached its apogee with the opening in 1993 of the United States Holocaust Memorial Museum on the National Mall in Washington. Yet the importance attached to the Holocaust in American Jewish identity also came under fundamental challenge, with many rabbis, scholars, and ordinary Jews criticizing the way the community had lost sight of positive Jewish values, beliefs, and culture in the reduction of Jewish identity to the reactive "never again" stance. Israel also became as much a source of vituperative divisiveness as it was a glue for peoplehood. With the outbreak of the Palestinian intifada in the late 1980s and the peace initiatives of the Clinton administration, American Jews split between militaristic "hawks," affiliated with the Israeli right, and peace movement "doves," affiliated with the Israeli left.

American Jewish Religious Practice

As Jewish Americans lost their distinctiveness culturally, and political and philosophical differences split American Jews in their secular relationships within the community, the experience of Judaism as a religion and the significance of religion in defining Jewish identity began to change. Within American Judaism, there were three major and two minor denominations, each divided internally, active in the 1990s: Orthodox, Conservative, Reform, Reconstructionist, and Renewal.

Orthodox Judaism was in the midst of a fundamental transformation; the modern orthodoxy that had prevailed in 20th-century America was being supplanted by ultra-orthodoxy, which rejected many of the tenets of the modern Orthodox movement. The change was significantly related to developments in Israel. American Orthodox customarily sent their youth for a year of study in Israel. But as the ultra-Orthodox had assumed more power in Israel, particularly in the yeshivas where Americans studied, American students returned home rejecting the modern orthodoxy of their parents. Meanwhile, the Orthodox struggled to contend with the difficulty raised by the growth of the Lubavitcher movement and its turn toward treating its deceased founder as the messiah—a heresy as far as the other Jewish denominations were concerned.

Conservative Judaism, always the denomination with the most tentative sense of itself as a coherent alternative to Reform and Orthodox, struggled in the 1990s with declining membership, debates over the movement's position on intermarriage and homosexuality, and, more fundamentally, a redefinition of Jewish identity among young people raised in Conservative congregations. Younger Conservative Jews, sharing in general American trends in religious practice toward increased emotionalism and spirituality, sought their Jewish identity in a spiritual religious practice, contrary to their parents' tendency to locate their Jewishness in community life and cultural Judaism. Young adults and younger boomers were also less concerned about preserving group identity. Intermarriage became the controversial focal point of the debate within the Conservative movement. For the postwar and post-Holocaust generation, marrying within the religion had been widely viewed as essential to Jewish survival in a hostile world. Official bodies of the Conservative movement remained largely opposed to intermarriage while individual congregations, in keeping with the opinion of congregants, tried to make synagogue life more hospitable to intermarried and converted families (Roof 2000).

Reform Judaism in the 1990s focused on finding a way to incorporate the new spiritual modes of religious experience into its liturgy and practice. These changes were met, within the movement, with dismay by some who believed that

Social Reforms in Judaism

Reform, Conservative, Reconstructionist, and Renewal Judaism all engaged in significant reforms during the 1990s. The Conservative movement issued a new prayer book and a new rabbi's manual, both employing gender-neutral language. But, reflecting its historical role seeking a traditionalist middle ground between Orthodox and Reform Judaism, Conservative authorities balked at other reforms adopted by the Reform movement and demanded by many of its members. The official bodies retained their position against homosexuality, rejecting homosexuals from the Conservative rabbinate and prohibiting rabbis from performing ceremonies blessing same-sex unions. On this subject, however, there was active resistance from Conservative synagogues and individual rabbis. The congregational board of the liberal B'nai Jeshurun in New York City cut off funding for the Jewish Theological Seminary when the latter refused to change their policy on admitting homosexuals to study for the rabbinate. Analogous protests and dissent occurred in California (Laderman and León 2003). (Not until 2006 did Conservative Judaism adopt a policy of full inclusiveness toward homosexuals.) In contrast, the official body of Reform Judaism allowed gays and lesbians in the rabbinate in 1990.

Changes in American society, of course, were of signal importance in stimulating such reforms. Yet, forces internal to Judaism were more decisive influences over the shape and character of the reforms. Many of the reforms had originated in the nondenominational Jewish Renewal movement where the effort to create a more egalitarian and social-justice oriented Judaism began and where the American turn to a deeper spiritual and emotional practice first became manifest. Jewish Renewal grew significantly in the 1990s, even as Reform and Conservative congregations adopted some of its innovations. Reconstructionism, also historically a pioneer of reforms, went the furthest in defining an inclusive community for non-Jewish spouses and children in intermarried families; it issued a new prayer book that omitted references to the biblical sacrifices and any reference to the chosen people. Orthodoxy, on the other hand, exercised a countervailing force against social and liturgical reform, most importantly through its institutional power in the state of Israel (Grossman 1999).

Reform Judaism was conceding too much to the traditionalism it had rejected at its founding. In 1999, "Ten Principles for Reform Judaism" was issued, widely condemned by many in Reform, and sent back for revision.

Diversity in American Buddhism

In the popular 1993 film on the life of pop music star Tina Turner, *What's Love Got to Do with It,* Turner converts to Buddhism in the wake of her abusive

A Western Buddhist monk in Cambridge, Massachusetts, makes a donation to a political campaign. (David Leskowitz)

marriage. Turner's conversion narrative was familiar to American audiences in the 1990s, who learned of Buddhism through the handful of celebrities who had embraced Buddhist practices. Celebrities such as Richard Gere and Harrison Ford used their bully pulpits in entertainment and the media to educate Americans about Buddhism and to awaken their conscience to the struggle of the people of Tibet. Through three Hollywood films and countless fundraisers, the spiritual and political leader of the Tibetan Buddhists, the Dalai Lama, became a familiar figure to Americans. Although he lived in India, he was probably the most important individual in American Buddhism in the nineties (Laderman and León 2003).

Yet the practice of Buddhism among American converts, though significant, was only a tiny part of the picture of Buddhism in America. In fact, most Buddhists in America were immigrants or the children of immigrants from Asia, whose native religion was Buddhism. They brought the three major branches of Buddhism—the *yanas,* or vehicles—from their native countries to the United States and adapted them once here, as all immigrants have done. Immigrants and their American-born children from Vietnam, Cambodia, Laos, Burma, Sri Lanka, and Thailand tended to be practitioners of Theravada—"Way of the Elders." Mahayana—"Great Vehicle"—Buddhism predominated in China, Korea, and Japan and among descendants of immigrants from these countries. Zen centers in the United States and the largest Buddhist organization in the nation, the Soka Gakkai International-USA, were part of the Mahayana tradition. In both of American Theravada and Mahayana Buddhism, although there were some native-born American convert practitioners, Asian immigrants and Asian Americans were in the vast majority. Mahayana Buddhism, nevertheless, was the only Buddhist tradition that attracted a sizeable number of African American and Hispanic, not just white American, converts. The most familiar Buddhist tradition in the United States was the Tibetan Buddhism of the Dalai Lama—the Vajrayan, or "Diamond Vehicle." With only about 3,000 Tibetans resident in the United States, American converts were the vast majority of Vajrayan practitioners. The 1990s represented, to scholars of American Buddhism, a "Third Great Awakening," set in motion by the 1965 Immigration Act ending

Table 5.3. Annual Spending on Entertainment

Form of Entertainment	Annual Spending (billions of dollars)
Toys and sporting equipment	65
VCRs, TVs, CD players, videotapes	50
Books, magazines, newspapers	50
Gambling	28
Cable television	19
Amusement and theme parks	14
Movie tickets and film/video rentals	13
Recorded music	10

Source: Kraft 1997.

the prohibition on Asian immigration, and one in which diverse strains of Buddhism from all over the Buddhist world flourished in America.

POPULAR CULTURE AND ENTERTAINMENT

In the 1990s, Americans worked hard, slept little, and entertained themselves with relish. Many of the leisure-time activities they engaged in were familiar and had long been settled habits. Spectator sports, television, movies, music, and shopping continued to occupy many hours of "down time." Other activities, such as gambling, "extreme sports," or videogaming, were new or newly popular.

There were divergent tendencies and paradoxes evident in popular culture and leisure activities. Americans took risks in the new extreme sports and gambling, yet they also became more and more "couch potatoes," as they watched movies and shopped from the comfort of home. Technological developments atomized society, yet many pursued the "interactive" possibilities of the new technology in videogaming, internet surfing, and chat rooms. Civic organizations shrank, but coffee bars and chain bookstores boomed as they became public gathering places. Popular culture became increasingly homogenized, with the commercial mainstreaming of hip-hop and grunge, and the diffusion of pop music to younger and younger audiences. Yet there was a renaissance in many supposedly high culture arts—jazz, serious fiction, theater, art film, and documentary. The national mood hovered between devil-may-care optimism and jaded cynicism, yet Americans ingenuously consumed apocalyptic movies and books and stocked basements with supplies to survive the anticipated Y2K virus. Within the increasingly strident Culture Wars, eclectic, multicultural, postmodernist cultural products achieved commercial and critical success. Critics decried "trash culture"—the ever-mounting focus on raunch, sex, personal troubles, and violence in the media. Yet complex dramas, sophisticated ironic comedies, and politically sophisticated music that dealt with controversial and troubling social themes gained unprecedented critical and commercial success. Indeed, many of the decade's most popular television shows—*Seinfeld, Roseanne, The Sopranos, NYPD Blue, Oprah*—creatively melded Americans' taste for violence, sex, other people's troubles, and raunch with a critically reflective social realism.

The Rise of Independent and Documentary Film

The brief rise in the 1990s of independent film to mainstream success was conditioned upon upheavals in the film industry that took place in the 1980s. The consolidation of media companies had led to a focus on high-grossing blockbuster movies, produced to maximize profit and minimize risk, and the reduction in the number of nonstudio movies. The consolidation of movie theaters, with the building boom for multiplex theaters in suburban malls and the decay and abandonment of independent movie theaters in small towns and urban centers, provided the conditions for the dissemination of the new studio model of production. The spread of the VCR into the majority of American homes allowed many to avoid theaters and enjoy movies in the privacy of their own homes. In sum, film culture had became more commercialized, more risk averse, and more privatized in the 1980s.

As these tendencies progressed, however, independent filmmakers who viewed film in ways distinct from studio executives began to finance, produce, and make movies outside of the industry system. These movies departed from the blockbuster formulas of action-packed, escapist stories with happy endings geared toward a suburban youth demographic. Instead, independent filmmakers drew on the long history of cinema verité and art film to create films that were socially or artistically challenging to their audiences.

The pivotal year in the mainstreaming of independent film was 1989. Michael Moore's rough-hewn, self-financed documentary *Roger and Me,* humorously and irreverently exploring the devastating subject of the industrial death of his home city Flint, Michigan, redefined the documentary genre. Breaking with the often-depressing seriousness of so many documentaries, Moore lit the path for socially conscious filmmakers to entertain viewers as much as to inform them, and thus win a mass audience for politically controversial material. Steven Soderberg's *Sex, Lies, and Videotapes* served a similar catalytic role for independent feature films. It was the first to cross over from the traditional independent film audience in urban art houses to mainstream popularity. Premiering at Robert Redford's small, quirky, and obscure Sundance Film Festival, it also helped turn the festival into one of the hottest annual international film events of the 1990s.

Independent film in the 1990s won big audiences and critical acclaim alike. A large part of the commercial success and broad diffusion of indies was due to the influence of Miramax Film. Harvey and Bob Weinstein brought their hard-driving New York concert promoter tactics, learned in the city of Buffalo, to the once effete world of art house cinema. For *The Crying Game* (1992), for example, they created buzz for the movie by cleverly enlisting the press in a successful effort to prevent anyone from revealing the plot twist. The movie earned critical raves and a profit, despite the fact that it sympathetically portrayed terrorism and an interracial, transgendered sexual relationship. Many of the most popular independent films of the 1990s, including *Pulp Fiction, Shakespeare in Love,* and *The English Patient,* were produced by Miramax.

Commercial success in the 1990s for many of the 1980s' pioneering independents, such as Oliver Stone, Spike Lee, and Steven Soderberg, was one sign of the mainstreaming of the independents and the decline of the Hollywood formula. Another was the artistic evolution of the titans behind the 1980s blockbusters. Steven Spielberg, justly celebrated for his technically inventive and compelling sci-fi movies, reoriented his career in the 1990s to accord with the independent sensibility to tackle artistically and socially challenging subject matter. In his movie *Schindler's List,* in which a German industrialist saves hundreds of Jews from extermination at Auschwitz, Spielberg employed all of his technological brilliance and story-telling powers to portray harrowingly vivid scenes of Nazi death camps.

As independent movies won commercial success, the major studios started to hone in on the field. Disney acquired Miramax in 1993, and by the end of the 1990s, most of the major studios had launched their own "independent" division. By the end of the 1990s, independent was more a marketing catch phrase than the description of a type of film. Predictably, tensions between filmmakers, independent producers, and the studios emerged anew in these industry conditions. The classic Hollywood tension between artists, who realize a film, and the executives of large corporations, who make movies as a business, was replayed in the second half of the 1990s.

The New Media and the News

New, and relatively new, technologies transformed the news media between the mid-1980s and the mid-1990s. The invention and then broad diffusion of cable television into American homes increased competition for market share in television viewing. Videotape, mobile minicams, and earth-orbiting satellites put into place the technological conditions for instant and constantly streaming news. Without actual changes in technology, the explosion of entertainment and news sources in this period would not have been possible. With their new forms of programming, the new sources redrew the boundary between private and public life.

Added to the economic and technological forces was politics. The Reagan administration deregulated the airwaves in its efforts to unleash the free market. In doing so, it had radically altered the manner and content of the news Americans received by the early 1990s. A 1997 study by the Committee of Concerned Journalists documented how "hard" news coverage in television, magazines, and newspapers had fallen and coverage of "soft" topics had dramatically increased since the late 1970s. Celebrities and other lifestyle topics received double the attention; coverage of national issues by two of the most popular news magazines dropped by a third (Johnson 2001).

Television news was the most powerfully transformed by the political and market changes. In the 1980s, the Federal Communications Commission (FCC) changed the longstanding public service requirements for licensing and allowed media companies to own more radio and television stations in local markets. Diversified corporate giants—many of which were primarily entertainment, not news, companies—raced to buy up local news stations and the three big networks themselves. General Electric bought NBC; Capital Cities Communications got ABC. Consolidation continued at a brisk pace in the 1990s. Time Warner, the corporation created from the merger of Warner's entertainment portfolio and Time Inc.'s publishing empire, got CNN. And then in the most colossal deal of them all, Time Warner and AOL merged. Cable news had brought new competitive forces to bear on the network news. Less regulated from the start, many cable news shows engaged in a journalism focused on scandal and salaciousness. (CNN had wed the new technology and old-style standards of network journalism to great critical acclaim, but it too quickly faced pressure from other cable networks.) For broadcast news, the economic bottom line became, contrary to tradition, the measure of success. What sold best on the news, according to Nielsen ratings, was celebrity, scandal, and tragedy—"if it bleeds, it leads" came into its own under this new economic, political, and technological structure (Johnson 2001).

The O. J. Simpson case was one of many such episodes in which the new media culture and a celebrity scandal came together in an explosive brew. The media's handling of the case became the template for covering those that followed, especially the Clinton-Lewinsky scandal.

The Media in the Trial of O. J. Simpson

The eerie scene remains vivid in the minds of many Americans who were alive in 1994. During the afternoon of June 17, 1994, every major broadcast and cable network aired video footage shot from helicopters above a Los Angeles freeway. The scene showed dozens of Los Angeles County police and California Highway Patrol cars following, not quite chasing, a white Ford Bronco. Commentators and news anchors informed viewers that O. J. Simpson was in the Bronco,

Helicopters film the police chase of O. J. Simpson in Los Angeles, June 17, 1994. (Rick Maiman/Corbis Sygma)

reportedly holding a gun to his own head. Viewers could also see that crowds of Angelinos were massing along the chase route, some to gawk, most to cheer on the sports and TV celebrity.

Everyone in the country, including many who were rooting O. J. on, knew that warrants for his arrest on two counts of murder had been issued that morning, and that he had failed, as arranged, to turn himself in to police. Five days earlier, O. J.'s ex-wife, Nicole Brown Simpson, and a friend of hers, Ronald Goldman, had been brutally murdered outside her home while the Simpsons' two children slept upstairs. She was found nearly decapitated, with multiple knife wounds to the head and neck. Goldman had been knifed more than 20 times. At the scene of the crime, Los Angeles police found a leather glove, a knit cap, and bloody footsteps leading from the open front door of the house.

As the chase proceeded, every television show was preempted to allow for live coverage of the unfolding drama. One hundred million viewers watched the spectacle (Johnson 2001). Their curiosity was motivated less by the unusual police chase of a well-loved celebrity than by the lurid fascination with whether this celebrity would commit suicide, live on TV. Two hours and 50 miles later at Simpson's Brentwood mansion, the suspense ended when Simpson finally surrendered to the police.

The subsequent nine-month-long televised trial of Simpson was the most covered and most watched event of the decade to that point. The so-called trial of the century was one that anyone with a television could see or hear commentary about at any hour of the day or night. The interest Americans' showed toward the case stands in an age-old tradition of fascination with spectacle, and spectacle it was. Only the delivery—through a media transformed—was different. The story of the trial and the media extravaganza surrounding it has been ably told many times, most interestingly by Haynes Johnson in *Best of Times* (2001).

Ultimately, the trial hinged on race. At first, however, in the weeks after the murders, it seemed rather that the case would shine public attention on the problem of domestic violence. Simpson had carefully nurtured a squeaky-clean, avuncular, harmless public persona. Soon after the murder, the press reported Simpson's record of physical and verbal abuse of his wife, the many calls Nicole Simpson made to 911, the many times the police have been called to the scene and left after doing nothing. Police reports and 911 tapes were leaked to the press. Attention shifted, however, when Simpson's defense team investigated the background of one of the police officers first to the scene of the crime. Mark Fuhrman, the officer who had discovered most of the incriminating forensic evidence, was revealed at trial to be a raging racist of the sort that many white Americans believed had gone extinct with the civil rights revolution. The defense team discovered audiotapes of Fuhrman that had been recorded by a screenwriter; they called her as a witness and played the tapes in court. Casually peppering his dialogue with the epithet "nigger," Fuhrman bragged on the tapes about beating African American suspects and framing innocent African American people, never quite making it clear whether he had done these things himself or simply found such actions amusing. Other witnesses testified to hearing similar racist boasts and epithets spoken by Fuhrman. Once Fuhrman's views were exposed in court, after he had lied about them under oath, a trial that had started as one about celebrity prerogatives, wealth, fame, and domestic violence became one about race and race alone, a kind of Rorschach test of the racial divide in America. For many African Americans, with this coming on the heels of the LAPD beating of Rodney King and the acquittal of the white officers by a jury in a notoriously racist white enclave of Los Angeles County, O. J. became the symbol of all the black men throughout American history who had been abused and framed by racist police and a racist judicial system. In the view of many white Americans, a celebrity had gotten away with murder because of the racism of African American jurors.

Music: The Sampling Decade

The Who's "[Talkin' 'Bout] My Generation" (1965) had served as an anthem and slogan of the 1960s counterculture; in the 1990s, "classic rock" radio stations broadcast the song regularly to millions of Americans of all ages. In 1990s' America, just about everyone from the age of seven to middle-aged boomers listened to pop music. Notwithstanding protests against gangsta rap, popular music was not a subject of deep social division, as it had been in the rise of so many popular music forms, from jazz to blues to rock. Popular music no longer served as the marker of generational divides but rather had developed into a unifying cultural force.

Popular music in America today is so ubiquitous and uncontroversial that it can be difficult to recognize the historic cultural shift this represents. The distance traveled can be glimpsed in Frank Sinatra's 1957 congressional testimony decrying the rise of rock. "Rock 'n' roll smells phony and false," he declared. "It is sung, played, and written for the most part by cretinous goons . . . the most brutal, ugly, desperate, vicious form of expression it has been my misfortune to hear" (Isserman and Kazin 2000, 533). Popular music derived from rock had been a defining element of youth culture in the 1950s and the youth rebellion of the 1960s. By the late 1970s, the animus expressed by Sinatra was no longer the majority view of adult America. By the 1980s, popular music was inescapable in American culture.

By the 1990s, conflict between the generations, once symbolized by sharp differences in musical taste, had been transmuted into different consumer preferences expressed by the very young, teenagers, younger adults, and the middle-aged, between girls and boys and men and women—but less and less in differences between black, white, and Latino. Grunge, hip-hop, punk, and heavy metal styles, which continued to embody the rebellious, innovative, and critical spirit of their forebears, appealed to some youths in their late teens and early 20s. Others of their peers preferred the classic rock of their parents' youth. Alternative or indie rock, ranging from less hard-edged grunge to folk-influenced singer-songwriters, had a wide audience among people in their mid-20s to mid-40s. Whereas heavy metal and much of hip-hop culture celebrated an exaggerated masculinity—with a strong dose of misogyny mixed in—women musicians possessing a sophisticated Third Wave feminist sensibility won unprecedented success and recognition. Highly commercialized pop girls and boys groups went after the preteen market. Latin "crossover" did exactly that, gaining a wider non-Spanish speaking audience in the 1990s. Country music incorporated more rock instrumentation and Hollywood-level production techniques, and, although still concentrated in the South and the West, won a national audience. Christian pop music allowed traditionalist Christians to participate in the cultural mainstream while being spared its unsavory sexual and secular themes. Conversely, classical music was no longer considered only for squares. People of all ages were likely to sample their music from different genres—classical, jazz, rock, country, and world music—rather than to rigidly define themselves by their taste in one type of music.

Histories of popular culture have an immense amount of musical activity to chronicle. From the perspective of social history, however, the 1990s stand out from the prior four decades for the paucity of cultural, artistic, intellectual, stylistic, political, or technological breakthroughs. Much of the internal dynamics at work in popular music in earlier decades continued unabated in the 1990s—styles developed out of and in reaction to earlier ones. Musicians' principles to stay authentic vied with their desires for commercial success and their real economic needs, and the media conglomerates were always on the lookout for the next commercial opportunity in authentic youth fads. Commercialization of popular music's various subcultures accelerated and intensified in the 1990s with the relentless entertainment industry consolidation of the mid-1980s to mid-1990s. Technological innovations had been critical to the transformation of popular music in other decades, but there was a lull in the impact of technological change on music in the 1990s. Video and MTV were of the 1980s. The technological foundation for the computerization of music—MP3 and related programs—was refined during the 1990s but only became important months before the millennium, when Napster began making music available online for downloading to computers. Portable digital players—the iPod and others—went on the market in 2001 and after.

The expansion of veritable amusement parks for rock and blues illustrates well the shift in the social and cultural significance of popular music. The House of Blues and the Hard Rock Cafe presented "legendary" blues and rock and roll performers in well-lit, air conditioned theaters, making accessible to everyone the hard-edged rock and blues that had originated out of distinctive historical experiences. The practice of repackaging black music for white audiences was ingrained at the birth of rock and roll, yet the entrepreneurs behind the House of Blues and Hard Rock Cafe chains took it to a new level. Branson, Missouri, advertised by its tourism board as the "family-friendly Las Vegas," performed a similar service for country music fans with its dozens of theaters geared toward tourists. The commercial and regimented "Woodstock" festival of 1999 stood at the apex—or to rock's devotees, the nadir—of this tendency.

Alternative styles and sensibilities, attuned to the rebellion and cultural criticism at the heart of popular music, did not disappear in the 1990s. Yet the reverence with which alternative musicians treated their forebears stood in ironic counterpoint to the spirit of innovation and rebelliousness they hoped to perpetuate. Emblematic of this position was the grunge band Nirvana, led by Kurt Cobain. Rebelling against the trend in popular music toward slick, Hollywood-style production values and commercialization, Nirvana's music was rough, home produced, and it foregrounded lyrics of rebellion, disaffection, and jaded detachment from the corrupted adult world. But rather than invent new musical idioms, explore new technologies, or otherwise innovate, Nirvana looked back to punk rock and new wave of the 1970s and 1980s, adding in influences of country and heavy metal. It was an unusual melding of styles, yet there was the whiff of reverence in Nirvana's rebellion. Punk music, the sine qua non of rock's innovative, rebellious character, continued to draw new youth into its

Hip-Hop and West Coast Gangsta Rap

Hip-hop, which melded artistic, technological, and intellectual inventiveness with the spirit of authenticity and rebellion at the heart of original popular music, was perhaps the only style to have bucked the pervasive cultural pattern described above. As the *Village Voice*'s 1988 pull-out section "Hip Hop Nation," put it, hip-hop "was the only avant-garde around, still delivering the shock of the new" (Chang 2005, 348). By the end of the decade, media consolidation, commercialization, conflicts internal to the community of rappers, and political controversy had mainstreamed hip-hop as just another highly profitable genre of youth culture and popular music.

In the late 1980s and early 1990s, hip-hop was one of the most popular styles of music among black and white young men, and a distinctive hip-hop subculture had arisen. Part of what appealed to black and white hip-hop fans alike was the style's realistic, dark, and graphic depiction of life in the post-Reagan inner city, where joblessness, the crack epidemic, gang rivalries, and gun violence prevailed. For many African American hip-hop fans, this was the reality they lived in. For those outside the inner city, hip-hop's "*attitude—that b-boy stance, with its brimming streetwise confidence, scowling generational defiance*" spoke to the disaffection of what would shortly be dubbed the "Hip-Hop Generation" (Chang 2005). Hip-hop provoked tensions, desires, conflicts, and debates similar to those that had marked the origins of rock. Rock had provoked virulent opposition in the 1950s in part because it flouted the color line in mainstream popular music between "race" records by and for black people and "white" music for the majority. White youth, in their attraction to hip-hop, were unwittingly imitating their boomer parents, who had also found in black music—in rock, in Motown, in blues—an expression of authenticity and vibrancy lacking in their own lives.

Hip-hop had first emerged among black youth in the Bronx in the late 1970s. In the late 1980s, a new genre of hip-hop, "gangsta rap," was born with the 1988 release of Ice Cube's "Gangsta Gangsta." Ice Cube and his rap group NWA (Niggaz with Attitude) lived in Compton, a working-class African American and Latino city in Los Angeles County in which deindustrialization had left many African American men unemployed, and the crack epidemic had landed many others in jail. NWA's songs included violent and sexually explicit lyrics, and the group became a magnet for controversy with its 1989 "F*** the Police," a song about police brutality in Los Angeles. Social critics were appalled at rappers' supposed glorification of sex, violence, race war, and misogyny and were deaf to the distinction between advocacy and the depiction of reality. In 1990, a federal judge in Florida ruled that 2 Live Crew's *As Nasty as They Wanna Be* (1989) was obscene, and Florida law enforcement authorities went after the group, arresting several members at a show. (The ruling was overturned and the musicians acquitted at their trial.) In 1992, Ice-T's song "Cop Killa" sparked nationwide outrage. The group's record company, Time Warner, succumbed to pressure and the threat of a boycott

Continued on next page

Hip-Hop and West Coast Gangsta Rap, Continued

by dropping the band and pulling the song from record stores. Around the same time, other labels cleaned up their lists and got rid of the artists and tracks that might unleash a similar storm against their company.

Censorship and backlash, ironically however, helped to push gangsta rap into the commercial mainstream. NWA's 1991 record became a Billboard top hit, although no radio stations or music video television shows would play it on air. Up until then, most hip-hop music was produced by independent producers and labels and publicized through journalists and writers who were avid fans. The major record labels realized that there was a profitable market to be tapped and began signing artists and buying up the independent labels. Over the course of the 1990s, the large media corporations producing hip-hop records increasingly adopted the Hollywood blockbuster format—a heavy capital investment in fewer and fewer products. Some artists, hip-hop producers, and entrepreneurs made huge profits as part of the major label system. As in other media, however, consolidation spelled a decline in diversity.

Gangsta rap was the most commercially successful of the hip-hop subgenres. It was a more complicated phenomenon than many of its critics made it out to be. Some of its leading musicians had indeed been involved in crime or gangs. Snoop Dogg had worked a low-wage job, served time in jail before he became a rap musician, and was tried for murder after he became a famous rapper. The men who founded Death Row Records and Ruthless Records were drug dealers. But others, such as NWA's Ice Cube and Dr. Dre, were never gang members. Rather they adopted the persona of gangsters as an artistic style and viewed themselves as engaging in an art form of social realism. Others straddled the line. Tupac Shakur, perhaps the most renowned hip-hop artist of the decade, combined a searing social realism and political critique with a life increasingly consumed with and finally ended by the violence he rapped about.

---

subculture, and the most significant development was the emergence of female punk musicians, in the Riot Grrrls, Bikini Kill, and other groups. But musically, politically, and culturally speaking, the practice of perpetual innovation took place within an established idiom. Indie rock remained popular on the edges of the mainstream, but only a few artists, such as Beck and Moby, broke new artistic ground.

Jazz

Jazz is arguably America's first and most distinctive contribution to music history. A small group of leaders in jazz—most notably Wynton Marsalis, musician and composer, Stanley Crouch, jazz critic, and Rick Burns, documentarian—worked tirelessly in the decade to transfigure jazz's conventional cultural image as a pop or bohemian form, and to elevate it to the status of high culture, as America's quintessential classical music. The jazz ambassadors invented a canon, won philanthropic support for performing it, wrote articles elucidating jazz's high culture bona fides, composed jazz symphonies, produced documentaries, sharply debated jazz aficionados who disagreed with them, and went on speaking tours in public schools, all to promote their cause. They succeeded. By the end of the decade, Lincoln Center had a permanent jazz orchestra under the conductorship of Marsalis; Marsalis was a widely known, familiar, and likeable teacher and performer; millions of Americans had viewed Ken Burns's PBS documentary on jazz; and jazz had been installed permanently in the pantheon of American high culture. Downplayed in this vision of the music and jazz culture was the more sordid lived experience of some greats like Charlie Parker and Billie Holiday, as well as the work of the more experimental jazz innovators.

Books and Reading

The diversity of Americans, their tastes, and their culture was particularly evident in the wide variety of books published, distributed, bought, and read in the 1990s. Despite the ever-persistent alarms that this or that new technology would displace reading, the book business went through a boom in the 1990s. Chain stores such as Barnes & Nobles and Borders, while putting many small bookstores out of business, provided environments that drew people into bookstores in unprecedented numbers. Oprah Winfrey's book club, begun in 1996, provided instruction and a welcoming forum for her devoted television viewers to explore books and writers they would probably not have known about but for her show. The later decade online stores, especially Amazon, provided incomparable convenience for book purchasing.

In accord with trends over the previous decades, self-help books were one of the most popular genres of nonfiction, and mystery/thriller and romance novels were the most popular types of fiction consumed by Americans. John Grisham and Danielle Steele each had two novels in the top five of the hardcover fiction and mass-market paperback best-seller lists for 1997. A new development in the 1990s was the popularity of books related to religion: Americans bought more books focused on religious and spiritual themes than on any other kind of fiction or nonfiction book in the 1990s (Garrett 1997). A popular Christian series was Christian Right activist Tim LaHaye's *Left Behind* series, published by his company, Tyndale House, after being rejected by other publishers. Premiering in 1995, the series adapted the biblical story of revelations and set the rapture and the apocalypse in modern-day America. By 2001, 27 million copies of books in the series had been sold (Unger 2005). LaHaye thus simultaneously tapped into the American public's cultural fascination with millennial and apocalyptic themes in the years leading up to 2000, and the small but fervent minority of premillennarian Christians who believed the end times were imminent. Not only Christian books did well; the Parallax Press, specializing in Buddhism, had a mailing list of 100,000 people interested in their list (Winston 1998). And then there were books such as the series *Chicken Soup for the Soul,* which straddled the religious and self-help genres at once. Literary fiction experienced something of a renaissance in the 1990s. The decade saw the publication of major new works by important writers—Thomas Pynchon's *Mason and Dixon,* Philip Roth's *American Pastoral,* Don Delillo's *Underworld,* John Updike's Everyman Library collection of *Rabbit* novels, and other well-received novels—and the award of the Nobel Prize to Toni Morrison.

Literary Fiction: From Ethnic to American Literature

While the Culture Wars attempted to polarize the American public on a purported opposition between American patriotism and multiculturalism, Americans demonstrated in their cultural fare that they found the distinction to be a false one. The broad popularity and official recognition of the writers Toni Morrison and Philip Roth suggest that many Americans had a more complex understanding of the relationship between ethnicity and Americanness.

Morrison and Roth broke through to win accolades as great American writers with, respectively, *Beloved* (1987) and *American Pastoral* (1997). In these novels, both authors pursued a theme common to their earlier life's work: the historically distinct experience of one's ethnic group as a supremely American story. Roth's purview was the experience of Jewish Americans in the 20th century from immigration through assimilation; Morrison's was that of the nearly 400-year history of Americans of African descent, from slavery, through Jim Crow and de facto segregation in the North, to the uncertain present of contemporary America.

American Pastoral and *Beloved* were showered with awards, won a far broader audience than was typical for serious fiction, and won their authors unusual fame. Morrison, after publication of *Jazz* (1992), won the 1993 Nobel Prize in Literature. She was the first American woman and first African American to have won the Nobel, and was one of only nine American writers to have ever won the prize. Although the novel *Beloved* was experimental in style and morally ambiguous in subject matter—two poisons in the marketplace—Oprah Winfrey produced and starred in a critically acclaimed film adaptation of the novel in 1998. Roth won the Pulitzer and a number of other awards for *American Pastoral.* Roth and Morrison, at the height of their careers, had certainly in their maturity perfected their craft. Yet it was as surely a sign of the post-ethnic times that those who had once been ghettoized as a "Jewish writer" and a "black woman writer" were considered to represent the pinnacle of American literature on the eve of the third millennium.

Spectator Sports

Football and baseball remained the most popular spectator sports for which millions of Americans felt a deep attachment. The Super Bowl always gained the highest television ratings for a spectator sport. The 1990s saw the soaring popularity of basketball as a generation of phenomenal players converged with the maturation of professional basketball into big business. Michael Jordan, one of the greatest players of all time, led the Chicago Bulls to six NBA championships. Yet nearly a dozen other players—Earvin "Magic" Johnson, Larry Bird, Shaquille O'Neal, Dennis Rodman, David Robinson, and others—were familiar household names.

Stock car racing won new fans during the 1990s, emerging as the fastest-growing spectator sport. Six million people attended the National Association for Stock Car Auto Racing (NASCAR) Winston Cup races in 1998, nearly double the number who had attended in 1990 (Oxoby 2003). Television broadcasts of NASCAR races increased, and TV coverage introduced new fans to the sport. Like more established spectator sports, the leading figures became national celebrities, well known beyond the circles of NASCAR enthusiasts.

Fans of baseball, the "national pastime," endured several collective mood swings during the decade. The opening of Camden Yards in Baltimore in 1992 symbolized the hopes and dreams residing in baseball's devotees. The stadium, consciously designed to evoke the classic baseball parks of the early 20th century—Chicago's Wrigley Field, Brooklyn's Ebbetts Field—promised to restore the glory and innocence of the sport. Truly a great venue for watching baseball, Camden Yards nevertheless testified to the powerful nostalgia residing in Americans' attachment to the sport.

Baseball fans' sense of the sport as an American tradition above crass interests was offended when players went on strike in the 1994 season, suspending the season. Few wanted to face the new reality of baseball as big business. But the following year, they exulted again, when Cal Ripken of the Baltimore Orioles broke Lou Gehrig's record for consecutive games, hitting home runs in the tying and the breaking games. Ripken embodied the image of the American pastime. He was widely known to be an honest, decent, and modest individual—in short, all the qualities that were in short supply in the decade of bad-boy celebrity athletes. Records broken later in the decade and various scandals deflated fans yet again. Mark McGwire broke Roger Marris's home run record in 1998, but many suspected that McGwire was using steroids.

The common theme running through all professional spectator sports in the 1990s was money. Tickets to events soared in price, and new corporate-named sports venues were built with private clubs and corporate boxes to separate the wealthy from other fans. Prices for these privatized areas ranged from $75,000 to $300,000. Advertising became ubiquitous within the sporting arena, and the merchandising of team paraphernalia and souvenirs added additional millions of dollars to the take of franchise owners. As owners' profits soared, so too did players' salaries. Deals between sports leagues and television networks for broadcast rights reached into the billions. Star athletes supplemented their multimillion-dollar contracts with corporate sponsorships. Tiger Woods, the decade's sensation in golf when he became the youngest player to win the Masters Tournament in 1997, received $24 million from sponsorships. While it all seemed wrong and unseemly to sports fans, they nevertheless continued to attend games in droves, purchase the teams' merchandise, and favor the brands endorsed by celebrity athletes (Oxoby 2003).

Women's Sports

As a generation of girls who had grown up under the advantages of Title IX (1972) reached the cusp of adulthood, for a brief moment in the 1990s, women's sports appeared ready to take off and rival men's sports. The Women's National Basketball Association (WNBA) started play in 1997 after the U.S. women's team had taken the gold medal in the sport at the 1996 Olympics. With the exception

Mia Hamm speaks to aspiring players at a soccer clinic in Colorado. (NewsCom)

of the women's baseball league during World War II and a short-lived basketball league, the United States had never before hosted professional women sports leagues.

The sensation of the decade in women's sports was the U.S. women's World Cup soccer team. Led by its star player, Mia Hamm, the team won the first and second women's World Cup championships in 1991 and 1999. Hamm and her teammates were idolized by young American girls, who joined youth soccer leagues in droves. In 2001, Hamm helped start the first professional women's soccer league in the United States. The financial backers of the league withdrew in 2003, ending the league. The fate of professional women's soccer suggested that Americans had not moved as far toward gender equality in sports as some had thought and hoped. Nevertheless, the new model of female athleticism and success embodied by Hamm and other young women athletes was destined to have a deep and lasting effect on American girls. And the WNBA continued to grow and in 2006 became the first professional women's league in the United States to reach the 10-year mark.

Gambling

Gambling shed its historical disrepute as a vice in the 1990s. Much like another historical vice, alcohol, moderate gambling was socially condoned, though some people had an "addiction" and were advised to abstain or offered help by Gamblers Anonymous. Gambling became such a normal and accepted part of American leisure activity that entrepreneurs transformed the experience into a family affair.

The earlier legalization and cultural legitimation of gambling was a precondition for developments in the 1990s. From the mid-1960s through the 1980s, states established lotteries to raise state funds, and states and the federal government legalized many forms of gambling in diverse locations. The 1988 congressional Indian Gaming Act, following a Supreme Court decision in 1987 allowing casinos on Indian reservations, gave powerful impetus to the proliferation of gambling. Gambling exploded thereafter. Riverboat gambling, for example, was extended from 3 to 16 states between 1990 and 1993.

Las Vegas led the way in the cultural repackaging of gambling. Always economically dependent on gambling as its primary local industry, Las Vegas in the 1990s thoroughly left behind its own history as the desert city built by gangsters. The key figure in the transformation of Las Vegas was Steve Wynn. An entrepreneur who described himself as "in the recreation business," Wynn literally blew up the old casinos on the Strip and built new family-oriented amusement park–like casino complexes in their place (Painton 1993). Gambling became just one of many activities for the parents on a family vacation. At his Mirage, an ersatz volcano erupted outside every 15 minutes while inside tourists could view rare white tigers in the shopping mall atrium. By the end of the 1990s, Wynn and his competitors had rebuilt and redesigned Las Vegas according to this new model. So much so that Americans could enjoy *Bugsy* (1991), a movie about Bugsy Siegel, the gangster founder of Las Vegas, and experience no qualms about taking the kids on a family vacation to the city.

BIOGRAPHIES

Tim Berners-Lee, 1955–

Inventor of World Wide Web

Software pioneer Tim Berners-Lee was the inventor of the World Wide Web. Berners-Lee was born in Great Britain and educated at Oxford University. While working for a British company in the summer of 1980, he produced a form of software that stored data through random associations. Although that software was never published, it became one of the building blocks of the World Wide Web more than a decade later. In 1989, he proposed creating a global hypertext project that would allow people around the world to share information through hypertext documents. In 1990, he wrote the programs that have remained the basic mechanism for the sharing of information on the Web. In doing so, he turned a communications system that had only been accessible to a technological elite into a form that could be used by the masses. The World Wide Web debuted in 1991. Unlike many Internet pioneers who converted their computer expertise into multimillion-dollar commercial enterprises, Berners-Lee remained a passionate advocate of the early democratic, noncommercial, decentralized vision of the Web and continued to devote his life to scientific research. In 1994, he founded the World Wide Web Consortium (W3C), based at the Massachusetts Institute of Technology with research centers operating worldwide. W3C works to preserve the openness of the Web by creating open-source standards, thus preventing the balkanization of the medium by competing proprietary systems. Berners-Lee continues to work at W3C and to conduct scientific research in the United States and Europe.

Kurt Cobain, 1967–1994

Musician

Kurt Cobain, the songwriter and lead of the band Nirvana, was one of the most innovative and influential popular musicians in the 1990s. Nirvana began as a garage band in Seattle, where the grunge movement originated. Like other musicians in his community, Cobain sought to return popular music to its roots and wanted little part of the world of commercial rock. The movement rejected the increasingly commercialized, highly produced conventions of music making then dominant in rock, as well as its corrupting world of celebrity. Stylistically, grunge was influenced by punk, rock, and heavy metal bands. Cobain had incredible gifts as a songwriter. Melodically, his songs were full of pop hooks that made them appealing to a broad audience. Lyrically, his work was much darker and more complex. His lyrics, dealing with subjects such as divorce, abortion, parents' drug use, and other taboo subjects, spoke to youth who viewed themselves as outsiders. Nirvana's first record was self-produced, made in a week at the cost of $2,000. In 1991, Nirvana was signed by a label and quickly put out *Nevermind*. The record included the song "Smells Like Team Spirit," which was an immediate hit and quickly seen as the anthem of Generation X. The album skyrocketed the group to international fame and went gold within a few weeks. Members of the band become millionaires and celebrities overnight. Over the following three years, they toured the world, their videos aired constantly on MTV, and they released a third album. Cobain, however, was ill-prepared to deal with the fame, fortune, and celebrity that so contradicted the vision of the Seattle music community where he had gotten his start. Cobain struggled with heroin addiction, and on April 8, 1994, he committed suicide shortly after escaping from a drug treatment center.

Larry David, 1947–

Co-creator of Television Comedy *Seinfeld*

Stand-up comedian and writer Larry David was a co-creator of *Seinfeld,* the most popular, most talked-about, most financially successful, and most critically analyzed television show of the 1990s. David was raised in Brooklyn and began performing comedy skits in New York in the 1970s, where he met and became friends with stand-up comedian Jerry Seinfeld. David and Jerry came up with the concept of the show while on trip to the grocery store. *Seinfeld* was famously "about nothing." For nine seasons, most of those in the Number one slot, the show chronicled the lives and friendship of four self-involved New York City singles. Many of the ideas for episodes came from David's life. As executive producer and writer, David picked up Emmys in 1993 for outstanding comedy series and outstanding individual achievement in writing in a comedy series. He stayed with the series until 1996, left on amicable terms, and returned to write the show's finale in 1998. A year later, David starred in and produced a largely unscripted special for HBO—*Larry David: Curb Your Enthusiasm*. That successful special led to a regular HBO series, *Curb Your Enthusiasm*.

Kathleen Hanna, 1968–

Feminist Punk Musician

Musician Kathleen Hanna was a pioneering figure in the Riot Grrrl feminist movement of the 1990s. Hanna began her artistic and political trajectory while studying photography at Evergreen College in Olympia, Washington, in the 1980s. Hanna and other women, frustrated with the lack of women's studies courses, sexism, and censorship of politically themed art, opened an art gallery in downtown Olympia. Olympia was the center of the incipient grunge movement, and Nirvana and others performed at the gallery. In the early 1990s, Hanna joined with Tobi Vail, Kathi Wilcox, and Billy Karen to form the punk rock band Bikini Kill. The band's songs were feminist and politically radical. Bikini Kill was one of the first successful female punk bands, and when they began, there was still sharp prejudice against women in punk. Teenaged and young women were huge fans of Bikini Kill, and the band inspired many radical women musicians of the 1990s and 2000s. The band, however, was hounded by antagonistic men in the audience, who often shouted obscenities and threw things at them during performances. In 1992, Hanna and fellow musicians and friends Allison Worth and Molly Neuman founded the Riot Grrrl collective in Washington, D.C. (named after a small fanzine already published by Worth and Neuman.) Riot Grrrl attracted teenaged girls and young women who were artists, feminists, and radicals. Groups sprouted up in cities throughout the country. The group published fanzines, trained each other how to produce concerts, held latter-day consciousness-raising sessions, and discussed feminist theory. It became a hub for emergent Third Wave feminism. Bikini Kill lasted until 1998. Hanna released a solo album and then founded other bands.

Michael Lerner, 1943–

Leader in Jewish Renewal Movement

Rabbi Michael Lerner, a philosopher, political commentator, and Jewish scholar, rose to prominence in the 1990s as leader of Jewish Renewal and as a political writer. After graduating from Columbia, he went to the University of California–Berkeley in 1964 for postgraduate work, and there he became involved with radical politics. He was active in the movement opposing the Vietnam War. With Ph.D.s in both philosophy and clinical psychology, Lerner later worked as a clinical psychologist and adjunct professor in the San Francisco area. He started the small progressive magazine *Tikkun* in 1986 and moved the journal's headquarters from Los Angeles to New York in 1992 because he wanted to be closer to the center of American Jewish life. As the editor of *Tikkum* and in his book *Jewish Renewal: A Path to Healing and Transformation* (1994), Lerner laid out the case for the Renewal movement, which argued for Jews to embrace the traditional social-justice tenets of Judaism, its concept of "*tikkun olam*"—to heal the world. At the same time, Lerner attracted political attention by coining the phrase the "politics of meaning." President Bill Clinton was intrigued by Lerner's ideas, and Lerner served as an informal advisor to the Clintons.

Tupac Shakur, 1971–1996

Rap Musician

Tupac Shakur had a meteoric rise to fame as one of the most popular and critically acclaimed rappers of the decade, and remains the best-selling rap artist of all time. Shakur's parents were Black Panthers, and troubles plagued the family before he was born. Shakur's mother, Afeni, was incarcerated during part of her pregnancy awaiting trial on a conspiracy charge. (She was later acquitted.) Shakur was born in New York and raised by his mother. She was poor and addicted to crack during his childhood, and they spent years moving frequently between the Bronx, Harlem, and occasionally into homeless shelters. At the age of 12, Shakur was cast in his first role as an actor in a production by a Harlem community theater. Shortly after, the Shakurs moved to Baltimore, and Tupac attended the School for the Arts, where he studied acting and ballet. He did well, but when his mother moved him to California, he dropped out of school. He continued performing in California with Digital Underground, and the record on which he made his 1991 debut as a rapper went gold. Later that year, his solo debut record, *2Pacalypse Now,* won him instant national fame as one of the leading voices of gangsta rap. The songs on the record depicted the life he had known living in so many of America's black inner cities. He made his first film, *Juice,* in 1992 and received favorable reviews. Shakur, who had articulated a philosophy of the "thug life," had a number of run-ins with the law, and his life increasingly began to resemble the persona he had invented in his music.

In 1993, he released *Strictly 4 My N.I.G.G.A.Z.,* which went platinum, spent 10 days in jail for assaulting another rapper with a baseball bat, and starred in the film *Poetic Justice.* In 1994, his life continued to follow two tracks: He released *Thug Life, Volume One* and earned critical praise for his film *Above the Rim,* and he barely survived an ambush by another rapper's gang. In 1995, he served a prison sentence for sexual abuse and released *Me Against the World,* which went multiplatinum. The legal case and civil suits connected with it had bankrupted him, and he agreed to sign with Marion "Suge" Knight of Death Row Records in exchange for Knight helping him out with his debts. Although he told friends that prison changed him, he was drawn back into the gangsta life at Death Row Records. In September 1996, he was shot as he rode through Las Vegas with Knight. He died from gunshot wounds six days later. Death Row Records released his last album, *The Don Killuminati: The 7-Day Theory,* posthumously in 1996. His murder remains unsolved, though it is widely believed to have resulted from a feud between East and West Coast rappers, specifically Knight's Los Angeles Death Row Records and New York Big Boy Records.

Oprah Winfrey, 1954–

Television Talk Show Host, Media Entrepreneur

Oprah Winfrey, talk show host and head of a media empire, was by the end of the 1990s one of the most famous, influential, and richest women in America. Winfrey grew up poor in rural Mississippi and Milwaukee. She revealed in 1991 that she had been repeatedly sexually abused by male relatives as a teenager. She became a delinquent, and after her mother could not get her into a school for delinquent children, she was sent to live with her father and stepmother. There she refocused on her education and won a full scholarship to Tennessee State University. She first began her career in high school as a newscaster in Nashville, and in college, she became anchor of the newscast. After graduation in 1976, she moved to a Baltimore station, where she soon co-hosted a talk show. In 1984, she took a job as the host of a morning talk show in Chicago. After her ratings surpassed Phil Donohue's, the show was renamed *The Oprah Winfrey Show,* and it went into syndication in September 1985. The show, with a viewership over 40 million, was the number one talk show for every year of the 1990s. As a talk show host, she became known for her ability to draw out authentic personal revelations from her guests and audience, as well as for confronting a broad array of controversial social issues. As her talk show gained popularity, she continued to take on acting roles and established her own production company, Harpo, Inc. She launched Oprah's Book Club in 1996; literary novels she recommended immediately catapulted to the top of best-seller lists. In 1998, she co-founded Oxygen Media, a cable television channel geared toward women. She introduced her own magazine, *O,* in 2000. Winfrey has become a notable philanthropist through her foundation.

REFERENCES AND FURTHER READINGS

Abma, J., G. M. Martinez, W. D. Mosher, and B. S. Dawson. 2004. "Teenagers in the United States: Sexual Activity, Contraceptive Use, and Childbearing, 2002." *Vital and Health Statistics* Series 23 (Number 24).

Altman, Lawrence. 2004. "Study Finds That Teenage Virginity Pledges Are Rarely Kept." *New York Times,* March 10.

Berube, Allan. 2006. "The Middle Class Is Missing." *New York Daily News,* July 8.

Berube, Allan, Audrey Singer, Jill H. Wilson, and William H. Frey. 2006. "Finding Exurbia: America's Fast-Growing Communities at the Metropolitan Fringe." In *Living Cities Census Series.* Washington, DC: The Brookings Institution.

Bianchi, Suzanne M., John P. Robinson, and Melissa A. Milkie. 2006. *Changing Rhythms of American Family Life.* New York: Russell Sage Foundation.

Chang, Jeff. 2005. *Can't Stop, Won't Stop: A History of the Hip-Hop Generation*. New York: St. Martin's Press.

Cox, Harvey Gallagher. 1995. *Fire from Heaven: The Rise of Pentecostal Spirituality and the Reshaping of Religion in the Twenty-First Century*. Reading, MA: Addison-Wesley.

Dorcth, Shannon. 1994. "Farewell to the Farm Report." *American Demographics* 16 (3): 21–22.

Friedan, Betty. 1993. *The Fountain of Age*. New York: Simon & Schuster.

Fukuyama, Francis. 1999. *The Great Disruption: Human Nature and the Reconstitution of Social Order*. New York: Free Press.

Garrett, Lynn. 1997. "Notes from the Marketplace." *Publishers Weekly,* November 10, 32.

Grossman, Lawrence. 1999. "Jewish Communal Affairs." In *American Jewish Year Book, 1999,* edited by D. Singer, 165–198. New York: American Jewish Committee.

Hatch, Julie, and Angela Clinton. 2000. "Job Growth in the 1990s: A Retrospect." *Monthly Labor Review* 123 (12): 3–18.

Hayden, Dolores. 2003. *Building Suburbia: Green Fields and Urban Growth, 1820–2000*. New York: Pantheon Books.

He, Wan, Manisha Sengupta, Victoria A. Velkoff, and Kimberly A. DeBarros. 2005. "65+ in the United States: 2005," edited by C.P.R. U.S. Census Bureau, U.S. Government Printing Office.

Hout, Michael, and Claude S. Fischer. 2002. "Why More Americans Have No Religious Preference: Politics and Generations. *American Sociological Review* 67 (2): 165–190.

Isserman, Maurice, and Michael Kazin. 2000. *America Divided: The Civil War of the 1960s*. New York: Oxford University Press.

Johnson, Haynes Bonner. 2001. *The Best of Times: America in the Clinton Years*. New York: Harcourt.

Katz, Bruce, and Jennifer Bradley. 1999. "Divided We Sprawl." *Atlantic Monthly,* December, 284 (6). http://www.theatlantic.com/issues/99dec/9912katz.htm.

Katz, Bruce, and Robert Lang. 2003. *Redefining Urban and Suburban America: Evidence from Census 2000*. 3 vols. Washington, DC: Brookings Institution Press.

Kilborn, Peter T. 2001. "Rural Towns Turn to Prisons to Reignite Their Economies," *New York Times,* August 1, A1, 12.

Kittredge, William. 1993. "The Last Safe Place." *Time,* September 6, 27.

Kraft, James P. 1997. "American Entertainment in the 1990s." *Business and Economic History* 26 (2): 805–811.

Laderman, Gary, and Luis D. León. 2003. *Religion and American Cultures: An Encyclopedia of Traditions, Diversity, and Popular Expressions*. Santa Barbara, CA: ABC-CLIO.

Lindner, Eileen W., ed. 2000. *Yearbook of American and Canadian Churches 2000,* edited by National Council of the Churches of Christ in the U.S.A. Nashville: Abingdon Press.

McGranahan, David A., and Calvin L. Beale. 2002. "Understanding Rural Population Loss." *Rural America* 17 (4): 1–11.

Meyer, Julie. 2001. "Age: 2000." In *Census 2000 Brief.* Washington, DC: U.S. Census Bureau.

Miller, Donald E. 1997. *Reinventing American Protestantism: Christianity in the New Millennium*. Berkeley: University of California Press.

Mishel, Lawrence R., Jared Bernstein, Sylvia Allegretto, and Economic Policy Institute. 2005. *The State of Working America, 2004/2005*. Ithaca, NY: Cornell University Press.

Oxoby, Marc. 2003. *The 1990s,* American Popular Culture through History series, edited by R. B. Browne. Westport, CT: Greenwood Press.

Painton, Priscilla. 1993. "The Great Casino Salesman." *Time,* May 3, 52–53.

Roof, Wade Clark. 1996. "God Is in the Details: Reflections on Religion's Public Presence in the United States in the Mid-1990s." *Sociology of Religion* 57 (2): 149–163.

Roof, Wade Clark. 2000. "Toward the Year 2000: Reconstructions of Religious Space. *Annals of the American Academy of Political and Social Science* 527 (Religion in the Nineties): 155–170.

Seltzer, Robert M., and Norman J. Cohen. 1995. *The Americanization of the Jews, Reappraisals in Jewish Social and Intellectual History*. New York: New York University Press.

Simmons, Tavia, and Grace O'Neill. 2001. "Households and Families: 2000." In *Census 2000 Brief.* Washington, DC: U.S. Census Bureau.

Spain, Daphne, and Suzanne M. Bianchi. 1996. *Balancing Act: Motherhood, Marriage, and Employment among American Women*. New York: Russell Sage Foundation.

Stephen, Elizabeth Hervey, and Anjani Chandra. 2000. "Use of Infertility Services in the United States: 1995." *Family Planning Perspectives* 32 (3): 132.

Therborn, Goran. 2004. *Between Sex and Power: Family in the World, 1900–2000, International Library of Sociology*. New York: Routledge.

Unger, Craig. 2005. "American Rapture." *Vanity Fair,* December 2005, 204.

U.S. Bureau of the Census. 2000. *Statistical Abstract of the United States, 2000.* U.S. Department of Commerce, Economics and Statistics Administration. Washington, DC: U.S. Census Bureau. http://purl.access.gpo.gov/GPO/LPS12567.

USDA, Economic Research Service. 2000. "United States Farm and Farm-Related Employment," edited by the U.S. Department of Agriculture. Washington, DC: USDA.

USDA, Economic Research Service. 2001. "America's Diverse Family Farms" (Agriculture Information Bulletin, No. 769), U.S. Department of Agriculture. Washington, DC: USDA.

USDA, Economic Research Service. 2005. "The 20th Century Transformation of U.S. Agriculture and Farm Policy" (Economic Information Bulletin, No. 3), U.S. Department of Agriculture. Washington, DC: USDA.

U.S. Teenage Pregnancy Statistics. 2006. Guttmacher Institute. http://www.guttmacher.org/pubs/2006/09/12/USTPstats.pdf.

Wald, Kenneth D. 2000. "The Context of Gay Politics." In *The Politics of Gay Rights,* edited by C. A. Rimmerman, K. D. Wald, and C. Wilcox, 1–30. Chicago: University of Chicago Press.

Williams, Donald C. 2000. *Urban Sprawl: A Reference Handbook, Contemporary World Issues.* Santa Barbara, CA: ABC-CLIO.

Wills, Garry. 1998. "How Odd of God." *New York Review of Books,* August 13.

Wilson Quarterly. 1997. "It Takes a Village." *The Wilson Quarterly* 21 (1): 121–123.

Winston, Kimberly. 1998. "Buying the Dharma." *Publishers Weekly,* September 14, 32.

Immigration and American Life

OVERVIEW

More people immigrated to the United States in the 1990s than ever before in the nation's history. Not only were the lives of the millions of people who made America their home powerfully transformed by their journey but native-born Americans too faced changes in their daily lives, changes that raised fundamental questions about community, public resources, and national identity. As they have done throughout American history, American citizens and immigrants in the 1990s struggled to find a way to accommodate each other in their local communities and in the national polity.

Just as the economic divide of the nation in the 1990s mirrored the Gilded Age of the 1890s, so too did immigration evoke many of the same hopes and fears that had arisen in the Gilded Age and the Progressive era. Did new immigrants fuel economic growth or did they take jobs away from native-born workers? Would they contribute to building the nation or would they undermine American government and drain public resources? Would they assimilate to the American way or would the American way be destroyed by their influence? Did they enrich American culture with their diverse practices or would the national identity be lost in the encounter?

The 13 to 14 million new immigrants and the more than 31 million foreign born in the 1990s were part of the era of "new immigration" dating to the Immigration Act of 1965. Immigration has increased in each decade subsequent to the act; the 1990s was a peak in immigrations numbers, to that point, but current trends suggest that the 2000s will surpass the 1990s. It is important, however, to maintain a historical and comparative perspective when analyzing the significance of immigration. Although more immigrants took up residence in the United States in the 1990s than ever before, the national population was also larger than ever. Immigrants thus accounted for a smaller proportion of the population than they had in the peak years of immigration from Southern and Eastern Europe in the Gilded Age and Progressive era. By a conservative estimate, new immigrants represented only 5.6 percent of the national population. By contrast, in 1910, immigrants accounted for 11.8 percent of the population, or more than double the percentage in the 1990s. The comparison for the foreign born as a whole is analogous. By 2000, 11.1 percent of America's residents had been born in a foreign country; in 1890 and 1910, 14.7 percent were foreign born. In a broader comparative perspective, it is also important to keep in mind that every advanced industrialized country received large numbers of immigrants in the last decades of the 20th century. Global mass migration was one of the defining features of the social history of the era (Passel and Suro 2005; Malone et al. 2003; U.S. Bureau of the Census 2000).

A historical perspective, nonetheless, must encompass the recent past as well as the longer historical trends and comparisons. With immigration, as in so many other areas of American life, the last 25 years of the century were markedly different from the postwar era. During the latter, the proportion of immigrants to native-born Americans had fallen to a low not experienced since before the Civil War. These decades of low immigration were also preceded by the virtual cessation of immigration during the era of depression and world war. In the last two decades of the 20th century, the American experience of immigration was a remarkable fact of life in part because the change was so dramatic. The mid-years of the 20th century had been the exceptional ones in this nation of immigrants; even though the country returned to its historical patterns in the 1980s and 1990s, the change was nonetheless jolting to many Americans whose life experiences had rarely included the encounter with people from another country and culture.

This chapter begins with an overview of the key facts of immigration: the numbers of immigrants, where they came from, why they migrated, who they were, and where in the United States they settled. Immigration is a national phenomenon, yet the consequences of immigration unfold in local communities. As in the decades before, most immigrants went to a few states, especially California, Texas, and New York. But a shift in the destination of an unprecedented number of immigrants created immigrant enclaves in regions and states where they had never existed before. At the same time, immigrants were arriving from more countries, and more diverse regions within those countries, than ever before. National and regional demographic information is presented and analyzed in the first section.

The chapter then turns to different aspects of immigration in American life, with a focus on the experience of immigrants themselves. Some common themes emerge within this discussion. An overarching one is the importance of globalization to the American experience of immigration. The changing character—in nationality, in numbers, in social origin—of immigrants and their experience in America were all conditioned by transnational demographic and economic developments. Another prominent theme is that of diversity itself. In the 1990s, a more diverse cohort of immigrants interacted in a wider range of locales with an ever-growing array of Americans. This chapter provides the essential demographic statistics on diversity and presents a number of portraits of diverse immigrants and the new relations among immigrants and Americans, from Guatemalan Mayan in Morganton, North Carolina, to Iranian and Korean businesspeople in Los Angeles. Another recurring theme is the contradictory nature of the American response to immigration, most pronounced in the seemingly insatiable demand for immigrant labor that combined with the political quest to prevent the full incorporation of immigrants into American civil society. This chapter provides the context and background for this internal national struggle and describes the nativist backlash against a perceived loss of American cohesion. More on this subject can be found in the discussion of California's Proposition 187 in the final chapter.

The movement of peoples is not free in the world community, and thus governmental policy and democratic politics exerted a formative influence on immigration and the social experience of immigration. Who migrates, to where, and for what are all determined not only by abstract economic forces, but also by governmental policies. Those policies also set in motion and shape the interactions of immigrants and native-born Americans. For the many Americans who did not meet immigrants in their daily lives, moreover, immigration policy has a far greater effect on their experience than the fact of immigration itself. From the spending of their tax dollars to the cost of consumer goods produced by immigrant labor, the effects of immigration ramify throughout American society. National policy—establishing how many immigrants are admitted and their rights once here, budgeting money to administer immigration laws or to prevent other would-be immigrants from migrating—profoundly shapes how most Americans will experience such a large-scale social trend. In the American system of representative government, immigration policy has always been tethered to the politics of immigration. The turning point of immigration politics and policy came with the passage in California of Proposition 187, a far-reaching punitive measure against immigrants. Cresting anxiety about high levels of immigration during the recession of the early 1990s produced this anti-immigrant backlash. National immigration policy, both the effects on 1990s' America of the landmark legislation of the 1980s and the tendencies and changes to policy in the 1990s itself, is analyzed in the following section. National policy, the federal budget, and the American debate about immigration have increasingly focused on the issue of "illegal" immigration. This chapter examines the flash point of this tension and the politics, ideology, and practice of "illegal" immigration into the United States across the Mexican border and across the Pacific Ocean.

TIMELINE

1990	The Immigration Act of 1990 is passed.
1991	In a settlement of *ABC v. Thornburg,* brought by advocates for Salvadoran and Guatemalan refugees, Guatemalans gain a temporary protected status.
1992	Republican presidential candidate Pat Buchanan denounces illegal immigration in presidential campaign.
1993	NAFTA is ratified, opening the U.S.–Mexico border to free trade.
	The World Trade Center is bombed and CIA agents are shot at by immigrants.
	The *Golden Venture,* carrying illegal Chinese immigrants, runs ashore in New York harbor.
	Operation Blockade inaugurates a new border policy.
1994	Proposition 187 is passed in California.
	Operation Gatekeeper (San Diego) begins.
1995	Unauthorized immigration exceeds legal immigration.
	President Clinton appoints a "Border Czar."
1996	The Illegal Immigration Reform and Immigrant Responsibility Act (IIRIRA) is passed by Congress.
	The Anti-Terrorism and Effective Death Penalty Act limits legal due process rights of immigrants.
	The Personal Responsibility and Work Opportunity Act (welfare reform) ends eligibility of legal immigrants to receive array of educational and social welfare benefits.
1997	Congress passes a limited amnesty for Central Americans who immigrated during the 1980s.

1999   The AFL-CIO formally adopts pro-immigrant resolution, changing decades-old policy advocating immigration restriction.

A West African immigrant, Amadou Diallo, is killed by New
York City police officers, which sparks mass protests against
police brutality.

IMMIGRATION BY THE NUMBERS

Somewhere between 13 and 14 million individuals immigrated to the United
States in the 1990s. In the same decade, the foreign-born population of the nation increased 57 percent to 31.1 million—two out of five of whom had entered
the country between 1990 and 2000. As had been true since the reform of immigration law in 1965, the new immigrants were overwhelmingly from Latin
America, Asia, and the Pacific Islands. Latin Americans, and Mexicans among
them, far outnumbered immigrants from other countries. Almost one-third of all
U.S. residents born abroad were from Mexico, and 4.4 million Mexicans newly
took up residence in the 1990s alone. China and the Philippines were the next
two highest countries of origin, together accounting for 9 percent of the foreign

*Approximately 4,000 immigrants are sworn in as citizens at the Los Angeles
Convention Center in 1996. (David Butow/Corbis Saba)*

born and 27 percent of the arrivals in the 1990s. India was a close fourth, with more than a million residents in the United States in 2000, half of whom had come in the 1990s. Many of the immigrants—7 million by Immigration and Naturalization Service (INS) estimates, more by other studies—residing in the United States during the 1990s had entered without proper legal authorization or had stayed in the country after temporary visas had expired (Passel 2005; Malone et al. 2003; U.S. Bureau of the Census 2000).

Historians of immigration speak of the "push-pull" forces that impel people to leave their home country and move to another. In the 1990s, the push to emigrate was felt most strongly by Mexicans. The peso crisis, the most serious economic recession in half a century, the reform of rural land tenure, political corruption, economic integration with the United States through NAFTA, and a devastating earthquake made it increasingly difficult for Mexicans to make a living at home, particularly in rural areas. But the pull was equally strong. A study by the Pew Hispanic Center of Mexican immigration analyzed the annual rate of Mexican migration in relation to the U.S. and Mexican economies and concluded that the availability of jobs in the United States was a more significant determinant of migration (Passel and Suro 2005). Many of the forces encouraging Mexicans to emigrate were consequences of globalization. For the most part, immigrants from other parts of the world were also motivated to emigrate primarily because of the economic hardship they were suffering at home, as the world economy continued to undergo profound transformation, and the United States beckoned with its millions of jobs for unskilled workers. It was logical that the larger forces of globalization acting in the local context would result in a greater number of Mexican immigrants to the United States because the countries shared a long land border, a wide disparity in wage rates, and a long history of trade and labor migration. On the opposite end of the spectrum of economic immigrants were those who came to the United States with high levels of education or experience as businesspeople.

Not all immigrants were what are called "economic immigrants." In the 1980s and early 1990s, the United States revised its policies for refugees and for family unification. These then provided a path for legal entry for individuals whose motives to emigrate were not necessarily economic. In the 1980s, wars in Central America—and the economic devastation and political terror resulting from them—had driven several million Salvadorans, Guatemalans, Hondurans, and Nicaraguans to the United States. Most immigrants from these countries who entered the United States in the 1990s did so to join a wife, husband, child, parent, or sibling. Political upheaval and turmoil in Haiti, Eastern Europe, the former Yugoslavia, Russia, parts of Africa, and other countries drove their citizens to migrate to the United States. For many of these immigrants, the political and economic causes of immigration were intertwined.

Most immigrants settled in areas in which generations of immigrants had been a part of the community for at least decades, if not for the entire span of their

What's in a Name?
The Language of Immigration

Immigration laws in the United States limit the number of visas annually distributed to foreign nationals wishing to immigrate to the United States. The demand for visas has outstripped the supply, especially since the early 1980s, and many immigrant hopefuls have established permanent residence in America without a valid visa.

U.S. government agencies deemed such individuals to be "unauthorized immigrants." Opponents of large-scale immigration called the same individuals "illegals," "illegal immigrants," or "illegal aliens." In response to this rhetorical equation of unauthorized immigrants with crime, immigrant advocates adopted the term "undocumented" to describe those who had entered America without a visa or had stayed after a temporary visa had expired. Although many people casually used the terms interchangeably, the terms originated in the political contest over immigration and were frequently clear guideposts about what side one was on in the debate. As such, from a historian's perspective, the two terms leave something to be desired.

Politics—in the broadest sense—will determine how Americans will conceptualize the place of the millions of these individuals living in the United States, what legal status they will attain, and what they will be called. For the time being, the bureaucratic term of the government, though inelegant, has the value of specificity and political neutrality. The term *unauthorized immigrant* will be used throughout this book, except where the context argues for using the political terms of debate.

---

history. The states of California, New York, and Texas were home to fully half of all the foreign-born residents of the United States. Those states, plus the three other leading destinations of Florida, Illinois, and New Jersey, were home to 68 percent of the nation's immigrant population. One-quarter of Californians were foreign born, as were one-fifth of New Yorkers. The foreign born were highly concentrated in a few cities—Los Angeles, Miami, Chicago, New York, and Houston—and proportionally large in some agricultural areas of California and in many border counties in the Southwestern states.

New patterns of settlement by a minority of immigrants in the 1990s, however, had a profound effect in parts of the country with virtually no history of incorporating non-Americans into their communities. Changes in the South were particularly dramatic. As a region, the South experienced an 88 percent increase in its foreign-born population as the foreign-born population grew from 4.6 million to 8.6 million. A few states in the Mountain West and Midwest, especially Colorado and Minnesota, went through a similar experience. Among the new immigrants to these unconventional destinations were many unauthorized immigrants (Passel and Suro 2005; Kochhar, Suro, and Tafoya 2005).

Unauthorized Immigrants

The number of unauthorized immigrants living in the United States doubled between 1990 and 2000. In January 2000, 7 million of the 31.1 million foreign-born residents of the United States were unauthorized immigrants, according to an analysis of Census Bureau and INS data performed by the INS. Of these, 5.5 million had entered the United States illegally or had overstayed visas in the decade of the 1990s, and another 1.5 million who had entered before 1990 were still in unauthorized status. Another leading source for information about unauthorized immigrants, the Pew Hispanic Center, included an additional 1.5 million immigrants in quasi-legal status in its count. INS, however, included those immigrants in the numbers of authorized immigrants.

Since the adoption of immigration restriction laws in the 1920s, which established the terms of legal and illegal immigration, there had always been some unauthorized immigration to the United States. There was a marked change, however, in the mid-1990s. Starting in 1995, more immigrants entered the United States without authorization than did so legally. Between 450,000 and 970,000 immigrants took up residence in the United States without authorization in every year of the 1990s. Yet as some of those already in the country gained legal residency or left the United States each year, the unauthorized population grew on average 350,000 per year. Although the INS stepped up enforcement during the 1990s, doubling the annual number of deportees, more people left the country voluntarily than were deported. In 1999, the year that the largest number—almost a million—of unauthorized immigrants newly took up U.S. residence, among the population already in the country, 183,000 emigrated, 63,000 were

Mexicans climb over the border fence separating Sonora, Mexico, and the U.S. city of Nogales, Arizona. (Les Stone/Sygma/Corbis)

deported, and 184,000 adjusted to legal status. Thus the growth in the unauthorized population in the 1990s was 3.5 million.

Most unauthorized immigrants came from Mexico. Among the 7 million unauthorized immigrants, 4.8 million were born in Mexico. The absolute numbers of new unauthorized entries by Mexicans increased in the 1990s, as well as did their share of the total unauthorized population. There were 100,000 or more unauthorized immigrants from six other countries—El Salvador, Guatemala, Colombia, Honduras, China, and Ecuador. Many Central Americans, Cubans, and others from the former Soviet Union who had entered illegally in the 1980s or before gained legal status through various legislative acts. Because of amnesty, the population of Salvadoran unauthorized immigrants actually decreased by more than 100,000 in the 1990s. China, India, and Korea provided most of the growth in the Asian unauthorized immigrant population.

Two-thirds of unauthorized immigrants lived in only five states, yet the population shifts that occurred over the decade with the total foreign-born population extended to the unauthorized immigrant population as well. In 1990, about four out of every five unauthorized immigrants lived in one of the big six settlement states. By 2000, two out of three did. One-third lived in California alone in 2000; however, the proportion of the unauthorized immigrant population living in California had dropped 9 percentage points over the decade. This trend accelerated in the early 2000s as the proportion of unauthorized immigrants living in states other than the big six rose from 12 to 39 percent. Recent developments suggest that a new settlement pattern, particularly among Mexican immigrants, originated in the mid-1990s. With the broader dispersion of immigrant communities, the political conflicts over immigration were nationalized as well (Passel 2005).

Vital Statistics on Immigration and the Foreign Born

Table 6.1. Overview of the Foreign Born Population: 1990–2000

	1990	*2000*
Foreign born population	19.8 million	31.1 million
New immigrants entering during previous decade	8.5 million	13.1 million
Unauthorized immigrants among foreign born*	3.5 million	7 million
Foreign born from Latin America/Caribbean	42.5%	51.7%
Foreign born from Asia Pacific	25.2%	26.4%
Foreign born from Europe	22.0%	15.8%
Foreign born as percent of total U.S. population	7.9%	11.1%

*Includes new arrivals and earlier immigrants remaining in unauthorized status.

Source: Census Bureau, Foreign-Born Profiles (STP-159), U.S. Census 2000.

Table 6.2. Immigration to United States by Country of Origin, 1980s and 1990s Compared

	Entered 1980–1989		Entered 1990–2000
Country	Number (rounded to hundreds)	Country	Number (rounded to hundreds)
1. Mexico	2,588,900	1. Mexico	4,443,600
2. China	476,000	2. China	672,200
3. Philippines	451,800	3. Former Soviet Union	590,670
4. El Salvador	369,600	4. India	562,300
5. Vietnam	333,100	5. Philippines	483,400
6. Korea	297,600	6. Vietnam	442,300
7. India	266,900	7. El Salvador	328,600
8. Dominican Republic	218,600	8. Korea	317,600
9. Cuba	175,000	9. Dominican Republic	297,200
10. Guatemala	171,000	10. Guatemala	236,900

Source: Census Bureau, Foreign-Born Profiles (STP-159), U.S. Census 2000.

Table 6.3. Destination of Immigrants Residing in the United States without Authorization: Regional Change 1990–2000

Thirty states experienced a more than 100 percent increase in the number of unauthorized immigrants making the state their home. The shift, in relative terms, was most significant in the South. In absolute terms, the increase was greatest in Colorado, North Carolina, and Georgia. Nevertheless, unauthorized immigrants continued to represent a relatively small proportion of the total of foreign born in all states, approximately 7 percent, except in Texas (14.9 percent) and California (31.6 percent).

State	Unauthorized Immigrants (2000)	Unauthorized Immigrants as Percent of Total Population	Percent Change 1990–2000
United States	7,000,000	2.5	100
California	2,209,000	6.5	50
Texas	1,041,000	5.0	138
New York	489,000	2.6	37
Illinois	432,000	3.5	123
Florida	337,000	2.1	41
Arizona	283,000	5.5	222
Georgia	228,000	2.8	132
New Jersey	221,000	2.6	571
North Carolina	206,000	2.6	692
Colorado	144,000	3.3	365
Washington	136,000	2.3	249
Virginia	103,000	1.5	115
Nevada	101,000	5.1	274

Source: U.S. INS Estimates of the Unauthorized Immigrant Population Residing in the United States, 1990–2000, http://www.uscis.gov/graphics/shared/aboutus/statistics/2000ExecSumm .pdf.

IMMIGRANTS AND THE AMERICAN ECONOMY

The lure of economic advancement has brought millions of immigrants to the Americas since the time of the European conquest. In the last decades of the 20th century, changes in the global economy impelled millions to leave their native countries as the restructuring of the U.S. economy and domestic demographic changes created opportunities for them in America. The majority of immigrants in the United States in the 1990s found those opportunities in unskilled or low-skill jobs for low wages, and a number of American industries became newly dependent on cheap immigrant labor. But migration to the United States had always involved more than just the "poor, tired, and huddled masses," and in the 1990s, many immigrants found work in management and the professions or established themselves in independent businesses.

Considered in terms of overall economic significance, the main impact of large-scale immigration was the creation of a new supply of low-wage, unskilled laborers. As the economic expansion of the 1990s gained momentum, the American economy generated these sorts of jobs in great numbers while the domestic workforce of unskilled workers was diminishing as high school graduation rates continued their long-term rising trend. At the same time, conditions in Mexico were making it increasingly impossible for rural Mexicans to survive. A long history of migration from Mexico to the United States, as well as a history

Hispanic migrant laborers harvest apples. (Corel)

Debates: Economists on the Effect of Immigration

The question of employment, and whether immigrants displaced American work-ers or depressed wages, was a more central concern to most Americans and to most analysts. Among those who viewed immigration as beneficial, experts ar-gued that immigrants did not displace American workers. With the rise in the proportion of American high school graduates, according to economist Gordon H. Hanson, immigrants labored in the many unskilled jobs that would have gone un-filled because of a domestic shortage of unskilled workers. Without immigrants willing to work minimum-wage manufacturing jobs, the United States would have seen even more of its domestic manufacturing sent overseas, explained Richard Rothstein, pointing to the Los Angeles garment industry as an example. The econ-omist David Card, who compared wage rates in cities with high immigration to those of cities with low immigration, concluded that immigrant labor did not lower the wages of native-born workers. Disagreeing with these studies, others con-ducted research that suggested that the presence of large numbers of immigrants depressed wage rates throughout the nation, especially for native-born unskilled workers. The economist George Borjas studied the national labor market of the 1980s and 1990s and concluded that the wages of native-born workers without a high school degree were reduced in the long run by 4.8 percent by competition with low-wage immigrant workers. Two other economists, Giovanni Ottavianno and Giovanni Peri, noting that native-born and immigrant low-skill workers tended to work in different low-skill jobs, concluded that the impact on the former was no more than 0.4 percent. In summary, although economists disagreed about the effect of immigrant labor on the wages of native-born workers, most academic studies, including Borjas's, concluded that the effect was relatively small and tended to affect primarily those workers who had little education. Pro-immigration and anti-immigration activists both used these studies strategically to argue for their position, at times against the intentions of the studies' authors (*Economist* 2006; Borjas and Katz 2005; Reimers 1998; Daniels and Graham 2001).

Nevertheless, from a broader perspective, which includes a consideration of politics and of class relations, the availability of immigrant workers throughout the nation enabled employers to recast labor relations and class relations in their favor. There were many trades and industries—drywalling, truck driving, meat-packing, to name a few—which had once provided well-paying, skilled work and had been highly unionized in the postwar era. Wage rates and unionization rates both dropped precipitously in many industries during the 1980s and 1990s in these and other industries. For example, meatpacking wages were higher than the national manufacturing average in 1980, but by the turn of the 21st century, when the workforce was largely made up of Mexican immigrants, it had dropped to almost a quarter below the national average. Over the same period, the per-centage of packinghouse workers in unions dropped from more than 80 percent to less than 50 percent. Efforts to unionize the new immigrant workers repeat-edly foundered in the 1990s as employers threatened to bring in the immigration

> ### *Economists on the Effect of Immigration, Continued*
>
> authorities should the workers associate with the union (Bacon 2005). The labor movement's belated conversion in 1999 to a pro-immigrant position was not only a stand on principle but also one born of pragmatism. To ignore immigrants was to consign a growing segment of the U.S. working class—immigrants—to heightened exploitation with little prospect of material improvement. Although immigration was but one of many interrelated causes allowing employers to enhance their power in the workplace, the presence of a vulnerable class of workers exerted a social, political, and economic influence on the national economy.

of dependence on Mexican agricultural laborers in California and Texas, combined with the specific economic forces of the late 20th century to create a seemingly inexorable force encouraging Mexican migration to the United States. Of the 4.4 million Mexican migrants to the United States in the 1990s, most were unskilled laborers from rural regions.

Immigrant workers dominated the workforce in certain industries, such as agriculture, as they had for decades. Immigrants also held virtually every job in some manufacturing industries that had outsourced most of their work overseas but maintained some limited production in the Unitied States. The few enclaves of garment manufacturing that remained in Los Angeles and New York had abandoned their unionized workers over the previous several decades. They reconstituted their American production with the most vulnerable of immigrants—undocumented, monolingual women. But the most significant development of the 1990s was the emergence of a majority-immigrant workforce in a widening range of industries and over an expanding geographic range. Midwestern meat packing, Southern poultry processing, Southern California port trucking, and many trades within the construction sector across the nation were employing mostly immigrants by the end of the century. Many industries in the service sector, such as hotels, restaurants, and janitorial companies, also employed large numbers of immigrants.

The large proportion of immigrants who were unauthorized profoundly shaped the conditions immigrants found at their places of work. Labor laws concerning wages, hours, health, and safety were routinely violated in industries—like the garment trade and restaurants—where the employers knew their workers would keep quiet because they feared reprisal by deportation. Immigrant workers nevertheless began to organize to improve their working conditions, in some cases joining unions but more often forming workers centers. The presence of large numbers of unauthorized immigrants, and employers willing to exploit their vulnerability, spawned a vibrant underground economy (Gordon 2005). One study by the Los Angeles Economic Roundtable concluded that there were almost 400,000 unauthorized immigrants working in the informal economy in Los Angeles County. More than 1 out 5 workers in manufacturing, more in the apparel industry, and 1 out of 11 workers in private households were working off the books. Many of the employers who skirted the law by hiring unauthorized immigrants evaded taxes and flaunted labor, wage, health, and safety laws as well (Haydamack et al. 2005).

In the debates about immigration, the question of the economic impact of immigrants was the one that most agitated Americans. The debate revolved around two questions: Did immigrants take jobs away from native-born Americans? Did the cost of providing social services to immigrant families cause an undue burden on taxpayers?

In the 1990s, those who wished to restrict immigration tended to focus more of their energy on the cost of public services. All Americans, they argued, were economically hurt by large-scale immigration because their taxes went to pay for public education, health care, welfare, and other social services to immigrants and their families. In the first half of the decade, when governments at all levels retrenched and cut many services, the charge was a politically volatile one. Those who favored immigration argued that immigrants contributed to the American economy. They countered that immigrants paid taxes also, and that the studies of the other side overstated the cost of providing them with public services. A conclusive answer to such a complicated calculus is difficult to reach—there is a wide range reported in the credible research studies on the subject—but the answer lies somewhere between the two extremes. Many of the anti-immigration studies inflated the costs by ignoring various contributions made by immigrants. But given the preponderance of low-income households among immigrants and that millions were working in the underground economy—in which neither they nor their employers fully paid into the payroll tax system—the cost of providing government services to immigrants was greater than what they contributed, and some of the pro-immigration studies overlooked this part of the equation.

Whereas the impact of immigration on the American economy was largely one of the long-term transformation of the unskilled service and manufacturing workforce, many immigrants themselves made their livelihood in different ways. Even among nationalities where most immigrants labored in low-wage industries, such as among Chinese and Mexicans, there were many individuals who were in business or the professions and prospering. Among other nationalities, such as Indians, most worked in highly skilled and highly paid professional, technical, and managerial occupations. Among other nationalities, starting a business of one's own was the common route to fulfilling the American dream. Immigrants from Iran and South Korea, for example, were much more likely than any other immigrant group to be self-employed. The reason for these national differences had mostly to do with the distinct forces at work in the countries of origin, which both drove and encouraged a different kind of person to migrate. For example, the American economy in the 1990s provided better career opportunities than did the Indian economy for English-speaking professionals with technical or scientific expertise. The establishment of an Islamic republic in Iran had prompted the flight of Iranians seeking political refuge; middle-class Iranians had a better chance of making the long and expensive trip, while poorer Iranians were more likely to favor the revolutionary government. Fewer in number and often geographically concentrated in urban or suburban ethnic neighborhoods, these immigrants were less visible to native-born Americans than were the Mexican and Central American workers who struggled to survive on low wages and whose presence was more pervasive and visible in the national economy.

Immigrants in Business: A Comparison of Korean and Iranian Immigrant Entrepreneurs

Among some nationalities, a significant proportion of immigrants went into business for themselves. Iranians and Koreans were the most entrepreneurial groups among immigrants. Comparing Iranian and Korean businesses in Los Angeles reveals new developments in the history of immigrant business in the era of globalization and suggests revisions to popular assumptions about cultural and national predispositions. Historically, most immigrant businesses began poor and small, and their viability depended on family labor and private loans from relatives and ethnic compatriots. In the contemporary age of globalization, however, many middle-class families migrate also. Personally possessing high levels of education, professional work experience, or capital, these immigrants have been able to establish themselves in business without the reliance on ethnic networks that traditionally have made the difference for immigrant businesses. Nonetheless, distinct national histories in a country of origin continued to have ramifications for even the best-situated immigrants.

About one-third of all Iranian and Korean immigrants to the United States lived in Los Angeles in the early 1990s, and about 1 in 3 Iranian and Korean Angelinos were self-employed. While the majority of Iranians and Koreans worked for wages like most other immigrants, the proportion of the self-employed was dramatically larger than it was among other groups in Los Angeles. For example, only 1 out of every 20 immigrants from Mexico was self-employed. Iranians and Koreans were also more entrepreneurial than native-born white Angelinos, of whom about 1 in 8 were self-employed.

What accounted for the apparent propensity of Koreans and Iranians to start their own businesses? The experience of immigrants in their country of origin and the cultural and economic resources they accumulated there did much to shape their fortune in America. Iranian and Korean immigrants to the United States

had certain things in common that enabled them to become successful entrepreneurs. First, many had college or advanced degrees; almost half of the Iranians and almost 40 percent of the Koreans were college educated, a much
higher rate than that for the native born in Los Angeles. Second, somewhat less
than half of the Iranians and somewhat more than half of the Koreans had worked
in their native county as business owners, managers, executives, and professionals. Among immigrants from both countries, less than 1 in 20 had held blue-
collar jobs at home. Many not only possessed such cultural capital but also had
savings or access to financial resources on which they could draw to finance a
business in the United States.

Thus, by American and by world standards, many of the Iranians and Koreans who migrated to the United States were middle class, and the educational
and financial resources with which they arrived enabled them to enter middle-
class occupations upon settling in America. Nevertheless, the differences between them were also significant and helped to determine the range of options.
Korean immigrants to America, almost all of whom were South Korean, had
held either managerial or professional jobs at home. They first arrived in the
United States after being educated in South Korea, and most spoke only limited
English. Koreans had difficulty finding jobs commensurate with their education
and experience. Their degrees were not recognized by American institutions and
employers, and they usually did not speak enough English to work as managers
in American firms. Koreans became entrepreneurs in Los Angeles generally for
lack of other options.

Iranian immigrants were better prepared to integrate into the American economy, and they arrived with a desire to be in business for themselves. In the later
years of the shah's regime in Iran, many Iranians had come to the United States
for college or graduate education in technology and the sciences to prepare for
professional work in Iran's oil-based economy. (There were more foreign students from Iran in U.S. institutions in the 1970s than from any other country.)
Although most of these students intended to return home, the Iranian revolution of 1978–1979 convinced many of them to stay in the United States instead.
They were soon joined by an additional wave of Iranians who were political
refugees fleeing the fundamentalist government. The post-revolution immigrants
were disproportionately made up of ethnic and religious minorities who feared
persecution, including Jews and Armenians, who had historically been in business in Iran. Among the Muslims who immigrated to the United States, a large
proportion were professionals who had formerly been educated in the United
States, and most had been either middle class or wealthy in Iran. Many Iranian
immigrants thus began their lives in America with educational degrees from
American universities, substantial business experience gained in a multiethnic,
multilingual environment, and a high degree of English fluency. Armenian and
Jewish Iranians, who had historically in Iran served as middlemen entrepreneurs,
were often continuing a generations-long family tradition when they started a

business in America. Muslim and Baha'i Iranians, with high levels of professional education from American institutions, easily found professional jobs in the United States but sometimes chose self-employment to earn more in their professions.

Self-employment, in sum, was for Koreans the result of limited opportunity. For Iranians, it was often the preferred path. While Iranians and Koreans, in comparison to some other immigrant groups, were in a favored position, the differences between them translated into quite divergent experiences. Although both were self-employed and entrepreneurial, the kinds of businesses they owned, the amount they earned from them, and the nature of their interactions with Americans diverged.

Koreans, who had less capital and less access to financial resources outside their community and were more culturally and linguistically isolated from native-born Americans, tended to take on business opportunities that were less desirable for native-born Americans. Korean business owners were concentrated in small retail and wholesale businesses, such as grocery and liquor stores, dry cleaners, or low-margin manufacturing such as garment subcontracting. The businesses tended to be labor intensive and only moderately profitable. Those in retail tended to serve other Koreans in Koreatown, or poor Americans and other immigrants in low-income urban neighborhoods where corporate retail institutions refused to go. As middlemen between the corporations of the mainstream

Two shoppers exit the Korean Korner supermarket that caters to the large Korean community in Wheaton, Maryland, 1995. (Paul A. Souders/Corbis)

American economy and the urban poor, their experience replicated that of previous generations of immigrant small business owners. And as in the past, the encounter generated mutual suspicion and hostility between the immigrant merchants and the residents of poor communities. By the early 1990s, Koreans had monopolized liquor stores, gas stations, and swap meets in South Central Los Angeles, and hostility, tension, and violence between African American residents and Korean merchants simmered. In the Los Angeles Riots of 1992, 2,300 Korean-owned stores were looted, damaged, or destroyed, and post-riot analyses revealed that Koreans had been specifically targeted by the rioters. Ironically, these new immigrants were the face of corporate America in poor, minority neighborhoods.

Iranians possessed a number of advantages that allowed them to assume more desirable positions, both in relation to American society as a whole and more remunerative in themselves. English-speaking Muslim Iranians with professional degrees could establish their own law, real estate, or medical firms serving middle-class and wealthy Americans. Iranian Jews and Armenians, whether they started professional businesses, manufacturing or construction firms, or stores, could take advantage of capital and social networks from the American Jewish and Armenian communities of Los Angeles. In this way, they escaped their traditional Iranian middleman position, yet they had learned from that experience how to better navigate the potential tensions of doing business as a minority within a majority culture. In general, Iranian businesses in Los Angeles were located in middle-class white neighborhoods and concentrated in professional, high-skill service, and capital-intensive businesses, such as real estate, medical firms, and construction. Iranian businesspeople rarely served minority customers, and although they experienced some social prejudice, they did not encounter the same sort of racialized conflict that the Korean businesspeople did (Min and Bozorgmehr 2000).

The Economic Condition of Immigrants

Whether an immigrant prospered or struggled economically in the United States had less to do with being an immigrant or with being one from a particular country or culture than it did with their personal condition in their country of origin. Comparisons among and within nationalities bear this out.

Census figures on the income and occupation of immigrants who entered the United States between 1990 and 2000 provide a portrait of their economic status and condition. Median family income for immigrants as a whole was $33,816, more than $20,000 less than the national median. One-fifth of new immigrant households survived on less than $15,000 a year, and one-quarter of new immigrant families with children lived below the federal poverty line. Low incomes and poverty, however, were not caused by the lack of jobs but rather from the low wages of employment. The unemployment rate for new immigrants was 5 percent, far below the unemployment rate for the native-born poor. Unauthorized immigrants, more than others, faced the likelihood of extremely low wages.

While most immigrants were in a comparatively disadvantaged economic condition, and most native-born Americans began to think of immigrants as a low-wage, unskilled workforce, the picture of the immigrant's condition was in part distorted by the overwhelming numbers of poorer Mexicans among the total immigrant population. Of the 13.2 million new immigrants in the 1990s counted by the census, 4.4 million came from Mexico. Of the Mexican-born population in the United States, close to half of whom entered in the 1990s, 70 percent had less than a high school education, and 38 percent of households earned under $25,000. The average Mexican male immigrant earned about $21,000 a year while a Mexican female immigrant earned about $16,500. Median family income was $30,689, 45 percent below the national median, and was reached only with two full-time workers in most households. Mexican immigrants were overrepresented in construction, agriculture, and manufacturing and underrepresented in management, the professions, and business. Only 4 percent of those born in Mexico were in the top income quintile for the nation while 25 percent lived below the federal poverty line.

Not all immigrants, however, were on the bottom rung of the economic ladder, and when each national group is looked at individually, a wide range of variation among immigrants becomes evident. Some immigrant groups were primarily in the professions and in business, as were many individuals, even among those nationalities where the majority were unskilled wage workers. Among the approximately 1 million immigrants born in India, 81 percent of whom had entered the United States in the 1980s and 1990s, 38 percent had a professional or graduate degree, and another 31 percent had a bachelor's degree. Two-thirds of Indians worked in management, the professions, or related occupations. Median income for Indian immigrants was $69,076, more than double the median income for new immigrants as a whole and higher than the national median. Few worked in low-wage jobs, only 2.7 percent were unemployed, and the poverty rate was half the national rate.

Immigrants born in Africa, half of whom arrived in the United States in the 1990s, were more likely than other immigrants to work in management, professional, office, and sales occupations and had high rates of college- and graduate-level education. Yet there was great variation by country of origin. While the median income for the foreign born from Mozambique, South Africa, and Tanzania was far above the median for the foreign born, half of the immigrants from Botswana and Somalia lived in poverty in the United States. Immigrants born in China and Taiwan were more evenly distributed along the socioeconomic spectrum, yet were overly concentrated at the top and the bottom, with comparatively few in the middle. Overrepresented among the top income quintile of the national population, with 24.6 percent earning more than $100,000 a year, they were even more overrepresented among the lowest quintile, with 28.7 percent earning less than $25,000 annually.

The range of economic conditions for Koreans was different. More than one out of six Korean immigrants had a graduate degree, but instead of being concentrated in management and the professions, Korean immigrants were three times as likely to own their own small business than the immigrant population as a whole. At the same time, many other Korean immigrants worked as employees for low wages. The high rate of business ownership placed many Koreans in the middle of the American income spectrum, yet with so many also working low-wage jobs, one-quarter earned less than $25,000 annually, leaving the community with a higher rate of poverty and lower median income compared to the nation as a whole (U.S. Bureau of the Census 2000).

IMMIGRANT LIFE

The vast majority of immigrants, despite the new diaspora throughout every region of the United States, lived and worked in a few large American cities, as most immigrants over the centuries had done. In the 1990s, Los Angeles, Chicago, New York, and Houston had the largest immigrant populations. In each city, immigrants encountered and then forged a particular social geography.

In Los Angeles, the destination of 11 percent of the nation's immigrants and recent immigrants, the historical presence and overwhelming numbers of Mexican immigrants produced a distinctively Mexican-dominated immigrant city within a city. In sprawling Los Angeles County, immigrants and their children became absolute numerical majorities in most of the industrial working-class neighborhoods. The symbolic heart of immigrant Los Angeles remained the historic Pico-Union district on the edge of the old downtown, which had been settled by Jewish immigrants earlier in the 20th century. In the 1980s, Central American refugees also had made it their home, and in the 1990s, it became the first stop of choice for new immigrants from Mexico and Central America. The neighborhood became almost exclusively Latino, and it boasted the largest concentration of Central Americans outside of those countries of origin. There one could find grocers selling native foods and botanicas mixing traditional remedies, purchase fake documents to present to employers, seek advice from attorneys specializing in immigration law, attend English-as-a-second-language classes, and receive job training at immigrant service organizations run by former Salvadoran and Nicaraguan revolutionaries. Immigrants also moved to many other areas of the city, particularly to ones like South Central Los Angeles, Inglewood, and South Gate, which had once been home to the African American working class. The hundreds of thousands of immigrants from other countries also tended to live together in ethnic neighborhoods. Recent immigrants from Armenia settled in Glendale within a large decades-old Armenian community; most Koreans lived, worked, or shopped in Koreatown, which abutted Pico-Union; Cambodians lived together in Long Beach; wealthier Chinese moved to the stately homes of the San Gabriel suburbs. To immigrants in a multiethnic city where white Americans were a minority and African Americans were a smaller proportion of the population than in any other primary immigrant destination, America was a place where different groups of immigrants lived out a good part of their lives with little interaction with native-born Americans. More than 100 languages were spoken by the students of Los Angeles's public schools. Nevertheless, the vast numerical majority of Mexicans shaped Los Angeles's multiethnic interaction. In Koreatown, for example, the majority of residents were immigrants of Latino descent, and Spanish, not English, was the second language of Korean business owners and workers.

New York, by contrast, imprinted its social history on new immigrants, rather than the other way around. No single national or ethnic group of new immigrants was in the numerical majority in New York, and new immigrants settled in working-class neighborhoods that had been built by generation after generation of immigrants. Neighborhoods and schools were multiethnic and polyglot, their boundaries overlapped each other and bordered nonimmigrant neighborhoods, and their businesses were run by second- and third-generation immigrants. Little Italy on the Lower East Side of Manhattan had become largely a tourist destination where one could consume ersatz Italian-ness, but new ethnic neighborhoods in the outer boroughs of Queens, Brooklyn, and the Bronx were home to new little Indias, little Kievs, and maturing and diverse West Indian, Puerto Rican, and Dominican communities (Foner 2005).

For immigrants, the 1990s was a decade of settling down in America, as political, economic, and cultural forces converged to persuade many to make a permanent home for their family in the United States. Although among immigrants there were still many young, single men, who spent most of their time working and sent their wages back to their families in their home country, three-quarters of the foreign born lived with family members, and close to half of all these families had children. Where immigrants lived in families, these families tended to be larger and closer than those of the native-born American population. As the American nuclear family atrophied, the extended family formed the foundation of many immigrant communities. Immigrants of most nationalities tended to have more children, live in multigenerational households, and socialize with extended family and families from their native countries.

The daily life and life cycle of immigrants shared routines with native-born Americans—of work, of education in public schools—but also was distinctive. Immigrants usually worshiped in congregations of their fellow nationals, even if they belonged to a religion practiced by native-born Americans. Guatemalan,

Salvadoran, and Korean evangelical Christians went to their own churches, not to American ones; most local Catholic churches reflected the population of its neighborhood while the larger ones became dominated by and directed toward Latino immigrants who were more religious than third- and fourth-generation American Catholics. Immigrant men played in football leagues with men of their home countries, watched the World Cup in bars and clubs with special international satellite hook-ups, and coached their sons in "soccer" leagues. For the most part, they disdained "American football" and ignored the Super Bowl. Mexican girls celebrated *quinceaneros* at church and with parties with their extended families while their American friends at school celebrated Sweet Sixteens with parties of teenagers only. Many Indian parents attempted to broker the marriages of their teenage children to suitable Indian or Indian American spouses while American teenagers began experimenting with Internet dating and extended the sexual revolution far beyond what their 1960s' parents ever imagined possible.

The difference between the native born and the new immigrants was partly one of national culture. But it was also, in some ways more significantly, a clash between traditional and modern culture. For the many immigrants from the rural less-developed world, it was even more exacerbated by the differences between rural and urban industrial life. Young men and women who had grown up in rural villages in Mexico, Central America, China, and Vietnam found themselves living and working in the most urbanized places in the richest industrial nation. A clash that was often interpreted in the United States as a collision of cultures was that, but it was also a classic case of the wrenching transition from agriculture to industry, from rural to urban, and from tradition to modernity.

The cultural difference between rural Mexico, Central America, or China and urban America was enormous, and immigrants faced tremendous pressure on their old customs. Life in America upended traditional familial hierarchies of husbands over wives and parents over children. Wives earned their own wages, which were sometimes more than their husbands' wages. Daughters went to college when their fathers had not even started high school. Children attended American schools and often spoke English better than their parents and navigated the American system more adeptly. Elders, religious leaders, and village authorities lost the ability to control and sanction the behavior of junior members of the community. High levels of multiethnic marriage among second-generation Mexican Americans and burgeoning gang activity among the same group were equally products of the urban immigrant experience. Grandchildren lost the ability to speak in the family's native tongue. It was an experience very much like the ones of Italian, Jewish, and Eastern European immigrants in the 1910s.

Just as debates about multiculturalism and American identity roiled the cultural landscape for native-born Americans, immigrants experienced the inexorable forces speeding assimilation and, in response, founded communal institutions to preserve ethnic, familial, and national customs. Immigrants established native-language schools as much so that American-born children could talk to their older relatives as to preserve the building block of one's native culture. They created cultural institutions, where the national traditions of art and dance were taught and where compatriots could meet and perform. They created mutual-aid societies, such as Mexican hometown clubs or Korean trade associations.

The greatest influence on immigrant communities, of course, was the particular American community of which they became a part. The mass immigration of the 1980s, though far smaller than that of the 1990s, had spawned a sense of crisis among many native-born Americans. The early 1990s witnessed the crescendo of the backlash of the 1980s. It was most extreme during the early-decade recession—which was deepest in California and New York where the most immigrants lived. It crested with Proposition 187, one of the most important consequences of which was the impetus it gave to future immigrants to avoid California. The currently available evidence (statistical and qualitative) strongly suggests that the large-scale immigration of Mexicans to the American South and Midwest was first set in motion by Prop 187. The new immigrant communities of these regions, the new encounter between Southerners, Midwesterners, and Latino immigrants, and everything that henceforth unfolds between them will likely date their birth to California's Prop 187.

Whether immigrants intended to integrate into American society or to subsist as culturally autonomously as they could, the politics of nativism propelled immigrants into the American political arena. As the legal context of immigration shifted rapidly in the 1980s and 1990s, immigrants began to forge a new relationship to the American political system. Ad hoc and volunteer groups that had been formed in the 1980s to help refugees from the Central American wars or to link Koreans in America to political struggles at home emerged into full-fledged institutions in the 1990s, offering an array of social services and community activities. With the rise of nativism, these organizations became the nucleus of a political movement for the citizenship rights of immigrants. Local incidents had similar effects on other groups, whether it was a newfound effort at political integration by Koreans in Los Angeles after the 1992 riots, or the mass protests against police brutality including whites, Latinos, African Americans and immigrants in New York City sparked by the killing of West African Amadou Diallo by New York City police officers. In short, tensions within America and the effort of nativists to drive immigrants from their midst spurred foreign-born Americans and their children to enter the political fray. By the end of the decade, millions of immigrants had become citizens and voters. In doing so, they were following in the footsteps of the Southern and Eastern European immigrants who had preceded them in facing down an earlier nativist backlash (Foner 2005; Rangaswamy 2000, 2007; Davis 2001; Portes and Rumbaut 2006).

Two young women wear traditional Oaxacan costumes during the celebrations of the Guelaguetza *in Los Angeles. (AFP/Getty Images)*

Culture and Community in Mexican Hometown Associations

Rural Mexican immigrants formed hometown associations to bring newly arriving migrants together with others from their village of origin and to help them adjust to life in America. Each club was organized as a home village club; as the clubs multiplied and matured, state federations, composed of all the village clubs of a particular Mexican state, were formed as well. Originating with dual objectives, to provide mutual support to fellow immigrants from their home villages and to ensure that one's home culture was not lost in the adopted homeland, the clubs evolved into multipurpose cultural, community, and political institutions. By the end of the 1990s, the Mexican immigrant communities of New York, Chicago, Dallas, and Los Angeles had each established between 100 and 200 local hometown associations.

The Mexican hometown associations bore many similarities to the mutual-aid societies of earlier immigrant groups. Members helped each other find jobs, maneuver through governing bureaucracies, and pay for hospital stays and funerals. Hometown associations had been formed in part because adult immigrants were worried about what was happening to the children who grew up in America. The clubs offered classes for the young in traditional dance and music and put on festivals celebrating native customs and rituals to help build knowledge and attachment to native customs and identity. As hometown associations grew, they raised money to send back to Mexico for rural development projects in their home village and provided legal and social services for members in the United States. And as they matured, they took on quasi-political roles, advocating on immigrant issues in American politics and serving as the voice of the expatriate community in Mexican national politics. They evolved, in short, into complex civic organizations with a political orientation toward immigrant rights (De La Garza and Hazan 2003).

Immigrant Farm Worker Women in Action

Líderes Campesinas was founded in 1992 by women farm workers in rural California. The organization, made up mostly of migrant women, organized and educated other women farm workers about the AIDS virus, domestic violence, and the dangers of pesticides to those working in the fields. Breaking the stereotype of the silent, long-suffering Mexican immigrant woman, the members performed skits and mounted demonstrations in public spaces in rural towns to publicize the issue of domestic violence. Líderes Campesinas was founded and led by Mily Treviño-Sauceda, a daughter of farm workers who began working in the fields of different Western states at the age of eight. Her family's involvement in the United Farm Workers (UFW) in the 1960s and 1970s first sparked her interest in community organizing, and she became active in farm worker and women's rights as a youth through a church youth group and the UFW.

Korean Americans and Immigrant Rights

A national alliance of Korean Americans was formed in the mid-1990s to educate and organize the tens of thousands of working-class Korean immigrants living in Los Angeles, Chicago, and New York. Originating with one foot in the politics of the South Korean democracy movement and one in the day-to-day problems faced by Korean immigrants in American cities, the alliance and its constituent centers grew in the 1990s to become one of the leaders of the mass immigrant rights demonstrations in 2006.

The National Korean American Service and Education Consortium (NAKASEC) was formed as an alliance of local Korean American groups, whose specific histories reflected the transnational histories of its founders and their particular experience in different cities in America. The Korean Resource Center of Los Angeles, founded in 1983, originally concentrated on connecting Korean Americans to the democracy movement in South Korea, conceiving itself as a progressive social justice and peace organization. At about the same time, Korean Americans in Jamaica Heights, Queens, were coming together around the problems facing Korean immigrants in the United States. Contrary to the image of Koreans as the "model minority" widely held by Americans, which conceived of Koreans (like other Asian immigrants) as uniformly successful at school and business, most Korean immigrants were working class. Working-class Koreans faced problems similar to those of other working-class immigrants, as well as distinct ones. Forming Young Korean American Service and Education Center in 1985, the new organization focused on immigrant rights and worker rights. It joined the coalition opposing Reagan-era legislation and led campaigns supporting Korean women garment workers in New York.

The Los Angeles Riots of 1992 and Proposition 187 of 1994 turned the attention of the two centers toward each other and toward the idea of a united response to the freshly exposed vulnerability and negative perception of Koreans in America. In 1994, they came together in a national alliance, NAKASEC. In Chicago at the same time, young, working-class Korean Americans began to meet. The following year, they formed the Korean American Resource and Cultural Center and joined NAKASEC. Like Mexican hometown associations, the three centers provided a range of services, educational projects, and cultural programs. Nevertheless, the Korean American centers originated out of a political program rather than a cultural project to sustain roots and solidarity, and community empowerment was the motivating objective from the start.

As nativist politics surged in California and beyond, the groups worked to protect Korean immigrants against the practical blows of local and national legislation enacted to appease nativist sentiment. The first political issue that the centers took on was the withdrawal of social welfare benefits to legal immigrants in 1996 national legislation, which affected elderly Korean immigrants. Elderly Koreans who were legal residents and who had worked in low-paying jobs found themselves on the edge of subsistence when the new law deprived them of supplemental security income. Working with other organizations, NAKASEC launched a national "Justice for Immigrants" campaign to influence welfare and immigration legislation. With actions such as advertisements in national newspapers, delegations to legislators, and mass letter-writing drives, organized and paid for by working-class Korean immigrant volunteers, they helped influence the legislation that restored some benefits to immigrants. Similar struggles over state benefits were occurring. After California governor Gray Davis threatened to veto funding approved by the legislature for state cash assistance to low-income elderly and disabled immigrants, 200 elderly Koreans performed a sit-in at the governor's Los Angeles office. News coverage of the protest, in which his office was reported to be preventing the protesters from using bathrooms and having food brought to them, prompted a barrage of phone calls, which then forced Davis forced to abandon his position.

As the three centers in New York, Chicago, and Los Angeles grew and established extensive networks within the Korean community, a strong presence in the Korean media, and alliances with other immigrant rights organizations, the scope of their political involvement expanded. By the late 1990s, nativist sentiment among native-born Americans had subsided, yet the problems faced by immigrants in the immigration bureaucracy—long waiting times for family unification applications and little availability of legal visas for the unskilled—had led more and more Koreans to come to or stay in the United States without authorization. Estimates of the number of unauthorized Korean immigrants living in the United States at the end of the decade varied widely, from the INS's estimate of 55,000 to one academic research study estimate of 190,000. NAKASEC and the centers began to devote their attention to advocacy for the legalization of unauthorized immigrants, to other legislative reforms on the state and federal level, and to building relationships with other immigrant rights, labor, and progressive organizations. Their accomplishments in the 1990s, in building community organizations among Korean immigrants and linking them to state and national political campaigns, made NAKASEC one of the most mature and experienced institutions of the immigrant rights movement, and placed them in a position to be influential in the mid-2000s upsurge. In late 2005, NAKASEC joined other immigrant rights organizations from throughout the nation to plan a joint strategy for achieving comprehensive immigration reform and opposing the punitive legislation that right-wing House Republicans had passed. Their work laid the foundation for the massive demonstrations of March 25, 2006.

NEW RELATIONS BETWEEN IMMIGRANTS AND AMERICANS

One of the most significant developments of the 1990s was the dispersion of immigrants to regions of the United States that had very little historical experience of incorporating immigrants into their local communities. After 1994, an increasing number of immigrants settled in mass in the South, the Mountain West, and the Midwest upon their arrival in the United States. Bypassing the classic gateway states and cities, these immigrants created a new nationwide diaspora and inaugurated a new era in American immigration history.

As was the case in the aggregate national numbers, most of the immigrants settling in new places were from Mexico. The core Mexican immigrant communities remained in California, but Proposition 187 and California's recession persuaded many prospective immigrants to settle in places where they believed Americans would be less hostile to them than they were in California. Then, following the pattern that has held true during every phase of immigration in history, immigrant communities grew larger through the informal transnational networks among immigrants and their compatriots in their countries of origin. The new settlement patterns resulted not only from the decisions of migrants but also from the needs of regional industries in the United States. After 1996,

United States Border Patrol agents at work. (U.S. Customs & Border Protection)

labor shortages in the Northeast, Midwest, and Southeast in such jobs as meatpacking, poultry processing, seafood canning, agribusiness, and construction motivated employers to hire and recruit immigrants. The militarization of the border, additionally, made it difficult for immigrants to enter California and Texas, thus reinforcing the already powerful tendencies for immigrants to settle in new destinations. The new border policy went into effect in 1993. Before 1993, 15 percent of unauthorized immigrants had settled outside main gateway destinations; after 1993, 45 percent settled elsewhere. In 1999–2000, one-quarter of all immigrants were going directly to new growth states (Passel and Suro 2005).

Advocates for Immigration Restriction

Demands for immigration restriction in the 1990s had roots in a new restrictionist movement that arose in the late 1970s and early 1980s. The movement, spearheaded by organizations such as the Federation for American Immigration Reform (FAIR) and the American Immigration Control Foundation (AICF), formed in reaction to the expansive post-1965 immigration policy and the mass immigration of largely Third World immigrants in its wake. In the early 1990s, more activist, militant, and grassroots organizations began to be formed on the local level, particularly in states bordering Mexico, where the largest numbers of unauthorized immigrants settled. The primary arguments advanced for restricting immigration were the need to limit population growth in the United States, the negative effects of immigration on the American economy, and fears about the loss of American identity.

Restrictionists differed among themselves and variously accented the distinct reasons for limiting immigration. The new restrictionism first emerged out of the population control wing of the environmental movement. FAIR was started in 1979 by Dr. John Tanton, the former president of Zero Population Growth (ZPG) and subsequently the founder of U.S. English (in 1983). FAIR spun off a research center, the Center for Immigration Studies, in the mid-1980s, which became the main resource for studies critical of immigration. In the mid-1990s, FAIR counted about 70,000 members and was the leading national immigration control organization. Other smaller restrictionist organizations were also primarily concerned with immigration as a population and environmental problem. Thousands of the rank and file of the restrictionist movement held as their core belief that immigration and population control were preconditions to averting an environmental catastrophe. But it was an idea that did not gain broad dissemination or significantly influence the broader debates (Reimers 1998). It is also worth noting that the environmental movement rejected the drive by some of its members to make their organizations oppose immigration.

Any movement for immigration restriction in the contemporary United States must contend with the history of immigration control in nativist, xenophobic, and racist movements, and the wholesale repudiation of these ideologies after World War II. Many participants in the new restrictionist movement of the late 20th century labored to distance themselves from an unsavory nativist legacy and frequently publicly repudiated signs of xenophobia and nativism in their midst. Leon Bouvier and Otis Graham, for example, presented principled reasons for restricting immigration that disavowed nativism. Avoiding nativist rhetoric about the degradation of American identity, they argued instead for preserving a common civic and national identity that had been shaped by immigrants too. Turning the conventional multiculturalist argument about the contribution of immigrants to America on its head, they argued instead that the period of restrictionism from the 1920s to the 1960s had allowed the descendants of immigrants and native-born Americans to adjust to each other to create such a pluralistic yet American identity. Bouvier wrote, "by the 1980s, the melting pot had worked quite well for immigrants from southern and eastern Europe. . . . In addition to different groups acting increasingly alike, a new population is in the process of forming—the 'unhyphenated Americans.'" The current immigration, however, which was so large and seemed unlikely to abate, led him to fear that "future cultural adaptation could easily regress into the more negative forms of cultural separatism" (quoted in Reimers 1998, 63). Graham, a historian and member of the board of FAIR, lobbied within the organization to focus on the economic case for immigration control, and to reject funding from the Pioneer Fund, a foundation with a history of promoting white supremacist causes and research (Reimers 1998; Daniels and Graham 2001).

Although all but the self-identified extremist right claimed not to be nativist, the second most important national organization of restrictionists, the AICF, indulged in rhetoric and actions that its critics reasonably charged were nativism in a new skin. (Those critics included other restrictionists.) Publishing books such as *The Path to National Suicide* and *The Camp of the Saints* and the newsletter *Border Watch,* AICF promoted apocalyptic visions of the destruction of America by an alien horde. Sometimes implicit, often explicit, the America that they wanted to save was the white, Protestant, and Anglo America founded by the patriots of the revolutionary era. Peter Brimelow, published by a mainstream press and contributing frequently to the *National Review,* gained the widest circulation of those who desired restriction for cultural reasons. In *Alien Nation* he wrote, "It is simply common sense that Americans have a legitimate interest in their country's racial balance. It is common sense that they have a right to insist that their government stop shifting it" (quoted in Reimers 1998, 115–116). As a writer, Brimelow worked assiduously to derail attacks on him as a racist, in one case writing, "Still, there's a certain lack of symmetry when one side in a debate can routinely make charges that would seem designed to drive their opponents out of public discourse and even destroy their chances of making a living if they work in journalism or academe. Is there a moral equivalent to their charges of xenophobia, nativism, racism, neo-Nazism, etc.? (Just to select a few from my own experience.) Yes. The morally equivalent charge is this: What the immigration enthusiasts are doing is, in the last analysis, treason" (Brimelow 1996). Among the grassroots activists, a new and convoluted rationale for cultural defense arose in the widely diffused theory of the Mexican "Reconquista." Glenn Spencer of Voices of Citizens Together (VCT) proposed that Mexico had launched a virtual war on the United States, threatening "white Americans with extinction" (quoted in Reimers 1998, 113). The logic allowed Spencer's own xenophobia to be couched as no more than pragmatic national defense. In the 1980s, this cultural wing of the restrictionist movement had focused on language and won "English-only" initiatives in almost half the states. In the 1990s, there were few English-only victories, and instead, the energy of those most concerned about assimilation and American identity went into a campaign to "defend" the border and stop "illegals."

The national immigration restriction organizations devoted most of their work to lobbying Congress, to reforming immigration law in a restrictionist direction, and to persuading the American public of the ills of immigration. Leaders of the restrictionist movement wrote many books during the 1990s while conservative publications such as the *National Review* and the Rockford Institute's *Chronicles* gave them a forum. Leaders of local and grassroots groups, such as Barbara Coe, of Save Our State and later California Coalition for Immigration Reform, and Glenn Spencer, of VCT, were more prone both to taking direct action and to expressing nativist and racist views. For example, Coe's group demonstrated near polling places in the 1996 election, giving out fliers warning that only citizens could vote and that "violators will be prosecuted" (Reimers 1998, 39). The Mexican American Legal Defense and Education Fund (MALDEF) sent out monitors to prevent them from intimidating Latino voters.

The restrictionist movement gained some victories early in the 1990s when harsh economic conditions soured the American public on immigration. Surveys and polls in the early 1990s indicated that a majority of Americans were concerned about the effect of immigration and hoped to limit it some (Reimers 1998). The passage of Prop 187 reflected this sentiment, but it was also the crescendo of anti-immigrant sentiment. Few restrictionists were passionate about the economic impact of immigration, which was what the American public cared most about. As the economy improved, immigration receded as a national issue, leaving pro-immigrant and anti-immigrant movements to battle with each other, largely unnoticed by the broader public. The gains and setbacks of each side were not an expression of popular will but rather of the momentary political influence of one party in a decade in which the political landscape constantly shifted.

The Maya of Morganton, North Carolina

Many of the new gateway destinations were like Morganton, North Carolina, a small industrial town bordering the Great Smoky Mountains, where the poultry-processing industry was one of the largest employers of the town's roughly 16,000 citizens. In 1989, with the economy booming in Morganton, the Case Farms chicken-processing plant was having trouble attracting local people to work for them primarily because it was well known how difficult, dangerous, and filthy work on the processing floor was. One of the Case Farms managers heard from an associate in the industry in Mississippi about a church in Florida that was helping Guatemalan refugees find work beyond the citrus groves of that state. The manager went to the church, interviewed Guatemalans, arranged work permits, and, the next week, drove 10 Guatemalan men back to Morganton. The Florida connection provided him with more Guatemalan workers over the next months, and soon, word spread by the Case Farms Guatemalan workers attracted others of their friends and kin to Morganton. In 1990, there were 58 Hispanics in Morganton, 23 of whom were Guatemalan. Most of the original immigrants were single men, many of whom had worked in agriculture in other states. By 1995, more than 350 Guatemalans were working at Case Farms' Morganton plant. As more Guatemalans came for work, more family members—wives, children, cousins—arrived as well, and although single men remained the majority, a community of families grew as well. The census of 2000 showed that the Hispanic population of Burke County had grown over the decade from 344 to 3,180, or an 894 percent increase (Fink 2003).

The Guatemalans in Morganton were indigenous Maya from the Cuchamatán highlands. They had left Guatemala because their region was being devastated by the military government's brutal suppression of a leftist guerrilla movement. In the Guatemalan civil war from 1962–1994, more than 200,000 Guatemalans, mostly indigenous Maya, were killed or disappeared. Almost all of the deaths were at the hands of the government's soldiers and quasi-military death squads associated with the military junta; violence peaked during the 1982–1983 dictatorship of Gen. Éfraim Rios Montt ("Memory of Silence" 1996). Most Guatemalan immigrants to the United States in the 1980s had entered the country without authorization and had applied for political asylum. In 1991, in a settlement of *ABC v. Thornburg,* brought by advocates for Salvadoran and Guatemalan refugees, Guatemalans gained a temporary protected status that allowed them to gain legal work permits while their asylum petitions were adjudicated.

The status of the Morganton Maya as refugees was viewed by their employers as an advantage that allowed them to run their plant at full capacity without worrying about disruption. As one manager told the historian Leon Fink, "I didn't want [Mexicans]. I got nothing against Hispanics . . . but Mexicans will go back home at Christmastime. You're going to lose them six weeks [*sic*]. And in the poultry business, you can't afford that. . . . But Guatemalans can't go back home. They're here as political refugees. If they go back home, they get shot" (Fink 2003, 20).

What Case Farms did not realize is that the same refugees who lived in the United States under the constraints of exile had historical experiences and memories from Guatemala that made them tenacious advocates for their rights as workers and bound them together in communal solidarity to strengthen their resolve. Since the 19th-century Spanish colonization of the indigenous Maya, Highland Maya had been collectively contending with those who held power over their lands and their livelihood. The first sign that the Maya were not exactly the docile workers the company desired came in 1991, when 20 men who hailed from the remote mountain village of Q'anjob'al walked out in protest over speed-up during the night shift. In 1993, about 100 workers—all Guatemalan except for a handful of Mexicans—staged an action in the plant's cafeteria, refusing to work and demanding that the company respond to their many charges of workplace wage, safety, and hour violations. Then, in 1995, after a manager had three representatives of the workers arrested for trespassing instead of meeting with them as they asked, 300 workers from Aguacatán rallied outside the plant and shut it down for four days. The 1995 action gained the attention of an established American union, the Laborer's International (LIUNA), which decided to launch a union campaign with the already mobilized workers.

The struggle to gain union recognition and negotiate a contract continued over the next seven years, as the management of Case Farms bitterly resisted the efforts of its immigrant workforce to exercise their rights as workers. Such persistence was unusual in the 1990s, as most labor campaigns crumbled under the increasingly sophisticated antiunion tactics of employers. Even though most of the Case Farms workers were immigrants, vulnerable because of their unresolved legal status and because of the dependence of their families in Guatemala on their wages, they brought to the effort social resources that undergirded their resolve. The campaign was led by Mayan immigrants who drew on their native heritage of radicalism, labor struggle, communal solidarity, and collective resistance. It was supported by sympathetic pastors in the local Catholic and evangelical churches and sustained by the local office of LIUNA, even as the national pulled out.

Nevertheless, among the Maya of Morganton, while traditional customs and relationships fostered collective strength in their new American community, they also kept alive conflicts that mitigated against solidarity. Preserving native customs in America—such as wearing *traje;* eating a traditional diet of beans, rice, tortillas, and chicken; using natural medicines and healers for most medical needs; and speaking one's native language at home and work—helped the Maya preserve deeper traditions of communal solidarity. But the population of Mayan immigrants in Morganton was divided by place of origin, by language, and by historical interethnic disputes. For example, the first work action had been organized by a small group from a highland village. They stayed out or actively opposed the larger union effort that came later. The union campaign, which ultimately attracted not just Mayan but also American and Mexican workers, was led by the urban and multiethnic Aguacatecos. Comparatively more cosmopolitan and modern than their compatriots from the rural highlands, they were able to mount and sustain a union organizing campaign and attract supporters beyond their own ethnic group. Even in this story of immigrant collective action, the complexity and the impact of the immigrant experience is evident. There was no automatic, or essential, unity that arose from the common Guatemalan national identity, and new identities and new political programs were forged in the encounter with an American employer and an American community in the South (Fink 2003).

IMMIGRATION POLICY

The lives of immigrants and the debates about immigration among Americans in the 1990s were shaped in part by the new stage of federal immigration policy set in motion with the Immigration Reform and Control Act (IRCA) of 1986. Between 1986 and 2000, another 15 immigration laws were passed, as were other bills that included items of profound importance for immigration. Of these, the most important were the Immigration Act of 1990, the Illegal Immigration Reform and Immigrant Responsibility Act (1996), and the provisions addressed to immigrants in the primary crime and welfare bills enacted in the mid-1990s.

Contemporary immigration policy derives from the effort to redesign the immigration system through IRCA. To understand developments in immigration in the 1990s, it is necessary to begin with an examination of IRCA and its effects. In its sponsors' view, IRCA sought to create a rational system of immigration regulation, one that would facilitate legal immigration and prevent illegal immigration. The legislation incorporated five primary means to regularize immigration: increased enforcement of border crossings by unauthorized immigrants; sanctions on employers who hired undocumented immigrants; amnesty for unauthorized immigrants who permanently and continuously resided in the United States; financial assistance to states to fund the process of legalization; and provisions specifically for agricultural workers.

IRCA's sanction on employers departed most sharply from previous U.S. immigration law. Since the 1950s, the enforcement of immigration law had been governed by a fundamental contradiction under the so-called Texas provision: it was illegal for an individual to work in the United States without a work visa or legal residency, but employers were permitted to hire that person. Businesses and immigrants alike opposed employer sanctions, yet experts and casual observers had long known that as long as there was demand for workers, immigrants would come, regardless of whether they had permission to do so. IRCA for the first time brought the two sides of the labor market equation into harmony by mandating that employers had to check a job applicant's authorization to work in the United States. The provision, however, was drafted in a way that made it impossible to verify whether papers were legitimate. Unauthorized immigrants easily obtained forged documents and employers were all too happy to look the other way. Furthermore, the resources devoted to enforcing the sanction on employers were laughably inadequate for the job—500 investigators for more than 8 million employers. Fraud was particularly rampant in the farm sector. Sanctions against employers was thus a dead-letter law almost as soon as it went into effect; nevertheless, the existence of employer sanctions profoundly affected labor relations in every industry in which immigrants—legal or not— were a significant proportion of the workforce.

In contrast, the amnesty provision of IRCA was widely implemented. Three million immigrants who were in the country without papers applied for temporary resident status. For the 2.7 million formerly unauthorized immigrants who successfully made it through the process, attaining the legal right to reside in the United States profoundly affected their lives. Once unauthorized immigrants gained temporary resident status, they were eligible to become permanent residents or citizens after going through certain steps, including paying fees and taking classes in English and civics. Among the legalized population, incomes rose, more moved up the economic ladder, and they and their children integrated more fully into American society and the political system. Many were also able to bring family members to the United States with the later passage of family reunification legislation. About half of all unauthorized immigrants, however, had moved back and forth between their home country and the United States and thus were not eligible to apply for amnesty under IRCA's specific requirements. They remained in unauthorized status. In addition, in the years following the amnesty, evidence that significant numbers of applications were fraudulent (particularly among farm workers) helped to harden opposition to more amnesty programs.

The third pillar of IRCA was to deter unauthorized immigrants from entering the United States, and to that end, additional funding was directed to border control. More illegal immigrants were apprehended crossing the border. Nevertheless, the focus on border control did little to staunch the rise in the number of unauthorized immigrants entering the United States.

The goals that Congress sought to achieve with IRCA—meeting the nation's economic demand for immigrant workers, cutting off illegal immigration, regularizing the immigrant population already residing in the United States—remained the core strategy of federal immigration policy in the 1990s. The achievements and failures of IRCA also were those of the era as a whole, as each component of so-called immigration reform proved to have paradoxical results. Amnesty had been included to resolve the problem of the millions of unauthorized immigrants, and, in a sense, to start afresh. It did much to improve the lives of the immigrants who were able to convert to legal status, and it allowed their employers, many of whom were going to employ immigrant labor whether it was legal or not, to comply with the law. But it also created a pull for more immigrants to come. By enabling once insecure immigrants to put down roots in communities, it created new immigrant networks to aid friends and relatives from home in finding jobs and adjusting to live in America—whether those compatriots had legal visas to enter or not. Employer sanctions did almost nothing to end reliance on undocumented workers but provided employers with a powerful threat against workers who complained about conditions at work or tried to form a union. Neither employer sanctions nor enforcement at the border stemmed the flow of unauthorized immigration. By the end of the 1990s, it was clear that IRCA had changed the terrain of immigration, had reshaped immigrant communities and the relations of immigrants and Americans, but not in the way in which it was intended (Daniels and Graham 2001; Meissner 2005).

Revising Immigration Law in the 1990s

Congress revisited immigration law soon after IRCA went into effect and in 1990 passed another major overhaul of immigration policy to correct the unforeseen problems created by IRCA. The Immigration Act of 1990 addressed a range of issues related to immigration, and, like IRCA, it simultaneously eased entry for legal immigrants as it threw up more obstacles to illegal entry into the country. The annual quota for legal immigrants was raised to 675,000. But a numerical cap was placed for the first time on the previously unrestricted category of family visas through a complicated formula keying it to the overall numerical cap. The 1990 act in effect expanded the refugee category, providing the government additional grounds on which to grant temporary protected status to immigrants from countries going through war or natural disaster. Four more categories for temporary workers were created, as was a provision to provide special visas to highly skilled workers to immigrate. It repealed the restrictions on "subversives" remaining from the Cold War–era McCarran Act (1952). It subtly sought to increase immigration from Europe by creating a category of diversity visas to be randomly issued; 48,000 of the 55,000 annual visas were reserved for natives of Ireland. On the punitive side, the border patrol was enlarged, jurisdiction over deportation and removal was transferred from the more liberal federal court system to the INS, and deportation of aliens with a criminal record was made easier.

While the act of 1990 represented an effort to adjust the immigration system along the lines of IRCA, as well as to accommodate to post–Cold War reality, by middecade, a more hostile mood toward immigrants in the states found expression in an increasingly punitive approach to immigrants in federal law. In addition, the national mood of middecade, with admonitions about personal responsibility accompanying large cuts in social services to a wide swath of the American public, flowed over into legislation on immigrants. Provisions of welfare reform and of the crime, antiterrorism, and death penalty bills of 1994 and 1996 targeted immigrants specifically, and many of the principles of those acts were incorporated into the decade's centerpiece of immigration legislation, the 1996 Illegal Immigration Reform and Immigrant Responsibility Act (IIRIRA). IIRIRA denied immigrants due process rights they had held since the early American republic, making it easier for immigration officials to prosecute and deport them. It expanded the type and number of offenses that would be classified as aggravated felonies, for which even a longtime legal resident could be deported. For example, skipping a fare on a New York subway—which cost about $1.50 a ride in the 1990s—was defined as a deportable offense. IIRIRA and the Personal Responsibility and Work Opportunity Reconciliation Act (1996) included provisions inspired by Proposition 187. They barred legal immigrants from receiving various forms of public benefits and public assistance such as food stamps or Supplemental Security Income. Illegal aliens were declared ineligible

Retired American artist Mike Monahan spends much of his time in Baja California, Mexico. This work references the warning signs erected in 1990 on Interstate 5 near the U.S.–Mexico border. The painting is constructed of remnants of discarded amateur American-made paintings sold in the second-hand markets in Baja. (Mike Monahan)

to receive social security benefits, even if they had paid taxes into the system, and the act limited their eligibility for benefits related to education, again, even if they had paid state taxes that funded public education. States were allowed to deny public assistance to both legal and illegal immigrants. Most of the federal effort and resources, however, went into border control, enthusiastically endorsed by politicians of both parties as they navigated the surging emotions of the American public on the subject of immigration.

The high tide of the decade's anti-immigrant surge came in 1996. Although illegal border crossings continued to be a source of political and social conflict, the stance toward long time immigrant residents softened in the last part of the decade. Congress restored some of the benefits, such as food stamps, that legal residents had lost in the 1996 acts. In 1997, Congress passed a new limited amnesty for roughly half million Central Americans who had been in the country since the 1980s but who were still in limbo in their legal status.

The Border

For those who have never traveled the freeways deep in southern California, the first trip presents a mystifying, if not disconcerting, vista. The sign first appears in Orange County, long before the San Diego–Tijuana border. Americans in the Northeast are accustomed to the signs that mark forest-lined roads reminding drivers to watch for bolting deer. On the road to Mexico, a sign with a silhouette of a man, woman, and child holding hands, in full sprint, hair streaming in the wind, warns that you have entered the zone of *La Migra,* and that the roadkill might be human. As you continue south, you start to feel like you have entered occupied territory. Miles before the official border, armed guards at checkpoints size you up, and wave you along or stop your car to ask questions and check papers. Long before the attacks of September 11, Southern Californians had become blasé about routine searches that would have outraged those who lived in other parts of the country where the freedom to travel unaccosted was still considered a simple right in a democracy. Mexicans dubbed the new border landscape the "tortilla curtain."

Such a militarized environment was the result of the utter transformation of the border between the United States and Mexico in the 1990s. At the start of the decade, a chain-link fence stood at a few spots along the nearly 2,000-mile-long border. By 2000, 76 miles of military-constructed walls and steel fences flanked by stadium-style, high-intensity-lighting towers separated the two countries.

For most of the 20th century, U.S. border policy had sought to resolve an impossible contradiction. Employers in the United States, particularly in agriculture, relied on migrant Mexican workers, but the American public often clamored to restrict immigration and railed against "illegal" immigration by Mexicans. Until IRCA in 1986, the solution was a hypocritical one that gave both sides what they

United States Border Patrol agents apprehend migrants who crossed the border illegally. (Gerald L. Nino/U.S. Customs & Border Protection)

wanted: the appearance of border control with the reality of high numbers of unauthorized Mexican workers working in the United States and seasonally migrating across the supposedly regulated border. Although different formal policies were adopted over the years, a stable system evolved whereby young male Mexican workers assumed the minimal risks and costs of border crossings, the border patrol presented the appearance of border control to the American public, and agricultural businesses had their labor needs met (Massey, Durand, and Malone 2002).

In the early 1980s, as Americans suffered economic troubles and the Reagan administration stepped up the Cold War, opposition to illegal immigration from Mexico gained a new and more intense political force. The 1984 Republican Party platform included, for the first time, a plank calling for a clampdown on illegal immigration. Meanwhile, Reagan spoke of illegal immigration across the Mexican border in a militarized rhetoric of "invasion" and "terrorism." In this political environment, Congress increased funding for border control in IRCA. Nevertheless, the border patrol remained the bush league of federal law enforcement, and there was little to deter an intrepid migrant from making it into the United States even at the most visible border posts.

Two developments in the late 1980s and early 1990s intensified the difficulty of border control while making activity at the border more politically visible.

The "Drug War" of the Reagan administration, by disrupting the airborne drug trade through the Caribbean and Florida, had unintentionally shifted the majority of trafficking to the U.S.–Mexican land border. At the end of the 1980s, a negligible amount of drugs had come across the Mexican border; by the late 1990s, 75 percent of the cocaine and much of the heroin, marijuana, and methamphetamines consumed in the United States were smuggled by car or truck over the southern border. In 1991, the first leg of the 10-foot-high corrugated steel fence between San Diego and Tijuana was built by the Navy Seals, ostensibly to deter drug trafficking.

NAFTA intensified the logistical difficulty of regulating the border. By encouraging the free trade of legitimate goods across the border, the agreement increased the level of traffic, legal and otherwise. NAFTA thus ironically made the task of interdicting drug traffic through Mexico more difficult because the economic imperatives of NAFTA—which required fast and smooth distribution of goods—prevented the level of searches that would have been effective in deterring the drug smugglers. The entire yearly consumption of cocaine in the United States in any year in the mid-1990s could fit in nine large tractor-trailers, whereas 220,000 vehicles crossed the border on an average day (Andreas 2000).

Despite the seriousness of the drug trade, border policy in the 1990s came to focus on putting an end to illegal crossings by would-be immigrants. Political demagoguery on the immigration question provoked the change in border policy. In 1991, Pat Buchanan made immigration a hot subject in his insurgent challenge in the Republican presidential primary. Holding a press conference in Smugglers Canyon near San Diego, he denounced the government's permissiveness toward the "illegal invasion" (Andreas 2000). In 1993, Clinton moved to co-opt the issue from Republicans and launched a new initiative to beef up INS and, especially, the border patrol. The passage of Proposition 187 in California in 1994 stimulated bipartisan acclaim for the law-and-order approach among anxious politicians throughout the nation. Prop 187 only heightened the Clinton administration's resolve to get in front of the immigration issue. Its new border initiative, "prevention through deterrence," doubled the number of border patrol agents and tripled the agency's funding over the course of the 1990s. In 1999, more than $1 billion annually was being spent to control the nation's borders.

The new policy shook up the long-existing patterns of illegal border crossings and changed the landscape of the Southwest. The first test of the new technique took place in September 1992 at the El Paso border with Operation Blockade. Agents employed a 24/7 surveillance of a highly trafficked point on the border to prevent migrants from crossing rather than, as in the past, pursuing them once they had reached U.S. territory. Judged a success—but retitled Operation Hold-the-Line after protests by Mexico—the strategy was expanded in 1994 to the other main crossing at San Diego in Operation Gatekeeper. In 1995, Clinton named a "Border Czar," and in 1996, Congress gave legislative approval to the "prevention through deterrence" strategy, which until that time had been evolving through administrative acts supported through the congressional appropriation process. By 1999, Operation Safeguard and Operation Rio Grande had been deployed from Douglas to Naco, Arizona, and from McAllen to Laredo, Texas. The new funds flooding into the INS were used to purchase high technology surveillance equipment, such as all-terrain vehicles, motion detector devices, infrared night vision scopes, and an automated fingerprinting system, and to construct steel fencing and stadium-type lighting towers. The physical barriers were built by the American armed forces, and many of the technologies adopted for use at the border originated in military industry. The new border patrol agents roamed the newly militarized areas where illegal crossings had once been concentrated.

The heightened policing almost eliminated illegal crossings at urban entry points, where most migrants had formerly attempted to cross illegally. But with little enforcement of other components of immigration law in the rest of the country, especially against employers eager to hire immigrants, the tactic did nothing to reduce the number of immigrants entering the country without authorization. Indeed, conditions at home impelled more Mexican and Central American nationals than ever to try to make the journey while the booming U.S. economy created an insatiable demand for unskilled workers. The border crackdown thus only drove those who were determined to enter the United States to do so in unpatrolled areas, and to place them at the mercy of professional smugglers.

In earlier times, a Mexican who wanted to enter the United States illegally would either make the journey on his own or with the help of a local "coyote." The intensification of border policing turned smuggling into a professional, and lucrative, big business. According to a U.S. task force, 10 to 12 family smuggling businesses controlled most of the illegal human traffic across the border. Professional smugglers developed increasingly sophisticated means of transport—tunnels under the border or hidden compartments in 18-wheelers. For a migrant, the price of a guide rose from $250 to $1,500. For the smugglers, the reward had grown with the risk, and one could reportedly earn $60,000 a year in the process. In addition, following the crackdown on human trafficking by sea after the *Golden Venture* incident, Asian traffickers diverted the final leg of their smuggling to a land crossing at the Mexican border. In the mid-1990s, it was estimated that 100,000 Asians annually crossed through this route.

For migrants, "prevention through deterrence" magnified the danger of the journey. One study concluded that in the four years after Operation Gatekeeper went into effect, close to 1,200 men, women, and children died from dehydration, drowning, or traffic accidents while attempting to cross the border. By the end of the decade, each summer brought reports of men, women, and children found dead in the desert, locked in trucks, or abandoned to die near the border by a smuggler.

Immigration Policy and the Question of Terrorism

Events in 1993 raised a new concern about the danger to the United States from ineffectual enforcement of its immigration laws. In January, a Pakistani who had entered the United States illegally and then applied for asylum opened fire outside the headquarters of the CIA. In February, a Kuwaiti who had entered the United States with a false Iraqi passport led the terrorist car bombing of the World Trade Center. In June, Sheik Omar Abdel Rahman, an Egyptian Islamic radical who had been issued a visa even though his name was on a list of suspected terrorists, was arrested for leading a conspiracy to blow up the Holland and Lincoln tunnels and the United Nations and was connected to the World Trade Center bombing. That same month, the *Golden Venture* beached in New York harbor sent vivid images to Americans about an underworld of criminal trafficking in human beings. In September, Sheik Abdel Rahman was indicted by a New York grand jury for leading a terrorist conspiracy, "to levy a war of urban terrorism against the United States." It was clear that it was not just the southern border that was porous. Some who slipped into the United States through other means posed a far more serious problem.

In 1997, the INS estimated that 41 percent of those in the country without authorization were people who overstayed their visas. After the World Trade Center bombing in 1993, the INS became concerned about a link between terrorist activity and students residing in the United States after the expiration of their student visas. The 1996 immigration act included a number of provisions to track the entry and departure of people on temporary visas, but disputes over its implementation delayed its adoption. In an additional effort to cut off this avenue for unauthorized immigrants, the INS opened offices abroad and worked to train consular officers and airline staff to detect fraudulent documents in an effort to reduce smuggling and trafficking. In 1999, a U.S. Customs agent at the Canadian–Washington State border arrested Ahmed Ressam, who was attempting to transport explosives across the border. He was tried and convicted in the spring of 2001 for plotting to blow up Los Angeles International Airport during the millennial celebration travel season. In response, the INS instituted a plan in 2000 for the Canadian border modeled on the southern border strategy.

With border patrol focused on the historical crossing points, immigrants crossing illegally attempted to enter in geographically remote areas. Small border towns in New Mexico and Arizona thus became the prime entry points to the United States; these towns then demanded border enforcement, more agents, and more fencing. In Douglas, Arizona, population 15,000, where apprehensions increased from 3,000 a month in 1995 to 27,000 a month in 1999, the mayor complained the situation was "making our town a militarized zone" (quoted in

Golden Venture *beached in Queens, New York, 1993. (Reuters/Corbis)*

Andreas 2000, 94). Others sought to take matters into their own hands, arming themselves, capturing the migrants, and keeping them under armed guard until the border patrol showed up to detain their quarry. On the eve of the new millennium, a nativist vigilante movement was emerging in exactly those areas once remote from the historical border crossings. On the Mexican side of the border, small towns were likewise transformed into nearly lawless way stations where smugglers freely sold their services to—and exploited—eager migrants. The unintended consequences of increased U.S. border policing, therefore, was to transform many border towns of the Southwest into 20th-century versions of the Wild West, replete with criminal syndicates, vigilantism, and vicious racial and ethnic politics.

Border policy from the early 1990s on thus was riddled with paradoxes. The United States embarked on a massive campaign to fortify its borders at the same time it strove to create an integrated North American market in goods, capital, and information. In 1998, 278 million people, 86 million cars, and 4 million trucks and railcars crossed the border legally. As the American and Mexican federal governments avidly hastened along their countries' commercial relationship, so too did American anxieties about smuggling mushroom. About half of the illegal drugs consumed by Americans came over the border, as had probably half of all the unauthorized immigrants living in the United States at the time. The intensification of border control had pushed migrants into the arms of international criminal conspiracies and had forced them to cross in treacherous areas where they were more likely to die. The danger of the journey in turn made them more likely to stay once they succeeded, hence creating more of an incentive for their family members to make the dangerous journey themselves. Border policy did not deter migrants. It only transferred the burdens of the crossing to communities far from official border towns, where there were neither the resources nor the will to meet the challenge. Rather than remove immigration from the political calculus of the Culture Wars, instead the reliance on border control generated more lawlessness and further polarized the immigration debate. On the eve of the 21st century, a century many anticipated would see the largest global migrations in world history, the politics of the border rendered Americans ill equipped to deal with the complex issues posed by immigration.

Surviving the *Golden Venture:* The Smuggling of Chinese Immigrants

On the night of June 6, 1993, a cargo steamer illegally carrying 286 Chinese immigrants in its hold ran aground in New York harbor, after the lead smuggler had failed to reach his contact in Queens and, at gunpoint, had taken over the navigation of the ship from its captain. Jolted by the collision, the 262 men and 24 women came up to the deck and saw the shore of America, the towers of the World Trade Center in the distance. Understanding their predicament, that they would be apprehended and deported, some jumped into the cold water and tried to swim ashore. By morning, 6 had made it to shore and disappeared into freedom and 10 had drowned; the coast guard had mounted a rescue operation, and the media was on the scene filming the cold and wet immigrants gathered on Rockaway Beach.

The passengers on the *Golden Venture* were attempting to enter the United States without legal papers. They had agreed to pay smugglers, known in the Chinese community as "snakeheads," up to $30,000 for the passage if they made it to America. Most of them were poor peasants from Fujian Province. They had spent four months in the dark, cramped, and damp hold of the ship, subsisting on little more than rice and water. To raise the fee for the smugglers, they had agreed to turn over their wages in the United States until the debt was paid off. As scholars had been warning, indentured servitude had returned in late-20th-century America, as the fees demanded by smuggling rings forced illegal Chinese immigrants to accept the most debasing work conditions in order to pay off their debts. If everything had gone right for those on the *Golden Venture,* they would have found themselves working in an underground economy organized in New York's Chinatown, and radiating throughout the country, where child labor, 84-hour workweeks, sub–minimum wage, and labor law violations were common (Kwong 1997).

The INS took the snakeheads, the crew of the ship, and the "snake people"—the immigrant hopefuls—into custody as the world watched and President Clinton declared, "We must not—we will not—surrender our borders to those who wish to exploit our history of compassion and justice" (quoted in Kwong 1997, 4). Clinton instructed the INS to take the asylum seekers into custody, reversing existing policy in which immigrants were released on bond until their case was heard and decided. Most of the passengers of the *Golden Venture* were detained in a federal prison in York County, Pennsylvania, while their applications for asylum were reviewed.

To win the right to remain in the United States, some claimed that they had been pro-democracy activists and would face political persecution, others that they would face prison or forced sterilization if they returned, for they had violated China's one-child policy. Some, who were Christian, explained that they feared religious persecution. Undoubtedly, some of the *Golden Venture* passengers had come to the United States solely because of economic hardship, but a statement to that effect would have led to immediate deportation. Back in the home villages from which the *Golden Venture* detainees had come, their families struggled to survive with new debts taken on to hold off the snakeheads; they failed to comprehend how the United States could imprison their relatives. As the passengers of the *Golden Venture* languished in U.S. prisons, some of the men began making sculptures from their meager supplies, constructing eagle-like "freedom birds" trapped in cages and a Statue of Liberty made from toilet paper (Herbert 1996). Vigils were held outside the Pennsylvania prison where most of the men were detained, bringing together an unlikely alliance of feminists, antiabortion activists, citizens of the town in which the prison was located, and the lawyers working pro bono to secure their release (Kohn 2006). Three-and-a-half years after the *Golden Venture* ran aground, the 53 detainees who still remained in prison were paroled by Clinton. The smugglers aboard the ship, in contrast, had been held for six months to a year and then released. After the release of the *Golden Venture* parolees, relatives in China reported that the smugglers demanded that the passage fees be paid, as agreed, for their family members' successful arrival in the United States.

Over a decade later, the fate of those involved in the episode reveals much about the challenges, contradictions, and inadequacies of U.S. immigration law. Despite the celebrations over the release of the 53 *Golden Venture* detainees, Clinton's parole had left them in a precarious situation because it did not grant them legal status, and the INS continued to pursue and deport them—as it does to this day. Of the original 268 passengers, only 37 obtained the legal right to remain in the United States—2 on artists visas and the others as political refugees. Another 50 or so who had been released on bond or parole disappeared from the sight of the authorities before their cases were resolved and were living somewhere in the United States. The United States deported 111 of the passengers. Twelve of the deportees who were Christians ultimately gained political asylum in Latin America through negotiations overseen by the Vatican. Of the remainder, about half illegally returned to the United States again. In 2006, about 220 of the original 268 passengers were living in the United States. The lives of the 220 residing in America varied tremendously. Some remained single, working long hours and sending most of their money back to their families in China. Others married, had children, who were American citizens, and became successful at business, including some of those still living in legal limbo or unauthorized status. Of the two leaders of the smuggling operation, the one based in Thailand was extradited and sentenced to 20 years in prison. The other, a New York Chinatown businesswoman who had financed the smuggling operation, was sentenced to 35 years in prison—but justice came only 13 years after the incident.

The case that most poignantly reveals the human toll of the clash between people willing to risk all to emigrate and the impersonal forces of the state attempting to stop them is that of Y. C. Dong. Dong was imprisoned for three years in the United States only to be deported in 1996 after an immigration judge denied his application for asylum. Dong was the father of three children in China and had thus broken the country's one-child law. The judge ruled that Dong's fear of reprisal was "subjective." When Dong returned to China, he was imprisoned, tortured, and sterilized against his will. In 1999, Dong paid smugglers $50,000—twice that for his *Golden Venture* attempt—and he illegally and successfully entered the United States by plane with a false passport. In 2006, he was living in Arkansas, working a 72-hour week as a cook in a Chinese restaurant. His re-petition for asylum had been rejected without review twice on the basis that his case had been settled by the 1996 ruling. "I almost feel that my life is out of hope," he told a *New York Times* reporter in 2006. "But I still hope one day I will live freely in this country" (Bernstein 2006).

The *Golden Venture* episode, with its image of international criminal syndicates dumping poor foreigners in America, was one of the events that galvanized anti-immigrant sentiment and forged it into a political juggernaut. The incident occurred within months of a shooting outside of CIA headquarters and the first bombing of the World Trade Center. Media sensationalism and political demagoguery converged to conflate the problem of terrorism with the problem of illegal immigration. It was a premonition of the debates post-9/11, in which the fate of the millions of mostly Latin American and Asian unauthorized immigrants would be subsumed into a debate about security and the danger to the country from radical Islamist terrorists.

BIOGRAPHIES

Sergey Brin, 1973–

Computer Scientist, Founder of Google

Sergey Brin co-founded Google in 1995 with fellow graduate student Larry Page. Brin was born into a Jewish family in the Soviet Union and immigrated with his family to the United States when he was six during the mid-1970s wave of Soviet Jewish emigration. Brin's father, Michael, was a mathematician, and his mother, Eugenia, was a research scientist. In the Soviet Union they faced anti-Semitism in their careers. After much debate, Michael persuaded Eugenia to immigrate to the United States. Applying for a visa to leave the Soviet Union came with the risk that they would be classified as refuseniks and lose their jobs and apartment. Both lost their jobs after he applied for the visa. After a year of struggling, they gained a visa in 1979 and immigrated to Maryland, where the Jewish community helped them get settled in the United States. Brin excelled in math and computers from the time he was a child. He won a National Science Foundation scholarship for graduate school and went to Stanford University to earn a doctorate in computer science. His particular interest was data mining, finding meaningful patterns in information. In 1995, Brin met Page and the two began collaborating to discover the means to search the World Wide Web more effectively. In 1996, they tried to find a buyer for their discovery and their fledgling start-up, Google, but no one was interested. The two took a leave of absence from graduate school, raised money from friends and family, bought a server, set it up in a garage in Menlo Park, and ran it themselves. Coasting out the dot-com boom and shakeout, Google did not do a public stock offering in the 1990s, and it was unclear how it was earning revenues. In 2004, Google went public, revealing for the first time the incredibly large revenues and profits it was amassing with the discrete ads popping up with searches. The company in 2007 was worth $150 billion, and Brin's net worth was around $15 billion.

Francisco Chang, 1965–

Korean Immigrant Activist and Labor Leader

Francisco Chang was an organizer in the multiethnic immigrant rights movement. Chang was born in South Korea. His father was a government worker who decided to emigrate because he was disgusted with government and societal corruption. The family joined an aunt in Argentina and stayed there for seven years, working first in garment factories and then eventually opening their own clothing store. When Chang was 17, he and his family moved to New York. Chang experienced an identity crisis, as he had lost his ability to speak Korean and only spoke Spanish. He eventually made friends in his mostly Korean high school and relearned Korean. After high school, he gravitated toward a religious career. Hoping to work with youth, he volunteered with the Young Korean American Service Education Center. He soon became politicized in their political arm, Young Koreans United (YKU), a group of young educated radical Koreans with ties to the democracy movement in South Korea. It was the mid-1980s, and YKU at the time was working with other political groups, especially within the Central American solidarity movement. The YKU recommended Chang for an organizer's job with the textile workers union in New York, and Chang was assigned to work as a "salt" in a nonunion factory to try to organize union members from the inside. Meanwhile, Chang experienced a classic immigrant generational conflict with his parents. They disapproved of his political activity, worried about his leanings toward communism, and were disappointed he was not going to college. Chang continued to work as a union organizer, and his parents eventually reconciled to his choice.

As a Spanish, Korean, and English speaker, Chang had unusual abilities for organizing the immigrant textile workers of New York. In 1992, Chang helped the union set up the Worker's Justice Center as an alternative model for organizing immigrants. Chang's experiences as a trilingual organizer made him understand the burning need for more organizers for the community, and he became one of the founding members of the Asian Pacific Americans Labor Alliance (APALA). APALA trains new organizers and facilitates alliances with other labor and ethnic organizations. In 1995, Chang left the center and the union to work for SEIU on its Justice for Janitors campaign. In 2000, he became a director with the public sector union, American Federation of State and County Municipal Employees (AFSCME) (Wong 2001).

Rojana Cheunchujit, 1971–

Enslaved Immigrant Worker

Rojana Cheunchujit was 1 of 72 Thai immigrants enslaved in a Los Angeles sweatshop. Cheunchujit was born and raised on a farm in rural Thailand. Hoping to help her family, she immigrated to the United States based on the promises of a Bangkok labor contractor that she would be paid high wages. Upon her arrival, she was shuttled immediately to an armed complex in the Los Angeles area, and her passport was confiscated. In 1995, the INS raided the garment factory in El Monte, a suburb of Los Angeles, where Cheunchujit was held. The factory was in an apartment complex barricaded with razor wire and sharpened iron guardrails and surrounded by armed guards. Some of the immigrants apprehended had been held in virtual slavery for as long as seven years, working 18-hour days, and paid $1.60 an hour to sew clothes for leading apparel brands. Cheunchujit and the others had been forced to work, sleep, eat, and live in the seven-unit building, and they were never permitted to leave. They slept on the floor, seven to a room, while rodents crawled over them. They were threatened by the sweatshop's operators that if they tried to escape, their relatives in Thailand would be murdered and their homes burned. The INS took the group of workers into custody and threatened to deport them. The advocacy group Sweatshop Watch and other community groups intervened and publicized their case, and the workers were released in a little over a week. Eight operators of the complex ultimately pled guilty to criminal counts of involuntary servitude and conspiracy and were sentenced to prison and ordered to pay fines. Two others fled. The advocates of the workers filed a civil lawsuit in federal court against the manufacturers and retailers contracting with the El Monte sweatshop. Cheunchujit began studying English immediately upon her release from INS custody, and she emerged during the case as one of the spokespeople and leaders of the formerly enslaved workers. She testified in front of the state assembly in favor of legislation designed to halt sweatshop production. The suits were settled and the workers won more than $4 million in damages. During the years the case proceeded through settlement, Cheunchujit married a professor, had three children, and began studying fashion design. Her ambition was to open a garment factory that treated its workers fairly and humanely.

Miguel Contreras, 1943–2005

Labor Union Leader in Los Angeles

Miguel Contreras was a labor union leader in Los Angeles who was instrumental in reversing American labor's century-long opposition to immigration. Contreras was born in the Central Valley of California into a migrant farm worker family. His father had entered the United States in the 1920s as part of the bracero guest worker program. During his childhood, he worked in the fields with his father and brothers. Contreras's father became active with the United Farm Workers in the late 1960s after attending a rally at which Robert Kennedy and Cesar Chavez spoke. At the age of 17, Miguel and his brothers were handing out leaflets in support of the grape boycott. Contreras described the awakening in an interview later in his life: "Mexican farm workers were seen as nothing more than agricultural implements, to be used and discarded like you would discard an old shovel or an old hoe. [Chavez] gave us a feeling of real self-worth and a feeling of breaking away those imaginary shackles you had to the grower and standing up for yourself" (quoted in *Los Angeles Times,* May 7, 2005). Contreras went to work as an organizer for the UFW, and then for the national Hotel Employees and Restaurant Employees Union (HERE). In the late 1980s, HERE sent Contreras to Los Angeles to sort out a controversy between the established leaders and insurgents in one of the HERE locals. The insurgents, mostly immigrant women, were led by Maria Elena Durazo. She was elected

Miguel Contreras, with striking grocery workers, speaks to a reporter, 2004. (Los Angeles County Federation of Labor, AFL-CIO)

president of the local, and she and Contreras soon married. In 1994, the year California passed Proposition 187, he became political director of the Los Angeles County Federation of Labor (the Fed). His focus in the position was to politically mobilize Los Angeles immigrants who were eligible to vote but had remained outside the political process. In 1996, Contreras was elected executive secretary, the top position, of the Fed. He was the first Latino and first nonwhite to serve in the post. He quickly transformed the countywide labor association, putting its resources into organizing nonunion workers, especially immigrants, and electing pro-labor politicians to office. He was instrumental in converting the somewhat moribund organization into a political powerhouse, and he was one of the most important figures behind the scenes in the political transformation of California from a conservative Republican to a liberal Democratic state. An incredibly gifted political thinker, Contreras expertly navigated the treacherous ground between his immigrant and labor constituents and the centrist, business-dominated politics of Los Angeles and the state. In 1997, to the dismay of immigrant rights activists, Contreras quashed a move to present a pro-immigrant resolution before the national AFL-CIO. He argued that the time was not ripe. In 1999, after convincing the AFL-CIO to hold its national convention in Los

Angeles, Contreras and like-minded local labor leaders turned out thousands of supporters to demonstrate for immigrant rights. Based on the convention's discussion, the AFL-CIO in February 2000 adopted a pro-immigrant resolution, reversing the anti-immigrant stance it had held for the past 100 years. Contreras remained head of the Los Angeles County Fed until his death in 2005.

Jennifer Gordon, 1966–

Immigrant Rights Organizer and Attorney

Jennifer Gordon, the founder of the Workplace Project in Hempstead, New York, was a leading advocate for the rights of immigrant workers. Appalled by the rebirth of sweatshops in 1990s suburban America, during her last year at Harvard Law School, she raised money to start a legal clinic for immigrant workers. In 1992, she established the Workplace Project in a prosperous suburban community in Long Island where low-wage immigrant workers had become a prominent segment of the local workforce. Immigrant workers were subject to discrimination and abuse and were frequently the victims of labor law violations. At first, Gordon devoted herself to providing the largely Hispanic low-wage immigrant workers with legal advice and assistance. Disturbed by the limited results of following a purely legal approach to labor abuses, she shifted the project's work toward immigrant organizing. The approach to organizing was based in the popular education, which emphasizes the importance of worker empowerment and critical consciousness to achieve social change. Immigrants who came to the center for assistance were first enrolled in the center's Workers Course where they learned about their rights in the workplace, labor law, immigrant and labor history, and organizing techniques. Through this course, immigrant workers were trained to become leaders of their own movement. Most who participated in the course chose to become members of the center. The immigrant workers of the Workplace Project had one of their biggest victories in 1997 in a case study of the value of grassroots organizing and empowerment. Working with two other workers' centers in New York City, immigrant workers developed, drafted, publicized, and lobbied for legislation to address the exploitative conditions in immigrant employment. The bill they drafted became law in New York State. The Unpaid Wage Prohibition Act increased penalties on employers who violated wage, hour, and safety laws. Gordon and the Workplace Project had convincingly argued that the former law was failing to act as a deterrent because penalties were not enforced or were minimal. Gordon left the Workplace Project in 1998 to raise her infant and write a book about immigrant organizing. That year she was awarded a MacArthur Genius Fellowship. She is currently a law professor at Fordham University's law school. She is the author of *Suburban Sweatshops: The Fight for Immigrant Rights,* published in 2005.

Angela Oh, 1955–

Korean American Activist

Angela Oh gained national attention during the Los Angeles Riots of 1992 as a spokesperson for Korean immigrants and the Korean American community. Oh was the daughter of Korean immigrants, and she was born, raised, and educated in Los Angeles. She was involved in community activism as a college student at the University of California, Los Angeles. Responding to the violence leveled at Korean business owners during the Los Angeles riots, Oh defended the Korean American community yet also interpreted it for a broader American audience. She wrote many articles and gave many speeches about the devastating impact of the riots on Korean Americans in Los Angeles and provided legal aid to many of those who lost their businesses. The California State Assembly appointed her to head a special committee investigating the causes of the "Los Angeles Crisis." In the course of her post-riot work, she became known nationally as a voice of reconciliation between African Americans and Korean Americans. From that experience she developed an acute sensibility about interethnic conflict resulting from new immigration and worked in many capacities to move the American dialogue about ethnicity and race beyond the historical black-white paradigm. President Clinton appointed her to serve on the advisory board of the "President's Initiative on Race." In writing about that work, Oh observed, "The challenge becomes how to see the humanity in one another. Today's generation of Americans see the world in terms of a duality: Black and White. But what might happen if a more expansive set of American experiences—beyond Black and White—were to penetrate the public discourse and policymaking debates: Would the dominant Black/White race relations discussion somehow give way to a modest examination of how other emerging populations may offer a way out of the intractable problem of racism in America?" (Oh 2002, 108–109). Oh's interest in "the question of human beings and racial divisions" led her to seek counsel with a Zen master and, ultimately, to be ordained as a Zen Buddhist priest (quoted in Kim 1999, 132).

John Tanton, 1934–

Leader in the Immigration Restriction Movement

John Tanton was a leader of the anti-immigration movement of the 1990s. An ophthalmologist by profession in a small town, Petoskey, Michigan, and a self-described progressive, Tanton became politically active in the 1950s in Planned Parenthood and in the 1960s as a conservationist. The cause at the root of these two activities was the effort to stop world overpopulation, an issue that briefly in the mid-1960s seemed one of the most pressing in the world. (Birth rates dropped precipitously in the 1970s and most demographic experts from that time on stopped worrying about overpopulation.) Tanton believed that birth control and conservation would both help to avert the mass famine predicted by the theorists of overpopulation. Tanton founded and chaired the population sub-committee of his local chapter of the Sierra Club in 1969. He also was involved with, and then became president of, Zero Population Growth (ZPG). As the U.S. birthrate dropped below replacement levels, Tanton began to argue that the source of the nation's overpopulation problem was immigration. Neither the ZPG nor the Sierra Club were persuaded by Tanton's increasing focus on im-migration, and in 1979, Tanton, Otis Graham, and other ZPG board members left the organization to found the Federation for American Immigration Reform (FAIR), which was devoted to stopping illegal immigration and reducing legal immigration. FAIR was the first of many similar ventures by Tanton. Over the course of the 1980s and 1990s, Tanton founded or spearheaded many of the lead-ing organizations and campaigns of the anti-immigrant movement: US English, NumbersUSA, the Center for Immigration Studies, and Social Contract Press. Over the course of his organizing from the 1970s to the 1990s, Tanton's case against immigration underwent a significant revision. In the 1970s and early 1980s, Tanton focused on the economic and environmental impact of immi-gration, a mainstream argument still advanced by some of FAIR's leaders. But in organizing to build a mass movement, Tanton discovered his natural allies tended to be nativists, worried about the cultural degradation of the nation, and fringe right-wing groups, including racist white supremacists. Tanton remains interested in disavowing those sentiments, but his own writings and the posi-tions his groups have taken are squarely in the nativist tradition (Hayes 2006). Tanton was and remains a controversial figure. Tanton's supporters viewed him as one who raised difficult and critical questions about the consequences of im-migration. Critics charged him with being a racist and xenophobe.

REFERENCES AND FURTHER READINGS

Andreas, Peter. 2000. *Border Games: Policing the U.S.-Mexico Divide.* Cornell Studies in Political Economy. Ithaca, NY: Cornell University Press.

Bacon, David. 2005. "And the Winner Is . . ." *The American Prospect,* Novem-ber, A12–A14.

Bernstein, Nina. 2006. "Making It Ashore, but Still Chasing U.S. Dream." *New York Times,* April 9, 1.

Borjas, George J., and Lawrence F. Katz. 2005. "The Evolution of the Mexican-Born Workforce in the United States." Cambridge, MA: National Bureau of Economic Research.

Brimelow, Peter. 1996. "Un-American Activities." *National Review,* November 25, 43–44.

Daniels, Roger, and Otis L. Graham. 2001. *Debating American Immigration, 1882–Present*. Lanham, MD: Rowman & Littlefield Publishers.

Davis, Mike. 2001. *Magical Urbanism: Latinos Reinvent the U.S. City*. Revised and expanded edition. New York: Verso.

De La Garza, Rodolfo O., and Myriam Hazan. 2003. *Looking Backward, Moving Forward: Mexican Organizations in the U.S. as Agents of Incorporation and Dissociation*. Claremont, CA: Tomás Rivera Policy Institute.

Economist. 2006. "Myths and Migration." *The Economist,* April 6.

Fink, Leon. 2003. *The Maya of Morganton: Work and Community in the Nuevo New South*. Chapel Hill: University of North Carolina Press.

Foner, Nancy. 2005. *In a New Land: A Comparative View of Immigration*. New York: New York University Press.

Gordon, Jennifer. 2005. *Suburban Sweatshops: The Fight for Immigrant Rights*. Cambridge, MA: Belknap Press of Harvard University Press.

Guatemalan Commission for Historical Clarification. 1999. "Guatemala: Memory of Silence." http://shr.aaas.org/guatemala/ceh/report/english/toc.html.

Haydamack, Brent, Daniel Flaming, Economic Roundtable, and Pascale Joassart. 2005. "Hopeful Workers, Marginal Jobs: LA's Off-the-Books Labor Force." Los Angeles: Economic Roundtable.

Hayes, Christopher. 2006. "Keeping America Empty." *In These Times,* April 24.

Herbert, Bob. 1996. "In America; Freedom Birds." *New York Times,* April 15.

Kim, Hyung-chan, ed. 1999. *Distinguished Asian Americans: A Biographical Dictionary*. Westport, CT: Greenwood Press.

Kochhar, Rakesh, Roberto Suro, and Sonya Tafoya. 2005. *The New Latino South: The Context and Consequences of Rapid Population Growth*. Washington, DC: Pew Hispanic Center.

Kohn, Peter. 2006. *Golden Venture*. Hillcrest Films.

Kwong, Peter. 1997. *Forbidden Workers: Illegal Chinese Immigrants and American Labor*. New York: New Press.

Malone, Nolan J., et al. 2003. "The Foreign-Born Population: 2000." In *Census 2000 Brief*. Washington, DC: U.S. Census Bureau.

Massey, Douglas S., Jorge Durand, and Nolan J. Malone. 2002. *Beyond Smoke and Mirrors: Mexican Immigration in an Era of Economic Integration*. New York: Russell Sage Foundation.

Meissner, Doris. 2005. "Learning from History." *The American Prospect,* November, A6–A9.

"Memory of Silence." 1996. Guatemalan Commission for Historical Clarification.

Min, Pyong Gap, and Mehdi Bozorgmehr. 2000. "Immigrant Entrepreneurship and Business Patterns: A Comparison of Koreans and Iranians in Los Angeles." *International Migration Review* 34 (3): 707–738.

Oh, Angela E. 2002. *Open: One Woman's Journey*. Los Angeles: UCLA Asian American Studies Center Press.

Passel, Jeffrey S. 2005. *Unauthorized Migrants: Numbers and Characteristics*. Washington, DC: Pew Hispanic Center.

Passel, Jeffrey S., and Roberto Suro. 2005. *Rise, Peak and Decline: Trends in U.S. Immigration, 1992–2004*. Washington, DC: Pew Hispanic Center.

Portes, Alejandro, and Rubén G. Rumbaut. 2006. *Immigrant America: A Portrait*. 3rd edition. Berkeley: University of California Press.

Rangaswamy, Padma. 2000. *Namasté America: Indian Immigrants in an American Metropolis*. University Park: Pennsylvania State University Press.

Rangaswamy, Padma. 2007. *Indian Americans*. New York: Chelsea House.

Reimers, David M. 1998. *Unwelcome Strangers: American Identity and the Turn against Immigration*. New York: Columbia University Press.

U.S. Bureau of the Census. 2000. *Census of the United States*.

Wong, Kent. 2001. *Voices for Justice: Asian Pacific American Organizers and the New Labor Movement*. Los Angeles: Center for Labor Research and Education, UCLA.

Conflicts

OVERVIEW

Conflict, division, and acrimony pervaded social relationships among Americans during the first half of the 1990s. Previous chapters on social movements, immigration, and politics explored the social groups and beliefs in which these conflicts were grounded. This chapter explores the conflicts and divisions themselves, with a particular emphasis on violence—whether as metaphor (as in the Culture Wars) or in deed (the Persian Gulf War, the Los Angeles Riots, and the Oklahoma City Bombing). Discussion of most of the significant events in the decade that were manifestations or expressions of division, with the exception of domestic political conflicts, can be found in this chapter.

The first section of this chapter addresses various episodes and consequences of America's relationship with the world. The topic focuses on those conflicts that had a significant effect on American life as lived by large numbers of Americans. War is, of course, the supreme expression of conflict, yet it ironically often serves as a unifying force in an otherwise divided society. This section examines the Persian Gulf War, the nation's opinion about it in the context of the post-Vietnam and post–Cold War world, and its long-term consequences. The section includes an examination of life in the U.S. military, transformed by foreign policy and military leaders who had been most concerned about the so-called Vietnam syndrome, and an examination of America's oil dependency and the international effort to arrest global warming.

The Culture Wars, the subject of the second section, had begun in the 1980s, persisted through the 1990s, and continue to this day. They are, in a sense, the stage on which the vast majority of American social and ideological conflicts are played out. The focus is on an examination of the contour of the core debates and the key issues, including abortion, race, gay rights, national history, and science and religion.

The following two sections focus on key conflicts of the decade: urban riots in Los Angeles and Crown Heights, New York; and the passage of the anti-immigrant Proposition 187 in California. A word on the California focus of these two sections is warranted. As the most populous and the most ethnically diverse state in the nation, it is not surprising that Americans looked to California as a model or cautionary tale for the nation. In the case of the Los Angeles Riots, speculation at the time that they foreboded urban disorder throughout the country turned out to be unfounded. California's political system, moreover, provided a critical vehicle for simmering hostilities to emerge as topics of public debate and political contest. In no other state are the Progressive era tools of direct democracy—initiatives, referenda, and recall—employed as frequently and with as monumental an impact. It is essential to underscore, however, that the issues that appear before Californians for a direct vote are rarely the result of an upsurge of popular will. In reality, a sophisticated multimillion-dollar industry of political consulting long ago arose in the state through which ideas are conceived, funded, and shepherded through to passage. The system heavily favors particularistic interests with bulging campaign war chests. But the mythology of direct democracy as the citizens' voice persisted, and initiative campaigns in California were routinely viewed by the rest of the nation as a bellwether of public opinion.

The chapter ends with an examination of the extremist right. A book on the social history of the 1990s that fails to examine extremism would not be complete. The vigilantism and terrorism of extreme rightists directly affected thousands of people in the decade—the individuals, the kin, and friends of those killed in the Oklahoma City Bombing, in the attacks on abortion providers, and in racist lynchings. But contrary to the fears of watchdog groups and some scholars, such extremists were a fringe minority in the United States, even if many of their ideas and practices had deep roots in other fringe movements in American history. It is particularly mistaken to include the extremist right in the broader conservative movement. Although extremists agreed with social conservatives on many of the flashpoints of the Culture Wars, the former were paramilitary warriors, the latter culture warriors brandishing words and legislation. The difference is important. Right-wing extremists were separatist, and their trade-in-kind was violence, prejudice, and hatred. The lead essay of the section addresses this question of separatism as well as the intersection of rightist ideology with other currents in American culture. The remaining sections describe some of the key events and figures in the loosely affiliated movement.

TIMELINE

1989   The Berlin Wall falls (November).

The United States invades Panama (December 20) in largest military operation since the Vietnam War.

Congress adds an anti-obscenity pledge to funding for the National Endowment for the Arts.

1990   The Supreme Court strikes down a federal flag-burning law by a 5–4 decision.

President George H. W. Bush declares a "New World Order" during the lead-up to the Persian Gulf War.

1991   The Persian Gulf War begins.

Riots take place in Crown Heights.

The videotape of Los Angeles police officers beating Rodney King is aired around the world.

The Soviet Union is dissolved.

A San Francisco ordinance establishes domestic partnerships for same-sex couples.

1992   Randall Weaver, prominent in the militia movement, resists a warrant for his arrest at his home in Ruby Ridge, Idaho. Weaver's wife and son are killed in a shoot-out with federal agents.

Riots take place in Los Angeles (April 30–May 3).

Hurricane Andrew hits Florida in the costliest natural disaster in U.S. history. The Bush adminstration is criticized for its inadequate response (August).

A mass pro-choice demonstration is one of the largest demonstrations ever held on the National Mall in Washington, D.C.

The Supreme Court upholds *Roe v. Wade* and the right to abortion in *Planned Parenthood v. Casey*.

1993   President Bill Clinton issues the controversial "don't ask, don't tell" policy on gays in the military.

Hawaii's state supreme court rules that it is unconstitutional to deny marriage licenses to same-sex couples.

Islamic radical terrorists plant a car bomb at the World Trade Center in New York City.

The federal siege at David Koresh's Branch Davidian compound in Waco, Texas, ends in the deaths of cult members (April 19).

Antiabortion group Operation Rescue stages a seven-city campaign.

David Gunn, a doctor who performed abortions, is assassinated by a pro-life fanatic.

Combat roles are opened to women in the U.S. military.

1994   Gunn's successor, Dr. John Bayard Britton, and a clinic worker are assassinated by a pro-life fanatic.

Congress passes and President Clinton signs the Freedom of Access to Clinic Entrances Act in response to violent protests and attacks by some pro-life activists.

The anti-immigrant Proposition 187 is passed in California.

The Bell Curve is published.

Conservatives campaign against the National History Standards developed by a group of historians under the auspices of the National Endowment for the Humanities.

1995   American right-wing extremists Timothy McVeigh and Terry Nichols bomb the Alfred P. Murrah Federal Building in Oklahoma City (April 19).

Controversy erupts over the Smithsonian's Enola Gay exhibit commemorating the U.S. atomic bombing of Hiroshima.

American troops are deployed to Bosnia in a U.N. peace-keeping mission.

1996   Centennial Olympic Park in Atlanta is bombed by right-wing extremist Eric Rudolph.

The Defense of Marriage Act, which denies federal recognition to same-sex marriages, is passed by Congress and signed by President Clinton.

Proposition 209, which bans affirmative action, is passed in California.

1997   The Kyoto Protocol on global warming is negotiated and signed by President Clinton but never sent to the Senate for ratification.

1998 National divisions coalesce around the Clinton-Lewinsky scandal and midterm elections.

Dr. Bernard Slepian is assassinated in his home by a pro-life fanatic.

Matthew Shepard, a young gay man, is murdered in a hate crime in Laramie, Wyoming.

1999 Clinton is acquitted in a Senate impeachment trial.

The Vermont Supreme Court rules that the legal benefits and protections of married couples cannot be denied to same-sex couples.

NATION: AMERICA IN THE WORLD

As the 1990s dawned, with the United States the putative victor in the Cold War, Americans gave themselves over to a heady mix of utopianism, opportunism, and national self-congratulation. But international events quickly disabused Americans of their optimism. The international crises that arose after the Cold War raised in a new way the historical tensions in America's foreign policy between engagement and isolationism, and between values and interests. With the halt to the standoff of the superpowers, why didn't the United States simply ignore the new regional conflicts? Indeed, some politicians, notably Pat Buchanan in 1992 and 1996 and George W. Bush in 2000, counseled a turn inward. One answer, as a rich historical literature on American foreign policy reminds us, is that the American position in the international arena is not solely a defense of principle; it is also an assertion of interests. Since at least the 1890s, the U.S. government has pursued an active role in the affairs of other countries in part to advance the economic interests of American citizens and American businesses. In assessing the causes and motives behind American foreign policy, historians energetically debate the relative importance of economic interests—for example, access to natural resources such as oil or the pursuit of trade advantages for American corporations—compared to more strictly military, strategic, and ideological considerations. But no serious analyst of American foreign policy doubts that national economic interests influence our relations with the world. Those considerations did not disappear in the post–Cold War world. Equally, many of the emerging conflicts tugged on the conscience of America. Surely the most powerful nation in world history could stop the genocide of Rwanda's Tutsis or the massacre of Sarajevo's Muslims. But, should it do so? The Cold War was over, but the world beyond the nation's borders pressed onto the national scene the difficult question of balancing values and interests.

The Persian Gulf War, 1991

On August 2, 1990, Iraq invaded Kuwait in an effort by Saddam Hussein to win control over the enormous revenues from oil produced in the small, oil-rich emirate and thus gain a stronger hand in setting prices in the world oil markets. With the assistance and cooperation of Saudi Arabia, President George H. W. Bush launched Operation Desert Shield, deploying a military force in the Persian Gulf to prevent Iraq from moving beyond Kuwait and to prepare for a larger military action should Iraq refuse to withdraw from Kuwait. Between early August and November, the United States won United Nations resolutions imposing economic sanctions on Iraq and authorizing the use of force if Iraq did not meet a January 15, 1991, deadline for withdrawal. Bush then won from Congress authorization to use force against Iraq if necessary.

The diplomacy and public rhetoric employed by the Bush administration powerfully demonstrated the tensions between and intersection of America's interests and values. Everyone understood that American access to the world's most important natural resource—oil—was central to the conflict. National sovereignty against foreign aggression was likewise a critical principle and a matter of practical importance to defend in the post–Cold War world. These were the primary considerations on which Bush and his secretary of state, James Baker,

Soldiers of the 82nd Airborne Division watch a CH-47 Chinook prepare to touch down during Operation Desert Shield. (Department of Defense)

were able to pull together an international coalition of 28 nations under United Nations auspices. Nevertheless, Bush also elevated the conflict in the Gulf into a defining moment for post–Cold War America and, in doing so, worked to shape the post–Cold War order according to his conception of American power and dominance in the "New World Order." He employed exaggerated rhetoric to define the conflict, likening Saddam Hussein to Hitler, and explaining American involvement as nothing less than a struggle of "good versus evil" (Johnson 1991).

In the days leading up to the January 15 deadline, Americans were apprehensive. Christians packed churches while Jewish congregations called for a day of fasting. On the night before the deadline for Iraq's compliance, 6,000 people participated in a peace vigil from the National Cathedral to the White House. Everyone anticipated a difficult war against Hussein's large army, in which chemical weapons might be used against American troops, the world's oil supply would be disrupted, and chaos would be unleashed throughout the Middle East. Perhaps the United States would be caught in a Middle Eastern quagmire, the way it had been in Vietnam. The United States had gathered an international coalition to defend an essential principle of international relations—national sovereignty against foreign invasion. But was Kuwait worth it? The national mood was such that those who questioned or opposed the war had to carefully calibrate their actions so as not to alienate their neighbors.

At 6:45 p.m. on January 16, Secretary of Defense Dick Cheney executed the order to the U.S. military to begin bombing Baghdad. A couple hours later, President Bush gave a televised speech, watched by 61 million households, in which he memorably defined the mission as one to shape a "New World Order."

The United States fought the Persian Gulf War with a heavy reliance on technologically advanced weapons systems, which exacted enormous damage on Iraq yet posed minimal danger to the lives of American troops. For the first 43 days of the 48-day war, U.S. missiles and bombs rained down on Iraq in so-called surgical strikes on the infrastructure of Iraq. When Hussein announced 100 hours after the ground invasion began that Iraq would leave Kuwait, the Bush administration decided that the mission was accomplished. Although the administration considered Hussein to be a brutal dictator who they would have preferred to see out of power, they thought the risk of becoming mired in a chaotic post-Hussein Iraq was one not worth taking. American casualties were few in the Persian Gulf War: 148 died and 467 were wounded in combat. On the Iraqi side, roughly 100,000 troops and civilians were killed.

The unexpectedly swift victory was greeted by Americans with relief while planning for elaborate official celebrations commenced. The Persian Gulf War momentarily swept away thoughts of domestic economic and political troubles. Bush's popularity, which had been sinking before the war, rose to the highest levels ever recorded for a president. But it did not take long for underlying problems and implications of the war to surface. The Bush administration had convinced other countries, especially Saudi Arabia, to pay for the war, thus temporarily masking the difficulties America would have in paying for its actions as the world's sole superpower. Hussein, who remained in power, launched brutal military campaigns against Kurdish refugees and Shiite opponents. The Bush administration did little to stop it, and the American people became quickly disillusioned about the war and, particularly, the high-minded rhetoric with which it had been sold. Within a month of the end of the war, polls showed that the percentage of Americans who believed the war to have been a "great victory" had already fallen by 20 percent (Johnson 1991).

The "Vietnam Syndrome" and the Persian Gulf War

In his nationally televised speech on January 16, Bush had promised, "I've told the American people before that this will not be another Vietnam, and I repeat this here tonight. Our troops will have the best possible support in the entire world, and they will not be asked to fight with one hand tied behind their back." As he announced the cease-fire, he rejoiced, "by God, we've kicked the Vietnam syndrome once and for all" (Cloud 1991).

The ghost of Vietnam—the country's bitter divisions over the war, the military defeat—haunted some members of the military and foreign policy establishment who were determined never again to allow such a blow to American prestige and power. Any new war had to be fought, reported, and pitched in a different way; most important, America had to win. Between Vietnam and the Persian Gulf War, a new military was forged, one in which every member of the armed services was a volunteer and new weapons systems were deployed that would minimize direct combat. Thus the draft and the body bags that had sapped America's will to win were averted. The military strictly limited press access to war zones and became more sophisticated in its own public relations. And, there was an effort to bring some military realism to bear on the more visionary advocates of American power. As the chairman of the Joint Chiefs of Staff, Colin Powell, articulated in what became known as the Powell Doctrine, if America was to enter a war, it had to have strong public support and the military must be allowed to use overwhelming force to accomplish victory. But America should use force only as a last resort, only if national security was directly imperiled, and only if there was a clear exit strategy.

Likewise, Americans who were opposed to the Persian Gulf War keenly felt the weight of the Vietnam era antiwar movement, while a majority of Americans who supported or were apprehensive about the Persian Gulf War were also anxious to put the past behind them. Appropriating the symbolic gesture originating during the Iranian hostage crisis, Americans put up yellow ribbons to demonstrate their support for the president and the troops. The small peace movement made great efforts to demonstrate patriotism and respect for the troops within its protests, and to be inclusive of all Americans. This time around, students, union members, veterans, and families of the troops would stand united in opposition to the war. Nevertheless, the passions that had flared in the Vietnam era—and other American wars—occasionally broke loose. As the bombing campaign dragged on, militant patriotism got the upper hand. Pro-war vigilantes vandalized and burned signs expressing opposition to the war; in one incident, they attacked two men driving a car with a peace sign, chanting at them "commie faggots," and rammed a flagpole through their car window ("It's a Grand Old [Politically Correct] Flag" 1991). CNN viewers deluged the station with more than 30,000 angry letters when Peter Arnett reported civilian deaths in the bombing of Baghdad (Zoglin 1991).

Divisions about the Vietnam War remained deep in the early 1990s. But the protagonists all agreed that Vietnam veterans had been treated shabbily on their return when the nation's shame about the war had been displaced and projected onto them personally. The return from the Gulf would be handled differently, and many communities organized celebrations for the Gulf veterans. The official national homecoming, however, was shaped by those who shared Bush's view of the Vietnam syndrome as something that needed to be vanquished for America to assert its rightful power in the world. The celebration staged by the national government was unabashedly proud, not just of the men and women who served, but of American power. Operation Welcome Home raised $18 million from individuals and corporations and received $6 million from the Pentagon to mount a homecoming parade in Washington, D.C., on June 17, 1991. Evoking World War II, rather than Vietnam, Gen. Norman Schwarzkopf, MA1 tanks, and Stealth fighters led a parade of 8,000 troops, and 200,000 Americans lined the route and cheered (Gibbs 1991).

The All-Volunteer Army

After ending the draft in 1973, the United States adopted an all-volunteer military. On the cusp of the Persian Gulf War, there were approximately 2 million men and women in the American armed services, all of whom were there by choice, not by conscription.

The choice to join the military, however, was powerfully shaped by economic constraints. In the Vietnam era, there were few ways for black, poor, or working-class men to escape the draft, and they served disproportionate to their numbers in the population as a whole. In the early years of the all-volunteer military in the 1970s, when wages were high and blue-collar jobs were available to high school graduates, the military could not fulfill its numerical goals for recruiting nor could it attract youths with the level of education it sought. The calculus for young Americans changed in the 1980s, with the combination of recession and industrial job loss on one side and, on the other, the increase in military pay, social services for military families, and educational aid to military personnel. The 1990s military continued to be disproportionately minority and working class, but more because the military could offer economic stability and career advancement for those with few other such opportunities in the civilian economy. In 1989, 9 out of 10 recruits were high school graduates—compared to 1 out of 2 in the late 1970s—and 20 percent were African American. But few college-educated or higher-income Americans were joining up. Emblematic of the change was that, as hundreds of thousands of American soldiers waited in the Gulf for the war to begin, not one member of the president's cabinet and only two members of Congress had children stationed in the Gulf. In contrast, in 1970, there were 74 children of congressmen stationed in Vietnam (Lacayo 1990).

In the change from a conscript to a volunteer force, the armed services had been transformed in other ways as well. Drafted single men had made up two-thirds of the armed forces in the mid-1950s; in the mid-1990s, two-thirds of service members were married, and about 10 percent were women. Many service members had children and nonmilitary spouses; 18,000 of them were single parents. To support the family-based military, the Reagan administration and Congress had funded and built a vast array of social services—indeed, as funding for low-income housing, education, welfare, job training and the like was slashed, a kind of ideal Great Society social safety net exclusively for the armed services was being forged. It was estimated to cost more than $25 billion a year out of the Defense Department budget (Ricks 1996).

The Persian Gulf War, during which 33,000 women members were stationed in the gulf, was the first in which women performed combat-related activities. Through the 1990s, debate continued about whether women should be deployed as combatants in warfare. The women members of the armed services favored it, but the military leadership still balked. In 1993, official policy was changed to allow women to serve in combat.

With the institutionalization of the all-volunteer military, a new relationship between African American and white military personnel arose, particularly in the Army. Historically, the armed services had bitterly resisted President Harry Truman's 1948 order desegregating the armed forces. But by the 1990s, black and white troops lived, worked, worshiped, and socialized together in a manner virtually unknown in other areas of American life. Black and white soldiers both reported that the discipline and camaraderie of military life quickly eroded ingrained prejudice, hostility, and suspicion. By statistical measures, as well, the Army was the most integrated institution in American society. During the Gulf War, African Americans constituted 20 percent of the armed forces; by 1996, the percentage had risen to 30 percent. Half of the women in the services were African American. Charles Moskos, a military sociologist, observed that the military was "the only place in American society where whites are regularly bossed by blacks" (quoted in "Inside Soldiers' Heads" 1996). There were 18,200 African American officers in the armed forces, including 26 of the army's 407 generals.

A military policewoman operates an M-60 machine gun mounted atop a Humvee, as other members of her company search for unexploded ordnance. Women comprised almost 7 percent of U.S. forces in the Persian Gulf War. (Department of Defense)

Two of the three women generals were African American (Lacayo 1990). Corporate America looked nothing like this. Powell, in his memoir, credited his rise to the mentoring he received from other African American officers. For African Americans, military enlistment provided an opportunity for economic stability and career advancement in short supply elsewhere in America.

Nevertheless, the military—especially the Special Forces—remained a preferred destination for individuals with violent inclinations. Timothy McVeigh and Eric Rudolph, two of the most notorious of America's own terrorists, were in the armed forces and had been rejected from the Special Forces. (Chua-Eoan 1995). In the Army, wives were abused by their husbands in uniform at a rate double that of their civilian counterparts (Thompson 1994). The harassment of and violence against gay men remained a problem (Cullen 2000).

Media and the Persian Gulf War

The senior staff advising President Bush were those who believed that America had lost the war in Vietnam because of a lack of will. If only the civilian government had given the military the resources and latitude to fight the war the right way, the United States would have been victorious. The analysis that the

Vietnam War had been unwinnable, pioneered by that era's antiwar movement and gradually adopted by the mainstream of the American public, was not their belief.

Military leaders such as Colin Powell and civilian ones such as Donald Rumsfeld and Dick Cheney believed that the nightly televised bloodiness and the daily body count of the Vietnam War had made Americans excessively squeamish and were responsible for the hesitancy displayed by the civilian leadership in pushing through to victory. Images of body bags and napalmed children had infected Americans with the Vietnam syndrome, and the architects of Bush's foreign policy were determined not to let it happen again.

The Persian Gulf War, or Operation Desert Storm as the administration preferred to call it, would be a televised war, but one where the U.S. military, not a feisty and competitive press, wrote the narrative. Independent journalists had been the bane of the Vietnam era military. For Bush's advisors, the first requirement was to control journalists' access to war zones, and the next was to ensure that military spokespeople controlled the stories and images dispensed to the public.

The Bush administration timed the bombing campaign of Baghdad to commence at the hour the nightly evening news shows aired. Before it began, the United States told all journalists to leave the city, and Hussein had evicted others—only CNN stayed and kept its line active. Americans stayed glued to their televisions in the first hours and days of the campaign and watched footage from U.S. military cameras of missiles launched from U.S. carriers in the waters off of Iraq, followed by a cloud of smoke in a satellite photo of Baghdad with a caption underneath explaining which of Iraq's military facilities the "smart bomb" had taken out. Narration by Powell or Gen. "Stormin'" Norman Schwarzkopf would explain that the strangely hued, out-of-focus footage showed laser-guided bombs dropped by invisible Stealth fighters destroying targets of vital military significance. When asked, military briefers would not answer reporters' questions about civilian casualties, leaving the impression that the new technology had banished death from warfare. A number of Orwellian phrases, introduced by the Pentagon, entered American usage during the war: the deaths of Iraqi civilians from smart bombs were "collateral damage." The carefully staged briefings during the weeks of bombing were crafted to instill Americans with confidence in the nation's ability to win the war and to dull them to the human toll of war for the enemy.

For the new public relations campaign to succeed, it was necessary to limit competing visions of the war. The Grenada invasion during Reagan's presidency had provided the experimental ground for a new system, ostensibly preserving a free press while controlling it to a greater degree than ever before. In that intervention, the Pentagon had created a "pool system," in which reporters would be chaperoned through war zones by military officials. Pools allowed a small group of correspondents, under Pentagon rules and supervision, to cover the first stage of military action. The method was adopted for the Persian Gulf War with limited success. News organizations, although willing to give the system a try, were dissatisfied and protested the efforts by the military to control the character of their reporting. The Pentagon attempted to extend the system to cover all journalists, not just pool journalists, but journalists found ways to evade it. By mid-February, a number of journalists were venturing alone into war zones in Iraq to investigate (Zoglin 1991).

Ultimately, the effort to control the news of the war had mixed results. For the most part, American military action that killed more than 100,000 Iraqis was perceived by most Americans to be a bloodless war. But the independent footage and reporting of some brutal parts of the war, and the condition of the abandoned Kurdish refugees in its aftermath, did play a role in Americans' quick disillusionment with the war and the president.

Natural Resources, Transportation, and Global Warming

The Persian Gulf War renewed Americans' attention to their dependence on Middle East oil in a way that had not been so vivid since the 1973 Arab oil embargo. Since that time, two competing solutions had been debated: conservation versus increased production. President Jimmy Carter, himself an engineer, had pioneered the conservation approach, installing solar panels on the White House to serve as a model to the nation. President Ronald Reagan had them removed and treated conservation as a hangover of the era of "malaise." Bush followed in his predecessor's footsteps. In the midst of the war, he proposed a new energy policy that included a call to open the Arctic National Wildlife Preserve to oil exploration. He did not advocate any measures promoting efficiency or conservation.

In 1988, a new complication was added to the ongoing problem of America's dependence on a limited natural resource. James Hansen, a NASA climate scientist, testified before the Senate Committee on Energy and Natural Resources during an excruciating summer heat wave about global warming, saying, "It's time to stop waffling so much and say that the greenhouse effect is here and is affecting our climate now" (quoted in McKibben 2006). That year, climatologists from all over the world, supported by government funding, formed the Intergovernmental Panel on Climate Change (IPCC) to review the scientific evidence about global warming.

Global warming emerged in the 1990s as one of the most important environmental problems facing the United States and the world. In 1995, the more than 1,500 scientists in the IPCC concluded that "the balance of evidence suggests that there is a discernible human influence on global climate" (quoted in McKibben 2006). In 2001, it stated this conclusion more forcibly and unequivocally.

In late-August 1992, southern Florida was hit by Hurricane Andrew. Causing 66 deaths and over $22 billion in damages, it was the worst natural disaster in U.S. history to date. The laggard response by the Bush administration in helping victims of the storm led to widespread criticism and contributed to his defeat in 1992. Scientific research in the late 1990s and early 2000s established that global warming was increasing the frequency and intensity of tropical storms—hurricanes, monsoons, and typhoons. (Federal Emergency Management Agency)

Science has clearly established that global warming is a man-made problem: The burning of fossil fuels—coal, oil, and gas—builds up carbon dioxide in the earth's atmosphere, which in turn prevents heat from radiating back into space. Rising temperatures, in turn, have multiple consequences for the earth's delicately balanced ecosystem—among them rising sea levels from melting ice sheets, more frequent and deadly storms, and changes to migratory patterns of species and diseases.

The United States, with 4 percent of the world's population and annually using between one-fifth and one-quarter of the total world consumption of oil, natural gas, and coal, has been responsible over time for almost 30 percent of the world's carbon dioxide emissions. During the 1990s, America increased its emissions of carbon dioxide by 15 percent. The 5.7 billion metric tons of carbon dioxide that the United States released into the environment was almost double of what the nation had emitted in 1960. Most of the increase was caused by emissions from vehicles because Americans drove more and the fuel economy of the vehicles they drove stagnated. Americans drove an average of 2 trillion miles per year in the 1990s; at the turn of the 21st century, Americans had, in 40 years, tripled the miles they drove annually (McKibben 2005; Williams 2000; Worldwatch Institute 2001; Hansen 2006).

The 1990s, in fact, witnessed a reversal of progress on oil conservation and carbon dioxide emissions reduction. In the wake of the 1973 oil crisis, Congress had passed fuel efficiency standards for cars. Oil consumption—and emissions— began to fall immediately, but then hit a plateau in the late 1980s. Oil consumption then soared again in the 1990s' economic expansion. The main cause of increased fuel consumption was the explosive popularity of sports utility vehicles (SUVs), which traveled roughly 14 miles on a gallon of gas, compared to a mandated average for cars of 24 miles per gallon. In 1990, Americans purchased 8.5 million new cars and fewer than 4 million SUVs. In 1993, there were 7 million SUVs on the roads; at the end of the decade, there were more than 20 million. In 2001, for the first time, Americans bought more SUVs and similarly inefficient larger vehicles than cars. Only when oil prices skyrocketed in the mid-2000s in the aftermath of the Iraq War did sales of SUVs fall, and then only slightly.

Global warming was an international problem, and in the 1990s, momentum grew for an international solution. America's leaders, however, resisted the changes necessary to stem or reverse global warming. On the eve of the 1992 Rio de Janeiro environmental summit, the first international effort in which global warming would be addressed, Bush declared, "The American way of life is not up for negotiation" (quoted in McKibben 2005). Although rhetorically President Bill Clinton expressed more conviction about the seriousness of the problem, he did little substantively to act to limit global warming. He failed to raise questions with automakers and auto unions about the industry's increasing dependence on the sale of SUVs and its abandonment of research and development on alternative fuel vehicles. In 1997, the world's nations negotiated a treaty to reduce greenhouse gas emissions in the Kyoto Protocol, which set a timeline of 2012 for the industrial nations to have reduced their greenhouse emissions to 7 percent below 1990 levels. Although the Clinton administration signed the Kyoto Protocol, expecting a defeat in the Senate, it decided not to submit the treaty for approval. Throughout the decade, energy industry–funded lobbyists and scientists spread the now-discredited idea that global warming was just a theory and that there was dispute among scientists about its very existence, sowing confusion among Americans about the nature of global warming (Gelbspan 1997). At the end of the 1990s, the notion that action to stem global warming must be balanced against the nation's economic health seemed fixed in American politics. Nevertheless, opinion seemed to be moving toward some action—both parties' 2000 presidential candidates promised they would act on global warming. President George W. Bush decisively tilted U.S. policy toward the position that curbing emissions would have too great a cost for the American economy. One of his first acts in office was to abandon U.S. participation in the Kyoto Protocol.

CULTURE WARS

With the possible exception of the so-called Clinton scandals, which were in fact a subgenre of the phenomenon, no subject received more media attention in the 1990s than the Culture Wars. The term "Culture Wars" encompassed a litany of issues, including abortion, race and affirmative action, gay rights, sex and violence in the media, prayer and sex education in school, assisted suicide, the flag and the pledge of allegiance, the teaching of history, and the government's support of the arts. The underlying commonality among these distinct and diverse issues resided in the definition of morality and identity, and the connection between them. Who were we as Americans? What did we stand for? What should we allow our fellow citizens to do?

The Culture Wars that preoccupied the press in the 1990s are only comprehensible in light of the social groups and movements that promoted them as public matters. The Culture Wars were initiated as a defensive strategy of the Right. Despite the political victory of conservatism in the 1980s, the social innovations of the New Left had advanced far in American society by the end of that decade. What had once been radical demands agitated by a cultural and political vanguard were by the 1990s unremarkable characteristics of American life. Feminist activism had won legal rights for women in the family and over reproduction, which upended traditional family hierarchies. The right to abortion was the most controversial issue, yet by the 1990s, it was supported by a large majority of the American public. Likewise, equality in the workplace had become a solid American value for most Americans, even if there was still some distance to travel to achieve it. Following on the heels of the civil rights movement, "identity" movements of Black Power activists and Chicano radicals had won legitimacy for "multiculturalism" in education and public life. Other ethnic groups had followed their lead, and most colleges offered courses in Black Studies, Chicano Studies, and Asian American Studies—not to mention in the burgeoning field of gender and sexuality studies. Gay activists had achieved a far broader acknowledgement of the civil rights of gays and lesbians and acceptance in American life. And finally, though distinct from the political movements of the 1960s, the "counterculture" movement of the generation had, with the help of America's boisterous consumer capitalism, exploded traditional strictures against premarital sex and the use of drugs.

Those who held to conservative and traditional values were on the defensive. Social and religious conservatives saw the family and sexuality as the front line of the struggle (Faludi 2006). No one put it more memorably than did Pat Robertson. Feminism, he asserted, "encourages women to leave their husbands, kill their children, practice witchcraft, destroy capitalism and become lesbians" (quoted in Ivins 1992). Social conservatives engaged in various campaigns throughout the decade to promote "family values" to restore the traditional family. They called on women to stop working and campaigned to make divorce more difficult to obtain. The nationalist branch of the conservative movement viewed issues relating to national identity as the most pressing concern. They attacked multiculturalism in schools and colleges for undermining a common national identity based in pride in the American past; they sought constitutional amendments to ban flag burning. Social, religious, and nationalist conservatives were in agreement about the baneful effect of indecency in American culture. They tried to stop National Endowment of the Arts funding for artists whose work they considered pornographic; they berated the music and movie industry for distributing artists whose works contained explicit references to sex, drugs, and violence. It is, however, important to note that free market, libertarian, and most traditional conservatives largely absented themselves from the battles of the Culture Wars.

The Culture Wars had an ambiguous effect on the daily lives of Americans. Many of the cause célèbres of the Culture Wars were essentially affairs of an elite. The media, the history profession, and leading conservative cultural warriors, such as William Bennett Jr. and Lynn Cheney, became deeply embroiled in the 1994–1996 controversy over the National History Standards. Few others cared, and history classes went on in much the same way they had before, with new scholarship very gradually diffused into high school classrooms, determined more by individual educators and the demographic make-up of the individual school than by dictates from committees and commentators. The controversial history standards were eventually adopted and distributed. Flag burning was reliably trotted out in every election and could be counted on to rile up nationalists and civil libertarians alike. But virtually no one was desecrating a flag anywhere in the United States. The battles of the Culture Wars did affect the lives and opinions of Americans on matters that struck closer to the heart and home, on issues such as abortion, homosexuality, teenage sexuality, and evolution where traditional religious doctrine clashed with national norms or individual practice.

Abortion

Abortion was the fulcrum on which the most virulent battles of the Culture Wars turned. For women and men who defended the right to abortion articulated in *Roe v. Wade,* the availability of abortion was an essential precondition for women's health and women's equality and a fundamental issue of the right to privacy enjoyed by Americans. For women and men who opposed abortion, the act of abortion was essentially murder, and nothing in American society more powerfully demonstrated the depths of the moral degradation wrought by feminism.

The preferred term by the combatants in the abortion debates obliquely gestured toward the underlying differences in value systems separating the two

Two months after the passage of the Freedom of Access to Clinic Entrances Act, police stand guard outside a Little Rock, Arkansas, abortion clinic during a pro-life protest by Operation Rescue. (Greg Smith/Corbis)

camps. The "pro-life" side was founded in a religious worldview derived from conservative Protestantism and Catholicism, holding that life begins at conception. Such a view, for many of its adherents, also proscribed traditional roles for women in the family. The "pro-choice" position, on the other side, derived from liberal feminism. Individual liberty and the individual's right to privacy were two of the supreme human values, and feminism elaborated on liberalism's promise of self-realization by claiming it for women also. A vast majority of pro-life activists viewed their protest against abortion as required and sanctioned by their religious beliefs. A vast majority of pro-choice activists worried about the imposition of one version of religious beliefs on all American women, and viewed that eventuality as a devastating blow to the gains toward equality women had made since the early 1970s. Between the two sides was a deep chasm concerning the proper structure of authority within the family, the role of religion in American society, and the appropriate sphere for women in society.

In retrospect, though the majority of Americans remained supportive of abortion rights and *Roe v. Wade* remained the law of the land, the antiabortion movement made significant advances—legislatively and culturally—in the decade. Abortion, though it remained legal, became more difficult to obtain, as the Supreme Court upheld restrictions on abortion, such as waiting periods or

The Status of *Roe v. Wade*

The Supreme Court reaffirmed *Roe v. Wade* in 1992 in *Planned Parenthood v. Casey,* which reviewed restrictions on abortion passed by the State of Pennsylvania. In a surprise alignment, Justice Sandra Day O'Connor joined Justices Anthony Kennedy and David Souter to explicitly uphold the constitutionality of the landmark case. Although they let stand two of the restrictions on abortion contained in the Pennsylvania law, they rejected the requirement that a woman notify her husband. In the ruling, they acknowledged that some justices were morally opposed to abortion, but "our obligation is to define the liberty of all, not to mandate our own moral code."

parental notification, or through federal funding restrictions. The raucous demonstrations by Operation Rescue intimidated clinic workers and women seeking abortions, and led many to decide to close shop or avoid the public glare. For women in many states, it was impossible to obtain an abortion without traveling to another state or far from one's home. Terrorism on the movement's fringe—the murder of seven doctors, nurses, and aides between 1992 and 1998, firebombing and acid attacks at abortion clinics—achieved the intended chilling effect. Fewer and fewer doctors and nurses were willing to perform abortions; medical schools dropped instruction in the procedure from their curriculum.

The mainstream of the antiabortion movement, nevertheless, pursued their goal to make abortion illegal by seeking to win over the hearts of Americans. The movement abandoned the early decade tactics of Operation Rescue, which had alienated the public and enabled Clinton to pass the federal abortion clinic protection law with little fear of public outcry. Although most diehard activists came out of religious traditions that condemned sexual activity outside of marriage and adhered to the belief that life begins at conception, they did not try to sway the American public with these arguments. Instead, they campaigned on issues that stood in the grey zone for most Americans. They succeeded in passing laws that required teenage girls to get parental permission for an abortion; they renamed a rarely performed surgical technique for late-term abortions—most of which were done for the health of the mother or because of severe problems with the developing fetus—"partial birth abortion." No matter that doctors disputed point for point the claims of the antiabortion campaign to outlaw the procedure, it was a public relations coup.

The talent with which the antiabortion movement crafted a message and an imagery to dramatize their view of abortion impressed many Americans. The rhetoric of choice, individual rights, women's health, and woman's autonomy simply did not carry the same emotional sway as pictures of human-looking month-old fetuses plastered on billboards and attacks on the gruesome "partial birth abortion." Opinion about abortion shifted significantly during the decade. In 1991, about 65 percent of Americans supported *Roe*. By 1998, that percentage had dropped to 57 percent. More than two-thirds also disagreed with a central tenet of *Roe* (that abortion was legal in the second trimester of pregnancy) and thought that second trimester abortions should be illegal (Taylor 1998).

The Resurgence of Biological Racism: *The Bell Curve*

Several controversial books that asserted that there were fundamental differences between the races received wide distribution and media attention in the first half of the 1990s. Garnering the most attention was *The Bell Curve* by Richard Herrnstein and Charles Murray (1994). Herrnstein and Murray argued in the book that there were racial and ethnic differences in intelligence caused by genetics, that intelligence predicted social behavior, and that the main determinant of social differences was genetic difference. In other words, they sought to establish that any observed inequality between white and black in the United States was caused by natural, biological differences and could not be fixed by social programs such as affirmative action. The book was refuted by most scientists and social scientists on many grounds. Critics noted its selective use of scientific studies, its uncritical acceptance of disputed theories of general intelligence, its scientifically questionable assumptions about biological race, and the social implications of its biological determinism (Fraser 1995). It was ironic that as the map of the human genome neared its completion in the 1990s, and scientific biological racism received its definitive comeuppance, the convergence of the Culture Wars and the new media elevated the pseudoscientific racism of *Bell Curve* to mass media truth. Scientists had long argued what the human genome project confirmed: that race was a scientifically meaningless concept. (Because there is more genetic differentiation within putative races—for example, among white people—than between them—for example, between white people and black people—there is no meaning to the idea that there are different races. The findings of the scientific research received far less media acclaim than did the works of Murray, Herrnstein, and other proponents of biologically based racial differences in ability.

Affirmative Action and California's Proposition 209 (1996)

Opposition to affirmative action had existed since it was first adopted by the Nixon administration as a means to remedy race discrimination. In 1996, opponents of affirmative action in California placed an initiative on the ballot to end all affirmative action programs by the state. Voters approved the measure by a vote of 54 percent to 46 percent. Proposition 209 abolished affirmative action in California state programs: it prohibited the State of California from employing preferences by race or sex in school admissions, the hiring of public employees, and government contracting.

The campaigns for and against Proposition 209 were emblematic of the national debate and the politics surrounding affirmative action. The proponents of Prop 209, the California Civil Rights Initiative, appropriated the rhetoric of fairness and equal civil rights to posit that affirmative action amounted to "reverse discrimination," a violation of the true spirit of the civil rights movement. In the language of the proposition, "a generation ago, we did it right. We passed civil rights laws to prohibit discrimination. But special interests hijacked the civil rights movement. Instead of equality, governments imposed quotas, preferences, and set-asides." Opponents argued that discrimination persisted and that the proposition would undermine protections against it (State of California 1994).

The end of affirmative action, accomplished by popular vote in the most populous state in the nation, represented a signal victory for affirmative action's critics. Since then, proponents of affirmative action have been on the defensive, trying to persuade a skeptical American public that discrimination against women and people of color persisted in modern-day America. Public opinion in the 1990s on affirmative action served as a signpost of the nation's journey since the civil rights movement. A majority of white Americans had come to believe that racial discrimination no longer existed, and that "preferences" for African Americans over others were unfair and un-American.

Gay Marriage

Petitioned by three gay and lesbian couples, the Hawaii Supreme Court ruled in 1993 that the state's denial of marriage licenses to same-sex couples was an unconstitutional form of sex discrimination under the state's equal rights amendment. The court's ruling injected the subject of same-sex marriage into the already heated Culture Wars, which on gay issues up until that time had centered on the issue of civil rights and discrimination.

The controversy was not one the gay and lesbian movement had wanted to provoke. Most gay and lesbian organizations had not been enthusiastic about the Hawaii case, anticipating that the court would reject the claim, as every court had done in the last two decades. The community was struggling to hold back popular initiatives limiting the civil rights of gays, and most believed that those would have to be won first, and agitation for gay marriage was premature.

In 1996, the Christian Right began a campaign calling for the adoption of bans on same-sex marriage. At a rally before the Iowa presidential caucus, eight religious groups, including the Christian Coalition, issued their Marriage Protection

Resolution, gaining the endorsement of all Republican candidates. Three months later, Republican representative Bob Barr introduced the Defense of Marriage Act (DOMA), which would deny federal recognition of same-sex marriages and allow states to deny recognition of those marriages performed in other states. The Hawaii Supreme Court had ruled that the issue was one of discrimination; the debate in Congress made it one of morality. "What is at stake in this controversy [is n]othing less than our collective moral understanding . . . of the essential nature of the family" (Lewis and Edelson, 193–216) intoned one representative during the House debate. Opponents of DOMA, of whom there were few, denounced the move as a blatant partisan one in the midst of a presidential election. Clinton announced that he opposed gay marriage, thought DOMA was unnecessary, but would sign the bill if it passed. Within seven months of the Iowa rally, DOMA had passed the U.S. Senate by a six to one margin and the U.S. House by a five to one margin (Lewis and Edelson 2000). The action at the state level was swift as well. By mid-1998, bans on same-sex marriage had been enacted in 31 states and had been considered in all but Massachusetts and Nevada.

State Legislation on Gay and Lesbian Issues

Acceptance of homosexuality increased significantly in the 1990s yet seemed itself to generate an even greater backlash against gays and lesbians by conservatives. From the mid-1990s on, there was tremendous activity in the states and local municipalities on gay and lesbian issues as gays and lesbians tried to ex-

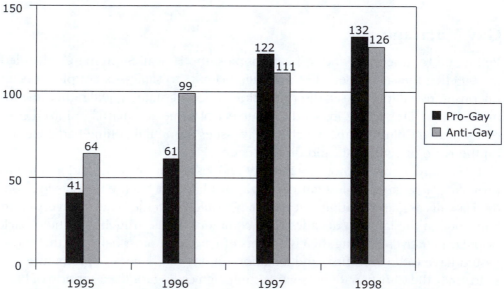

Figure 7.1 *Pro-Gay and Anti-Gay activity in the mid-1990s.* Source: *Haider-Markel 2000, 300-301.*

pand their rights and conservatives sought to constrain the social revolution in attitudes about sexuality. Pro-gay measures included the issues of hate crimes, domestic partnership, civil rights, and health, specifically on HIV/AIDS. The antigay measures included bans on same-sex marriage and efforts to prevent or rescind antidiscrimination statutes (Haider-Markel 2000).

Contested History and the Smithsonian Museum's Enola Gay Exhibit

In 1995, the battles that had raged over the teaching of American history the year before were rekindled in a controversy over how to portray America's use of the atomic bomb in World War II in a Smithsonian exhibit marking the 50th anniversary of the bombing of Hiroshima.

As the Smithsonian National Air and Space Museum (NASM) refurbished the plane that had dropped the atomic bomb on Hiroshima, the curators of the NASM planned an exhibit to accompany the display of the airplane. The curators of the museum had started in the mid-1980s to design exhibits that would provoke historical debate. They were strongly influenced by the new social history and various currents of revisionism that cast a critical eye on episodes in America's past. Historians and students of history, at least at the college level and above, disagreed about the right approach or the most persuasive interpretation of the past. But such debate was at the very heart of the discipline. Martin Harwit, director of the NASM, expressed the way that view affected public history museums when he wrote in a catalogue for an exhibit on the air war of World War I, "the principal task of an historical exhibition is to help a museum visitor understand the impact of key events on everyday life—how past experience has shaped today's world" (quoted in Gallagher 2000, n.p.). The curators' plans for the Enola Gay exhibit were to situate the display of the plane within a historical examination of the many political and ethical questions raised by the atomic bomb.

For those who viewed the study of the nation's history as primarily training for national citizenship, such debates were often viewed as un-American and those who engaged in them to be far-out leftist extremists. The earlier Culture Wars about the standards for teaching history had been confined to a debate among intellectuals, albeit one that drew a lot of media attention. The Enola Gay exhibit, in contrast, was a subject in which veterans' groups and the U.S. Air Force were deeply interested. To them, the plane symbolized American virtue and prowess, and, even more, the heroism of America's World War II veterans. Intensifying the potential for conflict was the fact that World War II was the last one in which there was a national consensus in the "good war." Probing questions about American conduct threatened to unravel the social fabric, already threadbare from the divisions over Vietnam.

Meetings between representatives of military groups and the curators of the museum began early in the process, but disagreement persisted. The military groups wanted the plane to be displayed "proudly" and began internally criticizing the curators for their "politically correct" pretensions and subversion of the Smithsonian's mandate. Tom Crouch, one of the exhibit's curators, asked the director of the museum in a private communication, in reference to the brewing controversy: "Do you want to do an exhibit intended to make veterans feel good, or do you want an exhibition that will lead our visitors to think about the consequences of the atomic bombing of Japan? I don't think we can do both" (quoted in Gallagher 2000, n.p.).

The internal debates were a window into the real differences of opinion among Americans in the 1990s. But the differences in this case only became part of the Culture Wars in March 1994 when the conservative newspaper the *Washington Times* published articles on the planned exhibit that were sharply critical of the NASM curators. In the following months, Congress, historians, the American legion, the pilot of the Enola Gay, and other prominent veterans entered the fray. The main professional organization of American historians issued an objection to political interference in museums that amounted to censorship. The U.S. Senate passed a nonbinding resolution opposing the exhibit. Revisions to the exhibit continued, with the NASM director and curators changing the exhibit to mollify critics. Ultimately, the planned exhibit was cancelled by the new secretary of the Smithsonian, who then announced his intent to mount a less controversial exhibit. Removed from the exhibit were photographs of the atomic blast and the wreckage in Hiroshima and artifacts that had been contributed by the Japanese government. The 600-page exhibit script, a catalogue, the display of testimony from survivors, debates about the morality of the dropping of the atomic bomb, and an examination of the factors weighed by President Harry Truman in the decision to use the bomb were likewise abandoned. In May 1995, the director of the NASM, Martin Harwit, resigned. In June, American University mounted an exhibit of parts of the originally planned exhibit, while the scaled-back Enola Gay exhibit opened at the Smithsonian, including only a part of the plane, a commemorative plaque, and a videotaped interview with the crew of the Enola Gay (Gallagher 2000; Harwit 1996).

The Revival of Creationism

Many Americans were surprised at the end of the 1990s to discover that the battle of the 1925 Scopes trial, between evolution and creationism, was still raging in the nation. In 1987, the U.S. Supreme Court had ruled that state public schools could not teach creationism. Thus, when fundamentalist Christian opposition to evolution and its teaching in American public schools reemerged in the 1990s, it did so in a new guise, that of "intelligent design" theory. In place of biblical literalism, intelligent design (ID) proposed instead a theory of the origins of life that conceded that evolutionary processes had played a role in the diversity of the species, yet maintained that life itself was created by an "intelligent" designer. The theory's core argument was that life was so complex, it could not have resulted from natural processes but could only have been created by an intelligent being capable of such complexity. Unlike earlier challengers of Darwinian evolution, the proponents of ID purported to base their views on science, not religion, and did not specifically identify the creator as the Judeo-Christian god. Working scientists universally rejected intelligent design on scientific grounds but were initially reluctant to enter the cultural controversy that exploded at the end of the decade (Orr 2005).

The movement for ID was allied with and funded by conservative Christian groups. Its main institutional promoter was the Discovery Institute, a think tank based in Seattle. In 1995, the head of the Discovery Institute, Bruce Chapman, and board member George Gilder convinced the Ahmanson family of Southern California to provide a grant to promote the teaching of ID against Darwinism, and they launched the Center for the Renewal of Science and Culture as a project of the Discovery Institute. The center struck an apparently moderate public pose: students should be taught that there was "controversy" over Darwinian theory.

The designs of the Discovery Institute were, however, far more sweeping— as a 1998 internal document that was anonymously posted on the Internet in 1999 revealed. The "Wedge" document laid out the vision, goals, and strategic plan of the Discovery Institute. (An illustration in the memo was titled "The Wedge.") It opened, "The proposition that human beings are created in the image of God is one of the bedrock principles on which Western civilization was built. . . . This cardinal idea came under wholesale attack by intellectuals drawing on the discoveries of modern science" (Center for the Renewal 1998, n.p.). Thinkers such as "Charles Darwin, Karl Marx, and Sigmund Freud portrayed humans not as moral and spiritual beings, but as animals or machines" in a world governed by "impersonal forces." This "materialism" bred moral relativism and "undermined personal responsibility" (Center for the Renewal 1998, n.p.). Everything bad in the modern world, from welfare, to consumer protection laws and modern criminal justice, stemmed from the corruption of materialism. The stakes involved were high: "We are convinced that in order to defeat materialism, we must cut it off at its source. That source is scientific materialism. This is precisely our strategy. If we view the predominant materialistic science as a giant tree, our strategy is intended to function as a 'wedge' that, while relatively small, can split the trunk when applied at its weakest points" (Center for the Renewal 1998, n.p.).

The writings of ID theorists, such as Phillip Johnson (*Darwinism on Trial,* 1991) and Michael Behe (*Darwin's Black Box,* 1996), the memo explained, were the "thin edge of the wedge." Ultimately, "design theory promises to reverse the stifling dominance of the materialist worldview, and to replace it with a science consonant with Christian and theistic convictions" (Center for the Renewal 1998, n.p.).

The Wedge document went on to describe a multipronged strategy of scientific research, education, publicity, and legal action. The final phase of the long-term plan was "cultural confrontation and renewal," and in the last year of the decade, it appeared that it had begun. In 1999, the Discovery Institute provided assistance to a Washington State science teacher who had substituted intelligent design readings for the state-approved curriculum on evolution. Parents, who were subsequently assisted by the American Civil Liberties Union, objected to the religious content of the teacher's lessons and threatened legal action if it did not end. The Discovery Institute charged that the teacher's academic freedom was being violated (Downey 2006; Orr 2005).

In the most publicized case in the 1990s, religious conservatives won a majority on the Kansas Board of Education. They voted to make the teaching of evolution optional in its state standards and eliminated requirements for teaching other scientific theories that conflicted with the biblical version of creation, such as the big bang theory and the age of the earth. At the same time, other states renewed proposals to teach the "controversy" over evolution and placed disclaimer stickers about evolution on the front of biology textbooks. In 2005, a United States District Court concluded in *Kitzmiller v. Dover Area School District* that "ID is a religious view, a mere re-labeling of creationism, and not a scientific theory" and its teaching violated the Supreme Court's prohibition against the teaching of creationism in the public schools.

Debates: The Culture Wars

The state of the literature on the Culture Wars continued in the mid-2000s to be largely bound up with the sociopolitical conflicts of the 1990s. The election of 2000, and then the attacks of September 11, aggravated the Culture Wars, and an even greater polarization and subjective involvement is evident in many post-2001 works.

On the left, where there was an almost apocalyptic sense of defeat after the election of Bush, the Culture Wars have frequently been interpreted as a political strategy of deliberate distraction from Americans' real material interests. In this analysis, Republicans on the right deliberately manipulate the cultural and religious beliefs of average Americans to win elections; Republican politicians thus elected then proceed to ignore the pressing issues of culture and to instead enact a pro-corporate agenda, which hurts their constituents economically. The 2005–2006 lobbying scandals involving Jack Abramoff and leading Republican social conservatives lent some support to this analysis. This version has been told most entertainingly by Thomas Frank in *What's the Matter with Kansas?* (2004).

Informative about the local political manifestation of the Culture Wars, it never-theless derives from several debatable premises—that material interests are in-herently and inevitably prior to other interests, and that voting based on other interests is evidence of false consciousness.

On the right, where the Culture Wars were declared, most writing on the Cul-ture Wars are indeed entries in them. Whether from the extreme—Ann Coulter, *Slander: Liberal Lies about the American Right*—or the Olympian—William J. Bennett Jr., *America: The Last Best Hope*—the Culture Wars are presented as a legitimate and worthy cause to which conservatives should devote their energy. Engagement in Cultural war is seen as a means to stamp out the polluted spawn of the New Left and liberals—cultural degeneration, social fragmentation, the decline of an ethic of personal responsibility, anti-Americanism, and amoral secularism (Coulter 2002; Bennett 1998, 2006).

Nonetheless, other works on the Culture Wars sought some distance from the battle. But that stance became more difficult over the course of the 1990s and into the present. The shift can be seen in the comparison between two ex-cellent works on the Culture Wars, Robert Hughes's *Culture of Complaint* and Haynes Johnson's *The Best of Times*. Hughes's book originated as a series of lectures given at the New York Public Library in January 1992. As he explained, "the clouded issues of 'political correctness,' 'multiculturalism,' the politiciza-tion of the arts and so forth had been moving from academe, the art world and the cultural magazines into American popular journalism, creating, on the whole, more heat and fumes than light" (Hughes 1993, xi). Analyzing the Cul-ture Wars on the cusp of its transformation from an elite preoccupation to a po-litical platform, Hughes dissects them in a passionate and provocative, yet nonpartisan, fashion. In subjecting the phenomenon to a historically and philo-sophically informed examination, Hughes produced a work that transcended the specific conflicts. In addition to its lively analysis, the book is a valuable document of the state of the Culture Wars in 1992—before the Republican Party made the Culture Wars the centerpiece of the 1992 presidential campaign (Hughes 1993).

Published as the new century opened, Johnson's book was both a bellwether of the corrosive effects of the Culture Wars and a clarion call to restore Ameri-can civil society to its pre–Culture Wars state (Johnson 2001). Johnson constructs his narrative on an interpretation of the intersection of the commercial and tech-nological transformation of the media, the politicization of the Culture Wars by the Republican Right, and the mood of the American public during the New Economy boom. Hughes's subjects are multiculturalism, political correctness, the arts, and the academy—an accurate taxonomy of the Culture Wars in the early 1990s. Johnson examines the media frenzy surrounding the O. J. Simpson trial and the alliance between the Right and a compliant media in the Clinton-Lewinsky scandal; it is a reflection of how significantly the stakes were raised over the course of the decade.

Political columnist Andrew Sullivan. (Shepard Sherbell/Corbis)

Johnson's work shares with many other late-decade entries on the Culture Wars a sense of alarm and urgency. Johnson is dismayed as much by the role of his own profession—journalism—in degrading American civil debate as he is by the politics of it all. For most of the other writers on the Culture Wars, it is all about politics. From the most partisan to the most academic, the political Culture War rages in the books about the Culture Wars.

A new genre of writing on the Culture Wars is currently emerging—works of memoir and biographically informed historical analysis—that promises to move our understanding beyond partisan interpretation. There are works such as former *New Republic* editor Andrew Sullivan's *The Conservative Soul* (2006). Sullivan is a different kind of conservative: he is gay and HIV positive, a passionate advocate of gay rights, and extremely worried about religious zealotry. To him, the Culture Wars are "our new wars of religion," of "fundamentalism against faiths of all kinds that are at peace with freedom and modernity" (Sullivan 2001). Sullivan is convinced that the Culture Wars are a dead end for conservatives and disastrous for the country. From the other end of the political spectrum comes a similarly reflective work by *The Nation* writer Eyal Press. Press's father was an obstetrics gynecologist in Buffalo, New York, who, after his friend Dr. Bernard Slepian was assassinated, was next on the hit list kept by antiabortion extremists. Rooted in personal experience, Press approaches the abortion wars from the perspective of social history. In American politics, Press writes, abortion is "a prism through which debates about sex and gender, religion and politics, and (less overtly but no less unmistakably) race and class have long played out. How those debates unfolded on the streets of Buffalo can tell us a lot about the nature of American politics in recent decades: the passions that drive it, the contradictions that riddle it, the cultural divisions that cleave it as sharply as any economic or racial lines do" (Press 2006, 3). A step or more removed from the battle lines, Press's, Sullivan's, and other works like these are not only valuable documents for future historians, but they also suggest the contours of future analysis.

What's in a Name?

Many residents of Los Angeles refer to the 1992 events as the "civil unrest" or the "civil disturbance." Such a circumlocution was motivated by a sense of the injustice of the verdicts in the Rodney King case and a desire not to stigmatize the entire community from which the participants in the "unrest" came. The "unrest" was thus a protest against a racist verdict, and justified as the reaction was, it would be wrong to call it a "riot." Among some on the activist left, the language used to describe the events even more emphatically signals one's solidarity with those who actively participated in the demonstrations, property destruction, and violent attacks on individuals. To these, the event was an "uprising" or an "insurrection." A survey after the events, albeit one that was ineptly phrased, suggests why Angelinos needed a means to navigate differences. Roughly two-thirds of African American Angelinos viewed the events as primarily a "protest" while only slightly more than one-third of Anglo Angelinos did (Baldassare 1994, 165). Fifteen years after the fact, etiquette in many circles requires one to avoid the presumably loaded term "riots." The euphemistic "civil unrest" persists as the preferred solution.

Although there is a centuries-old derogatory association of "riot" with "mobs," there is nevertheless also an equally well-established scholarly tradition analyzing "riots" as a form of collective protest. From this perspective, scholars propose that riots have been a form of collective behavior for social groups that have few other institutionalized avenues for effective social or political action. A central concern of this analysis is to provide a means to explain the very important distinction between organized and political forms of violence—the Boston Tea Party, for example—and the more or less spontaneous, collective outbursts of violence motivated largely by social grievances—the Paris Bread Riots in the years before the French Revolution, for example. The latter are routinely called riots in the historical literature, with no implied negative judgment on the actors. That standard scholarly usage will be followed here.

URBAN UNREST: LOS ANGELES, 1992, AND CROWN HEIGHTS, 1991

In the late spring of 1992, as working people throughout America's once-vibrant industrial centers sunk into unprecedented anxiety over their future in what economists and journalists were just beginning to call the "jobless recovery," and as the young and charismatic Bill Clinton campaigned to win the presidency from the ineffectual and unpopular elder George Bush, Los Angeles residents of South Central and Pico-Union took to the streets in a violent upheaval that would rank as the largest "riot," "insurrection," or "civil unrest"—depending on one's point of view—of 20th-century America.

To understand the Los Angeles Riots, it first helps to ask the question: why Los Angeles? When social conflict of this magnitude occurs, scholars typically attempt to identify the underlying social and economic conditions of the locale at the time, even if there is a wide range of opinion on the relative importance of such forces. In 1992, Los Angeles was in the depths of recession, its manufacturing base as if spirited away in the blink of an eye. The city's always-vibrant service sector was doing better, but in significant measure because of the mass influx of Asian, Mexican, and Central American immigrants and refugees who were paid a fraction of the wages previously earned by Los Angeles's black and white working class. The city's budget was deep in the red and Angelinos had already suffered through several years of closed or dilapidated parks and libraries, overcrowded schools, sporadic trash collection, and potholed streets. Gangs were daily multiplying their membership and crime had grown to unprecedented deadly levels. The city's poor and working-class minorities, its African American, Mexican American, and new immigrant residents, bore the brunt of the impact.

The same could be said, however, of many American cities in 1992—New York, Philadelphia, Detroit, Cleveland, Houston, Baltimore. In the mid-1960s, the mix of urban decay, political upheaval, and social discontent had served as a similar powder keg. In 1965, the Watts Riot in South Central Los Angeles had been one of many cases in which poor urban black residents had rioted. But in 1992, Los Angeles proved to be unique. Notwithstanding a few episodes during the days of the Los Angeles Riots of protests in San Francisco and Harlem and violent actions by small crowds in Atlanta, Madison, and Las Vegas, the Los Angeles Riots were neither preceded by nor did they precipitate other major protests, demonstrations, or riots.

The difference between Los Angeles and other cities in 1992 was the Los Angeles Police Department (LAPD). In the late 1980s alone, more than 2,000 complaints of police brutality had been lodged against Los Angeles police officers. Rarely were police officers punished. The catalyst for the Los Angeles Riots of 1992 was indisputably the acquittal of four Los Angeles police officers for beating an African American man the year before.

On March 3, 1991, Rodney King, a black man, was beaten by four LAPD officers after a high-speed freeway chase. In an apartment building with a view of the scene, George Holliday heard the fracas, took out his new Sony Handycam, and videotaped the remainder of the beating. The next day, Holliday turned the 82-second-long tape over to a local news station, which then ran it unedited as its lead story on the 6 p.m. news. The national and international news immediately picked up the footage, and within two weeks, 9 out of 10 Americans surveyed reported that they had seen the tape or heard of the Rodney King beating.

Public outcry over the beating pressured the reluctant chief of police, Darryl Gates, to call for the felony prosecution of the officers shown engaged in the beating: Stacey Koon, Laurence Powell, Timothy Wind, and Theodore Briseno. Koon and Powell had previous police brutality charges on their records. Mayor Tom Bradley impaneled the Christopher Commission (headed by Warren Christopher) to investigate the LAPD. Three months later, the Christopher Commission issued a report presenting a damning indictment of the LAPD. In one notable comment, the commission observed that "too many LAPD officers view citizens with resentment and hostility" (quoted in Domanick 1994, 401).

In the legal proceedings against the LAPD officers, after a series of reversals and the removal of the first judge on the case, a conservative judge ruled for a change of venue—a rare move in Los Angeles courts. The trial was removed from Los Angeles to the town of Simi Valley, approximately one hour north of Los Angeles, in Ventura County. Simi Valley, a conservative white enclave in a larger region that was multiethnic and liberal, was home to 4,000 active law enforcement officers and their families (Domanick 1994). When jury selection began, the jury pool of 264 individuals had only 6 African Americans within it.

The trial lasted from March 5 to April 29. On the afternoon of April 29, the jury announced its verdict, acquitting Koon, Wind, and Briseno on all counts. Powell was acquitted on all but one count, on which the jury deadlocked. At police headquarters, officers celebrated and went home for the day. Chief Gates immediately went off to a political fund-raiser to raise money to defeat a charter amendment on the June ballot that would institute the police reforms called for by the Christopher Commission.

Within hours of the announcement of the verdict, rioting began in the neighborhoods of South Central and Pico-Union. The mayor, leaders of the African American community, and 2,000 people gathered at the First African Methodist Episcopalian Church for a peace rally that evening, but their message fell flat as the violence escalated. Rioting soon spread through the city and continued for the next three days. At the close of the riot, 58 people had been killed, 2,383 injured, 5,633 arrested, and $1 billion worth of property had been damaged or destroyed. As Joe Domanick, a critic and historian of the LAPD explained, "The point in time when people say I won't take this anymore, I will fight back, I will seek retribution, had been reached. It was a feeling so widespread in South Central and Pico-Union that what was really amazing was not what broke out during those days, but that so many white people were totally blind to what had led up to it" (Domanick 1994).

To many in the poor and minority neighborhoods of Los Angeles, the beating of Rodney King and the acquittal of the police officers was symbolic of a decades-long pattern of impunity and unaccountability by the police. The Watts Riot, after all, had started in the same neighborhood and had been precipitated by a police action. On the streets of Los Angeles in 1992, observers told the few journalists willing to venture into the conflagration that "it's a black thing"

(Domanick 1994). But Pico-Union and South Central had become majority Latino neighborhoods with black minorities. Analysts looking at statistics about the event, which showed that half of those arrested were Latino and one-third were African American, ventured that the Los Angeles Riots of 1992 presaged a new era when multiethnic conflict would overtake historic black-white conflicts (Baldassare 1994). That prediction did not come true.

Korean Americans after the Los Angeles Riots

Korean-owned businesses in Los Angeles were the hardest hit by the riots, with one-third of the Korean-owned businesses targeted. More than 2,000 businesses were destroyed, most of them family owned, and many of them immigrant owned. Many of the business owners had no insurance, or were defrauded by phony insurers, and many were unable to get bank loans to start anew. Promises and plans to rebuild Los Angeles faltered, and as time went on, the lasting consequences of the riots on the Los Angeles Korean community largely receded from the broader public view. Many Korean families were never able to restore their businesses, and some individuals committed suicide in the wake of their tragedy (Baldassare 1994).

At the same time, as the activist Angela Oh observed on the 10-year anniversary of the riots, "Korean America was born on April 29, 1992. . . . After that

A Korean business burns during the Los Angeles riots, April 30, 1992. (Peter Turnley/ Corbis)

A Comparison of Crown Heights, New York, and the Los Angeles Riots

In August 1991, long-simmering tensions between the two dominant communities living in the Crown Heights neighborhood of Brooklyn, New York, erupted in rioting. Crown Heights was the world headquarters of the Lubavitcher movement, a Hasidic Jewish sect led by the Rabbi Menachem Mendel Schneerson. Lubavitcher Hasidim from around the world came to study and live in Crown Heights. The rest of the working-class neighborhood was home to a large West Indian immigrant community. The Lubavitchers, on principle, disdained contact with individuals and communities outside their movement—including other Jews.

On the night of August 19, one of the drivers in a Lubavitcher motorcade drove recklessly through an intersection in the neighborhood, killing a nine-year-old West Indian boy named Gavin Cato and injuring his cousin. Soon West Indians took to the streets in protest and rioting, which lasted for three days. The sequence of events remains hazy, but at the end of the riots, one Lubavitcher had been murdered, another had committed suicide, six stores had been looted, and almost 200 civilians and police officers claimed to have been injured.

The riots occurred at a time when the disintegrating state of "black-Jewish" relations was a subject of anger, sadness, and concern in both communities. Jews viewed several recent incidents of African American anti-Semitism as indicative of a widely shared prejudice among African Americans and felt betrayed, given their history of involvement in the civil rights movement. African Americans believed many Jews had abandoned the struggle for black equality by rejecting affirmative action and were blind to persisting racism, and they resented the expectation that every black person be held responsible for the statement of any other black individual. New York was the locus of the conflict because it was home to two of the largest African American and Jewish American communities, it had been the heart of the liberal political alliance of the civil rights era, and it had strong ethnic media and ethnic political machines.

Thus, although the conflict in Crown Heights was small compared to the urban riots of the 1960s and the Los Angeles Riots that would soon follow, it appeared at the time to symbolize the strained state of black-Jewish relations and to have ominous portents for the future. In reality, the hostilities and conflict between the West Indians and Lubavitchers of Brooklyn had little to do with the issue of black-Jewish relations as most people understood it. Lubavitchers were religiously orthodox and politically conservative, and they segregated themselves from the majority of Jewish New Yorkers. The tensions between West Indians and native-born African Americans, though less intense, were equally notorious. The affair had more to do with the typical causes of conflict in poorer urban neighborhoods: tensions between customers and shopkeepers, feelings that city government and the police showed favoritism to one poor community over the other, and a struggle for limited public resources and jobs.

day a new political community and collective consciousness was born" (Oh 2002). New organizations were founded, and those that were already in existence often shifted into a more direct engagement in American society, either through formal politics, or through the building of alliances and relationships with other ethnic groups.

RESTRICTING IMMIGRATION AND IMMIGRANTS: CALIFORNIA'S PROPOSITION 187

On November 9, 1994, California's voters approved Proposition 187, an anti-immigrant measure, by a three to two margin. Proposition 187 barred illegal aliens from the state's public schools and denied them all but emergency health care. The proposition required teachers, nurses, doctors, and other officials working in state agencies to investigate the immigration status of individuals seeking services, and to report anyone they suspected of being in the country without proper authorization to the INS and the state attorney general. The proposition was widely and correctly viewed as targeting primarily the large numbers of unauthorized immigrants from Mexico and Central America. Put before the voters of California in the year of the angry voter, during a deep recession and a fiscal crisis in the state, Prop 187 became the fulcrum of the emerging immigration debate. In historical perspective, it marks a turning point in the contemporary politics of immigration.

The Campaign for Proposition 187

Proposition 187 was placed on the ballot by people who had been active in the Orange County chapter of the California Coalition for Immigration Reform and other individuals active in restrictionist politics. Contrary to the prevailing expert opinion regarding the reasons for immigration, they asserted that the state's generous social services attracted illegal immigrants to California. Therefore, to deny immigrants these public benefits would serve to deter illegal immigration. Like many of those who have moved radical proposals through California's direct democracy machine, the pro–Prop 187 campaign projected a populist image of themselves as ordinary citizens arrayed against the powerful. *People* magazine, for example, profiled Barbara Coe, one of the leaders of the "Save Our State" (SOS) campaign committee, presenting her personal experience with the state bureaucracy as the catalyst for SOS, and quoted her likening herself to David battling Goliath. Nevertheless, among those leading the campaign to pass Proposition 187 were established organizations and prominent individuals. When it had looked like the proposition would not receive enough signatures to qualify for

Proposition 187:
Text of Proposed Law (Excerpt)

Section 1. Findings and Declaration.

The People of California find and declare as follows:

That they have suffered and are suffering economic hardship caused by the presence of illegal aliens in this state.

That they have suffered and are suffering personal injury and damage caused by the criminal conduct of illegal aliens in this state.

That they have a right to the protection of their government from any person or persons entering this country unlawfully.

Therefore, the People of California declare their intention to provide for cooperation between their agencies of state and local government with the federal government, and to establish a system of required notification by and between such agencies to prevent illegal aliens in the United States from receiving benefits or public services in the State of California.

the ballot, the Republican Party stepped in with funding. (California allows ballot committees to pay signature gatherers per signature and places no limit on the amount.) Two top officials in the INS during the Reagan administration, Harold Ezell and Alan Nelson, led an allied group and went on to found an organization to carry the measure to other states. Nelson, a co-author of 187, had previously worked for the leading national organization advocating restriction, the Federation for American Immigration Reform (FAIR). He had authored legislation to deny American citizenship to children born to unauthorized immigrants on behalf of a California Republican assemblyman. FAIR endorsed the proposition, although the organization no longer employed Nelson and sought to distance itself from some of the more extreme xenophobes within SOS. Politicians and businessmen who were veterans of right-wing Republican initiatives in California funded the cause and served as its spokespersons (Kadetsky 1994).

Although Proposition 187 ultimately won broad support for a number of reasons, the members of the committee that qualified and sponsored the initiative and led the campaign expressed views far more extreme than those of most Californians. Ron Prince, the businessman who was the sponsor of Prop 187, accused those who favored "illegal immigration" of being "anti-American," and rallied his supporters with vigilante dreams—"You are the posse and SOS is the rope." The media director of the Prop 187 campaign conjured fears of a Reconquista, a California overrun by Mexicans who then would vote "to leave the Union and annex California to Mexico." Ezell, in the 1980s, had become infamous for his remark that "illegal aliens" should be "caught, skinned, and fried."

Coe, one of the drafters of the proposition, and the person who more than anyone else became the public face of the pro-proposition campaign, expressed classic nativist fears of the loss of American identity. To her, illegal immigrants held
"our language, our culture, and our very history in contempt" (Johnson 1998).

Electoral Politics and Proposition 187

Although Prop 187 had originated in the more extreme branches of the immigration restriction movement, it gained notoriety because it became a driving
issue in the gubernatorial and senate races as the Republican candidates seized
on immigration as a wedge issue. Early in the campaign, incumbent Republican
governor Pete Wilson badly trailed his Democratic opponent, Kathleen Brown,
the state treasurer and the daughter of the revered former governor Edmund
"Pat" Brown. Although Wilson, during his tenure in the 1980s as one of California's state senators, had supported legislation easing entry for temporary
agricultural workers, in 1994, he revived his reelection prospects with a tough
stance against illegal immigration. Wilson likened the movement of unauthorized immigrants across the border to an invasion and demanded that the federal government pay the state back for the burden they imposed on California.
His television ads, which had been produced by the border patrol, showed immigrants racing across the border into oncoming traffic on Interstate 5, as the
narrator intoned, "They keep coming. Two million illegal immigrants in California. The federal government won't stop them at the border." The political ad-
vertisement touted Wilson's support for Prop 187 and his move to sue the federal
government over the cost of immigrants (Andreas 2000, 87). Democratic politicians, including gubernatorial candidate Brown, Sen. Dianne Feinstein, and President Clinton, opposed 187, but as in so many skirmishes in the Culture Wars,
they conceded the high ground in the contest of ideas to the Republicans, promising that they had a better, more pragmatic way to deal with the admittedly awful problem. Clinton, for example, used sharp rhetoric against illegal immigrants
and promised that the federal government would do more to help California
and other states carry the cost and defend the border.

The Coalition against Proposition 187

The proposition immediately galvanized immigrant rights and civil liberties organizations, teachers and other public employees, and the Latino community to
work hard to defeat the measure. Many saw in Prop 187 a dangerous nativism
and racism against all Latinos. Others were wary of the authoritarian aspects of
the proposition that seemed to violate traditional American civil liberties. Organizations such as the Mexican American Legal Defense and Education Fund
(MALDEF), the American Civil Liberties Union (ACLU), and the Coalition for

Symbolic Politics, Bureaucracy, and the Media

In anticipation of the post-Christmas travel of Mexican migrants returning from visits home to their jobs in the United States, the San Diego chief of the border patrol, Gustavo de la Viña, had a fence built from the Pacific Ocean to San Ysidro (the Tijuana–San Diego border) and stationed additional agents there to apprehend those crossing without documents. The border station at San Ysidro itself was the only unfenced part of the westernmost stretch of the border. Those who wanted to cross therefore tried to go around the barricades. Soon, enterprising smugglers decided to take advantage of the large numbers of migrants massed in one spot. They organized "banzai runs" in which 50 or more people would rush the border; the odds were that more would make it across than if agents could pick them off one or two at a time. Viña of the border patrol was also enterprising. He videotaped the runs, which were a reaction to policies he instituted, and distributed the resulting public relations video under the title "Border Under Siege." Wilson took his campaign commercial footage from this video.

Humane Immigrant Rights of Los Angeles (CHIRLA) participated in the electoral campaign to defeat the proposition at the polls while also preparing for the legal battle should the initiative pass. Teachers, doctors, social workers, and other state employees who served immigrants opposed the proposition, and their organizations and unions ran most of the television ads against Prop 187. As election season kicked into high gear in October, African Americans, Asian Americans, other labor unions, and religious coalitions joined the public campaign, calling attention to the implications for their communities and to the broader civil rights struggle involved. Japanese Americans, for example, drew on their history of internment during World War II to underscore the danger of the proposition. Cardinal Roger M. Mahony, the highest-ranked official of the Catholic Church in California,

Students rally during a demonstration against Proposition 187 on November 8, 1994, in Los Angeles, California. (Getty Images)

criticized the measure as a "devastating assault on human dignity." John Mack, the leader of the Los Angeles Urban League, warned, "There are black people and other minority people who are at odds over jobs. But if you're black and you vote for 187, you're not just voting against Hispanics, but you're also voting for the kind of thing that has been used against blacks since time began" (Ayres 1994).

The Final Weeks of the Proposition 187 Campaign

Prop 187 led by huge margins in the summer of 1994, but by the fall, the opponents of the measure had marshaled their forces and seemed to be turning the electoral equation around. As the campaign against the proposition entered a phase of heightened activism, members of the coalition found themselves disagreeing about tactics to combat the initiative. A number of the larger organizations in the coalition opposed to 187 worried that any mass action might provoke a backlash while others believed just as strongly that the campaign needed a boost from mass protests. On October 16, 125,000 people demonstrated against Prop 187 in Los Angeles. It was the first mass demonstration since the Chicano Moratorium of 1970, and it was the largest held to date in the city. Within several days, high school students throughout Southern California were engaged in a wave of walkouts. In the two weeks before the election, more than 15,000 junior high and high school students joined in the walkouts, and the Los Angeles Police Department went on tactical alert. The effect of the demonstrations was mixed. While they buoyed the spirits of the opponents of the proposition, and likely boosted voter turnout among them, polls also showed that support for the proposition began to increase again after the demonstrations.

Just as division over tactics beset the opponents of Prop 187, the Republican Party experienced an embarrassing and potentially dramatic rift over the proposition and immigration in general. A few weeks before the election, two of the party's up-and-coming conservative leaders, both with presidential ambitions and renowned as men of ideas, issued a public rebuke to the nativists among their allies. Jack Kemp and William Bennett defended legal immigration and invoked classic ideas of America as a nation of immigrants. They warned their fellow party members that, from a pragmatic view, the Republicans had more votes to lose than gain in this battle. Immigrants, with their "entrepreneurial spirit and self-reliance, hostility to government intervention, strong family values and deeply rooted religious faith," were a natural constituency for the party (Martin 1996). The conservative *National Review* disagreed. An open immigration policy threatened the "balkanization" of America and the loss of its distinctive national identity, argued John O'Sullivan. "Of course, the original Americanism was enriched by the influences of immigrants from other cultures. Just as Christianity is the universalization of Judaism, so Americanism is the universalization of British culture. And in being universalized that culture changed to produce a distinctive American culture and identity" (O'Sullivan 1994). The debate revealed a serious fracture within the Republican Party between its free market individualists and its traditional conservatives, one that would continue to bedevil the Republicans over the next decade.

On Election Day, California voters passed Proposition 187 by a vote of 59 percent to 41 percent. With the exception of Latinos and Jews, a majority of every ethnic group voted to pass Prop 187. Elections in California tend to split along regional lines, but in the case of Prop 187, with the exception of eight San Francisco Bay counties, all counties approved the measure. Votes did split along party lines, with Democrats opposed by a margin of 64 percent, and Republicans in favor by a margin of 78 percent. Turnout among Republicans and Democrats was roughly equal, and in this context, unaffiliated voters (independents) helped push 187 to victory.

The day after the election, Governor Wilson moved to put Prop 187 into effect, ordering prenatal clinics and nursing homes not to care for undocumented immigrants, but his act was in vain. Throughout the campaign, opponents and supporters alike had warned that the proposition was unlikely to withstand legal challenge. A 1982 Supreme Court decision (*Plyler v. Doe*) granted illegal immigrants the right to public education, citing "the lasting impact of its deprivation on the life of a child" in its reasoning. Attorneys working for the campaign against 187 had spent the night of the election putting the final touches on their legal briefs and, the next morning, went into court and won a temporary injunction against the provisions of 187 denying access to health and education. In all, eight legal challenges were filed in state and federal courts in the immediate aftermath of the measure's passage. A few weeks later, a federal judge ordered the injunction to remain in force for most provisions until a full hearing and decision could be issued. Proposition 187 as a practical measure was in limbo.

In California, division and uncertainty reigned in the weeks after the passage of Prop 187. Immigrant rights groups received many complaints of harassment and discrimination. With the proposition under legal review, public officials who had opposed the proposition refused to implement its provisions. The elected board of the Los Angeles Unified School District filed a legal challenge to Prop 187. The backers of Prop 187, in response, tried to no avail to launch a recall campaign against them. Students at almost every institution of higher education in California protested against the proposition. The governor and proposition supporters were eager to reap the fruits of victory and enforce Prop 187 while opponents planned a multipronged strategy of opposition.

The proposition had captured national attention in the final weeks of the campaign, and the reverberations of its passage were national as well. A week after the California election, Save Our State Arizona announced a Prop 187–type campaign at a press conference. The supporters tried to export the campaign to Florida, Illinois, New York, and Texas as well. The new Republican majority in Congress began immediately to plan its immigration strategy. Although the Contract with America had been silent on immigration, by 1996, the Republicans in the House were trying to bar illegal immigrants from public schools, hoping to trigger the Supreme Court to overturn its earlier position. At its most extreme, Texas representative Lamar Smith held hearings about denying children of unauthorized immigrants American citizenship. In California, the wedge politics driving Prop 187 shifted into a campaign for a proposition barring state affirmative action programs, as Republicans sought to capitalize on the white male backlash revealed in the national 1994 elections. Opponents in other states threatened to punish California with boycotts while the student demonstrations in California spread to institutions throughout the nation.

The Impact of Proposition 187

Proposition 187 never went into effect because most parts were declared unconstitutional over the following several years. Nevertheless, the measure and the campaign around it had important consequences for American politics. Coinciding with the Republican sweep in the 1994 elections, the core tenet of Prop 187 became enshrined in federal law, as the Democrats tried to stanch their future losses in the uncertain political climate between the 1994 and 1996 elections. Stepped up border control and the provisions of welfare reform denying immigrants many forms of public assistance were both the progeny of California's Prop 187.

But Proposition 187 did not live up to the hopes of its authors. Campaigns in other states withered during the 1990s in part due to the uncertainty of the measure's legality. Most important, anger about immigration itself subsided in the midst of the economic boom of the late decade, when jobs were plentiful and state and federal coffers were flush. There was little to be gained politically by pushing an anti-immigrant agenda, and the movement for restriction withered to include only the hard-core, long-term activists.

The most significant consequence of Proposition 187, however, was also the most ironic. After the election of 1994, there was a surge in naturalizations and in Latino voter turnout. Few Mexican immigrants had taken advantage of the opportunity to become U.S. citizens in the past. But with the passage of 187, its de facto incorporation into federal law, with public benefits cut off to legal as well as unauthorized immigrants, many long-term legal residents decided that naturalization was necessary to protect one's basic legal rights, and that political mobilization must be one of the strategies in repelling the political attack on immigrants. The change was helped along by the decision by the Mexican government, in 1998, to allow dual citizenship for Mexican nationals residing in the United States. As Kemp and Bennett had cautioned, Proposition 187 backfired for Republicans. The Republicans were swept out of power in California in 1996 on the new wave of Latino voters. By the election of 2000, the party was trying to keep its nativists quiet while the nominee, George W. Bush, was promoting his enlightened view of immigrants, Hispanics, and Mexico as the trademark of the pragmatic, nonideological "compassionate conservative" style he was projecting to voters.

THE EXTREMIST RIGHT

Racist and anti-Semitic white supremacists, religious extremists who separated themselves from mainstream society, paramilitary groups, and xenophobic nationalists were all active in the nineties (Atkins 2002). The extreme right has a long history in 19th- and 20th-century America, and many elements of the extremist right exhibited a deep cultural affinity with historical movements. Nevertheless, a newly evolved ideological position provided coherence, if not unity, to the far-flung groups and factions and the disparate issues that agitated them.

That new ideology was what the historian Garry Wills described as "constitutional anti-governmentalism" (Wills 1995). Those attracted to extremist right issues shared a belief that there existed a sinister government conspiracy to deprive Americans of their rights and that it was being carried out by a repressive government bureaucracy. They challenged the very legitimacy of federal police powers, taxation, the jury system, and government regulation of economic activity, arguing that these measures were designed to strip Americans of their freedom. The religious among the extremists extended the Christian Right's criticism of secular humanism in the schools to propose that a conspiracy was afoot to brainwash Christian children as a means to control the entire population. They and their brethren in the Patriot movement, in the Christian Identity movement, and other groups were the true protectors of the U.S. Constitution against the usurpation of the federal government and its intrusive bureaucracies. To resist the clutches of the government, they called on their followers to homeschool their children, form citizen's militias, stockpile weapons for self-defense, and retreat to survivalist communities where the authority of the federal government could be ignored and denied.

Two bungled federal police actions in the early 1990s ignited the wrath of right-wing extremists and served for them as proof positive of their darkest suspicions. When federal agents attempted to arrest Randy Weaver, a leader in the white supremacist Christian Identity movement, on an illegal weapons possession warrant, Weaver resisted arrest and fired on the agents. In the shoot-out that ensued at his home in Ruby Ridge Idaho, Weaver was wounded and his wife and son died. The dramatic and deadly standoff between federal agents and the

Branch Davidians in Waco, Texas, in 1993 intensified extremists' paranoia and fury. Extremists viewed Weaver as a true American, defending his property and family, not as a fugitive from justice. Likewise, David Koresh exemplified self-reliant, Christian, patriarchal Americanism; he was not, as the public believed, a delusional and murderous cult leader. In the eyes of its perpetrators, the deadliest domestic terrorist act ever, the 1995 Oklahoma City Bombing, was payback for Waco.

In the aftermath of Oklahoma City, some critics accused conservatives of encouraging extremism and terrorism. Newt Gingrich, notorious for his hyperbolic rhetoric against government and liberals, justifiably protested the insinuations that his antigovernment position encouraged the Oklahoma City terrorists. There was in fact no alliance and no substantive communication between extreme rightists and New Right conservatives. They did, however, share fears. As Wills explained, "The suspicion that government has become the enemy of freedom, not its protector, crosses ideological lines. . . . Much of the appeal of the new extremists comes from the fact that they take a generalized discontent and spell out, in hard terms, what the consequences of such vague feelings could be" (Wills 1995).

Waco: David Koresh, the Branch Davidians, and the Federal Government, 1993

David Koresh was a cult leader who preached to his followers that he was Jesus Christ, that his seed was divine, and that the end was near. Calling themselves the Branch Davidians, Koresh and his followers lived communally at an armed compound in Waco, Texas. Branch Davidians surrendered all their possessions upon entry into the cult. Koresh withheld food as a means of control and publicly beat followers as punishment for disobedience. He proscribed celibacy for men while he considered all women in the group eligible to be his sexual concubine. Koresh sexually availed himself of girls as young as 11 years old. Most of the children in the cult were his own, fathered with the 19 women in the cult he claimed as his wives (Lacayo 1993).

Following reports that the Branch Davidians were stockpiling weapons and constructing explosive devices at their compound, the Federal Bureau of Investigation's (FBI) Bureau of Alcohol, Tobacco, and Firearms (ATF) prepared to serve a warrant on Koresh. The Branch Davidians got word of the upcoming raid, armed all of the adults in the compound, and greeted the federal agents attempting to serve the warrant with a volley of automatic fire, killing 4 and wounding 16 ATF agents. In the ensuing confrontation that day, up to 10 Branch Davidians were killed. Thus began the 51-day ATF and FBI siege that ended in the deaths of 85 cult members when the compound was consumed in fire on April 19, 1993. Among the more than 75 dead were at least a dozen children.

The Branch Davidians' Mount Carmel compound near Waco, Texas, engulfed in flames. (Reuters/Corbis)

Attorney General Janet Reno took responsibility for the FBI's mishandling of the siege but laid responsibility for the deaths on the Branch Davidians, who had set a massive and fast-moving fire within the compound as the agents were set to end the siege. Most Americans processed the news from Waco as another sorry episode of American cults' proclivity for mass suicide, although many were also disturbed by the way the FBI handled the siege. Assertions emanating from the right wing began to circulate charging that the FBI had fired something into the compound, and that the fire had been ignited by that. The government maintained that it had not used any device that would spark a fire, only tear gas. A federal independent investigation ensued. A report by special counsel John C. Danforth issued in 2000 cleared the government of any wrongdoing and confirmed the long-standing position of the government that agents had neither shot at the Branch Davidians nor set the fire, and laid responsibility for the deaths squarely on David Koresh. Danforth criticized the handling of Waco by the FBI, yet explicitly rejected the charges of conspiracy and cover-up that had circulated for seven years and had been fanned by the militia movement. But among antigovernment rightists, especially in the militia and Patriot movements, the conspiracy theory that the government had deliberately murdered the Branch Davidians lived on.

Vigilantism and Hate Crimes by the Extremist Right

Right-wing extremists committed a number of brutal murders in the 1990s in keeping with their ignominious history of lynching and vigilantism. Three white supremacist soldiers stationed at Fort Bragg, North Carolina, killed two local African American men in 1995 (Chua-Eoan 1995). Ex-convicts trying to establish a white supremacist group in Jasper County, Texas, chained an African American man, James Byrd, to their pickup truck and dragged him for three miles to his death (Fredrickson 1999). A former guard of the neo-Nazi Aryan Nations attacked a Jewish community center in Los Angeles, shot and wounded three children and two adults, and killed a mail carrier while fleeing the scene. Although there were other victims of prejudiced brutality—in the new lingo of the 1990s, "hate crimes"—these stand out for having been committed by individuals who were part of movements that advocated the extermination of their enemies.

A new turn was taken in the 1990s by the extremist right toward both systematic and larger-scale terrorism. Figures on the fringes of the antiabortion movement published literature and maintained Web sites that asserted that the murder of a person who performed abortions was a righteous act. The extremist right and antiabortion fanaticism met in the murders, physical attacks, and bombings of abortion providers and abortion clinics throughout the decade. The most egregious act of right-wing extremism was the 1995 bombing of the Federal Building in Oklahoma City, an act of domestic terrorism still unparalleled.

The Oklahoma City Bombing, 1995

When Americans learned on the morning of April 19, 1995, that a truck bomb had been detonated at the Alfred P. Murrah Federal Building in Oklahoma City, killing 168 persons, including 19 children who attended a federal day care program in the building, many jumped to the conclusion that radical Islamic terrorists were responsible. CNN falsely reported that three Muslims had been taken into custody—and even provided their names. It was, after all, only two years since the bombing of the World Trade Center by Islamic radicals.

Within hours of the bombing, the FBI was circulating "John Doe" sketches of two white men seen at the scene of the crime. Investigators had determined already that the bomb was made of ammonium nitrate (fertilizer) and had been delivered in a rented Ryder truck that had been parked in front of the building. Two days later, Timothy McVeigh and Terry Nichols, two other suspected conspirators, were in federal custody on suspicion of carrying out the bombing.

McVeigh and Nichols were right-wing extremists, participants in the white supremacist Patriot movement. McVeigh was a veteran of the Persian Gulf War, who after failing to win entry into the Army Special Forces, left the armed forces and gravitated more and more into the underworld of militant antigovernment activists. He commonly wore his army fatigues, stockpiled arms, always carried a gun, sold guns at gun shows, expressed his disgust with the government to co-workers and acquaintances, and practiced building bombs. He subscribed to *Soldier of Fortune* and was deeply moved by the *Turner Diaries,* the classic American neo-Nazi novel that advocated the overthrow of the government and the extermination of Jews and African Americans. Nichols, an army friend of McVeigh's, also held extreme antigovernment views—he had returned his voter registration card to the county with an angry letter, he refused to participate in federal farm aid programs, and he too stockpiled arms on his non-working farm in Oklahoma. Both were gun fanatics and obsessed with Waco and Ruby Ridge. McVeigh listened to the shortwave radio broadcasts of Mark Koernke, leader of the Michigan Militia movement, who preached that Waco was a "call to arms," and together they gravitated toward the Michigan Militia movement (quoted in Gleick 1995).

Search and rescue crews work to save those trapped beneath the debris, following the Oklahoma City Bombing, April 26, 1995. (Federal Emergency Management Agency)

When identified as John Doe I and questioned by the FBI, McVeigh gave his name, rank, and serial number; claimed he was a prisoner of war; and refused to say anything more.

Within a few weeks, the FBI had concluded that the Oklahoma City Bombing did not involve a larger conspiracy and was the work of the amateurs McVeigh, Nichols, Michael Fortier, and possibly one other man. All circulated on the fringe of various right-wing Patriot movement groups. (Although conspiracy theories continue to this day to circulate, there is no basis for them.) McVeigh went on trial in 1997 with Fortier, under a plea bargain, acting as the government's key witness. McVeigh's lawyers argued at the trial that he was a patriot, and although his actions were an overreaction, they were justified by the government's horrible deeds at Ruby Ridge and Waco. "Somehow, somewhere, in the midst of Mr. McVeigh's misplaced . . . horrifyingly out-of-proportion beliefs" about Waco, his lawyer told the jury, "there is a reason for all of us to have concern. That we have not expressed that concern before this tragedy means that we all bear some responsibility for Oklahoma City." The jury rejected the logic of that theory out of hand, voting unanimously in single votes each for conviction and execution. "What he represents to me is a terrorist-someone with no regard for human life," one juror declared. "He represents a twisted view of the intentions of the government and the principles that this country was founded upon" (Annin and Morganthau 1997). McVeigh was convicted of the crime, sentenced to death, and executed in 2001. Nichols, who had been part of the conspiracy but was not in Oklahoma City on the day of the bombing, was convicted in federal court in 1998 of conspiracy and manslaughter. In 2004, in a separate state trial, Nichols was convicted on 161 counts of first-degree murder. In both cases, juries deadlocked over whether to impose the death penalty, and Nichols was sentenced to life in prison without parole.

The Oklahoma City Bombing briefly raised alarm about homegrown militia and white supremacist movements. The bombing also helped to draw a distinction between mainstream conservatives and extremists and briefly made Americans less willing to tolerate extreme rhetoric from their elected politicians.

BIOGRAPHIES

William J. Bennett Jr., 1943–

Secretary of Education and Conservative Critic

William J. Bennett Jr. emerged in the 1990s as one of the most prominent conservative Culture Wars critics. In the 1980s and early 1990s, he had held high-level positions in the administrations of Reagan and Bush, including education secretary and "Drug Czar." Through these positions, he sought to advance a traditional conservative morality, such as when he advocated a constitutional

William Bennett Jr. (George Bush Presidential Library and Museum)

amendment designed to overturn the Supreme Court's ruling banning prayer in public schools. In 1990, after declining an invitation to serve as chairman of the Republican National Committee, he turned to writing and speaking about culture, American patriotism, and morality. He edited and contributed to 12 books during the 1990s. Several addressed the proper course in educating America's children, and some were children's books intended to inculcate traditional American and Christian ideals. Most of his work directly or indirectly targeted against social liberalism, the legacy of the New Left, and what he believed to be the moral relativism of liberals. *The De-Valuing of America,* published in 1992, argued against multiculturalism; he testified in favor of an end to government funding of the National Endowment for the Humanities and the National Endowment for the Arts in 1995. One of his most popular works was *The Book of Virtues,* in which he identified 10 important character traits and illustrated them with fables, poems, and other narrative forms. The book was turned into an animated children's show and aired on PBS in the 2000s. In the wake of the Clinton-Lewinsky scandal, Bennett took Americans to task in *The Death of Outrage: Bill Clinton and the Assault on American Ideals.* Bennett, who became a common talk show guest and a highly paid speaker on the lecture circuit, eventually hosted his own daily radio show. In 2003, Bennett's opponents charged him with hypocrisy after reporters for *Newsweek* and the *Washington Monthly* revealed that he was a heavy gambler, and that his losses amounted to up to $8 million (Green 2003).

Ward Connerly, 1939–

Anti–Affirmative Action Activist

African American businessman Ward Connerly became one of the nation's most prominent opponents of affirmative action during the 1990s. In 1995, as a member of the University of California Board of Regents, Connerly successfully pushed the university system to put a stop to any policies that gave preferential treatment based on race. A year later, he spearheaded a successful statewide drive for Proposition 209, which banned discrimination by race, gender, or ethnicity in public education, public employment, and public contracting. These changes profoundly reduced minorities' admission to the more widely esteemed universities within the state system. Connerly, who has a history of offering financial support to Republican candidates, was appointed to the board of regents by Republican governor Pete Wilson in 1993 and served until 2005. In his autobiography, *Creating Equal: My Fight Against Race Preferences,* Connerly describes an impoverished childhood followed by a difficult climb to business success; however, members of his family have argued that his upbringing was very much in the African American middle class. In addition, investigative reporters for the *San Francisco Chronicle* uncovered evidence that Connerly took advantage of affirmative action early in his career by getting publicly funded consulting jobs for his company as a minority contractor.

James Hansen, 1941–

Climatologist on Global Warming

James Hansen, a climatologist for the National Aeronautics and Space Administration (NASA) and director of the Goddard Institute of Space Studies in New York, has played a leading role in the science of climate change. Beginning with congressional testimony in 1988 that diagnosed a "greenhouse effect" that was causing global warming, Hansen has provided the model on which other scientists have built theories about damage to the planet's environment. Using a computer model, Hansen showed that since the Industrial Revolution, gases produced by industrial operations and manufacturing products have been trapping heat within the atmosphere. In early 1990, Hansen made a wager with a colleague that 1990, 1991, or 1992 would be the warmest year on record—and he won that bet when 1990 shattered all-time records. Hansen has since become one of the leading scientists on climate change, as well as a forceful advocate of dramatic measures to reduce carbon emissions. As a scientist in the government's employ, his work has been censored and revised against his protests. The administration of President George H. W. Bush edited his congressional testimony on global warming. In 2005, Hansen revealed that the administration of President George W. Bush attempted to censor his statements. Because of the criticism after the incident became public, NASA issued a new policy saying that its employees could speak freely about their work and their viewpoints. Hansen was named among the world's 100 most influential people by *Time* in 2006.

Jack Kevorkian, 1928–

Right-to-Die Activist

Pathologist Jack Kevorkian became the face of the right-to-die movement during the 1990s. The Michigan doctor created a machine that made it possible for patients who were terminally ill or living in misery to bring about their own deaths peacefully through the use of intravenous drugs. In June 1990, he first assisted in the suicide of Janet Adkins, an Oregon woman suffering from Alzheimer's disease. Instead of attempting to hide his role in patients' deaths, Kevorkian reported his involvement and argued fiercely that patients deserved the right to end their lives in dignity. He did not keep an exact count of the cases in which he was involved, but he may have attended more than 100 assisted suicides during the decade. His actions generated intense debate about whether seriously ill patients had the right to end their own suffering and whether physicians should help them in this process. Kevorkian faced criminal charges in several of these deaths; however, the vagueness of Michigan law enabled him to avoid imprisonment until 1998. At that time, he personally injected a fatal dose of drugs into Thomas Youk, who had Lou Gehrig's disease. His actions were taped and broadcast on the TV newsmagazine *60 Minutes*. Because this seemed to be clearly a case of euthanasia—not assisted suicide—Kevorkian was convicted of second-degree murder and sent to prison in 1999. He was paroled June 1, 2007.

Rodney King, 1965–

Victim of Los Angeles Police Brutality

On March 3, 1991, Rodney King, an African American man, was beaten by four Los Angeles police officers following a car chase. The beating of King and the exoneration of the police officers responsible triggered the Los Angeles Riots of 1992. When King stopped and exited his car, 27 officers, 10 with their guns drawn, surrounded him. King, then on parole after a year in prison for second-degree robbery, had been speeding and driving erratically and had decided not to stop. (He much later explained he was afraid of being sent back to prison.) King was stunned with a Taser gun, and as he writhed on the ground, officers beat him on the head and face with a solid aluminum baton and kicked and punched him in the head, ribs, and other parts of his body. King's injuries included 11 fractured bones at the base of his skull, a broken cheekbone, permanent damage to the bones around his eye socket, facial nerve damage, and a concussion.

A little over a year later, four LAPD officers put on trial for beating King were found not guilty. That afternoon, the Los Angeles Riots erupted. Defense attorneys had portrayed King as a dangerous criminal, strung out on drugs, who had evaded and resisted arrest. King, himself, remained a cipher, for he did not testify at the trial and did not speak to the public during the entire period. Two days into the riot, King spoke publicly for the first time since his beating. On nationally broadcast television, he pleaded, "People, I just want to say, you know, can we all get along? Can we stop making it horrible for the older people and the kids?" His words became one of the folk expressions of the 1990s. In the spring of 1993, a federal trial of the LAPD officers for the violation of King's civil rights ended in the conviction of two of the officers and the acquittal of two others. King won a $3.8 million settlement from the City of Los Angeles. He avoided the public role many wanted to thrust on him. He had several encounters with the law in subsequent years, including a conviction for drunk driving and a guilty plea to spouse abuse.

Eric Rudolph, 1966–

Domestic Right-Wing Terrorist

Eric Rudolph was responsible for several extremist acts of violence in the 1990s, and his life illustrates the nexus between various extremist right causes and organizations. Rudolph's first known attack was the bombing on July 27, 1996, at Centennial Olympic Park in Atlanta in which one woman was killed and 111 people were injured. Six months later, Rudolph planted two bombs at an Atlanta suburban office building; a family planning clinic was located in the building. One month later, Rudolph planted an explosive device packed with nails in a gay and lesbian nightclub in Atlanta, wounding five people. Eleven months later,

Rudolph targeted another abortion clinic, this time with fatal results. After being identified as a suspect in a Birmingham bombing, Rudolph fled before authorities had an opportunity to question him. He lived as a fugitive for five years before being apprehended in 2003.

Rudolph was raised in a white supremacist, anti-Semitic, and religious extremist family, and he traveled in those circles since his childhood. After his father died, his mother moved the family to North Carolina, living on property found for the family by an antigovernment survivalist prosecuted for stockpiling weapons. As a teenager, he and his mother lived for a few months with a fundamentalist, white supremacist Christian Identity group in Missouri. Christian Identity doctrine asserted that white Europeans were the Bible's true chosen people, Jews were the descendants of Satan, and all other races were "mud people." Some of its proponents advocated the use of violence to combat the evils of abortion, homosexuality, and interracial marriage. Returning to North Carolina, Rudolph and his family were close to a Christian Identity minister in their area. Before launching his spree of extremist attacks at the age of 30, Rudolph had briefly enlisted in the military, hoping to join the Special Forces, but had left after 18 months. He then lived with his brother in North Carolina and made his living by selling marijuana. His former sister-in-law speculated in an interview with a Southern Poverty Law Center reporter that Rudolph bombed the lesbian bar because of his anger over his youngest brother being gay and that he bombed the abortion clinics because he thought white women were committing race suicide. "In his mind, Eric believes that what he's doing is right, just like Osama bin Laden thinks what *he's* doing is right. Eric's striking out on his own, thinking that he can draw attention to certain situations in this country," she explained (SPLC 2001).

While he was a fugitive, he became a folk hero to extremists who wore T-shirts touting "Run, Rudolph, Run," and who saw him as a valiant freedom fighter against an oppressive government. Rudolph left letters at each of the bombing sites, except the Olympic bombing, claiming that the Army of God was responsible. In fact, Rudolph, although inspired by incitements on the Internet to murder abortion providers, worked alone. Although many speculated that he had left the country, he spent his fugitive years subsisting on acorns, lizards, and game in the North Carolina woods. He was apprehended in 2003 scrounging for food in a grocery store dumpster by a local police officer. In 2005, federal prosecutors reached a plea agreement with Rudolph shortly before he was to go on trial in a capital case for the Birmingham bombing. In exchange for life in prison, Rudolph provided information to authorities on the location of 250 pounds of dynamite, which he was stockpiling for future actions. (The prosecutors defended their offer of a plea bargain as necessary to recover the explosives hidden near residential communities.) Authorities discovered two fully constructed bombs and detonators, in addition to dynamite, at Rudolph's hiding spot (Dewan 2005).

Anna Deveare Smith, 1950–

Playwright, Actor, Professor

Anna Deveare Smith, a playwright and actor, was one of the ablest chroniclers of the decades' ethnic, racial, and sexual tensions. In 1992, she won an Obie Award and a Drama Desk Award for *Fires in the Mirror,* a play about the Crown Heights Riots. A year later, she won a Tony Award for *Twilight: Los Angeles, 1992.* To create her one-woman plays about the Crown Heights and Los Angeles riots, Smith interviewed dozens of witnesses, participants, and social analysts. The dialogue of the plays was taken wholly from her interviews, and she performed them solo, switching seamlessly between characters. Transforming herself into a Lubavitcher student, or a West Indian child, or Reginald Denny, or Mayor Dinkins, or Police Chief Gates, she demonstrated the essential individual humanity residing in our differences. Smith has had roles in a variety of movies, including *Philadelphia* and *The American President.* She became more widely known to audiences through her role in the popular television show *West Wing,* in which she played the president's National Security Advisor. The plays are a testament to her gifts as a storyteller and social critic, and to the power of art to convey the deep meaning of social history (Smith 1994, 1997).

REFERENCES AND FURTHER READINGS

Andreas, Peter. 2000. *Border Games: Policing the U.S.-Mexico Divide.* Cornell Studies in Political Economy. Ithaca, NY: Cornell University Press.

Annin, Peter, and Tom Morganthau. 1997. "The Verdict: Death." *Newsweek* 129 (25): 40–42.

Atkins, Stephen E. 2002. *Encyclopedia of Modern American Extremists and Extremist Groups.* Westport, CT: Greenwood Press.

Ayres, B. Drummond, Jr. 1994. "Minorities Join California Fight." *New York Times,* November 1.

Baldassare, Mark, ed. 1994. *The Los Angeles Riots: Lessons for the Urban Future.* Boulder, CO: Westview Press.

Bennett, William J. 1998. *The Death of Outrage: Bill Clinton and the Assault on American Ideals.* New York: Free Press.

Bennett, William J. 2006. *America: The Last Best Hope.* Nashville, Tenn.: Nelson Current.

Center for the Renewal of Science and Culture, Discovery Institute. 1998. Untitled ["The Wedge Strategy"]. Seattle. http://web.archive.org/19980514072337/www.discovery.org/crsc/aboutcrsc.html.

Chang, Jeff. 2005. *Can't Stop, Won't Stop: A History of the Hip-Hop Generation*. New York: St. Martin's Press.

Chua-Eoan, Howard. 1995. "Enlisted Killers: A Double Murder Raises the Specter of Race Hatred in the Military." *Time*, December 18, 44.

Cloud, Stanley W. 1991. "Exorcising an Old Demon." *Time*, March 11, 52–53.

Coulter, Ann. 2002. *Slander: Liberal Lies about the American Right*. New York: Crown.

Cullen, Dave. 2000. "Conduct Unbecoming." *Salon.com*, March 10. http://archive.salon.com/news/feature/2000/03/10/gays/index.html.

Danforth, John C. 2001. "Testimony before the Senate Judiciary Committee," June 20.

Dewan, Shaila. 2005. "Suspect in Blast at '96 Olympics to Plead Guilty." *New York Times*, April 9, A1.

Domanick, Joe. 1994. *To Protect and to Serve: The LAPD's Century of War in the City of Dreams*. New York: Pocket Books.

Downey, Roger. 2006. "Discovery's Creation." *Seattle Weekly*, February 6.

Faludi, Susan. 2006. *Backlash: The Undeclared War against American Women*. New York: Three Rivers Press. First edition, 1991.

Frank, Thomas. 2004. *What's the Matter with Kansas? How Conservatives Won the Heart of America*. New York: Metropolitan Books.

Fraser, Steve. 1995. *The Bell Curve Wars: Race, Intelligence, and the Future of America*. New York: BasicBooks.

Fredrickson, George M. 1999. "Jasper, Texas: A Historical Perspective on a Brutal Killing." *The Journal of Blacks in Higher Education* (23): 136–137.

Gallagher, Edward J. 2000. "The Enola Gay Controversy." Lehigh University Digital Library. http://www.lehigh.edu/~ineng/enola/.

Gelbspan, Ross. 1997. *The Heat Is On: The High Stakes Battle over Earth's Threatened Climate*. Reading, MA: Addison-Wesley.

Gibbs, Nancy. 1991. "Making Sense of the Storm." *Time*, June 17, 22–26.

Gleick, Elizabeth. 1995. "Who Are They?" *Time*, May 1, 44–51.

Green, Joshua. 2003. "The Bookie of Virtue." *Washington Monthly*, June. http://www.washingtonmonthly.com/features/2003/0306.green.html.

Haider-Markel, Donald P. 2000. "Lesbian and Gay Politics in the States: Interest Groups, Electoral Politics, and Policy." In *The Politics of Gay Rights*, edited by C. A. Rimmerman, K. D. Wald, and C. Wilcox, 290–346. Chicago: University of Chicago Press.

Hansen, Jim. 2006. "The Threat to the Planet." *New York Review of Books*, July 13, 12–16.

Harwit, Martin. 1996. *An Exhibit Denied: Lobbying the History of Enola Gay*. New York: Copernicus.

Herrnstein, Richard J., and Charles A. Murray. 1994. *The Bell Curve: Intelligence and Class Structure in American Life*. New York: Free Press.

Hughes, Robert. 1993. *Culture of Complaint: The Fraying of America*. New York: Oxford University Press.

"Inside Soldiers' Heads." 1996. *The Economist* (U.S.), January 13, 25–26.

"It's a Grand Old (Politically Correct) Flag." 1991. *Time,* February 25, 55.

Ivins, Molly. 1992. "Notes from Another Country." *The Nation* 255 (7): 229–231.

Johnson, Haynes Bonner. 1991. *Sleepwalking through History: America in the Reagan Years*. New York: W. W. Norton.

Johnson, Haynes Bonner. 2001. *The Best of Times: America in the Clinton Years*. New York: Harcourt.

Johnson, Kevin R. 1998. "Immigration Politics, Popular Democracy, and California's Proposition 187." In *The Latino/a Condition: A Critical Reader,* edited by R. Delgado and J. Stefancic, 110–117. New York: New York University Press.

Kadetsky, Elizabeth. 1994. "'Save Our State' Initiative: Bashing Illegals in California." *Nation* 259 (12): 416–422.

Lacayo, Richard. 1990. "Why No Blue Blood Will Flow: On the Front Lines, a Disproportionate Number of Troops Hail from Minorities and the Working Class." *Time,* November 26, 34.

Lacayo, Richard. 1993. "Cult of Death." *Time,* March 15, 36–39.

Lewis, Gregory B., and Jonathan L. Edelson. 2000. "DOMA and ENDA: Congress Votes on Gay Rights." In *The Politics of Gay Rights,* edited by C. A. Rimmerman, K. D. Wald, and C. Wilcox. Chicago: University of Chicago Press.

Martin, William C. 1996. *With God on Our Side: The Rise of the Religious Right in America*. New York: Broadway Books.

McKibben, Bill. 1999. *The End of Nature*. New York: Anchor Books.

McKibben, Bill. 2005. "Changing the Climate." *The American Prospect,* October, A10–A12.

McKibben, Bill. 2006. "The Coming Meltdown." *New York Review of Books,* January 12, 16–18.

O'Sullivan, John. 1994. "America's Identity Crisis: Why Kemp and Bennett Are Wrong." *National Review* 46 (22): 36–43.

Oh, Angela E. 2002. *Open: One Woman's Journey*. Los Angeles: UCLA Asian American Studies Center Press.

Orr, H. Allen. 2005. "Devolution." *The New Yorker,* May 30, 40–52.

Press, Eyal. 2006. *Absolute Convictions: My Father, a City, and the Conflict that Divided America.* New York: Henry Holt and Co.

Ricks, Thomas E. 1996. "The Great Society in Camouflage." *Atlantic Monthly* 278 (6): 24–28.

Smith, Anna Deavere. 1994. *Twilight—Los Angeles, 1992: On the Road: A Search for American Character.* New York: Anchor Books.

Smith, Anna Deavere. 1997. *Fires in the Mirror: Crown Heights, Brooklyn and Other Identities.* New York: Dramatists Play Service.

SPLC. 2001. "Intelligence Report." Southern Poverty Law Center. Interview with Deborah Rudolph. http://www.splcenter.org/intel/intelreport/article.jsp?aid =161. Accessed October 4, 2006.

State of California. 1994. "Prohibition against Discrimination or Preferential Treatment by State and Other Public Entities." Initiative Constitutional Amendment. http://vote96.ss.ca.gov/BP/209.htm.

Sullivan, Andrew. 2001. "This Is a Religious War. *New York Times Magazine,* October 7, 44.

Sullivan, Andrew. 2006. *The Conservative Soul: How We Lost It, How to Get It Back.* New York: HarperCollins.

Taylor, Humphrey. 1998. "Support for *Roe v. Wade* Still Solid, but Not Overwhelming, on Twenty-fifth Anniversary of Supreme Court decision." Harris Poll, January 21. http://www.harrisinteractive.com/harris_poll/index.asp?PID =198.

Thompson, Mark. 1994. "The Living Room War." *Time,* May 23, 48–52.

Williams, Donald C. 2000. *Urban Sprawl: A Reference Handbook, Contemporary World Issues.* Santa Barbara, CA: ABC-CLIO.

Wills, Garry. 1995. "The New Revolutionaries." *New York Review of Books,* August 10.

Worldwatch Institute. 2001. *Vital Signs, 2001.* New York: W. W. Norton.

Zoglin, Richard. 1991. "Jumping Out of the Pool." *Time,* February 18, 39.

People and Events in the 20th Century

THE 1900s

THE 1910S

THE 1920s

THE 1930s

THE 1940s

THE 1950s

THE 1960s

THE 1970s

THE 1980s

THE 1990s

1990s Index

About the Author

Dr. Nancy Cohen is a historian, writer, and teacher. She is the author of *The Reconstruction of American Liberalism, 1865–1914* (University of North Carolina Press, 2002). She is a visiting scholar at the University of California, Los Angeles, Institute for Research on Labor and Employment and is a lecturer in the Department of Political Science at California State University, Long Beach. She is a featured blogger on The Huffington Post. Her blogs and additional writings can also be found at www.nancycohen.org. She lives in Los Angeles with her two daughters.